CULTURE, BODIES AND
THE SOCIOLOGY OF HEALTH

Culture, Bodies and the Sociology of Health

Edited by
ELIZABETH ETTORRE
University of Liverpool, UK

ASHGATE

Published by
Ashgate Publishing Limited
Wey Court East
Union Road
Farnham
Surrey, GU9 7PT
England

Ashgate Publishing Company
Suite 420
101 Cherry Street
Burlington
VT 05401-4405
USA

www.ashgate.com

British Library Cataloguing in Publication Data
Ettorre, Elizabeth, 1948-
  Culture, bodies and the sociology of health.
  1. Human body--Social aspects. 2. Health attitudes.
  I. Title
  306.4'61-dc22

Library of Congress Cataloging-in-Publication Data
Culture, bodies and the sociology of health / [edited] by Elizabeth Ettorre.
    p. cm.
  Includes index.
  ISBN 978-0-7546-7756-7 (hbk) -- ISBN 978-0-7546-9499-1 (ebook)
  1. Human body--Social aspects. 2. Health--Social aspects. I. Ettorre, Elizabeth, 1948-

  HM636.C855 2010
  306.4'61--dc22

2010007972

ISBN 9780754677567 (hbk)
ISBN 9780754694991 (ebk)

HMVK
7
⟨ c ⟩
c - 1

Mixed Sources
Product group from well-managed
forests and other controlled sources
www.fsc.org Cert no. SA-COC-1565
© 1996 Forest Stewardship Council
FSC

Printed and bound in Great Britain by
MPG Books Group, UK

Contents

PART III ABJECT BODIES

Notes on Contributors

Shirlene Badger (Ph.D., Sociology, Cambridge University). Her doctoral research explored what happens when a group of children who are severely obese and their families participate in a 'genetics of obesity' study and potentially receive a genetic diagnosis for obesity. Currently, she is doing research concerned with families' experiences of obesity and their recruitment to complex interventions and medical/scientific studies.

Peter Conrad (Ph.D., Sociology, Boston University) is Harry Coplan Professor of Social Sciences at Brandeis University where he has been on the faculty since 1979. He is the author of over 100 articles and chapters and nine books, including the awarding winning, *Deviance and Medicalization: From Badness to Sickness* (with Joseph W. Schneider) and his most recent book, *The Medicalization of Society: On the Transformation of Human Conditions into Treatable Disorders* (2007).

Elizabeth Ettorre (Ph.D., Sociology, London School of Economics) is Professor of Sociology and Social Policy, University of Liverpool. Her work focuses on women and health with special reference to reproduction, drugs, embodiment, autoethnography and depression. Her most recent publications are *Revisioning Women and Drugs: Gender Power and the Body* (2007) and *Reproductive Genetics, Gender and the Body* (2002).

Rui Gomes (Ph.D., Sociology of Education, Technical University of Lisbon) is currently Professor of Sociology of Education and Sociology of Leisure, University of Coimbra, Portugal. His work focuses on body, health and leisure and he has developed specific interest in embodiment, health and subjectivity. His most recent publications are: *The Government of Education in Portugal* (2005), *Sites of Leisure* (2005), and *Leisure Landscapes* (2007).

April Dawn Henning is a Ph.D. student at the Graduate Center of the City University of New York. She is currently conducting research in the Sociology of Sport.

Ciara Kierans (Ph.D., Anthropology, National University of Ireland, Maynooth) is a cultural anthropologist working as a Lecturer and Director of Postgraduate Research in the School of Population, Community and Behavioural Sciences at University of Liverpool. In 2001, she was a Fulbright Fellow at Harvard University and explored issues of culture and embodiment in transplant technologies. She has, since, conducted ethnographic and narrative research on chronic conditions, new medical and information and communication technologies, gender and health and urban communities.

Ashley Rondini (MA, Social Policy, Brandeis University; MA, Women's Studies, University of Sussex, UK) is a Ph.D. candidate in the departments of Sociology and Social Policy at Brandeis University. Her work focuses on race, gender, social stratification, and qualitative research methods with special reference to youth, identity, health, and education. Her dissertation research examines the social meanings of education within families of low-income, first generation college students at elite universities.

Jason L. Powell (Ph.D., Social Gerontology, Liverpool John Moores University) is Reader in Sociology and Social Policy at the University of Liverpool. He is best known for his work on Foucauldian approaches to social gerontology. His research extends to theorizing the ageing body and its relationship to health and social care policy and practice. He has authored over 141 professional publications including *Social Theory and Aging* (2005) and *The Welfare State in Post-Industrial Society: A Global Perspective* (2009) (with J. Hendricks).

Carole Sutton (MSc Social Research, University of Plymouth) is a Senior Lecturer in Quantitative Methods at the School of Psychosocial Sciences, University of Plymouth. Her research interests include using secondary data in research, the sociology of the body and sport, and the contribution of autoethnography to research. Her most recent publications are: *Social Research: The Basics* (2004) and *Moving Bodies in Running in Gendered Journeys, Mobile Emotions* (2009).

Acknowledgement
The editor and authors would like to thank Neil Jordan, Commissioning Editor at Ashgate Publishing for his continual support in the production of this volume.

Introduction
Re-shaping Bodies in the
Sociology of Health

Elizabeth Ettorre

'Fleshing Out' Sites of Illness, Leisure and Risk

Twenty-first century bodies are located in age, gender, race, ethnic, able bodied and class ranked positions, while these bodies are shaped simultaneously as sites of health, disease, leisure, technology, labour, emotions, attractiveness, consumption, style and risk. The body is a central element in the construction of the social and the focus of the private sphere, while the body has become the template upon which cultural identities are fashioned and through which public emotions and social problems are being played out. Embodied persons are 'productive bodies' capable of activities that change the nature of their lives, while also being 'communicative', 'powerful' and 'thinking' bodies (Burkitt 1999: 2) located in relations that transform their natural and social worlds. With regards embodied persons within biomedicine, there has been a lack of attempts to deconstruct 'the mobilising signifiers of health and disease' and more importantly, no one is able to exist as a fully embodied subject *vis-à-vis* medicine (Shildrick and Price 1998: 4–5). *Culture, Bodies and the Sociology of Health* is dedicated to the question of the body in health and illness and brings together critical scholars who interrogate bodies within the broad field of the sociology of health and illness. Our aim is to begin to open the discourses which fabricate our bodies and our health and illnesses and to demonstrate that our embodiment is 'provisional' (Fox 1998: 30).

The biomedical discourse on the body has become embedded in our modern culture over the past 300 years. Critical of medicine's lack of attention to the notion of lived bodies as fragmented, political sites, social science scholars have begun to situate bodies and issues of embodiment centrally within the domain of sociology of health and illness. Nowhere are these embodied matters more clearly demonstrated than in relation to health and illness (Williams 2004: 73). See also Frank (1991, 1995, 2004), James and Hockey (2007), Lupton (1994), Lyon and Barbalet (1994), Nettleton and Watson (1998), Shilling (2005), Turner (1986, 1992), Williams and Bendelow (1998), Williams (2003). In this context, Kelly and Field (1996) argue that in most types of sociological narratives about chronic illness, the body remains theoretically elusive and that medical sociology has understated the central facts of bodily difficulties which are entailed in illness and disability. They contend that the existence of the body is seldom denied but its presence has a kind of ethereal quality forever gliding out of view (p. 242). At the same time, clinicians, experts and others working in the field of biomedicine continue to devise ways to transform the boundaries of healthy and sick bodies and to medicalize them.

Medicalization of the body is a dramatic part of the pervasive industrialization of the body; it is the 'apogee' of the modern political economy in which the human body is simultaneously celebrated and degraded under the banner of production, consumption and social governance (O'Neill 2004: 66–67). In an excellent piece on medicalized bodies, Hughes (2000) discusses how for biomedicine the body is 'pre-social' and has no history and furthermore, that sociological bodies differ from the medical body in that the former is contested while the latter is 'real' with an objective, scientific status (pp. 12–13). In referring to Foucault's *Birth of the Clinic*, Hughes contends that medicine becomes biomedicine when its scientific endeavours focus on charting the contours of normality and that biomedicine is concerned with a regular functioning of the bodily organism and identifying where this body has deviated, what it was disturbed by and how it is able to be brought back to working order (p. 15).

In a real sense, biomedicine has privileged a type of technoscientific, biological determinism to explain social injustice as natural and necessary, while economic inequalities, resulting in the experience of disease, inequalities in health, the subordination of women and people of colour, and the untimely HIV-related deaths of millions on a global scale are considered an epiphenomena of biology (Urla and Terry 1995: 2). Examining the links between the body and deviancy, Urla and Terry contend that biomedicine has been instrumental in privileging 'embodied deviance', the term they give to 'the scientific and popular postulate that bodied of subjects classified as deviant are marked in some recognizable fashion' (p. 2). Their main contention is that medicine along with the other modern life sciences with their powerful and outdated Western epistemologies has surveyed, observed, assessed and reported on bodies, while at the same time clinicians construct bodies through particular investigative techniques and culturally lodged research goals (p. 3). These authors (Urla and Terry 1995: 3) demonstrate quite forcefully that bodies are not natural entities with a generic core; rather bodies are effects, products or symptoms of specific techniques and regulatory practices – bodies are points on which and from which the disciplinary power of scientific investigations is exercised. The clear lesson we learn from this work is that bodies, whether sick or ill, bad or good, moving or stationary, are never free of relations of power. This is because medical and lay discourses always already bind bodies into larger systems of knowledge production and moral discussions.

While it is true that medical sociology has produced important contributions to the renewal of the body's conceptualization (Berg and Akrich 2004), an emergent and indeed important task of social scientists interested in health and illness is to bear witness to all forms of embodied oppressions and to contextualize both the 'healthy' and 'ill' body as a politically, morally inscribed entity, its biology and histories/herstories shaped by practices of surveillance, containment and control. Medicalized bodies are bodies embedded in moralities of health and illness, appearing as shaped by the 'individuality', 'freedom' and 'rationality' concerns of conventional bioethics. Yet, at the same time, post conventional moralities of health locate classed, raced, ethnic, gendered, disabled and aged, bodies as being 'leaky bodies' that is as bodies which undermine traditional binaries and challenge ontological and epistemological closure (Shildrick 1997) as well as biomedical fixity. When moral judgements are made about how ill health and health 'in bodies' affects relations of power, inclusion and exclusion (Ettorre 2005), bodies become more malleable and unstable as they are designated as healthier and less sick or vice versa.

While 'health' and 'ill health' are terms that are culturally and socially defined, all cultures have known concepts of these terms. These concepts vary from culture to culture according to how sick and healthy bodies become visible and more importantly, the magnitude and breadth of what Rosi Braidotti (1994) calls the scopic drive – a drive compelling bodies to be deeply involved in an 'ethics of risk' (Shildrick 1997: 212). Whether sick or healthy, bodies within biomedicine are viewed as empirical objects to be quantified, classified, surveyed and ultimately, controlled. Alongside these complex processes, new forms of social mediation are being developed under the guise of biomedicine. Late modern medicine or the new public health privileges risk and widens the relevant points of contacts between professionals and patients into different sites, locations and social interactions toward the social body (Bunton and Burrows 1995: 207).

As implied above, bodies, whether ill or healthy, normal or pathological, etc. are never free of relations of power. That drug use or obesity can be seen as examples of 'dis-ease' which stigmatize sufferers and that these sufferers may be rejected by a 'healthy', 'normal' population, tells us that the medical and lay discourses on health and illness or the scientific and popular ways of representing healthy and ill bodies are never value free. This is why Frank (1995) calls for an 'ethics of the body' as a model for those who are suffering or ill to embody empathy and 'be' with others in 'communicative' bodies. He contends that we need to research suffering and map stories which allow ill people to connect their stories to others and to recognize what stories they have not yet told (Frank 2001: 361). While Frank exposes how sick bodies are able to maintain ethical communication in the midst of corporeal 'breakdown', Braidotti (2006: 111) contends that an ethical view of communication is always already about accepting the impossibility of mutual reciprocity, central to neo-liberal forms of ethics and neo-liberalism itself. Braidotti argues for a bio-centered egalitarianism which undermines the individualism and sameness (i.e. we are all the same) of neo-liberal forms of ethics. For her, a bio-centered egalitarianism attempts 'to think the interconnection of human and non-human agents' and re-think the ethical and political position of 'a non-unitary subject' (p. 111). In effect, she replaces the unitary subject of neo-liberalism with a non-unitary subject of bio-centered egalitarianism who experiences co-dependency and multiple belongings and redefines responsibility as a commonly shared sensibility (p. 149). Thus, for Braidotti, when we communicate with each other, we must respect our mutual co-dependency and accept at deep levels each others' multiple belongings (i.e. gender, class, race, ethnicity, age, health, nationality, and ability). Most importantly, we must accept diversity within the context of the neoliberal craving to keep us all the same. In the face of the spectacular effects of contemporary technological transformations in our world particularly in the field of biomedicine, we need to reassure those we communicate with how our lives are mediated by technologies and that it is 'OK' to feel overwhelmed given that we are surrounded by multi-layered and internally contradictory phenomena. Furthermore, history shows us that technologies become embedded in customs, procedures and societal structures (of which biomedicine is a part) that seem to inscribe themselves on the actions and identities of embodied individuals and often appear as fixed to new generations – the development of 'technological bodies' has long been steered by warfare and the economy (Shilling 2005: 179–80). Here, we need to present to others an honest picture of the technologies we use and why we use them. As Briadotti (2006: 160) implies, we need to be ethical subjects of sustainable becoming, that is we need to develop a sensibility to transformations and be able to sustain these transformations without cracking. Thus, our ethical becoming aims at joy and not destruction.

In an enlightening piece on how some feminist post-structuralist critiques have little to offer as an epistemological foundation for feminist health activism, Kathy Davis (2007: 61) contends that feminist theory does not need to distance itself from feminist health activism in order to develop an improved critique of science. Rather, in order for this gap between theory and action to be bridged, three reconceptualizations in feminist embodiment theory need to occur – reconceptualizations of 1) the body, 2) embodied experience and 3) epistemic agency. While acknowledging that this gap results from some feminist theorists rejecting experience as a 'suspect concept', Davis argues further that experience, specifically women's experience, provides an essential starting point for understanding the embodied and material effects of living under specific social and cultural conditions (p. 57). While *Culture, Bodies and the Sociology of Health* is implicitly feminist, Davis's contentions are useful for constructing this text's epistemological framework within current sociological thinking on health, illness and medicine. Simply, 'pondering experience' and attempting to deconstruct the key signifiers of health and illness provide useful tools for retrieving embodied experience as a theoretical resource when considering medicine, culture and society. To retrieve analyses of embodiment as concretely lived and experienced, the theoretician acknowledges how changes in 'techniques of ontological abstractions' (i.e. shifts in technological forms) are caught up with shifts in self understanding along with reconceptualizations of the embodied self (Cregan 2006: 7). The astute theoretician observes these shifts through historical comparisons within a culture or society or across different, contemporaneous social or cultural forms, thus wanting to avoid obsolete or Eurocentric notions of the body and uphold contradictory forms of embodiment (p. 7). Aware that modern medicine is extremely technocratic, contributors to *Culture, Bodies and the Sociology of Health* draw on different bodies in different contexts and cultures as a resource for what it feels like to be healthy or ill, normal or pathological, good or bad, and moral or immoral.

Whether we see sufferers of ill health or 'dis-ease' as Frank's ethical communicators in the midst of corporeal collapse or Braidotti's ethical subjects of sustainable becoming, experiencing co-dependency and multiple belongings and redefining responsibility as a commonly shared sensibility is not the point here. Rather, the main focus is on the fact that medical discourses always bind bodies into larger systems of knowledge and ethics production. In an age of biopower, many disciplinary strategies (i.e. techniques of measurement, visualization and classification technologies) surround the body in a constant, continual never ending effort to construct and normalize bodies (Braidotti 1994: 60). *Culture, Bodies and the Sociology of Health* is an attempt to show that while our current social realities are entirely medicalized and medical sociology has not played a pivotal role in the theoretical progress of sociology (Turner 1992: 159–60), we want to change this state of affairs and offer contributions which require greater theoretical reflexivity. This demands a sufficiently grounded reflexive and critical sociology linked to the project of modernity and favouring the decolonization and rationalization of the lifeworld through active engagement in civil society and the public sphere (Scambler 1996 cited in Scambler 1998: 63).

A key issue addressed by contributors concerns how social science scholars should begin quite reflexively to situate bodies centrally within the sociology of health and illness. In particular, contributors focus their attention on a key question: How are social scientists best able to contextualize the notion of 'healthy' embodiment and to understand the conditions and experiences of 'healthy' embodiment *vis-à-vis* organ donor recipients' (Chapter 1), 'doped' (Chapter 2), running (Chapter 3), consuming (Chapter 4), medicalized (Chapter 5), ageing (Chapter 6), 'obese' (Chapter 7) and pregnant drug using (Chapter 8) bodies? As can be seen, these issues reflect the specific embodied focus of each chapter in the book.

If, as we know, medical and other sociologists (Charmaz 1983, Frank 2001, Wilkinson 2005) are able to transform a somewhat restricted medicalized view of the chronically ill person's pain into a broader view of suffering, social scientists pursuing a quest for a greater understanding of health and illness should create wider, more stylized 'infirmity identities' and embodiments that defy closure, while resisting scopic regimes, such as medicine, which authorize and legitimate a morality of health. In his/her own ways, each contributor contextualizes the boundaries between bodies and society and how these boundaries are becoming increasingly obscured. Thus, the particular focus of this book is more on how the construction of these boundaries structure power relations under the banner of health and how bodies of healthy and ill people have been shaped through various biomedical discourses, their morphologies transformed into 'alien' subjectivities.

While numerous, complex issues are raised in these chapters, each one reveals in its own way, the body, as being inscribed by culture and indeed, secured by culturally embodied differences. In this context, the boundaries between bodies and society with special reference to health are examined through the cultural meanings of kidney transplantation (Chapter 1); pathologizing of elite athletes (Chapter 2); non-elite road running (Chapter 3); perusal and use of fitness magazines (Chapter 4); the cultural gaze of the internet (Chapter 5); gerontological theory, gender and the body (Chapter 6); the 'genetics' of obesity (Chapter 7) and pregnant drug-using bodies as polluted (Chapter 8). While the main focus of this book is on the body in the sociology of health, the chapters are arranged under three broad headings, bodies and technoscience, bodies and representation and abject bodies.

Bodies and Technoscience

Contemporary biomedicine upholds various technologies as emblematic of how successfully medical expertise has been able to manage, alter, control and 'cure' the human body. In contemporary society, we are witnessing the immense explosion of medical technologies into many areas of modern social life. Cultures have become increasingly dependent upon advancements in technoscience. In turn, these resultant advancements sustain biomedicine as a dominant paradigm on the body in Western thought, as biology becomes increasingly the filter through which humans are expected to interpret the world (Lundin 1997). Interestingly enough technologies, such as genetic technologies, affirm political processes and in the field of reproductive genetic technologies, we can speak of 'prenatal politics' (Ettorre 2002). Most definitely politics are embedded in the use of medical technologies and we need to map out the implications of medical technologies for the material practices, complex processes, embodied experiences and cultural and social formations they produce. On the one hand, subjects of technologies are situated at intersections of the medical world, individual interest and relational obligations as well as being co-producers of technological practice (Cambrisio, Young and Lock 2000: 11). On the other hand, the application of specific ideological beliefs, knowledge and medical procedures are seen to be played out on 'docile bodies', viewed as the visible, organic or 'raw' material needed to fulfil the successful implementation and employment of various technological processes. The workings of technocience in biomedicine expose a modern unease that technological interventions on human bodies transform sick bodies from fragmented subjects with concerns for 'sustainability', 'responsibility', 'agency', and 'empathy' to fixed objects of medical care focused on 'beneficence', 'sameness', 'mutual reciprocity' and 'rationality'.

Within the context of the donation of kidneys in the Republic of Ireland, Ciara Kierans in Chapter 1, 'Transplantation, organ donation and (in) human experience: re-writing boundaries through embodied perspectives on kidney failure', demonstrates how discursive practices on transplantation bring together organs, donor bodies, recipient bodies, identity, kinship and the public as a coincident location or biosocial space. For her, the convergence of the self and others through 'dead' and live organ donations has been accomplished through the convergence of ontological, biological and social domains in the discourse on transplantation. Key issues for her are the embodied consequences of dialysis and harvesting from the brain dead; the ontological implications and status of hybridity for bodies of organ recipients as well donor bodies and the immune system as the embodied ground of transplantation. Within the context of biomedicine, kidney transplantation has deep cultural consequences for human embodiment, social identity and medical governance. Most importantly, it has the power to shift our comprehension of the boundaries of life itself. Drawing on ethnographic work on kidney transplantation which Kierans conducted in the Republic of Ireland, she shows recipients' accounts of transplantation and introduces a new type of embodiment, the 'body-in-transplantation'. Her theoretical stance employs the notion of cyborg as a sensitizing concept indicating that science and technology continue to weaken the boundaries separating flesh and machine (Shilling 2008: 1). She contends that cyborg concepts have been both key practical and conceptual devices for describing the associated embodied, social and political implications of organ transplantation. The main aim of her paper is to uphold the importance of the recipient who has been traditionally absent from theorizing in much of the anthropological literature on organ donation and transplantation. She demonstrates quite effectively that the renal recipient does not necessarily encounter transplantation according to the hopes of clinicians, the public or researchers. As a final appeal, she asks those, social scientists in particular, involved in analysing this area of research to take a moral stance and be vigilant in ensuring that the embodied sufferings of all involved in this area become visible.

Taking a different tack on bodies and technoscience, the authors of the next two chapters view the body as a location for sport, positioning embodied subjects differentially within this cultural sphere (Shilling 2005: 104). Partaking in sporting activities implicates bodies engaging in cultural, material practices that give new meaning to temporal movements in social space outside biological, physiological and morphological body features and functions. Traditionally in popular culture, the movement of the body combined with the continual improvement in the efficient function and form of for example, a running body, emphasizes the body as a machine. A continuum of technologies from the banal to the spectacular capture this body and the idea of 'going to the gym' would not exist without the idea of the body as a high performance machine (Howson 2004: 89). Here, the concentration is on improving this 'machine'. Improving and maximizing performance, in particular for competition is the key. The focus of the sporting body on functioning, objectification and quantification implies that while this body can in principle be for leisure, play or recreation it is increasingly rationalized into a self-disciplined and self-regulated labouring body. In sport, social practices labour upon, discipline and transform the body (Shilling 2003: 96–7). In the course of this process of embodiment, gendered, aged and 'abled bodied' bodies are marked out and altered by existing social inequalities that form women's and men's bodies, young and old bodies and disabled and 'able bodied' bodies. This process appears to strengthen normalized body images.

With regards biomedicine, the health of the body is not one that can be simply measured by being disease free but is one that must also be able to demonstrate its fitness through the appropriate body pursuits to achieve a desired, healthy body image. Biomedicine directed towards sports requires the existence of highly trained, highly paid, drug-free, record breaking bodies, while these bodies provide a basis on which rationalization in society can be naturalized and viewed as the fulfilment of human destiny rather than as a technologically directed process imposed on humans (Shilling 2005: 113). This is regardless of the fact that these bodies undergo multiple, biotechnical measurements of their physiological capacities such as blood volume, heart rate, oxygenation, etc. (Lorber and Moore 2007: 71). For an athlete, adding drugs and foods known as 'nutracueticals' to one's diet does not seem like a major step or technological intervention; it is just another part of the training routine (p. 71). However, being a 'juiced up' or a chemically improved, sporting body means an athlete is not adhering to anti-doping regulations.

In this context, Chapter 2, 'Normalized Elites: Rethinking Doping as Abnormal Practice' by April Henning focuses on the emergence of sports medicine, the subsequent trend towards medical technology as a training tool for elite athletes and the chemically enhanced, sporting body through what has been termed over the years as 'doping'. Hemming shows how issues of doping encircle most elite sports and how elite runners' bodies are concurrently classified as 'top athletes' by a number of key stakeholders as well as in the media. She draws a great deal on reporting on elite runners in the US-based specialist running magazine *Runners World* and other media. It becomes quite clear that athletes' bodies were gradually becoming a captive group of subjects as they provided indispensable promise for investigations by medical researchers. Looking critically at the regulatory regime of anti-doping in sport, she unearths a fundamental dilemma. Elite athletes as a grouping are both pathologized and normalized within the anti-doping culture. On the one hand, their bodies may depend on any available technology to enhance their performance which goes directly against the anti-doping culture, on the other hand, if their bodies do not depend upon any available technology this embodied 'lack' removes them from the expected values and practices within the culture of elite athletes. This is regardless of the fact that their lifestyles and values vary from those of non-elites athletes. Hemming's exposé signals the need for an understanding of athletes by anti-doping agencies – an understanding that is open to the defining features and representations of elite athletes' bodies as shaped in different way from the rest of the population.

In Chapter 3, 'Embodying a Healthy Running Body in a British Non-Elite Road Running Community', Carole Sutton also focuses on the running body but she does this primarily within the genre of autobiography. Her story is all about how she has attempted over the years to embody a 'healthy running body'. This 'running story' is embedded in the method of autoethnography, which had its origins in anthropological work with the notion first being used by David Hayano (1979) in conjunction with the related notion, 'ethnographic autobiography'. While writing autobiographically is often seen negatively as a form of inexcusable self-indulgence, especially in academia, it is especially important for women to construct an authentic self in opposition to distorting cultural ideas in academia which shun the text as constructing subjectivities and corporeality as a subject of discourse (Oakley 2007: 23). Employing the method of autoethnography, Sutton opens up key concerns which enveloped her body's passage from an inactive to an active lifestyle. To set the scene, she examines initially the attractiveness of running in an international framework. She also reflects on the self-regulated running body within the context of consumer culture. Here, the modern individual in consumer culture is made conscious that he/she speaks not only through his/her lifestyle which becomes a 'healthy' life project but also through the aestheticization and stylized effect of his/her body on changing cultural contexts (Featherstone 1991: 86). While she uses an autoethnographic approach, she can be seen to identify herself alongside other 'postmodern witnesses' who have opened the way for health researchers to use autoethnography as a viable research tool (see Ettorre 2006). Certainly, in the last ten years, the area of health autoethnography has grown considerably, particularly in the field of nursing research (Foster, McAllister and O'Brien 2006, Ettorre 2010). By drawing upon personal data from her running diaries, she is able build a powerful embodied narrative of her running experiences and illustrates her, at times difficult, progression from a lone runner to a member of a non-elite road running club. One subtle theme which emerges is how while running may provide socially approved opportunities for both men and women to engage in such displays, there are definitely discernible gendered codes of conduct concerning degrees and forms of display (see Howson 2004: 75) for running bodies. In the end, we see how the intimate material she presents us with becomes the springboard for her further research on contemporary running bodies.

Bodies and Representations

The authors in this section of the book focus on social representations of the body, body practices and disciplinary regimes related to consumption, the internet and the discourse of gerontology, respectively. What is key here is how bodies are represented in order to be manipulated, managed and normalized through the relentless and constant engagement with the techniques of power, biopower. Shilling (2005: 2) argues that new forms of cultural consumption exhibit the sort of discipline, physical control and stylization commensurate with the display of a hyper-efficient embodied, performing self in consumer society. The rise of consumer society has given rise to a new body – the consuming body, a site for the nurturing of taste, the production of desire and the selling and consuming of goods, services, and pleasures (Falk 1994). Consumption involves the pursuit of embodied lifestyles through the acquisition of desired goods that suggest shared symbolic meanings and codes of stylized conduct. Identifiable regimes of modification or discipline are used to improve or perfect our bodies. We can identify bodily regimes of dieting, weight-watching, self-starvation, body-building, weight training, running, cosmetic surgery, reconstructive surgery, liposuction, yoga, competitive sport, military drills, meditation work, taking drugs – laxatives, and so on.

In Chapter 4, 'The Visible Body: Health Representations in a Consumer Society', Rui Gomes' bold contention that the moment we are living in, 'contemporaneity', emerges as a new visual regime marked by the growing power of visible techno-representations of present day bodies. His ideas on 'contemoraneity' shape his conceptions of body experiences as a product of medical-normative and moral discourses on the body. Doing a content analysis of media discourses in social identities construction in Portugal, he contends that uncertainty is a sign of the present day body crisis which appears alongside the image of a perfectible body. Gomes argues that images of (un) regulated bodies are not only empirical characteristics of these 'deviant bodies' but also the effect of discourses about bodies which emphasize the importance of the links between body shape and health in our consumer societies. Also important are 'new' body leisure activities such as yoga, tai-chi, bio-energy, relaxation techniques, etc. which are emblematic of the contemporary fascination with the embodied self. Gomes argues that this narcissistic fascination implies conquest of one's body 'innerness' and is the basis for self representations of one's embodied performances. For him, these are relatively novel self-representations which articulate a normative narcissism. These body leisure activities or self-knowledge technologies produce 'prerogatives' of the self from which emanate a movement of consciousness as well as an awareness of cultural responsibility. His conclusion is that we must contest the belief that each body is solely accountable for his/her condition, improving his/her body's reliability, remaining 'young' and his/her commitment to self-preservation.

While the majority of us are engaged in some kind of body project, body training or body discipline, this may reach an extreme or excessive level in one's efforts to perfect the body. If we strive for this ideal or perfectible body, we may be seen as well disciplined but we may also be seen as 'sick'. This is because biomedicine has identified anxieties, phobias, and obsessions underlying various illnesses. Two of these anxieties, phobias, or obsessions, self-starvation and the desire to amputate part of a limb, are analysed in Peter Conrad and Ashley Rondini's work, *The Internet and Medicalization: Reshaping the Global Body and Illness* (see Chapter 5). They begin their piece with the assumption that the world wide web has become a medium for endorsing or criticizing medicalized approaches to human troubles. Indeed, the internet has facilitated the extension of medicalization debates on a global scale. The individuals involved in Conrad and Rondini's two embodiment quandaries employ the world wide web to advance their opinions and assert their demands. Anorexics search for demedicalization and a certain amount of legitimacy, while wannabe amputees desire the opposite, medicalization in order to be cured. The authors contend that web activities of pro ana sites demonstrate the emergence of a global 'counter narrative' in opposition to the medical opinions that are accessible universally. On the other hand, 'wannabe amputees' or 'transabled bodies' share their desire to having their 'disorder' recognized as a medical problem, Body Integrity Identity Disorder or BIID. While the former group's bodies may be emblematic of our culture's obsession with non attainable ideals of attractiveness and conventional body shape and size, the latter group challenges established conceptions of disability, choice and medicalized bodies. While all of us experience the social and cultural burden to shape our bodies according to precise body images, pro ana bodies expose identifiable regimes of conceivably excessive discipline and bodily control, while 'transabled bodies' depict particular regimes of possibly extreme bodily modification – all done in the context of improving or perfecting one's body. What the construction of these bodies tells us is that while there may appear a variety of social bodies to choose from in society, the sorts of regimes in which medicalized bodies are conceived have different meanings for different individuals. Throughout human history, and in different cultures, we have decorated, clothed and modified our bodies in different ways to fulfil particular cultural and social purposes. Indeed, the body is a bearer of symbolic value and a form of physical capital: a possessor of power, status and distinctive symbolic forms that is integral to the accumulation of various resources (Bourdieu 1984). Nevertheless, individuals and groups have unequal opportunities for producing symbolically valued bodily forms and converting them into other resources. In this sense, medicalization may appear as an additional extra, but it appears as essential in helping to shape the desires and body practices of both anorexic bodies and wannabee amputees.

Most dominant groups in society tend to have the ability to define their bodies and lifestyles as superior, worthy of reward, and as, metaphorically and literally, the embodiment of superiority. One group which suffers from this embodiment of superiority is older people who are typically regarded as lacking rigour and intelligence and often become object of derision and ridicule (Biggs 2002: 167). With these ideas in mind, Jason Powell looks at how the ageing body acquires meaning as well as the uncertain representations of the ageing body in western culture in Chapter 6, 'The Ageing Body: From Bio-Medical Fatalism to Understanding Gender and Biographical Sensitivity'. To understand gender and the ageing body, Powell speaks to the question as to how a meaningful body is able to relate to social and cultural exertions. Of particular interest is his desire to consider the significance of the ageing body and ageing identity *vis-à-vis* feminist theory as an interconnector of gender and aging. In addition, he demonstrates why a biography of ageing is needed in the field. Powell deconstructs traditional gerontology and exposes the notion of the lifecourse as a linear trajectory, time as a finite resource, ageing as a one-way process (Featherstone and Hepworth 1998: 149) and getting old or increasing in age as an unchanging set of life 'stages'.

Powell's awareness of the need for an embodiment view on ageing reveals that the modern discourse on the ageing body as in decline or dying is yet another discourse imposed by medical science (p. 153). His challenge directed towards gerontology, specifically American gerontology, is an attempt to expose the fundamental ontological problems with disengagement theory. He contends that at heart, disengagement theory helps to mould negative cultural narratives, images and representations of ageing. The problem is not only disengagement theory's functionalist roots but also the effective ways it obscures how older people can 'intertextually' create positive narratives of old age by re-constructing these negative representations and explain more clearly their own embodied representations of their own identities. The evocation to consider biography as being essential when considering gendered older people's meanings and experiences of embodiment is innovative and refreshing. It is a confrontation with traditional gerontology with its paradigmatic, 're-territorialization' of the ageing body which denies difference, agency, subjectivity and the material body to old people, mirroring the embedded traditions of bioscience and contemporary cultural practices towards ageing. For Powell, to appreciate biography in this field is to re-construct gerontology into a more reflexive study which is deeply aware of the limits of gendered representations and perhaps, more importantly which is fully cognisant of how effective social science needs to clarify our grasp of the relationship between states of individual consciousness and social and cultural life.

Abject Bodies

In relationship to the body, biomedicine tends to overlook difference, agency, subjectivity and the cultural implications of materiality. In contrast, a more recent social science mandate has been to bring whole, sentient bodies back into our social consciousness. One key aim has been to generate an awareness that the traditional neglect of the body reproduced in a non-reflexive, imperialistic, hegemonic sociology naturalized bodies and legitimated control of privileged bodies over less privileged ones. In this context, feminists have documented the types of regulation, restraint, provocation and resistance experienced by gendered bodies. Anne Witz (2000: 2) contends that our disembodied sociological heritage includes a history of 'her excluded body' and 'his abject body' and she cautions that the recuperated body in sociology is in danger of being the abject male body. This is a warning which must be heeded. While we need to reclaim the lived experiences of both the excluded and abject body, we should become increasingly aware that what bodies experience, feel, suffer, bear, desire and consume should be the foundation stones for our sociologies (Frank 1995).

Regardless of the culture, society or defined social space in which certain individuals find themselves, some are viewed as more abject than others. Here, abject refers to the realm outside of culture which threatens to reduce culture to chaos; 'it is shapeless, monstrous, damp and slimy, boundless and beyond the outer limits' (Brook 1999: 14). Being abject places the one who is perceived as being abject in a liminal state. Being abject emphasizes that one has failed as an acceptable member of society and confirms the essential monstrosity of one's body – their abjection. As long as the monstrous remains the absolute other in its corporeal difference it poses a few problems and can be clearly put into an oppositional category of 'not me' (Shildrick 202: 2–3). Abject is not about affirming positive aspects of embodiment and subjectivity. Rather, abject denotes negativity. In examining the relationship between abjection and disgust, Ahmed (2007: 88) argues that when we think about how bodies become objects of disgust, we come to see how disgust is crucial to power relations and how becoming an abject body is all about the powerful role disgust has in the 'hierarchising of spaces as well as bodies'.

The notion of abject bodies as referring to the space outside of culture is clearly shown in Chapter 7, 'Where the excess grows': demarcating 'normal' and 'pathologically' obese bodies by Shirlene Badger. Badger shows how obesity is viewed as a public sickness, in everyday parlance as well as a corporeal manifestation. She contends that regardless of complicated knowledge bases regarding the causes of obesity between and within various disciplines, the obese body is perceived to be fairly obvious circling around a straightforward 'equation of input and output'. Her chapter demonstrates quite clearly that representations of this abject, obese body hold progressively more power in political, health, scientific and lay discourses. Those with obese bodies connect with these representations in a variety of ways and Badger argues that there is an array of norms that can be ascribed to these bodies – normalizing some body parts, while pathologizing others. This occurs through a wide range of regulatory regimes as well as become embedded in the subjective experiences of those with obese bodies.

Badger uses data drawn from an ethnographic study that focused on 'genetics of obesity'. The study included observations of obese children and their families interested in investigations on genetic causes for obesity. Embodiment runs throughout her chapter as she concentrates on the bodies of obese children and how they perform in different contexts. Abjection also is at the central core of her arguments. In this context, abjection is a kind of sickness; a horror at the body's vulnerability to a blurring of self (O'Connell 2005: 218). Thus it is not surprising that the sorts of images which emerge about respondents' bodies are both bizarre and commonplace. By plotting stories using snapshots from her ethnographic work, Bader designs these stories as two types of moments: fictional and political and she does this in order to demonstrate that these moments are proof of the 'generalizability' and 'assumed knowing-ness that is inferred on the obese body'. In this chapter, 'The Bridget Jones moment' helps to merge fiction and reality to highlight the numerous ways the obese body that can be played out at any given time. For Badger, the disease of space and preoccupation with the obese body of the younger generation conflicts with the specifically normalized opinions of the older generation about the larger body. This is an issue which needs to become more visible in contemporary society.

In Chapter 8, 'Bodies, Drugs and Reproductive Regimes', Elizabeth Ettorre looks at the reproducing body as a 'type of embodiment' that is available to drug using women within the regulatory regime of reproduction. For a woman drug user, being abject involves her body being disciplined by specific rituals and regulations of containment, invoking notions of embodied, monstrous deviance, abnormal activities, inexcusable performances and involvement in what is perceived as 'bad' material practices. While the cultural representations of pregnancy and drug use are presented, the author analyses the regulatory regime of reproduction with special reference to the power of normativity surrounding pregnancy and drug use. The author makes visible the 'real' material sites upon which the 'madness' and disorder of female drug use are inscribed. Many discourses (e.g. biomedical, legal, media, drugs, etc.) regulate this gendered body and shape it as a deviant, abject and 'monstrous' – one to be disassembled and reassembled and coded into diseased objects of knowledge and sites of intervention (Urla and Terry 1995).

In this chapter, we come to understand that the pregnant drug using body is not only the abject body who threatens to leak but also the 'bad' body whose leakiness contaminates the rational, public world of the logocentric economy. This body infects or contaminates the intimate, private spaces related to goodness and badness, inside and outside, self and other and mother and fetus. Reproductive bodies, both drug using and non-drug using, are necessary within 'the somatic society' as they become visualized through the 'scopic drive'. A main aim of the chapter is to see the importance of resistance to the dominant ideologies of reproduction by those, such as pregnant drug users, who can be seen to embody a political identity, opposition to this sort of visualization and a type of adversarial consciousness. In a 'cyborgian' sense, this means that many, if not all forms of women's embodiment are deeply related to their adaptation to normality and cultural management on a global scale. Female bodies do matter in this global assimilation or manipulation. Attitudes towards, values about, discourses on and tools of prevailing technologies surrounding pregnancy and drug use enforce and shape novel cultural relations for women's bodies on this global scale. A cyborg identity gives potential embodied agency to those declined secure 'race, sex and/ or class membership' such as women drug users who are able to have the cultural know-how in interpreting networks and/or technologies of power. What becomes clear from this chapter is that the drug field cannot retreat from these systematic regulatory practices. That the technologies surrounding drugs use and the scientific discourses about drugs are employed to inflict enforced representation and constant abuse on the basis of race, gender and class may appear at first glance as shocking. However, it is a truth which needs to be told.

While we will see in reading the work in *Culture, Bodies and the Sociology of Health* how medicalized bodies are pressed into constant normativity, those with ability to read 'webs of power' may champion their own survival and social justice. Yet, resistance is not always cultivated by those who are subjects to biomedicine. While the chapters in this book are empirical and theoretical explorations which illustrate the importance of contextualizing the body as a cultural entity, they demonstrate that the spaces and boundaries between healthy bodies are becoming more diverse than ever before on a global level. A key element of these explorations is how a morality of health embedded in our cultures has been concerned with constructing the material, fleshy body as well as surveying, managing and controlling it and its movements. After reading these texts, we become clear that uncovering the more hidden aspects of the cultural fabrication of health requires detailed examination of the regulatory practices used by experts in biomedicine and the material requirements of our global consumer culture which target bodies. This development involves an understanding of the intricate processes by which the age of modernity marks the emergence of the material bodily self at the centre of our theoretical attention. Re-shaping bodies in the sociology of health means that we must re-shape our political awareness of the body as well – a goal which has scholarly interest for all social scientists interested in embodiment theories and reflexivity.

References

Berg, M. and Akrich, M. (2004). Introduction – bodies on trial: performances and politics in medicine and biology. *Body and Society*, 10: 1–12.

Biggs, H. (2002). The ageing body, in M. Evans and E. Lee (eds) *Real Bodies: A Sociological Introduction*. Houndmills, Basingstoke: Palgrave, pp. 167–84.

Bourdieu, P. (1984). *Distinction, A Social Critique of the Judgement of Taste*. London: Routledge and Kegan Paul.

Braidotti, R. (1994). *Nomadic Subjects: Embodiment and Sexual Difference in Contemporary Feminist Theory*. New York: Columbia University Press.

Braidotti, R. (2006). *Transpositions: On Nomadic Ethics*. Cambridge: Polity Press.

Brook, B. (1999). *Feminist Perspectives on the Body*. London: Longman.

Bunton, R. and Barrows, R. (1995). Consumption and health in the 'epidemiological' clinic of late modern medicine, in R. Bunton, S. Nettleton and R. Burrows (eds), *The Sociology of Health Promotion*. London: Routledge, pp. 206–22.

Burkitt, I. (1999). *Bodies of Thought: Embodiment, Identity and Modernity*. London: Sage Publications, Ltd.

Cambrisio, A., Young, A. and Lock, M. (2000). Introduction, in M. Lock, A. Young and A. Combrisio (eds) *Living and Working with the New Medical Technologies: Intersections of Inquiry*. Cambridge: Cambridge University Press, pp. 1–16.

Charmaz, Kathy. (1983). Loss of self: a fundamental form of suffering in the chronically ill. *Sociology of Health and Illness*, 5, 2: 168–95.

Cregan, K. (2006). *The Sociology of the Body*. London: Sage Publications.

Davis, K. (2007). Reclaiming women's bodies: Colonalist trope or critical epistemology? In C. Shilling (ed.) *Embodying Sociology: Retrospect, Progress and Prospects*. Oxford: Blackwell Publishing/*The Sociological Review*, pp. 50–64.

Ettorre, E. (2002). *Reproductive Genetics, Gender and the Body*. London: Routledge.

Ettorre, E. (2005). Gender, older female bodies and medical uncertainty: finding my feminist voice by telling my illness story. *Women's Studies International Forum*, 28: 535–46.

Ettorre, E. (2006). Making sense of my illness journey from thyrotoxicosis to health: an autoethnography. *Auto/Biography*, 14, 2: 153–75.

Ettorre, E. (forthcoming). Autoethnography: making sense of personal illness journeys, in Bourgeault, I., De Vries, R. and Dingwall, R. (eds) *Handbook on Qualitative Health Research*. Thousand Oaks: Sage Publications, Inc.

Falk, P. (1994). *The Consuming Body*. London: Sage Publications.

Feathersone, M. (1991). *Consumer Culture and Postmodernism*. London: Sage Publications.

Featherstone, M. and Hepworth, M. (1998). Ageing, the lifecourse and the sociology of embodiment, in G. Scambler and P. Higgs (eds) *Modernity, Medicine and Health: Medical Sociology Towards 2000*, London: Routledge, pp.147–75.

Foster, K., McAllister, M., and O'Brien, L. (2006). Extending the boundaries: Autoethnography as an emergent method in mental health nursing. *International Journal of Mental Health Nursing*, 15: 44–53.

Fox, N. (1998). The promise of postmodernism for the sociology of health and medicine, in G. Scambler and P. Higgs (eds) *Modernity, Medicine and Health: Medical Sociology Towards 2000*. London: Routledge, pp. 29–45.

Frank, A. (1991). *At the Will of the Body: Reflections on Illness*. Boston: Houghton Mifflin.

Frank, A. (1995). *The Wounded Storyteller: Body, Illness and Ethics*. Chicago: University of Chicago Press.

Frank, A. (2001). Can we research suffering? *Qualitative Health Research*, 11, 3: 353–62.

Frank, A. (2004). *The Renewal of Generosity: Illness, Medicine, and How to Live*. Chicago: University of Chicago Press.

Hayano, D. (1979). Auto-ethnography: paradigms, problems, and prospects. *Human Organization* 38: 99–104.

Howson, A. (2004). *The Body in Society: An Introduction*. Cambridge: Polity Press.

Hughes, B. (2000). Medicalized bodies, in P. Hancock, B. Hughes, E. Jagger, K. Paterson, R. Russell, E. Tulle-Winton and M. Tyler (eds) *The Body, Culture and Society*. Buckingham: Open University Press, pp. 12–28.

James, A. and Hockey, J. (2007). *Embodying Health Identities*. Houndmills, Basingstoke: Palgrave Macmillan.

Kelly, M.P. and Field, D. (1996). Medical sociology, chronic illness and the body. *Sociology of Health and Illness* 18, 2: 241–57.

Lorber, J. and Moore, L.J. (2007). *Gendered Bodies: Feminist Perspectives.* Los Angeles: Roxbury Publishing Company.

Lundin, S. (1997). Visions of the body, in S. Lundin and M. Ideland (eds) *Gene Technology and the Public.* Lund, Sweden: Nordic Academic Press.

Lupton, D. (1994). *Medicine as Culture: Illness, Disease and the Body in Western Societies.* London: Sage Publications.

Lyon, M.L. and Barbalet, J.M. (1994). Society's body: emotion and the 'somatization' of social theory, in T.J. Csordas (ed.) *Embodiment and Experience: The Existential Ground of Culture and the Self.* Cambridge: Cambridge University Press, pp. 48–66.

Nettleton, S. and Watson, J. (1998). *The Body in Everyday Life.* London and New York: Routledge.

Oakley, A. (2007). *Fractures: Adventures of a Broken Body.* Bristol: The Policy Press.

O'Connell, K. (2005). The devouring: genetics, abjection and the limits of law, in M. Shildrick and R. Mykitiuk (eds) *Ethics of the Body: Postconventional Challenges*, London: MIT Press, pp. 217–34.

O'Neill, J. (2004). *Five Bodies: Re-figuring Relationships.* London: Sage Publications.

Scambler, G. (1991). Medical sociology and modernity: reflections on the public sphere and the roles of intellectuals and social critics, in G. Scambler and P. Higgs (eds) *Modernity, Medicine and Health: Medical Sociology Towards 2000.* London: Routledge, pp. 46–65.

Shildrick, M. (1997). *Leaky Bodies and Boundaries: Feminism, Postmodernism and (Bio)Ethics.* London and New York: Routledge.

Shildrick, M. (2002). *Embodying the Monster: Encounters with the Vulnerable Self.* London: Sage Publications.

Shildrick, M. and Price, J. (1998). Introduction: Vital signs: texts, bodies and biomedicine, in M. Shildrick and J. Price (eds) *Feminist Reconfigurations of the Bio/logical Bbody.* Edinburgh: Edinburgh University Press, pp. 1–17.

Shilling, Chris. (1993). *The Body and Social Theory.* London: Sage Publications.

Shilling, Chris. (2003). *The Body and Social Theory.* (Second edition) London: Sage Publications.

Shilling, C. (2005). *The Body in Culture, Technology and Society.* London: Sage Publications.

Shilling, C. (2008). *Changing Bodies: Habit, Crisis and Creativity.* London: Sage Publications.

Turner, B. (1986). *Medical Power and Social Knowledge.* London: Sage Publications.

Turner, B. (1992). *Regulating Bodies: Essays in Medical Sociology.* London: Routledge.

Urla, J. and Terry, J. (1995). Introduction: mapping embodied deviance, in Terry, J. and Urla, J. (eds) *Deviant Bodies: Critical Perspectives on Difference in Science and Popular Cultures.* Bloomington, Indiana: Indiana University Press, pp. 1–18.

Wilkinson, I. (2005). *Suffering: A Sociological Introduction.* Cambridge: Polity Press.

Williams, S.J. and Bendelow, G. (1998). *The Lived Body: Sociological Themes, Embodied Issues.* London: Routledge.

Williams, S.J. (2003). *Medicine and the Body.* London: Sage Publications.

Williams, S.J. (2004). Embodiment, in J. Gabe, M. Bury, M.A. Elston (eds) *Key Concepts in Medical Sociology.* London: Sage Publications, pp. 73–76.

Witz, A. (2000). Whose body matters? Feminist sociology and the corporeal turn in sociology and feminism. *Body and Society*, 6, 2: 1–24.

PART I
Bodies and Technoscience

Chapter 1

Transplantation, Organ Donation and (In)human Experience: Re-writing Boundaries through Embodied Perspectives on Kidney Failure

Ciara Kierans

New Medical Technologies: Biopolitical Arenas

Organ transplantation is one of the most potent symbols of what social scientists have come to term 'the new medical technologies'; powerful tools, treatments and procedures that emerged as a result of rapid technological development, innovation and the shift to the paradigm supplied by the new genetics. They have, in turn, profound implications for human embodiment, social identity, forms of medical governance, the distribution of medical resources and our understandings of the borders of life itself (Casper 1994, Davis-Floyd 1994, Dumit 1997, Lock et al. 2000, Rabinow 1996, 2000). In all their various forms, medical technologies involve deeply embedded ways of organising and reorganising the parameters of health, healing and the human body. Integral to contemporary biomedicine, and part of the 'taken-for-granted' background against which it operates, medical technologies have been, for some time now, a critical resource for social scientists who wish to examine the complex ways in which the practices and productions of medical knowledge connect up with power relations, the human experience of health and illness and new possibilities for living and dying (Foucault 1998 [1976], Latour 1993, Rabinow 2000). This chapter elaborates on these themes, providing an introduction to work in this area with specific emphasis on the technologically mediated relationship between the reconfigured body-in-transplantation and the experiencing subject.

'The Shock of the New': Lessons from the Past

A few words of caution are needed before proceeding. The growth of social scientific studies of technology and medicine in recent years testifies to our contemporary preoccupation with the new. It is critical, however, that we do not fetishise technology as an exclusively contemporary problem. It is important to remember that current attempts to think systematically through the multiple ways in which technology impacts upon society owe a great deal to work that came before. Discussed at length by both Marx and Durkheim, and representing central themes at all stages in the development of sociology and anthropology, technologies have long been recognised as both determinants of social structures and as phenomena forged within the crucible of social relationships (Durkheim 1982 [1912], Marx 1968 [1852], Turner 2007). Within early work on this subject, a key role was given to the body-in-society, as the productive source of technological innovation (Marx and Engels (1940 [1846]). At the same time, the body was also increasingly cast as a key site at which power could be exercised, as bodies come to be increasingly invested, invaded and reconstructed by processes made possible by technological innovation and advancement – principally those associated with the rise of the modern factory system and the disciplinary forces it was able to harness (Foucault 1977).

When carried forward and applied to the new medical technologies (the focus here), these insights about the duality of technology, as both master and slave, product and cause, agent and effect of socio-cultural change, retain their validity. Indeed, it is precisely these ways of thinking about the social, cultural, economic, political and embodied implications of technological practice, which reflect what the philosopher Michel Foucault sought to capture through his studies of 'biopolitics' and the production of 'bio-technico-power' (Foucault 1998 [1976]). This modality of power centralises the ways in which the human body, individually and collectively, can be altered and augmented 'making good the deficiencies and finitude of one's natural endowment' (Jackson 2005: 120). Tracing biopower thus helps us to see the complex network of connections between, on the one hand, developments in medical knowledge and innovations in medical practices and, on the other, the various social and cultural systems these developments emerge within but which also, once in place, part determine the shape those developments will go on to take and the points at which those processes will terminate.

Turning from theoretical questions to more substantive empirical ones, the main methodological lesson to be drawn is this: when setting out to understand practices like transplantation the researcher must move beyond restricted conceptions of either the medical setting or technical act alone, to take up positions where it becomes possible to see the role those practices play in much larger socio-medical processes. This is easier said than done. These larger processes are highly complex and their significance deeply contested. As a result, the new medical technologies have come to represent, at one and the same time, material promises of utopian futures as well as harbingers of coming human-generated catastrophes (Turner 2007). From bioengineering to nanotechnology, scientists, engineers and doctors conjure the prospect of 'living forever' through awe-inspiring advances in such diverse fields as therapeutic cloning, stem cells and 'immortal' cell-lines, 'smart' pharmaceuticals, and micro-medical disease detection processes that operate at the molecular level (Turner 2007, Williams 2003). Meanwhile, those working at the other end, on the development of reproductive technologies, tell us that we are progressively extending our ability to control the manner in which human life comes into the world by removing the residual uncertainties which surround our entrance on the stage through the gradual 'taming' of the 'wilder' aspects of conception, pregnancy and birth (Casper 1995, Davis-Floyd and Dumit 1998, Rapp 2000). As Marx prophesised, our biological 'species being', our 'bios', appears to be being brought under our direct control (Arendt 1969, Marx 1970 [1846]). At the same time, however, those self-same technologies have given rise to deep-seated anxieties about the hubris of knowledge, captured in speculation about unforeseen dangers: fears about iatrogenetic risk in nanomedicine exacerbated by uncertainties in the ways we evaluate the toxicity of nanoparticles (Renn and Roco 2006); about increased population surveillance as genetic screening becomes further embedded as a technology of government (Armstrong 1995, Kaufert 2000); over the bioprospecting of cell lines and the struggle between indigenous communities and multinational biogenetic companies over 'rights' to genetic 'property' (Lock 2007); over the commodification of the body parts used in organ transplantation (Scheper-Hughes and Wacquant 2002). All these fears and more besides combine to suggest that if the new medical technologies provide a map of the future, it is one in which monsters lie.

Utopian visions and dystopian anxieties notwithstanding, these technological advances, according to Paul Rabinow, stand to be a greater force for reshaping society and life itself than the revolution in physics, because of their far reaching consequences for identity, kinship and reproduction, what Rabinow has termed 'biosociality' (Rabinow 1996). The human genome project, to take one of the more remarkable examples, has forever altered our understandings of biology and nature, once viewed as immutable and fixed, but now fundamentally repositioned within the domains of society and culture, collapsing prior and held-to dichotomies of nature/nurture, science/culture, human/machine, individual/group and local/global (Hellman 2007, Rheinberger 2000). Moreover, how we understand this 'power'-full domain, has, according to Jackson, been somewhat too restrictive to medicine, obscuring the wider influences of venture capital, political and corporate imperatives. Michael Jackson suggests we have too often neglected how new medical technologies are embedded in the structures of global capitalism, 'particularly, in the ways in which corporate and state interests in the north compete for control over this new form of power – in roughly the same way that the terms eugenics – the "old genetics" – once disguised insidious state programmes for the manipulation of individual fates and national destinies' (Jackson 2005: 120). As a consequence, for Jackson, analysis of the new technologies must begin 'not with an attempt to evaluate their ethical, economic and political implications for our future, but with a critique of the ways in which these technologies are already implicated in global patterns of inequality and injustice' (Ibid, 120). These position-takings seem to call for clear-eyed evaluation on biomedicine, one neither rejectionist nor duped. However, the extent to which the social sciences might go about providing this is a matter for debate. What I want to do next is look at the main ways in which social scientists have gone about orienting to these problems.

To do this, I want to propose three analytical starting points from which a range of social theorists have chosen to open up the problematics attached to technologies. They will form an analytical backdrop against which my later discussion on organ transplantation and 'recipiency' will be placed.

New Medical Technologies: Key Methodological and Analytical Constructions

Some key analytical positions have been drawn upon to help us make sense of this rather dispersed domain of inquiry incorporating many biomedical specialities, theoretical concerns and methodological standpoints. Representing alternative ways of addressing similar sets of problems, but beginning from different starting points and moving in different directions, they, in turn, help us to think about how transplant technologies have come to be written and understood within the social sciences. Just as importantly, they also highlight what has been neglected or rendered invisible through the production of debate. While not wishing to review an entire field of research, I want to draw attention to these three dominant modes of thinking about technologies as they relate to intersecting bodies of academic work. For the purpose of this chapter, they will be considered in terms of (1) assemblages, hybrids and cyborg constructions; (2) the social practices and procedural work of biomedicine and (3) anxieties, transgressions and boundary concerns.

Assemblages, Hybrids and Cyborg Constructions

A core construct is that of the cyborg. Cyborgs may be considered as sensitising concepts, theoretical and rhetorical devices that force us to look at the new social relationships produced through biotechnical and biorobotic practices, and the human body as neither entirely natural nor artificial. In her *Primate Visions*, Donna Haraway defines the cyborg as an entity in which,

> ... two kinds of boundary are simultaneously problematic: 1) that between animals (or other organisms) and humans, and 2) that between self-controlled, self-governing machines (automatons) and organisms, especially humans (models of autonomy). The cyborg is the figure born of the interface of automation and autonomy (Haraway 1989: 139).

Haraway draws on Marx, to show that cyborgs become a route to looking at 'the new social means of technoscientific production'; new ways in which we organise our lives (Haraway 1989). This has involved an inevitable re-evaluation of our changing positions as subjects-in-the-world by focusing on the new forms of embodied experience that have become possible through social-technological relations. In health and medical arenas, cyborgs emerge as the result of a wide range of interventions from prostheses, sensory technologies and implantable devices alongside technologically aided ways of seeing, scanning, screening, testing, researching and so on (Casper 1995, Davis-Floyd 1994, Ihde 1990, 2007).

Among the many examples to chose from, Monica Casper's work on reproductive technologies has been particularly instructive of what we get from using the cyborg concept. Through an examination of the ways in which pregnancy and the bodies of women are put to an increasing range of uses, and with consideration for both the ontological and epistemological construction of cyborgs, Casper questions why we should classify anyone or anything as a cyborg in the first place. While Haraway talked about the new social relations of techno-scientific production, she was not simply talking about the degree to which technology penetrates our everyday lives, she also meant that there are real social, political and economic outcomes to these processes, that necessitate us keeping power as central to our understanding of the cyborg. Casper's work does just that, as she charts some of these outcomes in relation to the highly contested uterine space of a pregnant woman's body (Casper 1995). In doing this, she draws on six ways in which cyborg theory can be used to critically examine current developments in medical practice and reproductive technologies and the ways in which pregnant women come to be redrawn into these hybrid ontologies. These include: (1) technologies of vision, such as ultrasound, which enable a foetus in utero to be seen by those outside; (2) technologies of diagnosis, such as amniocentesis, which transforms the foetus into clinical data, and re-configures when pregnancy might be considered to start or end; (3) technologies of life, through postmortem maternal ventilation, altering our understanding of motherhood from a natural embodied state; (4) technologies of death, for example abortion, and the ways in which foetal cyborgs acquire new uses for research and therapy; (5) technologies of pain, such as foetal wound healing mechanisms or cosmetic surgery, where foetal cyborgs are reconstructed through research on animals and in vitro simulations; (6) technologies of healing. Incorporated here are are numerous examples of standardised technological interventions in the course of prenatal care which lead to the construction of medical cyborgs, such as, the use of pharmacological agents, nutritional supplements for foetal development, foetal blood sampling and so on and the prospective inclusion of gene therapy, foetus-to-foetus transplantation and experimental foetal surgery. Casper argues that these technological practices have made possible the emergence of a plethora of foetal cyborgs and technomoms transforming them from natural, organic entities into a very different kind of site within medical practice. These technological complexes change what it is to be a mother and help us to recognise that mothers are not everywhere the same.

Turning to organ transplantation, in very similar ways cyborg concepts have been both key practical and conceptual devices for describing the associated embodied, social and political implications. These include the ways in which the boundaries of the body profoundly change through dialysis (Hables Gray 2001) the reconstitution of categories of life and death through technologies of harvesting from the brain dead (Agamben 1998, Hogle 1999, Lock 1996); the reconstruction of the relationship between self and other through cadaver and live organ donation (Sharp 2006); the ontological implications of hybridity for the experiences of organ recipients (Kierans 2005) and the ontological status of the donor body (Hogle 1995a).

That transplantation practices impact profoundly on the organic unity of the body have for some authors been seen as a threat to the embodied self, an end point in biomedical dehumanisation (Young 1997). For others, cyborg possibilities can be experienced as a means of embracing new conditions for living through extending the boundaries of embodiment. In her attempts to fully engage with hybrid forms, Donna Haraway conjures a vision of the future which suggests ' ... a cyborg world might be about lived social and bodily realities in which people are not afraid of their joint kinship with animals and machines, not afraid of permanently partial identities or contradictory stand points' (Haraway 1991: 154). In contrast to the horrors, hybridisation can be considered part and parcel of the human existence and social life in societies and cultures, past and present.

> We are all Creoles of sorts: hybrid, divided, polyphonic and parodic, a pastiche of our Selves. The contemporary body-self is fragmentary, often incoherent and inconsistent, precisely because it arises from contradictory and paradoxical experiences, social tensions and conflicts (Van Wolputte 2004: 263).

As I will go on to show these aspects of contradiction, partiality and disjuncture are useful for thinking about organ 'recipiency' and how renal patients, in particular, piece together new ways of living and experiencing their bodies. Hybrid lives not only reveal new ways of being alive and living, but profoundly alter the phenomenology of bodily experience and bodily processes. These are brought dramatically into relief through the technologies of dialysis and transplantation, where the body's internal mechanisms are no longer concealed but visible, audible and tangible (Kierans 2001, 2005, Leder 1990).

Social Practices and the Procedural Work of Biomedicine

There has been a tendency to see new medical technologies as constellations of material objects. Social scientists have reacted to this by treating them as phenomena brought into being as the outcomes of particular cultural and institutional practices (Barnes and Bloor 1996, Knorr-Cetina and Mulkay 1983, Latour 1987, Rabinow 1996, 1999, Latour and Woolar 1986). These authors have been major contributors to a growing body of ethnographic work with a concern for how science and technology gets 'done', is put to work, within their local contexts and have been hugely influential in helping us to navigate the disjunctures between bodies of knowledge and knowledge construction and the differences between the reconstructed logics of scientific knowledge versus the logics-in-use of scientific practices (Kaplan 1968, Rabinow 1996, 1999). For sociologists of scientific knowledge, scientific communities – like any other community – are characterised by networks and forms of social interaction, and their work – like any other forms of work – couple the informal and accidental along with the formal and procedural.

Consequentially, biomedicine, technology and disease are in no way independent formations, privileged a priori as external to culture. Medicine and its objects are not objects-in-themselves, but, as Anne Marie Mol explains, objects-in-action, enactments, ways of doing things, part of the highly differentiated and mundane work of those who practice medicine (Mol 2002). It is through these everyday practices, that the objects of interest here, diseases, organs, body parts, pharmacological processes, technologies, interventions, organisational rules and bureaucracies, come into being, emerge or recede, becoming matters of concern and action for specific groups of people.

Transplantation technologies therefore emerge as part of a complex socio-technical apparatus, an assemblage composed of bureaucracies, bioethical legislation, power relations, different types of medical personnel, cultural constructions of death, dying and the body, specialist diagnostic methods, technical procedures, pharmaceuticals, machines and regulatory frameworks, and so on, all of which work to make transplantation possible. The distinctions between scientific protocols or procedures and ways of implementing and applying them have also been fruitfully problematised by researchers of this kind and there are key examples which focus on transplantation and organ procurement.

In a paper focusing on how protocols for organ procurement are 'worked through' at the local level, Linda Hogle, for example, describes how the standards in assigning donor cadaver status – which are assumed to be employed uniformly across institutional settings – are very often reinterpreted, modified or resisted in local contexts (Hogle 1995b). Veena Das provides a similar account of the disjuncture between 'rules and their execution' in her work on transplantation in India, where she describes the complex cultural interpretations which are brought to bear on the legislation on brain stem death (Das 2000). She points out that protocols and rules are not descriptions of events, but subject to intense negotiations between different stakeholders in the clinical environment. Margaret Lock makes similar points when comparing transplantation practices across cultures. With attempts to 'pin death down' in the debates on brain death, Lock explains that while standardised criteria for determining death in Europe and North America have been in existence for two decades, the guidelines and procedures are not necessarily referred to in the same ways, with often conflicting accounts about the value of confirmatory procedures (Lock 2000). When comparisons are made to societies like Japan, the ground of argument becomes even more contested:

> In North America ... a brain dead body is alive, but no longer a person, whereas in Japan, such an entity is both living and a person, at least for several days after a declaration of brain death. Because, in the Japanese case, the social identity of brain dead patients remains intact, a brain dead body cannot be easily made into

an object and commodified, but continues to be invested with 'human rights' (Lock 2000: 256).

In discussing the surgical management of organ procurement in the US, Sharp remarks on the unusual fact that though organ donors have legally and officially been declared brain dead, they are nonetheless given anaesthetic. When exploring the matter further through interviews, Sharp's questions were met by a wide variety of responses, from the need to suppress residual spinal activity to the importance of relaxing the donor body so that it will not move during surgery, to quelling residual anxieties among surgical staff (Sharp 2006).

What people who have adopted these perspectives on science and technology have taught us is that we should be cautious in accepting that pictures of complex technocractic processes are necessarily guides to how they operate. Representations, as a result, only acquire their meanings within systems of practice (Wittgenstein 1953). On their own, they tell us nothing. This body of studies helps to produce an understanding of technologies in-use, designating for them a cultural and human ground of action. They also enable us to move technology out of the 'black box', where it often resides as a specific kind of object with discernable causes and effects (Latour 1987).

Anxieties, Transgressions and Boundary Concerns: Technology at the Intersections

As was discussed earlier, it is almost impossible to introduce the subject of technology without concern for the anxieties provoked and unsettling worries that something precious has been transgressed. In discussing the ambiguities attached to technology with reference to genetically modified crops and gene technologies, Jackson, for example, returns to the fact that we find little that is actually new in current debates about the dangers posed by advanced technologies. Biotechnology, in Jackson's view,

> simply updates and re-dramatises the human anxieties that have always come with new technologies – anxieties that express deep misgivings about our human ability to comprehend and control any new phenomenon. In the case of gene technologies, the manifest lack of consistent and confident institutional or governmental control only exacerbates this crisis of agency. One simply does not know enough about the new technology to be able to feel that one can manage or predict its repercussions (Jackson 2005: 112).

Technologies embody our fantasies and our fears. They are both a fountain of hope and a font of despair, with the potential for profits *and* losses (Williams 2003). Margaret Lock has described the Shiva-like character of prevasive biomedical technologies as 'potential creators of happiness, but destroyers of society as we know it' (Lock 1995: 391).

Technologies, in other words, are increasingly being treated as mediators in struggles between the 'old ways' and 'new ways', giving rise to endless polarisations in attempts to make sense of, resolve, or resist their effects on our lives. Indeed, this has become a common rhetorical starting point for many theorists, part of their efforts to elaborate the borders or boundaries between uncommon zones of activity and the ways in which they have come to be breached (Brodwin 2000, Younger 1990, Fox 1993, Scheper-Hughes 1998). These arguments have tended to trade on our understanding of the body as inherently symbolic of social processes, which as Mary Douglas puts it, is 'a model which can stand for any bounded system', whose 'boundaries can represent any boundaries which are threatened' (Douglas 1968: 38).

Organ transplantation is exemplary in this regard as it tests many different boundaries at once: the borders between the immune system and the environment (foreign organisms); between machines, humans and animals; between the biological and the social-cultural; between procurement and 'recipiency'; and between altruism and gain. A complex domain of medical techniques and technologies, transplantation traverses the lines drawn between nations, cultures, economies, and the divisions between rich and poor, reconfiguring in the process what it means to be a person. Transplantation has raised, and continues to raise difficult bioethical and cultural questions about the status of the dead body, understandings of personhood, and, particularly as the demands for organs rise, the criteria we use to distinguish life from death. In one way or another, these multi-level boundary concerns draw our attention to a range of interconnected sites at the local and global level where issues relating to transplantation practices – i.e. procurement, organ selling, donation and 'recipiency' – serve to reorganise the relationship between self and other, private and public, resentment and gratitude, sickness and health. These relationships are, in turn, made more problematic by such things as the unevenness of access to life-saving procedures and the shortage of organs globally, problems increasingly rendered as public health crises and so matters for collective action (Randall 1991).

In relation to this, Lesley Sharp has questioned the responsibility the transplant industry bears in generating its own patients and creating a technological imperative, thus increasing the national demand for organs and exacerbating shortages. According to Sharp, 'transplantation is in essence the capitalist's dream because the supply can never answer the pressing and ever-increasing social desire for these coveted goods' (Sharp 2006: 18). This alters the construction of transplantation as an altruistic, patient-centred enterprise to an increasing international and extraordinarily expensive for-profit market-based industry (Williams 2003). The commodification of organs in particular, and body parts in general, though far from a new problem, has given rise to a darker side to organ procurement, captured in stories of organ-stealing (Sheper-Hughes 1996, Younger

1990). What Haraway treats as a positive becomes a negative when exploited for monetary gain, as body parts acquire financial utility.

Commodifying organs has become a rhetorical starting point for many researchers, reflecting how 'global capitalism, advanced medicine and biotechnologies, have incited new tastes and desires for the skin, bone, blood, tissues and reproductive and genetic material of the other' (Scheper-Hughes 2002). Nancy Scheper Hughes, Lawrence Cohen and their colleagues at *Organs Watch* in the University of Berkeley have been particularly active in drawing attention to an array of problems associated with the global exchange of organs. These include:

- race, class and gender inequalities and injustices in the acquisition, harvesting and distribution of organs;
- the widespread violation of national laws and international regulations against the sale of organs;
- the collapse of cultural and religious sanctions against body dismemberment and commercial use of body parts in the face of enormous market pressures in the transplant industry;
- the emergence of new forms of debt peonage in which the commodified kidney occupies a critical role;
- the coexistence of 'compensated gifting' of kidneys within extended families and coerced gifting of kidneys by domestic workers and by prisoners in exchange for secure work and reduction in prison sentences;
- popular resistance to newly mandated laws of presumed consent for organ donation;
- violations of cadavers in hospital morgues and police mortuaries in which organs and tissues are removed without consent for barter or sale;
- wasting of viable organs in the context of intense competition between public and private transplant units;
- medically substantiated allegations of kidney theft from vulnerable patients, mostly poor and female, during routine surgeries (Scheper-Hughes 2001: 35–6).

The traffic in organs described above can easily be mapped to global inequalities in capital and labour, and show organ procurement to be a social justice issue with repercussions for different populations across the globe. It goes without saying that as a social justice issue, these are critical concerns. However, it is also an area where it is hardest to draw unambiguous lessons from. This is because anthropologists, in reflecting on these anxieties and concerns, become participants in the very processes they are commenting on and as a result problematise the status of what they are talking about. What is presented are evaluative points not descriptions of empirical phenomena. My point is not simply a methodological one, but also a moral and an ethical one.

We need to think about the ways in which these points are made. The polemical rendition of organ givers and organ receivers might be considered an analytical short-coming with moral consequences. It can sensationalise and prioritise procurement, while masking the problems of recipients and disguising the fact that inequalities and suffering characterise relationships at both ends of the chain of supply and demand. In much of the anthropological literature on organ donation and transplantation, the recipient is curiously absent from theorising, with little presence beyond the part they play in the biomedical narratives that are being ruthlessly critiqued. They typically feature as caricatures: privileged western consumers, cherished patients, their biographies and medical histories known, and their proprietary rights over the bodies the poor, living and dead, are virtually unquestioned. They are juxtaposed with those who through poverty and necessity are forced to sell the organs upon which their health depends or as grateful patients, media items in the broader transplant success story. This is not dissimilar to ways of constructing medical professionals and biotechnical entrepreneurs as unambiguously 'the bad guys' in the contemporary story. The problem with polemical stances such as these is that as one takes positions, the problem, under-fire, is taken-for-granted. It is uncritically accepted.

In trying to cope with the anxieties surrounding transplantation, these polemical renderings persist, invoking age-old distinctions between self and other, body and machine, science fiction and scientific fact. The arguments suffer from what George Marcus and Willis before him cautions as 'anaemic' analysis (Marcus 1998, Willis 1976). In other words, in the attempt to deliver a unified, ethnographic counter-narrative to dominant representations of organ transplantation, researchers produce a 'bloodless' account where the phenomena investigated come to be caught in the borders between different zones of human affairs, and the researcher politically positions their thinking to highlight some issues at the expense of others. This has made it difficult to fully understand transplantation as moral, bioethical and biopolitical phenomenon across a range of interconnected arenas at both the local and global level and at the sites of donation and 'recipiency', which are inevitably interconnected.

What this means is that we need to see the human body as more than a 'soft machine' animated by powerful interests (although it is that too), but as an important empirical site for examining the embodiment of culture, society, power, economic relations and technology. Jackson argues – in a similar fashion to Haraway – that we need to consider the ambiguity and complexities that arise from technologies, less as a conceptual problem or logical anomaly, but as what he refers to as 'an inherent condition of intersubjective transitivity – where we are one moment merging with another (or another thing), the next distancing or separating from it' (Jackson 2005: 125):

> This fluent experience of being self only in relationship to not-self, of subject only in relation to another that is 'object' sets the scene, in my view, for the ambivalence we experience when confronted by new technologies – for a technology is, intersubjectively speaking, no different from another person, a tool, a thing, a stranger, or the earth; it has the potential to become a part of us, a

condition of the possibility of being ourselves, but it is also a perpetual reminder of what we stand to lose in any relationship with what we see as 'other' (Ibid 2005: 125).

There is no denying that the anxieties thus provoked help us to understand the implications of new medical technologies and highlight a wide range of concerns. However, the tendency towards juxtapositions makes some aspects of the transplantation story poorly understood. This has been particularly true in the case of renal recipients. In the next section, while drawing on these approaches, I will focus on a concrete example, showing how the discussion thus far helps us to think about the subject position of the renal patient.

Renal Transplantation: Technological Grounds and Embodied Consequences

The renal patient's experience is one totally mediated by technological factors from the moment a fistula[1] is fitted to make dialysis possible. From very early on, the patient experience is one characterised by unique and altering embodied states. During dialysis, for example, the body is enormously elaborated and dramatically thrown into relief. The cleansing of our blood, a process, ordinarily visceral, hidden and largely taken-for-granted is the problem that dialysis is organised in response to. On dialysis, internal bodily processes seem to be turned inside out, creating both existential anxieties and possibilities. This relationship between patient and machine is one with radical consequences for all aspects of everyday life: eating, drinking, cleaning one's body, sexual intercourse, working, leisure activities, travelling, conducting personal relationships, making plans and so on. Thomas Csordas reminds us in his presentation of a 'paradigm of embodiment' that the body is our existential ground (Csordas 1990). It is correlative with our cultural world. What shows up for us, therefore, in our world, is constituted only in so far as we bodily connect with it (Merleau-Ponty 1943). What shows up in the experiences of renal patients is profoundly constituted by the body's newly acquired technological dependencies. And as I will continue to describe, nowhere is this more pronounced than in transplantation. Here the cultural logics which extend from transplant technologies have profound, often unexpected and controversial consequences for the subject positions and lived experiences of renal recipients and the wider community.

---

1   A fistula is an access point usually created in the wrist by connecting a vein to an artery. This helps generate an increased blood flow through the vein causing it to enlarge and become thick, providing ease of access for needless and a sufficient blood flow to make dialysis possible.

The Immune System: The Embodied Ground of Transplantation

It is important to describe the significance of the immune system, designated here as the embodied ground of transplantation. The immune system structures the relationship between an organism and its environment, organising the relationship between self and other; donor and recipient. The immune system also provides us with a conceptual apparatus for thinking about the biopolitical character of transplantation: how medical knowledge, innovations and practice have particular implications for social and cultural processes.

Described by Emily Martin through metaphors of disease-as-combat, a cellular army with an arsenal of fighter cells, the immune system functions by the capacity to discriminate between self and non-self, recognising 'foreign entities' that enter the body by means of antigens and (r)ejecting them by the production of antibodies (Martin 1994). This mechanism of self/non-self discrimination is key to the protection of the organism and lies at the foundation of modern immunology. However, it also presents a paradox. The work of the immune system is to respond to threats to the organism; it is there to protect the body. However, in organ replacement therapies, the immune system becomes a barrier to treatment and healing. It is both an ally and an obstacle. In order for transplantation to occur, the immune system has to be suppressed, it has to be tricked into treating what is other or foreign as part of the self. This inevitably has the effect of reducing the organism's capacity to protect itself. This compromised status will have dramatic consequences for the organ recipient, consequences they are little prepared for.

The tangle of issues centred on the immune system and its role in contemporary medicine have drawn the interests of a number of theorists across the social sciences. Both Martin and Haraway, for example, have focused attention on the immune system as paradigmatic of major shifts within the sciences more broadly (Haraway 1993, Martin 1994). It is readily designated as a postmodern object: eminently ambiguous and contradictory, challenging any assumption that there can be a single way of thinking about biological objects. Haraway explains that the immune system has no single point of presence. Its signification is distributed throughout the body. It is multi-local, without borders (Haraway 1993). For her, it is

> a map, ... a plan for meaningful action to construct and maintain the boundaries
> for what may count as self and other in the crucial realms of the normal and
> pathological (Haraway 1993: 79).

As Haraway notes, ways of playing with the immune system displayed in transplantation practices point to the massive expansion and growing confidence in techniques that enable us to construct and reconstruct bodies as we see fit. Transplantation practices therefore reflect a world in which it is possible to think of the human body as an assemblage of interchangeable parts, created using sophisticated genetic tool kits; a world where the body has come to be constructed as a coded text whose 'secrets' yield only to the proper reading conventions (Haraway 1993). Transplantation is one area in which scientists are imagined to manipulate and play with immunological signifiers and processes, strategically interrupting them where necessary. However, rhetoric and practice have a tendency to diverge. Despite the promise of immunological recognition and tissue typing for the rise of an effective transplant medicine, one that could work with the body on its own terms, scientists have actually had to work with it on their terms and that has been a very different proposition. Transplantation is less about the recognition of molecular sameness and difference but the suppression of the entire system, though the advances gained with immunosuppressive drugs, like cyclosporine. This is about disenabling the body rather than enabling it. It is this process of misrecognition, based on immune-suppression, and the use of cyclosporine which has allowed transplantation to develop so quickly over the last twenty years.

Anthropologists like Lawrence Cohen have pursued the implications of immunosuppression on donor populations, and explains that because we no longer have to screen large populations for suitable blood and tissue matches, many more persons can now serve as donors. He refers to this as marking a shift from a biopolitics of *recognition* to the more pragmatic biopolitics of *suppression*, disabling the recognition apparatus so that operability and not sameness/difference becomes the criterion of the match (Cohen 2002). However, as stated earlier, I do not wish to reflect the established polemics constructed between organ givers and organ receivers but recognise how a biopolitics of suppression has implications for both. I focus attention specifically on the profound implications suppression has for the bodies of recipients and the re-contoured worlds they find themselves navigating.

In suppressing the recipient's immune system, the renal patient is more susceptible to infections and viruses. The side effects of daily immunosuppressive drug therapy can be devastating – changes in body image, weight gain, excess bodily hair, a range of new conditions, recurring sickness – ongoing problems that the patient may never escape. Sickness continues in addition to ongoing cycles of medical intervention, testing and check-ups. As a consequence, the body responds aggressively. Far from being the docile object theorised within the sciences, it proves to be willful, recalcitrant and subversive.

The renal recipient does not always encounter transplantation according to the hoped-for expectations of medical practitioners, the general public or even social scientists. Transplantation involves a parallel reconstruction of the local cultural worlds of these patients to that of the local biologies implied in immunology. In otherwords, both locals are compromised through receipt of the new organ. To demonstrate this, I want to draw on some of my own ethnographic work on kidney transplantation conducted in the Republic of Ireland and to show, through narrative extracts, how renal recipients piece together their accounts of transplantation. Paying attention to the particular, culturally sited ways in which the boundary line between the biological and social comes to be blurred through transplantation, provides us with insight into how the human experience of suffering is constituted and the ways in which patients make sense of therapeutic outcomes, and the notion of a 'gift of life', that transplantation is expected to extend to renal patients.

At the time of interview:

Lilly was a married woman in her sixties, from Co. Galway. She had undergone four transplantations up to the time of interview.

I could only but feel negative. I had been on dialysis for so long and was more secure there. My friends were there ... and all my support. For me transplantation means leaving all that and being with people who don't understand. It's impossible to stay in the unit but to be asked which makes me happiest, I have to say that I felt so much better in myself on dialysis.

Padraig was a married man in his fifties from Co. Wicklow. He received his kidney from his sister which was considered to be a good match.

Life after transplantation was a huge high. I just couldn't do enough living. Everything in my life improved, my relationship with my family, my work, my leisure activities. But after about five months of euphoria, life slipped backwards, and the problems everyone else has to cope with crept back into my life. I worry about rejection ... It's there as a constant reminder that I am always going to be a renal patient. It particularly springs to mind when I catch a cold or get a chest infection. We are all afraid of dying – the whole meaning of life changes. I don't think these thoughts are shared by the healthy.

Jack was in his sixties and lived in Co. Cork. He was retired and separated from his wife.

After the transplant, changes took place I ... I have a different perspective. We are not the people we were before. It's the whole condition. I can't separate one stage from the other. I'm always questioning the side-effects of the medication ... I had a parathyroidectomy. They took out three and a half that had grown to the size of golf-balls. After transplantation, your calcium rises. It's the reverse to being on dialysis. My bone pain was so severe that I was unable to walk and had to use crutches. I had my transplant on 2nd January, 1989, my parathyroidectomy in March and was on crutches until December of that year. If anyone touched me, I was a babbling wreck.

I knew I'd have to look after it – I did respect it and I never miss out on the medication, but I didn't know there'd be all these drugs beforehand – I thought once you were transplanted that was that. I didn't know the names of any of these drugs or told they were anti-rejection drugs.

Derek was in early fifties, married with children and living in Dublin

I was put on immuran, cyclosporine, steroids, blood pressure medication and lasix. The cyclosporine caused my gums to grow down over my teeth, hair to grow, weight gain and tremors. The steroids had the effect of giving me a false appetite and putting weight on my neck and abdomen.

I have been damaged in some way and something that is damaged is not going to last long. I have a plan, which is to retire in five years time and to hopefully have a good quality of life. My family worry about me and they ring up after every check-up. I have gout again and that worries them. My friends are always concerned. I don't think I would be as concerned if it was somebody else and that makes me feel guilty. I have mood swings and feelings of being tired. I get symptoms as if I were going back into failure. That said, my quality of life is better since transplantation.

Julia was single in early forties and living in Co. Louth
I had panic attacks after the transplant. It was reinforced by my rising blood pressure. I turned to prayer – something outside of myself … I never think of myself in the future now, that's the biggest change. I won't even plan a week ahead. I won't even plan holidays. Even if longevity was guaranteed, I don't think it would change. I worry about my nieces and my nephews regarding the genetic aspects. I have a sense of vagueness. I want to feel in control, independent. The future is a hazy prospect for me. I feel pressurised when I have to come up with a plan. Where I am, for the moment, is fine for me, but it is often not good enough for others.

Anne was single, living in Dublin and in her early thirties.
Of course, it is wonderful to be freed from dialysis. No one can argue about the benefits of having a new kidney. But … well, it's not that simple… After the surgery, I felt so protective about my new kidney. I hardly wanted the doctors to go near it. I remember, they had to do a biopsy on me and I was so frightened that they would damage it … I don't agree with the notion that transplantation is some great renewal of life. The side effects of immunosuppressants are very hard to live with. It is especially hard, y'know, for women to cope with extra weight and all the body hair that cyclosporine causes. I know it really affects me. I hate getting my photo taken. I don't even like looking at myself in the mirror. Since my transplant my family treat me as being well. People have forgotten. They make demands on me, do y'know. You are always misunderstood and when you try to explain your difficulties. Some people say, '[s]ure couldn't you get killed crossing the road' or '[a]ren't you lucky that they can do this for you'. The expectation is that you should be over the moon, but being upbeat is difficult. Terrible fears just can't be acknowledged. I worry in ways that I never did on dialysis….
    I don't plan much anymore – I can hardly think of myself in the future.

There are clearly many different issues involved here, but I want to draw out some commonalities. Like many patients with chronic conditions, what backgrounds the illness experience is a complex socio-technical apparatus, not fully visible to the participant (Mol 2002). Medical interventions and therapeutic outcomes for the chronically ill do not come to final end points. They continue to be underpinned by an array of seen and unseen medical procedures, protocols and practices incorporating, for example: a complex and changing legislative and ethical framework governing organ procurement, which includes criteria for selecting suitable donors and for assigning brain-death (Sharp 2006); technological innovations such as the ventilator and dialysis machine without which transplantation would be impossible (Lock 2000, Younger 1990); the informal and subjective decisions and working schedules that shape doctor-patient interactions and the selection criteria for placing dialysis patients on transplant waiting lists; the localised cultural criteria that shapes national legislation favouring live donation in some countries and cadaver donation in others. What has to always be kept in mind is that transplantation is a phenomenon caught within systems of practice, and in relation to which, the renal patient's experience is far from under their control.

The lived experience of renal 'recipiency' is without doubt a contradiction to medical and public expectations. It is also a marked divergence from the expectations the same patients have while on dialysis. As stated in earlier publications on dialysis (Kierans 2001, 2005), people look forward to transplantation, seeing it as the route to a 'new lease of life', a time where they will no longer have to depend on a machine. Dialysis patients describe themselves as future-oriented, and it is this capacity to project into the future that enables them to cope with their regimen. Once transplanted, however, there are growing concerns that one can no longer lay claim to a clearly-defined future, that the kidney might reject, that one might return to dialysis or die. This lack of resolution or disjuncture is what Haraway explains as a function of hybrid or cyborg embodiment. As a result, people talk about disengaging from the future; a continual experience of the present; a dissolution of the border between past and future. This is often attributed to the ways in which transplantation is conventionally constructed through biomedical discourse, emplotted around horizons of hope and held in place by the idiomatic expressions employed within society, donor awareness groups and physicians: 'a new lease of life'; 'a gift'. This is what patients are offered; an understanding that they will be healed; that they will be well again. They embrace collective narratives spun around transplantation practices, only to find that the reality is often quite different.

The 'gift of life' metaphor dominates personal and public expectations about transplantation. But as the anthropological record testifies, from culture to culture gifts bind giver and receiver, and necessitate reciprocity (Mauss 1967). One does not get something for nothing. There are new pressures on the renal patient post-transplant, that of being a good recipient. This carries responsibilities that are regularly described as unbearable, the responsibility to be well when one is not; to be healthy; independent; to be champions of donor campaigns; to fulfil a powerful medical narrative, and, in so doing, to mask and silence the continued sickness and suffering and the devastating consequences of immunosuppressive drug therapy and changes to body image. These are experienced in connection to the guilt that someone may have died to give them this new lease of life, but also in relation to the complaint that family and friends often disengage from the continued suffering and psycho-social affects of 'recipiency', unwilling to see them still as patients.

Renal recipients describe not being the people they once were, and it is not uncommon to hear remarks, like those made by Anne and Julia, of having a vague or hazy sense of oneself. Renal recipients emplot their accounts around the unexpected lack of an ending and the dismantling of their expectations. New worries about graft rejection, the isolation of recipient experience and the necessity of having to cope with the side effects of immunosuppressive drug therapies have created an extra burden of suffering, made worse by the fact that few wish to engage with it.

In reflecting back over her condition, Julia said,

> Throughout this condition, we tend to stack things ahead of ourselves … You see the road ahead isn't a straight one … It is a lesson we all have to learn and that is that transplantation is not the be all and end all and people often feel cheated by that – they are sold an idea that things are going to be perfect and they are not.

Many of the patients, however, who offered painful accounts of their experiences of transplantation, were also the same patients who regularly talk at patient support meetings, in the media and at donor awareness campaigns. I listened to them publically espouse and promote the benefits of transplantation and privately complain about their fear, loneliness and continued experiences of sickness. These contractions and grey zones are a fact of transplantation's ambiguities, and reasons while the polemical renditions provide no access to the complexities of the human experience. It is not surprising that these contradictions also reflect the institutionalised commitments and obligations patients feel towards their doctors, the donor, donor families and to their own family and friends. The compromised status of 'recipiency' captures the essential character of transplantation and demonstrates that a lost physiological sovereignty has it implications not only at the level of a compromised immunology and physiological vulnerability but extends its reach to the existential and social world of the patient. As Mary Douglas reminds us, anxieties arise at precisely these points of intersection, where social and cultural organisations meet personal experience (Douglas 1970).

Conclusion

It is not easy to tell a straightforward story about transplantation. This is not a phenomenon easily packaged in terms of its gains or losses for different populations but perhaps as researchers we should not try, partly because in Jackson's terms '… we can never grasp intellectually all the variables at play in any action or all the repercussions that follow from it, partly because they are so variously and intricately nuanced, and partly because they are embedded in singular biographies as well as social histories' (Jackson 2005: xxv).

We do know, however, that transplant technology and its associated techniques, in addition to improvements in immunosuppressive drug therapy and diagnostic procedures, are increasingly sophisticated and reliable. They are also more widely available, and to more people, than ever before and are being used to treat an expanding range of diseases. We cannot say that these are *not* welcome and, practiced in the right way, they can be an important tool for human benefit. National debates about the quickening in the demand for and distribution of organs, and the creation of durable but morally questionable links between patient-recipients and donor-populations, have taken a variety of different forms, raising newly problematic distinctions and boundary concerns. In order to navigate these issues, it is important that these controversies are situated in the lives of its protagonists and participants and underpinned by an ethics of care reflected by a concern for all those lives affected by these practices.

To do this, we might take our methodological cue from Appadurai (1986) and follow the 'social life' of organs as they operate within these technoscapes, crossing different borders in different parts of the world and the costs and benefits associated with every stage of the journey they make. This means we need to work outward from the technologies themselves, tracing those implications for the practices, processes, experiences and social formations they thus engender. Our analytical task is to a large extent a moral one and that is, in light of the new medical technologies, to learn what is at stake for others (Kleinman 1999), but to be cognisant of the ways in which we insert ourselves as researchers, advocates, humanitarians and practitioners into the ethnographic story lest, in our efforts to do good, or in the production of a juxtaposition, we render visible the embodied sufferings of some at the expense of others.

References

Agamben, G. (1998). *Homo Sacer: Soverign Power and Bare Life*, trans. Daniel Heller-Rpazen. Stanford, CA: Stanford University Press.

Appadurai, A. (1986). *The Social Life of Things*. Cambridge: Cambridge University Press.

Arendt, H. (1969). *The Human Condition*. Chicago: University of Chicago Press.

Armstrong, D. (1995). The rise of surveillance medicine. *Sociology of Health and Illness* 17(3), 393–404.

Barnes, B., Bloor, D., and Henry J. (1996). *Scientific Knowledge: A Sociological Analysis*. London: Athlone.

Brodwin, P. (2000). *Biotechnology and Culture: Bodies, Anxieties, Ethics*. Bloomington: Indian University Press.

Casper, M. (1994). At the margins of humanity: fetal positions in science and medicine. *Science, Technology and Human Values*, 19(3): 307–23.

Casper, M. (1995). Fetal cyborgs and technomoms on the reproductive frontier: which way to the carnival?, in *The Cyborg Handbook* edited by C. Hables Gray. New York: Routledge.

Cohen, L. (2002). The other kidney: biopolitics beyond recognition, in *Commodifying Bodies*, edited by Scheper-Hughes, N. and Wacquant, L. London: Sage.

Csordas, T. (1990). Embodiment as a paradigm for anthropology. *Ethos*, 18, 5–47.

Das, V. (2000). The practice of organ transplants: networks, documents, translations, in *Living and Working with the New Medical Technologies: Intersections of Inquiry*, edited by M. Lock et al. Cambridge: Cambridge University Press, 263–87.

Davis-Floyd, R. (1994). The technocratic body: American childbirth as cultural expression. *Social Science and Medicine* 38: 1125–40.

Davis-Floyd, R., and Dumit, J. (1998). *Cyborg Babies: From Techno-sex to Techno-tots*. New York: Routledge.

Dumit, J. (1997). A digital image of the category of the person: PET scanning and objective self-fashioning, in *Cyborgs and Citadels: Anthropological Investigations in Emerging Science and Technology*, edited by G. Downey et al. Santa Fe, NM: School of American Research Press, 83–102.

Durkheim, E. (1982 [1912]) *The Elementary Forms of Religious Life*, trans. Joseph Ward. London: Allen and Unwin.

Haraway, D. (1991). A cyborg manifesto: Science, technology, and socialist-feminism in the late twentieth century, in *Simians, Cyborgs and Women: The Reinvention of Nature*. New York: Routledge, 149–81.

Helman Cecil (2007). *Culture, Health and Illness*. 5th ed. London: Hodder Arnold.

Foucault, M. (1977). *Discipline and Punish: The Birth of the Prison*. London: Lane.

Foucault, M. (1998) [1976]. *The History of Sexuality Vol. 1: The Will to Knowledge*. London: Penguin.

Foucault, M. (1980). Body/power, in *Michel Foucault: Power/Knowledge,* editor C. Gordon. Brighton: Harvestor.

Fox, R., (1993). An ignoble form of cannibalism: reflections on the Pittsburgh Protocol for procuring organs from non-heart-beating donors. *Kennedy Institute of Ethics Journal* 3: 231–39.

Hables Gray, C. (2001). *Cyborg Citizen: Politics in the Posthuman Age*. New York: Routledge.

Haraway, D. (1989). *Primate Visions: Gender, Race, and Nature in the World of Modern Science*, Routledge: New York and London.

Hogel, L. (1995a). Tales from the crypt: technology meets organism in the living cadaver, in C. Hables Gray (ed.) *The Cyborg Handbook*. London: Routledge. 203–16.

Hogel, L. (1995b). Standardisation across non-standard domains: the case of organ procurement. *Science, Technology and Human Values*, 20(4): 482–500.

Hogel, L. (1999). *Recovering the Nation's Body: Cultural Memory, Medicine and the Politics of Redemption.* New Brunswick, NJ: Rutgers University Press.

Ihde, D. (1990). *Technology and the Life World.* Bloomington: Indiana University Press.

Ihde, D. (2007). *Listening and Voice: Phenomenologies of Sound.* 2nd ed. Albany: SUNY Press.

Jackson, M. (2005). *Existential Anthropology: Events, Exigencies and Effects.* New York: Berghahn Books.

Joralemon, D. and Cox P. (2003). Body values: the case against compensating for transplant organs. *Hastings Center Report* 33(1): 27–33.

Kaufert P.A. (2000). Screening the Body: the pap and the mammogram, in Lock, M. et al. *Living and Working with the New Medical Technologies: Intersections of Inquiry. Cambridge:* Cambridge University Press, 165–83.

Kierans, C. (2001). Sensory and narrative identity: the narration of illness process among chronic renal sufferers in Ireland, *Anthropology and Medicine* 8(2): 237–53.

Kierans C. (2005). Narrating kidney disease: the significance of sensation and time in the emplotment of patient experience, *Culture, Medicine and Psychiatry* 29: 341–59.

Kleinman, A. (1999). Experience and its moral modes, in (ed.) Perterson, Grethe *The Tanner Lectures on Human Values.* Salt Lake City: University of Utah Press.

Knorr-Cetina, K. and Mulkay, M. (1983). *Science Observed.* London: Sage Publications.

Latour, B. (1987). *Science in Action: How to Follow Scientists and Engineers through Society.* Cambridge, Mass., Harvard University Press.

Latour, B. (1993). *We Have Never Been Modern.* Hemel Hempstead: Harvester Wheatsheaf.

Latour, B., and Woolgar, S. (1986). *Laboratory Life: The Social Construction of Scientific Facts.* New Jersey: Princeton University Press.

Leder, D. (1990). *The Absent Body.* Chicago: University of Chicago Press.

Lock, M. (1995). Transcending mortality: organ transplants and the practice of contradictions, *Medical Anthropology Quarterly* 9(3): 390–93.

Lock, M. (1996). Death in technological time: locating the end of meaningful life, *Medical Anthropology Quarterly* 10(4): 575–600.

Lock, M. (2000). On dying twice: culture, technology and the determination of death in *Living and Working with the New Medical Technologies: Intersections of Inquiry*, edited by M. Lock et al. Cambridge: Cambridge University Press, 233–62.

Lock, M., Young, A., and Cambrosio, A. (2000). *Living and Working with the New Medical Technologies: Intersections of Inquiry*, Cambridge: Cambridge University Press.

Lock, M. (2007). Alienation of body parts and the biopolitics of immortalised cell lines, in *Beyond the Body Proper: Reading the Anthropology of Material Life*, editors M. Lock and J. Farquhar. Durham and London: Duke University Press.

Marcus, G. (1998). *Ethnography Through Thick and Thin*. New Jersey: Princeton University Press.

Martin, E. (1994). *Flexible Bodies: Tracking Immunity in American Culture from the Days of Polio to the Age of AIDS*. Boston: Beacon Hill Press.

Marx, K. (1970). *Economic and Philosophical Manuscripts of 1844*. Trans. by Martin Milligan. London: Lawrence and Wishart.

Marx, K. (1968 [1852]). The eighteenth brumaire of Louis Bonaparte, in *Marx Engels: Selected Works in One Volume*. London: Lawrence and Wishart.

Marx, K. and Engels, F. (1940[1848]). *The German Ideology*. London: Lawrence and Wishart.

Merleau-Ponty, M. (1943). *Phenomenology of Perception*. Trans. by Colin Smith. London: Routledge and Keegan Paul.

Mol, A. (2002). *The Body Multiple: Ontology in Medical Practice*. Durham and London: Duke University Press.

Rabinow, P. (1996). *Essays on the Anthropology of Reason*. New Jersey: Princeton University Press.

Rabinow, P. (1996). *Making PCR: A Story of Biotechnology*, Chicago: University of Chicago Press.

Rabinow, P. (1999). *French DNA: Trouble in Purgatory*. Chicago: University of Chicago Press.

Rabinow, P. (2000). Epochs, presents, events, in *Living and Working with the New Medical Technologies: Intersections of Inquiry*, edited by M. Lock et al. Cambridge: Cambridge University Press, 31–48.

Randall, T. (1991). Too few human organs for transplantation, too many in need ... and the gap widens. *Journal of the American Medical Association* 265 (13 March), 1223–7.

Rapp, R. (2000). *Testing Women, Testing the Fetus: The Social Impace of Amniocentesis in America.* New York: Routledge.

Renn, Ortwin and Roco, Mihail, C. (2006). Nanotechnology and the need for risk governance, *Nanoparticle Research,* 8(2), 1–41.

Rheinberger, J.J. (2000). Beyond nature and culture: modes of reasoning in the age of molecular biology and medicine, in *Living and Working with the New Medical Technologies*, edited by Lock, M. et al. Cambridge: Cambridge University Press, pp. 19–30.

Sharp, L. (2006). *Strange Harvest: Organ Transplants, Denatured Bodies, and the Transformed Self.* Berkeley: University of California Press.

Scheper-Hughes, N. (1996). Theft of life: the globalisation of organ stealing rumours. *Anthropology Today* 36: 409–40.

Scheper-Huges, N. (1998). The new cannibalism: international traffic in human organs, *New Internationalist* 300 (April).

Scheper-Hughes, N. (2001). Commodity fetishism in organs trafficking. *Body and Society*, 7, 2–3: 31–62.

Scheper-Hughes, N. and Wacquant, L. (2002). *Commodifying Bodies*. London: Sage.

Scheper-Hughes, N. (2002). Bodies for sale: whole or parts, in *Commodifying Bodies*, edited by Scheper-Hughes, N. and Wacquant, L. London: Sage.

Turner, B. (2007). *Culture Technologies and Bodies: The Technological Utopia of Living Forever*. London: Blackwell.

Van Wolputte, S. (2004). Hang on to your self: of bodies, embodiment, and selves. *Annual Review of Anthropology* 33: 251–69.

Young, K. (1997). *Presence in the Flesh: Body in Medicine*. Cambridge: Harvard University Press.

Williams, S.J. (2003). *Medicine and the Body*. London: Sage.

Willis, P. (1981). *Learning to Labour: How Working Class Kids Get Working Class Jobs*. New York: Columbia University Press.

Wittgenstein, L. (1953). *Philosophical Investigations*. (Ansxombe, G.E.N trans and editor). Oxford: Blackwell.

Younger, S. (1990). Organ retrieval: can we ignore the dark side? *Transplantation Proceedings* 22: 1014–15.

Chapter 2

Normalized Elites: Rethinking Doping as Abnormal Practice

April D. Henning

In October 2007, former Olympic gold-medalist Marion Jones pleaded guilty to lying to federal prosecutors when she was asked about her use of performance enhancing drugs in her quest to become a champion sprinter (Zinser and Schmidt 2007). In early 2008 Jones was stripped of her five Olympic gold medals and sentenced to six months in prison (Schmidt 2008). Shortly following Jones' case, 2008 Olympic marathoner Deena Kastor gave an interview to *Runner's World* magazine where she was asked her views on Jones' sentencing for doping violations. She responded saying, 'It was very disappointing. Anytime you have fame and money on the line, you're going to have people who cheat to get to the top ... What makes it even more troubling is that she [Jones] was such a hero for so many people; to have cheated her way into their hearts is just awful' (McDowell 2008). Kastor's view of doping violations is a common one, as elite athletes in all sports who are found to be in violation of anti-doping regulations are often condemned and vilified by fans, the media, and other athletes. They are viewed as cheaters, stripped of awards and medals they have won, and face punishment by governing bodies, and sometimes face federal prosecution. At the same time, however, that athletes are being attacked by a chorus from these several audiences, there are voices in another crying out against anti-doping regulations, calling for the removal or partial removal of current restrictions against doping. Herein lies the problem with the current system of anti-doping: elite athletes are pathologized as a group with values and beliefs deviating from social norms, while at the same time they are treated as if they are normal members of society who share normative views about values and lifestyle by anti-doping agencies. These two very different views raise the question, what has shaped the current system of anti-doping and the surrounding debates?

There is an underlying tension between the two ways elite athletes have been characterized in the media: normal and abnormal. Elite athletes face a paradox when it comes to how they are characterized by the media. On the one hand they are expected to conduct themselves in a way that is considered 'clean' by non-athletes, including avoiding doping practices or any behavior that would make a competition unfair. In short, they are expected to be like normal non-elite athletes, except to post results worthy of the elite title. On the other hand, they are expected to fulfill the role of elite by taking advantage of a lifestyle that includes professional coaching and medical support and training techniques not available or accessible to non-elites. Consumers of elite athletic competitions understand that these athletes are not ordinary, run of the mill recreational athletes, but are professional competitors who train to compete at an elite level. By definition, elites are removed and set apart from the categories of average or normal that most recreational athletes and non-athletes would fall under. However, fans, media, and governing bodies still hold elite athletes to a somewhat normative standard regarding how they train and compete and this standard is problematic when issues of doping arise. When an elite athlete is found to have violated anti-doping regulations the image of the normal athlete collides with its abnormal counterpart, leaving the athlete in a sort of limbo. On one side relying on any available technology to improve performance deviates from expectations of fans, officials, and the media, while on the other not relying on any available technology deviates from accepted values and practices within the elite athletic subculture.

Though questions of doping surround most elite level sports, the focus here will be on elite runners and how these runners are simultaneously cast as normal and abnormal by themselves, coaches, medical professionals, and in popular media. Elite runners have a well-documented history of debates surrounding performance enhancement and questions of doping within the sport, and these situations exemplify the challenges elite athletes across the spectrum of sports have faced. Drawing heavily on coverage of elite athletes in the specialty running magazine *Runner's World*, as well as other media outlets, I will interrogate what developments have led to both the view of the athlete as abnormal, as well as that of the elite lifestyle as normal or analogous to non-elite athletes. I argue that the tension between these two opposing views results from the differentiation of elite athletes from non-elites by coaches, medical professionals, and athletes themselves on the one hand, while the media and strict anti-doping advocates downplay these differences on the other. To illustrate this argument I will first offer a short background of the rise of sports medicine and the trend towards medical technology as a training tool, as well as a look at the movement towards the current system of anti-doping in sport. The next section will demonstrate how elite runners' lifestyles and values differ from those of non-elites, as well as how elite runners have been normalized through the media. I conclude by calling for an understanding of athletes by anti-doping agencies that is responsive to the differences of elite athletes from the rest of the population.

Background

Athletes, Medicine, and Technology

Physicians are now a fixture on the sidelines of most elite sporting events, and many athletes have an entourage of medical professionals to aid in their training. Though the bond between the two fields is now firmly in place, medicine and athletics have not always been so entwined. In his volume on sports medicine, Ivan Waddington (1996) argues that two processes, the medicalization of sport and increasing competitiveness, brought about a change in the way athletes train and are viewed by the medical establishment. Waddington sees the medicalization of sport—making medicine relevant to participants in sport when it had not been previously—as largely responsible for the development of the field of sports medicine following World War II. In this period medicine changed from having a tangential interest in athletic bodies to making medicine and medical interventions necessary for athletes.

John Hoberman (1992) notes that beginning in the interwar period, medical professionals were interested in athletic bodies as a source of information about human physiology. Sports medicine began as a chapter within medical books before moving on to become its own field within the medical profession (Waddington 1996). Citing an early text on sports medicine by J.G.P. Williams, Waddington argues that from very early on in the establishment of the sports medicine field, physicians regarded athletes as chronic patients whose physiological differences from the average person made them more similar to the traditionally invalid population than to non-athletes (Ibid). Viewing athletes as more prone to injury and illness than non-athletes, medical researchers' focus on working with elites worked to bring athletes into the medical subculture. Athletes became reliant on the medical establishment to be repaired when injured, to stay healthy, and to realize their natural physical potentials (Ibid). Athletes became permanent patients, viewed by the medical profession as a population inherently needing the aid of medicine even in the absence of a specific condition or ailment (Ibid). A second development in the era following the war was an increase in competitiveness of sport and the importance of sport to politics (Ibid). The new political pressures brought on by the Cold War increased the desire for more effective medical interventions that could give athletes an edge over the competition. The increased competitiveness of sport, coupled with the rise of sports medicine and the medicalization of athletes led more athletes to turn away from traditional methods of athletic training, and these methods were replaced and supplemented gradually by new technologies coming from sports medicine and other associated fields (Ibid).

As regular access to medical professionals and treatments increased, athletes began to undertake treatments, techniques, and use supplements developed with the goal of some type of enhancement in mind. Though athletes themselves have long sought ways to gain a winning edge, Barri Houlihan (2003) argues that it is since the rise of performance enhancement as a goal of sports medicine that the search for supplements for athletic bodies expanded. Supplements for athletic bodies have come in the form of dietary supplements, sports nutritional supplements, and medical interventions (Waddington 1996).[1] Dietary supplements, therefore,

---

1   The National Institute of Health (NIH) defines dietary supplements using a four part definition developed by Congress in the Dietary Health and Supplement Education Act. According to the NIH, a dietary supplement 'is intended to supplement the diet; contains

are intended to install from the outside what the body is missing on the inside. For athletes, supplements provide a way to build upon traditional training and dietary methods—concentrated, drinkable protein powders in place of eating large quantities of food, for example. By the early 2000s the sports-supplement industry had become a multi-billion dollar industry with nearly $20 billion in sales within the United States alone in 2007. While supplements are used by non-athletes as well as athletes, Baume, Hellemans, and Saugy (2007) cite several studies that suggest many athletes, both elite and recreational, use dietary supplements with the belief that they may have performance benefits. The main reasons for athletes to take supplements are: 1) supplementation of a food-based diet 2) performance enhancement 3) fulfillment of an exercise-specific nutrition requirement 4) achievement of a specific sports related goal 5) correction of a nutrient deficiency (Baume, Hellemans, and Saugy 2007).

Anti-doping

As the medicalization of athletic bodies and efforts to medically enhance performance increase, defining doping in a way that clearly distinguishes between what is legitimate sports medicine and what crosses the line into doping territory has become increasingly difficult. Early suggestions for a clearer definition of doping by differentiating between those substances and practices that are 'natural' and banning anything 'unnatural,' or in terms of food vs. non-food were made without success (Gardner 1989). Doping is often considered a problem in that it constitutes a form of cheating (Houlihan 2003, Miah 2007). The anti-doping movement gained momentum amid concerns by athletic governing bodies that the spirit of sport and competition was being undermined by the use of doping agents, such as anabolic steroids and synthetic hormones, and growing concerns of participants and governing officials over athletes cheating by artificially enhancing their performances in competition or doping. In response, athletic governing bodies, such as the International Olympic Committee (IOC) called for monitoring of athletes use of certain substances believed to be performance enhancers. Following this call, national governments, sporting organizations, and international governing agencies adopted new policies against doping, known collectively as anti-doping.

Houlihan (2003) traces the evolution of these policies and the rise of testing agencies, most notably the World Anti-Doping Administration (WADA). Established in 1999, WADA is comprised of a Foundation Board, an Executive Committee, and several sub-committees. The Foundation Board and each committee is composed of equal numbers of representatives from both the Olympic

---

one or more dietary ingredients (including vitamins; minerals: herbs or other botanicals; amino acids; and other substances) or their constituents; is intended to be taken by mouth as a pill, capsule, tablet, or liquid; and is labeled on the front panel as being a dietary supplement' (NIH 2007).

Movement and governments (WADA 2009a). The IOC created WADA for several purposes: to define what specifically the problem of doping entails; to institute regulations around doping practices and substances; and to conduct biological tests of competitors to ensure that they are in compliance with the anti-doping rules of competition (Houlihan 2003). Houlihan notes that there were several fundamental justifications for the anti-doping movement, including protecting the spirit of the competition, to protect the health and well-being of the athletes, and to protect those who model their behavior after elite athletes' (Ibid).

The current definition of doping developed by WADA is based on its prohibited list. This list, updated annually, lists all those products and procedures that are considered doping agents or practices (WADA 2009b). WADA differentiates between what is banned while 'in-competition,' 'out of competition,' and at all times, as well as defining some sport-specific bans (Ibid). WADA is the body that sets international standards which member organizations then use as a guide in developing anti-doping testing programs. For track and field the International Association of Athletics Federation (IAAF) is the body responsible for collecting blood and urine samples and administering tests to determine if doping agents are present (IAAF 2009b). The IAAF plans out testing procedures, schedules, and sets parameters for what constitutes a positive test for a banned substance. The IAAF also keeps track of athletes' whereabouts to ensure random testing can and does occur, and sets up testing protocols to ensure samples are not compromised before, during, or after the sample is taken and the test is administered (IAAF 2009b).

Scholars have taken two sides in the debate over the current anti-doping regulations: 1) doping is an ethical problem and public health risk that must be controlled, 2) doping has become a part of sport and current policies attempting to regulate and prevent doping are futile and must either be abandoned or modified. Thomas H. Murray (1983, 2008) looked at the how the fear of being left behind the competition forced drug use on athletes in an attempt to understand under what circumstances an athlete would engage in doping practices. Murray concluded that athletes were often pressured to take performance-enhancing drugs and that the decision was often not an independent undertaking by athletes. Murray further argued that anti-doping programs and policies are necessary to prevent athletes from being coerced into taking performance enhancers, especially if they do not want to engage in the practice but feel they cannot compete otherwise (Murray 2008). In his view, anti-doping is also a necessary development to maintain the level playing field that athletes seek for competition (Murray 2008).

Ben Mitchell (2008) considers gene doping as posing serious risks for young and/or amateur athletes. These risks are both in terms of the health risks and problems it may pose to young athletes, and in terms of maintaining an ethic of fairness in competition. Similarly, Pipe and Hebert (2008) considered the pharmacologic nature of many doping agents and contended that these products represent a deviant set of values that could erode public trust and pose possible health risks. They, like Murray, view anti-doping programs as a necessary component in protecting and promoting the values of fair play in sport (Pipe and

Hebert 2008). Each of these researchers has taken the view that doping poses some sort of potential risk to athletes and their health, and to sport and the value placed on fair play.

Conversely, researchers such as Eugen Konig (1995), Shogan and Ford (2000) have argued doping practices are a constituent part of sport—they are part and parcel of elite competition. In Konig's view, practices and agents considered to be doping are actually consistent with the use of other accepted technologies that have come to be defined as a natural part of sport. Konig asserts that these technologies are viewed as fair or natural only because they do not violate the current rules of play and not because they are essentially different from those labeled doping. Similarly, Andy Miah (2006) argues that 'human enhancement technologies can enrich the practice of elite sports rather than diminish them.' In Miah's view, the need to protect individuals from enhancements is lessened by the breadth of enhancements available to elite athletes.

Hoberman (2007) looked at doping in endurance events, such as marathons and endurance cycling events. He noted that only a handful of positive doping tests have been found in marathoners while a much higher proportion of cyclists have been found guilty of doping violations. He argues that the principles behind current anti-doping philosophies are grounded in the allegedly prudish and rigid Victorian idea that there is a contradiction between high level performance and doping. However, this idea is not consistent with the historical record of these endurance events, as they, according to Hoberman, have long records of doping. Yet modern marathoners post low rates of positive tests for doping agents, leading Hoberman to question whether they are simply not being caught rather than cutting back on a historically common practice. Each of these views questions the current anti-doping programs based on the organizations' presumptions about what sport should or should not be. These researchers find fault with the logic that underpins many anti-doping policies, finding them insufficient at best and harmful to sport and the athletes at worst.

Taken together, these views encompass both sides of the debate surrounding doping in sport. The approach adopted by current anti-doping agencies, including WADA and its affiliate organizations such as the IAAF, largely reflects former view on athletic doping. In its mission statement, WADA describes part of its goal as working 'towards a vision of the world that values and fosters doping free sport' (WADA 2009c). WADA views doping as an ethical matter within sport that requires a strict code of regulations and rigorous enforcement. In this system, all athletes are held to a uniform standard of conduct that prevents them from exceeding the bounds of what is deemed acceptable behavior and practice.

Based on these differing positions of doping and anti-doping issues, I argue that there are two conflicting portrayals of elite runners that have led to the debate surrounding the current system of anti-doping. The first is that elite runners lead different lifestyles from non-elites and, as a medicalized population, they subscribe to the view that technological and medical advances to aid in performance are useful, acceptable, and normal. This scenario lends itself to views like those of Konig and Miah, that sport is not harmed by doping, but that doping is an extension of what runners already do legally. The second view is that elite runners are really not that different from the non-elite population in their goals and lifestyles and should therefore be content to compete, and value competition, without the aid of performance enhancers. This view follows a logic similar to that proposed by Murray and Mitchell, i.e., that athletes should be protected from pressures to use performance enhancers and that sport should be protected from the upset to the rules of fair play that athletes have come to expect and value. These opposing views of elite runners, as both normal and abnormal, have collided and are reflected the current debate over doping and anti-doping policies.

Dueling Views of Athletes

Pathologizing Athletes

The view of athletic bodies as something distinctly different from non-athletic bodies came about, in part, through the field of sports medicine. As described above, sports medicine emerged as a way to treat athletic bodies in ways that had not been previously considered for non-athletes. The medical establishment's shift from viewing athletes as research subjects or patients with specific injuries to viewing them as permanent patients, brought performance enhancement to the fore of sports medicine (Houlihan 2003). Physicians were no longer treating or fixing acute injuries or specific ailments, but were focusing efforts on improving the performance of the uninjured athletic body in competition. This contrasts to other areas of life that have been medicalized. The current US medical system is focused on repairing the sick body, while preventative medicine focuses on well bodies and maintaining health (Park 2009). Sports medicine is unique in that it takes well, very fit bodies and attempts to not only maintain them, but to improve on them through medicine and technology. Athletic bodies are then differentiated further; not only are they treated by medical professionals as having different needs from the normal population, but these differences are highlighted by both further medical interventions and by training methods that demand a non-normative lifestyle and mind-set.

As such, the medicalization of sport coupled with the adoption of non-traditional training methods has led to the pathologization of elite runners and their bodies both medically and socially. Coaches and medical professionals recognize athletes, including elite runners, as different from the rest of the population. Two examples of programs that actively seek to set potential elite runners apart from non-elites are the Nike Oregon Project and the Hansons-Brooks Distance Project. These programs are designed to recruit distance runners with the best prospects of maturing into champion distance runners, seeking to relocate runners to project 'campuses' in order to train exclusively with other recruits on the team. These teams are housed and supported by the program sponsors, Nike and Hansons-Brooks (Tilin 2002, Hansons-Brooks 2008).

In order to be invited to participate in programs like Nike's or Hansons-Brooks', prospective runners must have already distinguished themselves from mainstream, non-competitive runners in some way. Hansons-Brooks listed the following time requirements (male/female) for participation on its website, 'The standards these athletes had to meet to be eligible for the Olympic Development program are 29:00/33:45 for the 10k, 14:00/16:15 for the 5k, and 2:20/2:42 for the marathon' (Hansons-Brooks 2008). As the program focuses on post-collegiate recruits, these requirements serve as a mechanism to separate the good, but average runners from the good, potentially great runners. In describing its goals, Hansons-Brooks states that, 'This opportunity provided by the Hansons is the best out there for runners coming out of college who have demonstrated the ability and wish to continue running, but haven't quite advanced to the next level ... Everything here focuses around time to train. Our lifestyle is most accurately described as being like college only we don't have classes or homework' (Hansons-Brooks 2008). Hansons-Brooks also cites the desire to form a community of runners within the community they are located to foster excitement about running. These goals demonstrate that the Hansons-Brooks programs focus is on removing those deemed to have the potential to become professional elites from a more normative lifestyle and transplanting them into a fully athletic lifestyle.

Central to these running projects is the all-encompassing focus on training that provides potential elites with an environment where they can focus solely on becoming competitive. To become competitive at the elite level, runners are expected to undertake physical training and diet regimens that are often much more strict and demanding than the average non-athlete. Runners' bodies are worked and trained to become not only fit, but fit in an activity-specific way. Simple caloric, vitamin, and mineral intake needs are higher in elites than in non-elites due to the former's extra expenditure of energy. These differences mean that the lifestyle requirements for elite runners' bodies to maintain health and fitness are far different from the average person. Kara Goucher, elite distance runner and member of the Nike Distance Project, described these differences in recalling her training for the New York City Marathon: 'While training for New York, my watch alarms went off at 8 a.m. and 5 p.m. I'd get up, work out, eat, and go to sleep. Then I'd wake up at 5 and do it again' (Rinkunas 2009: 71). Elite runners involved with the Nike Oregon Project often run twice daily, and many run near the 100-mile per week mark with some logging even more miles (Rinkunas 2009). Such intense training schedules are all-consuming, even for elite runners in running projects, and would be far less practical to maintain outside a setting where training were central to daily life.

Knowledge of and access to cutting edge technologies that can improve their performances over the competition also sets elite runners apart from non-athletes. In a sport like elite, competitive running where winners and losers are often separated by tenths or hundredths of a second, coaches and runners realize the potential value in using technologies to further set themselves apart from both non-athletes and other elites. The Nike Project is coached by former elite distance runner Alberto Salazar, a convert to relying on technological advances to aid in distance training. As he described his training philosophy from his time as a competitor to *Wired* magazine, 'I had a blood-and-guts mentality. I didn't think I needed sports drinks or water' (Tilin 2002). Now a vocal advocate of using technological and medical advances to aid runners, Salazar's influence is seen on the campus of the Nike Oregon Project. Discussing his use of technologies, Salazar says, 'As you improve, you have less room for improvement ... That's when you really start adding things. You don't leave any stone unturned' (Ibid). As a medicalized population, this willingness to add new technologies to traditional training methods is expected, as members of medical subcultures often value new discoveries in ways that those outside of the subculture do not need to.

Elite runners, especially those subscribing to the view that more technology is better, have access to technologically advanced training equipment and facilities not usually afforded to non-athletes. The Nike facilities include state-of-the-art equipment not found in the average fitness center or gym, including equipment such as antigravity treadmills, heart-rate analyzing software, vibrating muscle platforms, hyperbaric chambers, and altitude rooms and houses (Tilin 2002, Rinkunas 2009). This equipment is not often feasible outside of elite training or medical facilities, partly due to the cost and labor required to purchase and maintain the equipment. An Alter-G treadmill like the ones used at the Nike facility can cost $75,000 to buy outright, compared to regular non-antigravity treadmills which can be purchased by non-elites for a fraction of the cost (Alter-G 2009).

Salazar and the Nike project also use a training technique involving living high and training low, whereby athletes live at high altitudes, either simulated or actual, and train at lower altitudes. The goal of this method is to increase the athletes' hematocrit, the ratio of red blood cells to the total volume of blood (Tilin 2002). The increase in red blood cells is intended to increase the capacity for oxygen carrying and delivery in the blood. More efficient delivery of oxygen to muscles allows athletes to develop speed and strength more quickly, as well as reducing bodily recovery time (Houlihan 2003). Physiologists employed by Nike collect and analyze blood samples to determine what the athletes' blood make-up looks like to determine the best living and training altitudes for maximum performance. This live high, train low technique is not realistic for most non-elite athletes. Nike provides the Oregon Project athletes with homes that have rooms, often bedrooms, that are sealed off and have high altitudes simulated with altitude machines (Tilin 2002). Altitude machines, like other training equipment available to members of the running projects, are expensive and pose potential health risks. Programming the machines incorrectly can lead to problems associated with altitude sickness—potentially serious problems that can include headaches, fainting, and nosebleeds. Athletes living in a Nike Project house have experienced some of these effects after the altitude had been mistakenly set at a near-Himalayan 14,000 feet, not 12,000 as they thought. One runner reported difficulty catching his breath, while another suffered from sleeplessness and low energy (Ibid). What the live high, train low method offers is a way around WADA's ban on blood-doping. Blood-doping can take several forms; the most common type used by athletes involved the removal of athlete's blood and the separation of the red blood cells from the rest of the blood. Shortly before competition the blood cells are then transfused back into the athlete. WADA determined that such blood doping measures constituted doping and placed the practice on the prohibited list. However, WADA has placed no such ban on altitude training, including the use of altitude simulation machines. The live high, train low program used athletes such as the Nike runners thus serves as a way to raise the runners' hematocrit without violating doping regulations. While the effect of the two practices is similar, WADA has seen fit to distinguish between blood doping and altitude training.

As medicalized athletes, elite runners have regular contact with medical professionals to keep their bodies healthy and to enhance their performances. Goucher described her entourage of medical professionals that aid in her training: a chiropractor/active release therapist, a sports psychologist, and a massage therapist (Rinkunas 2009). To this entourage Goucher adds a regular, full-time coaching staff, a personal trainer, and a Pilates instructor. This level of access to and frequency of medical care not associated with chronic illness is one that is rarely found outside of a fully funded, professional athletic setting.

As described above, the shifting view of athletes as patients that need repair to patients that can be enhanced laid the groundwork for the development of supplements intended to give athletes a boost in training and competition. Gatorade is one supplement that was designed with the intent of improving athletic performances. Now a mainstay in the sporting world, including at fluid stations during elite running races, Gatorade was designed in 1965 by medical researchers at the University of Florida who wanted to develop something to aid the University's football team, the members of which often suffered from the stifling heat and humidity of Florida's climate (Gatorade 2009). The result was a drink that contained a solution of electrolyte and carbohydrates to replace those that are lost in the course of play. Athletic bodies were considered so different from non-athletic bodies in their levels of exertion in the harsh conditions, that they required their own innovation to replace fluids and carbohydrates lost while they were training or competing, and medical researchers were happy to oblige. Other products, including gels, liquids, bars, and chews, have followed Gatorade's lead and designed supplements geared toward athletes and improving performance. These supplements and replacements are set apart from regular food in their nutritional content and their form. Gels, for example, often come in small, easily transportable packets that are designed to be taken on the run. The jelly-like texture and highly concentrated formula of carbohydrates and electrolytes serve to make them unappetizing and unnecessary for many non-athletes. WADA currently has no bans on these supplements, though it has banned the use of some others, such as ephedrine (WADA 2009b). It has also regulated some substances such as caffeine, placing it on the list of agents in its monitoring program in 2004. Initially placed on WADA's prohibited list, medical researchers continued to study and debate the effects of caffeine in enhancing athletic performance. In 2004, WADA determined that caffeine did not enhance performance in a significant enough way to keep it on the banned list (Ibid). The initial ban of caffeine was curious, as it is a naturally occurring substance commonly found in food and drink. WADA has banned the use of other naturally occurring substances, including an athlete's own red blood cells as described previously.

Coaches, medical professionals, and athletes themselves recognize that elite runners are different from non-athletes. They have different bodily needs from non-elites—they require more sleep, have greater caloric and nutritional needs, and specialized medical staff to aid their physically demanding life and training styles. These differences from the average person are highlighted in each article and interview to show readers, in part, that these athletes do not lead a lifestyle commensurate with that of non-elites. Their lifestyle differences are pointed out in medical terms—their rigorous lifestyle needs and their seemingly high need for access to and actual contact with medical professionals—and in social terms— these athletes do not have the same daily life experiences as most non-elites.

Normalizing Athletes

Those who follow a more normative, non-elite athletic lifestyle make up much of the readership of the popular magazines, newspapers, and websites that discuss athletes' lifestyles. While there are plenty of column inches devoted to highlighting the extraordinary characteristics of athlete's lifestyles and training regimens, sportswriters and interviewers also have a second purpose in their coverage of elite athletes: to normalize them. This normalization happens in several ways in sports writing, and these efforts seem to directly contradict the way elites are set apart, both in sports writing and in actuality, from non-elites.

First, portions of elite athletes' lifestyles are displayed in broad strokes to show how they are similar to non-elite athletes. Miniature food journals showcasing what an athlete's average meal or weekly food log would look like are one technique used in popular literature, especially showing up in *Runner's World*. These lists include the regular foods that any person could or would eat for any of the three meals or snacks in a day—even desserts and box devoted to so-called 'Guilty Pleasures' appear (Lorge Butler 2008b). Absent are the specialty food products and vitamin, mineral, or herbal supplements. The inclusion of food that is easily recognizable sends a message to the non-elite athlete reader that these athletes really are not that different from them. They eat apples, bananas, sandwiches, and even sneak in a cookie or dessert here and there, just like a normal person might. The omission of the specialty foods and supplements—those things that set elites apart—are almost unnoticeable, as the food log seems so average.

Even with the omission of specialty foods in these articles, many are not hard to find. As more and more products and supplements are developed for athletes, many become available to mainstream consumers. Sports bars, gels, and shakes are now mainstays at recreational, non-elite races and events, and Gatorade is carried in supermarkets and drug stores. Marketing these products as scientifically formulated for athletes lets the non-elite consumer into the elite world for a brief time. Bringing these and other products to the mainstream makes them less revolutionary and less mysterious. When non-elite runners use these products they become familiar. No one questions the fairness or legality when watching a runner guzzle Gatorade or other sports drinks, the way no one questions eating a post-run banana. Even some products that promise to enhance an athlete in some way, such as the energy drink FRS, which is endorsed by elite cyclist and two-time marathoner Lance Armstrong, are benign in a society where energy drinks are ubiquitous (FRS 2009).

In a similar vein as food journals are miniature training logs of elite athletes. Often these appear in the context of larger articles on an elite's recent success or preparation for an upcoming race. The elite training logs show the basics of a workout schedule such as distance and type of workout on which days, while leaving out details as to how fast or at what pace elites run the distances. Again not only are the details that set apart the elite workout from the non-elite—the speed—mostly left out, but so is the entire context. There is no mention of the accompanying medical entourage, training technologies, or personal coaching that elite runners have at their disposal. A similar section in *Runner's World* titled 'The Workout' features miniature versions of workouts done by elite runners or recommended by well-known elite coaches (Rinkunas 2009). Once more the lack of details such as the pace for the workout, or the full-scale warm up to cool down details, work to show how similar the elite training plans are to the ones used by non-elite runners. Adapting the elite workouts for the non-elite runner is intended to aid the non-elite with training ideas to improve their own performances, just like the workouts are intended to do for elites. Juxtaposing the broad training schedule with an elite success story sends the message to the reader that if he or she can train like an elite and maybe obtain similar results. This portrayal is in stark contrast to articles that feature the aforementioned devices and training equipment used by elites, as there is no mention of employing underwater running, hyperbaric chambers, or altitude training in 'The Workout' recommendations.

To fill in some of the gaps, several well-known running coaches have written books to guide non-elites to running better. One of the first of this kind is *The Runner's Handbook* first published in 1978 by coaches Bob Glover and Jack Shepherd. One feature of all editions of this book is that it lays out training programs and workouts in detail, including target paces and times in neatly organized charts. The charts run from near-world record paces down to the much more pedestrian first-time runner paces (Glover and Shepherd 1996). According to Glover and Shepherd, the difference between elite and non-elites is simply a matter of pace, strategy, and proper preparation in the form of training, diet, and cross training. Seemingly, anyone following the principles and guidelines in Glover's book can achieve elite levels of speed without one of the specialized lifestyles afforded to the runners involved with the Nike Oregon Project or the Hansons-Brooks Distance Project.

The increasing number of road races and the opening of former qualify-only marathons to mass runners may have also lessened the perceived distance between elite and non-elite runners. Since the first charity runners, a Team in Training group, ran the New York City Marathon in 1988, other races have included participant slots for charity runners (TNT 2009). The five marathons that make up the world marathon majors series—Berlin, Boston, Chicago, London, and New York City— all now have a non-qualifying time option for entry into the race (WMM 2009). Each race sets aside a designated number of slots for these charity runners, who do not have to meet any qualifying standard other than membership with one of the associated fundraising groups. Since each of the world majors has an elite field of both male and female runners, non-elite runners are able to feel as if they are running in the race with, or against, the elite field. Adding an entry component not based on qualifying times not only opened races to a wider audience, but it also normalized the idea of running a marathon. No longer was it something only elites or competitive non-elites could do, it is something in which anyone willing to raise money for charity could partake.

Highlighting the similarities of family and work demands between elite and non-elite runners further closes the gap between the two groups. Far different from the lifestyle differences focused of the sort discussed above, these articles and interviews focus on the 'real world' pressures faced by elite athletes that are similar to what non-elites face. The working mother narrative, where elite female runners with children are portrayed as a normal working mom, is one that allows the fastest growing demographic of new runners, women over 40, and others in similar positions to relate to the plight of the woman who seeks to be a mother and to have a professional career. A *Runner's World* feature in the September 2008 issue focused on female runners who were not full-time elite runners (Lorge Butler 2008a). Titled 'Olympic Effort,' the main thrust of the article was how these women, all of whom qualified to run in the Olympic qualifying marathon, balanced their training with children and full-time careers outside of running. Three of the five women in the article are mothers, four of the five have professional jobs away from running and all discuss how they fit training into their daily routines. What is striking about this feature is that it exemplifies the tension between being an elite and a non-elite. The women are elite in one specific way—that they all qualified to run the Olympic marathon qualifying race. However, none of them are elite in the sense that none of them were expected to or did qualify for the Olympic team, while the women who did qualify were experienced, professional runners. The runners featured in 'Olympic Effort' were simultaneously highlighted for both the ordinariness and their extraordinariness—they exemplify the attempt to narrow the divide between the two.

While elite runners often recognize that they are not like non-elites, some come to view these otherwise abnormal behaviors as commonplace. Altitude machines and twice a day training runs become the norm. An early member of the Nike Oregon Project Karl Keska described his feelings toward the program: 'I'd like to do well in an Olympic marathon. As frightening as it sometimes sounds, this seems like a very natural and normal environment for helping me reach my goal' (Tilin 2002). Salazar himself takes the view that if all the technologies and equipment become normal, elites will be more willing to follow the technologies further to greater success. As he told *Wired*, 'If they [elite runners] improve a lot, then they'll say, gee, yeah, let's take another look at that vibration platform' (Tilin 2002). In this view, when the attitude that doing whatever it takes to get faster, to win, becomes the norm, new devices and technologies would become easier to adopt.

Tension

Casting elite runners as both normal and abnormal results in a conflict that has led to the current debates over doping and anti-doping. On one hand, elite runners are often portrayed as more similar to non-elites than different. Coverage of elite athletes highlights the routines and techniques that are similar and familiar to non-elites. They must do things that all individuals must do to stay healthy and competitive in their chosen fields, and often they must face obstacles such as family pressures, injury, and other traumas that can get in the way of even the best laid plans. This view, exemplified by Deena Kastor's shock and disappointment that an athlete would step outside the bounds of normative behavior and take or use something to enhance their performance, echoes those scholars who hold that doping should be treated as an ethical issue within sport. The normative view of organized sport is that it is a space where 'fair play' and the 'level playing field' are valued above all (Murray 2008). Therefore, a set of regulations is necessary to determine what is and what is not allowed in sport and to then enforce these regulations.

On the other hand, elite runners have a completely abnormal lifestyle. Elites who participate in professional running projects are literally set apart from non-elites, as they reside in special housing in a specified area, provided by their sponsors, with the intent to focus primarily on their training (Hansons-Brooks 2008). As a medicalized population, elite runners become used to relying on medicine not only to treat an ailment, but for new ways to become better, faster runners. This lifestyle and the attitudes that value technology and scientific progress for enhancing performance become norms within this subculture. Viewing elite runners, as well as other elite athletes, as not conforming to a normative lifestyle and value system is the basis for stances taken by scholars such as Miah and Hoberman. The use of performance enhancers is simply an extension of the technological approaches that are already undertaken by elite runners and other elite athletes. The expectation that a population that has come to rely on and value medicine and technology will suddenly cease their current practice and return to more traditional methods is unlikely.

Detractors leveled further critique at agencies such as WADA because of the seemingly arbitrary and sometimes contradictory nature in which agents and techniques have been identified as doping. Some practices are banned while others that have the same basic effect are not, such as the prohibition on blood transfusions but not on altitude training or the use of altitude simulation machines. Banning one set of practices because the effect is considered unfair but allowing another that has the same effect is not only confusing, but also contradicts the rationale behind anti-doping efforts: to protect the 'level playing field' notion of fairness these agencies feel is foundational to sport.

Anti-doping agencies have not completely ignored the argument that athletes are different from non-athletes. The flexibility in the way doping has been defined by these agencies leaves open the possibility for change and does not necessarily preclude any substance or practice *a priori*. Current definitions of doping rely upon and assume rules regarding anti-doping, and offer no fixed or concrete example of what constitutes doping; doping is violating anti-doping, anti-doping is preventing doping. These circular definitions can be problematic in terms of understanding what doping is, how a substance or practice becomes defined as doping, and what the implications of these prohibitions are. However, what can be easily understood is that doping and anti-doping are fluid and dynamic terms without fixed meanings. WADA's definition of doping is based on engaging in an activity banned by WADA in its list of prohibited substances and practices. The prohibited list is reviewed, altered, and reissued on an annual basis, with substances and practices added to or removed from the list each year. This review process allows for the addition of newly discovered substances to the list, as well as the removal of previously banned substances or practices. This means that if something labeled a doping agent is found to not have the effect or pose the threat it was originally thought to, it can be removed from the list.

Though some flexibility does exist in these anti-doping programs, critics of this approach hold that there are so many potential enhancements available that anti-doping programs based on strict codes of ethics will ultimately be insufficient in the effort to stymie usage as athletes will seek ways around the prohibitions (Miah 2006). As athletes continue to rely on new advancements in medicine and training technologies, medical researchers will continue to seek new ways to improve athletes' performances. Due to the value placed on the use of technology to enhance performance by many coaches and athletes, programs seeking to monitor these technologies must walk a tightrope between the two extreme views of this debate—that anti-doping programs should be ever more rigorous and athletes should be strictly monitored, or that anti-doping is doomed to be ineffective and all restrictions lifted.

It is for this reason that I argue for a reordering of the way anti-doping agencies view athletes in their consideration of what practices and substances athletes should be allowed to utilize to enhance their performances. This new way of looking at includes, first, recognizing that elite athletes are not normal in terms of their lifestyles and attitudes towards medicine. By definition elite athletes are different from everyone else—they represent the upper echelon of sporting achievement. As they are expected to perform in their chosen sport in a way that is not expected of non-elite athletes, it follows that their lifestyles would reflect this difference. They train more frequently and with more intensity and focus than non-elites. As a result of their being brought into a medical subculture via the rise of sports medicine, they have come to rely on, and value, medicine and technology to aid in this pursuit of excellence. As non-elites do not engage in the same practices or utilize the same technologies as elite athletes, it should not be surprising that the two groups have different attitudes regarding what is a logical extension of techniques and practices already in use and what is considered extreme. Recognizing that athletes are not normal in these ways can clear the way to understanding that what would be viewed as abnormal for non-elites may actually be standard practice among elites.

Second, anti-doping agencies must recognize that there is and can be no real standard of normal among elite athletes, as the ultimate goal of elites is to be as abnormal as possible. Elite athletes compete to be the best in their field, and being the best also means being the most different from everyone else, including other elites. In order for elite athletes to achieve this ultimate goal they adopt highly abnormal lifestyle and training techniques. If they train in the same way as everyone else they cannot become different—competition is built on the pursuit of the special, the different, the abnormal.

An understanding of athletes that takes these two ideas into consideration may work to create a system of anti-doping that does not fear, but instead respects the non-normative lifestyle and values of elite athletes. The system of anti-doping that can walk this tightrope between two extreme views of athletes and how they should be regulated must be open to acknowledging and incorporating technologies and values that may not be fully understood or appreciated by those outside the culture of elite athletes. However, a system that works within these differences and not against them has the potential to be more effective at protecting the spirit of sport and competition than the current approach.

References

Alter-G. (2009). *How to Buy*. [On-line]. Available at: http: //www.alter-g.com/ alterg/buy.aspx [accessed: 11 August 2009].

Baume, N., Hellemans, L., Saugy, M. (2007). Guide to over-the-counter sports supplements for athletes, *International SportMed Journal*, 8(1), 2–10.

FRS. (2009). *FRS Healthy Energy*. [On-line]. Available at: http: //www.frs.com/ [accessed: 9 August 2009].

Gatorade. (2009). *History*. [On-line]. Available at: http: //www.gatorade.com/ history/ [accessed: 15 July 2009].

Glover, R. and Shepherd, J. (1996). *The Runner's Handbook*. New York, New York: Penguin Books.

Hansons-Brooks. (2008). *About the Hansons-Brooks Distance Project*. [On-line] Available at: http: //www.hansonsrunning.com/index.php?option=com_conten t&view=article&id=63&Itemid=59 [accessed: 19 August 2009].

Hoberman, J. (2007). History and prevalence of doping in the marathon. *Sports Medicine*, 37 (4/5), 386–88.

Houlihan, B. (2003). *Dying to Win*. 2nd Edition. Strasbourg, Germany: Council of Europe Publishing.

IAAF. (2009). *Athletes Guide*. [Online: International Association of Athletics Federations]. Available at: http: //www.iaaf.org/mm/Document/ imported/38877.pdf [accessed: 18 July 2009].

IAAF. (2009). *Anti-Doping Regulations*. [Online: International Association of Athletics Federations]. Available at: http: //www.iaaf.org/mm/Document/ Antidoping/Rules&Regulations/03/30/46/20090105051202_httppostedfile_ 2009regulations_7948.pdf [accessed: 18 July 2009].

Konig, E. (1995). Criticism of doping: the nihilistic side of technological sport and the antiquated view of sport ethics. *International Review for the Sociology of Sport*, 30(3), 247–60.

Lorge Butler, S. (2008). Olympic effort. *Runner's World*, May, 94–100.

Lorge Butler, S. (2008). Secrets of the Olympians. *Runner's World*, September, 76–9.

McDowell, D. (2008). Everybody's favorite. *Runner's World*. September, 90–91.

Miah, A. (2006). Rethinking enhancement in sport. *Annals of the New York Academy of Sciences*, 1093(1), 301–20.

Miah, A. (2005). From anti-doping to a 'performance policy': sport technology, being human, and doing ethics. *European Journal of Sport Science*, 5(1), 51–7.

Mitchell, C.B. (2008). Genetically enhancing athlete? *Ethics & Medicine: An International Journal of Bioethics*, 24(1), 5–6.

Murray, T.H. (1983). The coercive power of drugs in sports. *The Hastings Center Report*, 13(4), 24–30.

Murray, T.H. (2008). Doping in sport: challenges for medicine, science and ethics. *Journal of Internal Medicine*, 264(2), 95–98.

NIH. (2007). *Dietary Supplements*. [Online: National Institute of Health]. Available at: http: //dietarysupplements.info.nih.gov/factsheets/dietarysupplements.asp. [accessed: 30 April 2009].

Park, A. (2009). This doctor does not want to see you. *Time*. [Online]. Available at: http: //www.time.com/time/specials/packages/article/0,28804,1903873_ 1903925_1903787,00.html [accessed: 2 September 2009].

Pipe, A. and Hébert, P.C. 2008 Doping, sport and the community. *CMAJ: Canadian Medical Association Journal*, 179(4), 303.

Rinkunas, S. (2009). Fast learner. *Runner's World*, May, 70–72.

Schmidt, M.S. (2008). Marion Jones gets 6 months in doping case. *The New York Times*, 11 January.

Shogan, D. and Ford, M.A. (2000). New sport ethics. *International Review for the Sociology of Sport*. 35(1), 49–58.

TNT. (2009). *History*. [Online: Team in Training]. Available at: http: //www. teamintraining.org/firsttimehere/themissionandhistory/ [accessed: 2 September 2009].

Tilin, A. (2002). The ultimate running machine. *Wired*. [Online]. Available at: http: //wired.com/archive/10.08/nike_pr.html [accessed: 11 August 2009].

Waddington, I. (1996). The development of sports medicine. *Sociology of Sport Journal*. 13(2), 176–96.

WADA. (2009). Governance. [On-line: World Anti-Doping Agency]. Available at: http: //www.wada-ama.org/en/dynamic.ch2?pageCategory.id=258 [accessed: 15 April 2009].

WADA. (2009). Prohibited list. [On-line: World Anti-Doping Agency]. Available at: http: //www.wada-ama.org/rtecontent/document/2009_Prohibited_List_ENG_Final_20_Sept_08.pdf [accessed: 15 April 2009].

WADA. (2009). World Anti-Doping Code. [On-line: World Anti-Doping Agency]. Available from: http: //www.wada-ama.org/en/dynamic.ch2?pageCategory. id=250 [accessed: 15 April 2009].

WMM. (2009). *Charity*. [On-line: World Marathon Majors]. Available at: http:// www.worldmarathonmajors.com/US/charity/ [accessed: 30 August 2009].

Zinser, L. and Schmidt, M.S. (2007). Doping: admitting to doping, Marion Jones enters guilty plea. *The New York Times*, 6 October.

Chapter 3

Embodying a Healthy Running Body in a British Non-Elite Road Running Community

Carole Sutton

Introduction

In this chapter I explore some of the issues surrounding my body's journey from a sedate comfortable lifestyle in my early 30s to a more physically active and sporty lifestyle by my late 30s. The chapter first documents the popularity of running in a global context. I then consider the self-regulated running body, nature and consumer culture. Using an autoethnographic approach allows me to explore some of my personal running experiences and reflections, drawing upon personal data from running diaries which recorded training sessions, race results, and some limited comments on how I felt at the time. I have used these running diaries as the basis for remembering and re-remembering the past as an embodied narrative. I chart my own journey as a lone runner and my progress as I join a non-elite road running club. Finally, I consider some of the emerging themes in relation to the literature and my future research.

Setting the Scene: The Rise of Long-distance Running by 'The Masses'

As I moved from a non-runner to a marathon runner I was aware of the development of road running both professionally and as a mass participation sport, particularly in relation to the marathon. Since the 1970s this growth is evidenced by the increasing prevalence of city marathons and the number of participating competitors, both men and women and across a wide age range. The modern marathon distance of 26.2 miles or 42.196 km was established in 1908 at the London Olympic Games (Bryant 2005). Despite women participating in city marathons and European athletics championships it was not until the 1984 Olympics that the first women's Olympic marathon was held. Outside of the Olympic movement large city marathons, for example, London, New York, Paris and Amsterdam are interesting examples of where both elite and non-elite competitors, club and non-club runners, tread the same route, albeit in different finish times, and for different rewards. These races have also become a vehicle for raising charity money with some organisers reserving places for charities who in turn allocate to fund-raising participants. Some of these participants will have been previous non-runners who have been motivated to start running as a way of raising money for their preferred charity. Another example of this type of charity running includes in the United Kingdom the women-only Cancer Research 'Race for Life' 5km series. They started in 1994 as one race with 680 women and have grown to 230 races in 2009 with an estimated total of 750,000 women participating. Similar charity raising events are held in other countries around the world, for example, the American Cancer Society 'Relay for Life' with 3.5 million participants.

An examination of road running results 'capture' the emergence of women's increasing participation in running and a snapshot of the underlying upward trend can be found in participation statistics from the New York City, Paris, Amsterdam and Helsinki marathons. The following statistics were obtained from the respective marathon organisations' websites. In 1970 the New York City marathon had a total of 127 starting participants and only one was a woman. By 1980 the participation numbers had risen to 14,012 of which 14 per cent were women. By 1990 there were 25,797 starters with 20 per cent being women and these figures continued to grow as in 2009 there were 43,660 runners of which 35 per cent were women. Similar growth and proportions of women can be found when examining the data of finishers for recent London marathons. In 2004 there were 29,770 finishers of whom 24 per cent were women and in 2009 there were 35,351 finishers, 31 per cent were women. Data from the Helsinki marathon for 2004 revealed similar proportions where 24 per cent of the 4,939 finishers were women. Data from the 2005 Amsterdam marathon show that 16 per cent of the 5,336 finishers were women; this being a similar proportion to the 2009 Paris marathon finishers where 16 per cent of the 30,334 finishers were women. The smaller proportions of women at Paris, Amsterdam and only slightly less at Helsinki may be due to structural factors relating to the registration process. These three marathons operate a direct registration system whereas both London and New York operate a more complex system that is partly ballot based in an attempt to manage the excessive demand for places. It could be argued that the quota regime adopted by the ballot systems may result in proportionally more women applicants getting actual places (figures on applications were not available) though this then leads to the inevitable question of why aren't there equal proportions of men and women. The direct registration systems may better represent the general level of participation in women's running however even direct registration with its 'first come first served' approach inevitably excludes individuals, especially as online web-based registration and card payment becomes the norm (e.g. 51 per cent of the 2006 Paris marathon registrations were made via their website).

Examination of the finishers' data from the 2009 New York City Marathon shows that distance running attracts men and women from across the age range. The age gender profile for the New York City Marathon 2009 is shown in Figure 3.1. The profile for men and women is different with a higher proportion of women finishers in the younger age groups compared to men. This may reflect the growing popularity of women only races, especially those run by charity

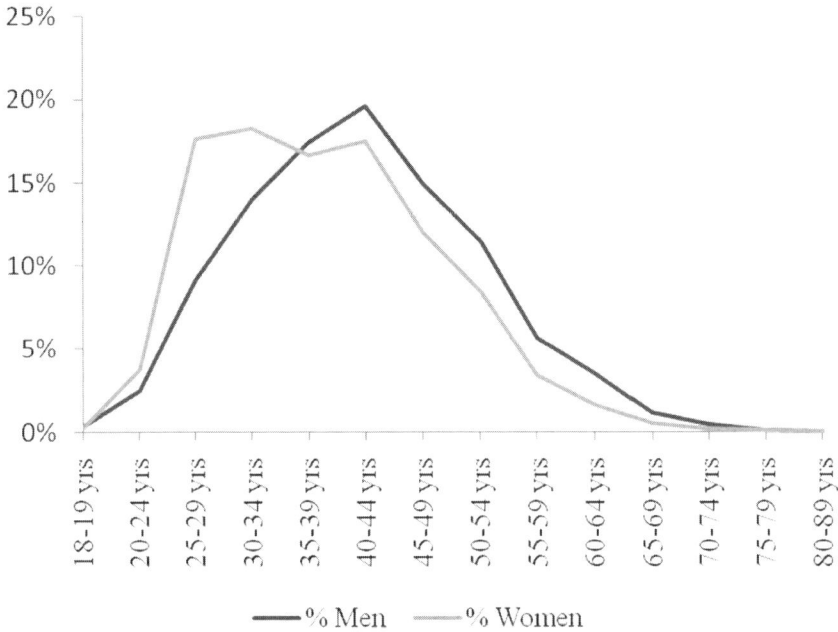

Figure 3.1   Age profile of men and women finishers: New York City Marathon, 2009

Source: Data taken from the New York City Marathon Demographics on Finishers statistics http: //www.nycmarathon.org/results_finisherDemographics.htm. Accessed 01/12/2009. Total finishers: men = 28,485; women = 15,175. Chart compiled by the author.

organisations, as well as reflecting family or child care responsibilities with the noticeable decline in women aged 35–39 years.

In summary the evidence from race statistics highlights the rising popularity of running and global marathon endurance running events. While woman have also increased their participation it has not reached equity with men. Having established the popularity of road running in the next sections I will explore the relevant literature relating to the running body as self-regulation and a consuming body.

The Self-regulated Running Body in Sport, Fitness and Health

In the following section I examine some of the literature related to understanding the body, focussing in particular on technologies of the body, gender and the body, how sporting activities are organised and measured, and finally, the consuming body.

Technologies of the Body

Similar to other social activities participation in a sporting pursuit whether for leisure or competition involves the body engaging in social practices that give new meaning beyond simply biological characteristics (Shilling 1993). The movement of the body in running and athletic coach training manuals, for an example see Noakes (2001), emphasises the body as a mechanistic hierarchical system where episodes of running or training are concerned with the continual improvement in the efficient function and form of the running body. The focus is on improving the cardio-vascular system, body strength, biomechanics and fuelling of the body. These texts often include chapters on the psychology of sport to improve and maximise performance, in particular for competition. This whole subject area is often referred to as Sport and Exercise Science, SES (Brackenridge et al. 2005), with its scientific knowledge and approach replicated in the popular press, sporting magazines and internet sites. The focus of the body on objectification and quantification suggests that while the sporting body can in principle be for leisure or play it is increasingly rationalised into a self- regulated work like form. Sport and Exercise Science (SES) has tended to give a limited consideration of the everyday social and natural environment in which the biological body functions. It is social practices that labour upon and transform the body, a process that Connell refers to as 'transcendence' (Shilling 1993: 110). Through this embodiment gendered bodies are both defined and transformed by existing social categories. As the work of Connell suggest these categories form women's and men's bodies that reinforce masculine and feminine images (Schilling 1993: 106). From a review of sociological research on women and sporting activities, Markula (2003) concluded that separating the dominant technologies of power from technologies of the self is problematic; and, recommended that women need to engage in a critical self-awareness of dominant technologies on their sport. In Foucault's concept of 'technologies of the self' the concern was with the actions and practices that an individual performs on their own body, sometimes with the help of others to:

> permit individuals to effect by their own means or with the help of others a certain number of operations on their own bodies and souls, thoughts, conduct and way of being, so as to transform themselves in order to attain a certain state of happiness, purity, wisdom, perfection or immortality (Foucault 1988: 18 cited in Markula 2003: 88).

In the review Markula concluded that the concept of technologies of the self had been interpreted slightly differently in the research projects of women in the different sporting activities analysed (these were gymnastics, rowers and body-builders). The review focused on research that examined the role of diet regimes of sports persons as dieting is used by individuals in many sports to achieve the ideal body image for premier performance. Markula concluded that it was difficult to separate the technology of the self from other power processes. Some research concluded that the process of dieting, as a transforming practice, enable athletes to fulfil the sporting discourse of achievement as an act of personal freedom and choice, however other research concluded that personal dietary choices were made within the bio-medical discourses of sports science and gendered images of the ideal body.

One framework for understanding the growth in activities such as running is to consider how health and fitness have become intrinsically linked in everyday life. The idealised body that is lean, toned and 'visually' healthy is one that both men and women, particularly from the middle class, strive for. The self-regulation required to achieve such an aesthetic disciplined body also becomes the body image of someone who is able to demonstrate self discipline, healthy and virtuous behaviour lifestyle. The act of running as a highly self-regulated activity is one form of a fitness activity that seeks to uncover or reveal the 'fit' individual body through rationalised activity and to cope with a rapidly changing world (Glassnor 1989). In this context, Lupton (1995: 143) contends.

> This concept of exercise is strongly linked with the concept of health as a 'creation' or an accomplishment of the self. It is also related to broader contemporary notions of the 'ideal' body as one that is tightly controlled, contained in space, devoid of excess fat or flabby muscle.

The therapeutic benefits of exercise and sport have also been explored with research evidence to suggest an association between emotional well-being and regular physical exercise and health life style (Steptoe et al. 1997), and that aerobic exercise is an effective treatment over no treatment in mild to moderate depression (Martinsen 1994, Estivill 1995). Further evidence suggests that exercise can be one element of an effective therapeutic approach (Laitinen et al. 2006, 2007) and that the social support network surrounding exercise behaviour (Oman and Oman 2003) also contributes to well-being.

Gender and the Body

The earlier analysis of marathon statistics suggest that men and women marathon runners also engage differently across the lifecourse and comparative research on choices in sport participation have revealed differences in men's and women's participation. Patterns of sport participation are generally accepted as being established at a young age.

Research into participation in sporting activities suggests that men/boys have not only been encouraged to take part in sport but that they are directed to sport that is masculine in terms of its emphasis on strenuous and competitive activities. Women/girls have not been so encouraged; instead definitions of fitness are based around performing everyday tasks, less on taking part in sport or exercise for fun and more on body image. Historically women's participation in sport was limited by biological determinism in order that they should fulfil their duties of motherhood. This approach advocated the less vigorous sports activities which were not built around competitiveness and muscular bodies. Exercise, health and morality became intertwined with sports appropriate for women, for example, croquet, stressing the cultured, gentle recreational leisure activity that was good for health and not the competitive sport of men (Hargreaves 1994).

Women are less likely to see themselves as 'sporty'(Choi 2000: 5) and research by Scratton (1996) suggests that this low participation rate, in the UK at least, can be located in the education system from secondary school onwards. Scratton's research found that the majority of young women in her study of UK schools lost interest in physical education from secondary school onwards. Reasons given include dislike of feminine sporting activities offered which are seen as low status, the school sports kit, getting sweaty and communal showering/changing. Where women do participate in sport/exercise there is a tendency for the emphasis to be on regulating the body to achieve an acceptable body image and shape built around a cultural slenderness which in order to achieve requires tight self-regulation (Bordo 1990). Deem's (1987) research on sport in women's leisure also highlights that participation or non-participation should be understood within the wider context of women's limited leisure time, due to structural and ideological factors such as the accessibility and location of organised sport, demands of women's gendered role in households, biology, physiology and sexuality. Fasting (1987) highlights that in Norwegian society women's participation in sporting organisations takes place on men's terms and Hargreaves (1999) notes that in women's organisations there is an under representation of women form all social backgrounds.

Organisations and Measurement

There has already been much research undertaken in exploring how individuals work on their bodies to bring about changes, for example, gym users (Crossley 2004, Sassatelli 1999), bodybuilding (Monaghan 1999) and aerobics (Markula 1995). Running can also be gym-based with fitness centres offering stationary running on treadmills. Like body builders and gym users the emphasis for runners is on individual engagement with a series of activities which are different from team-based events (e.g. football, netball) or sporting events that require a high level of skill (e.g. tennis, golf). The very nature and form that running can take also makes it a complex activity to research. While it is certainly true that running is a highly individualised action it can, should the individual chose, also involve the social and team elements of other sports. Individuals can chose to run as part of a running club organisation and take part in team based running events. Alternatively they may prefer to run alone or with friends. For example, a group of club runners may train together or attend a formal training event at a local track. Non-club runners may build a running network through friendships and work. Running clubs have their own rules and regulations. Some are formalised through the club constitution and like other sporting activities are focussed on the avoidance of conflict and injury. Club organisations can bring people together in a positive environment, although Huizinga (1970) identified that they also serve to regulate and structure what was once a playful creative activity (cited in Cashmore 2000).

The standard measurements of performance in running are time, distance and race position. In the professional athletic world statistical data recording personal best performances, games records, national records, and world records are scrutinised and interpreted. 'They define achievement and progress – progress towards the record. They are also said to serve as universal athletic currency, enabling unambiguous comparisons to be made between places and regions.' (Bale 2005: 24). Within local running clubs this practice is also adopted to include the recording of individual performance times and club record holders, with local athletes using this running currency to provide a common language between individuals of different abilities and commitment to running. Even for those runners that do not take part in races or do not belong to a formal club, the completion of a recreational run is often personally measured in time and/or distance, as a means of logging performance and progression. Research undertaken by Smith (1998) suggests that both the general public and runners themselves sub-divided runners into different 'types' based upon the level of regulated activity that the individual participates in. In a study of road running and racing, three types of runner were identified, 'athletes', 'runners' and 'joggers'. Those individuals whose speed enabled them to win or come highly placed in road races were 'athletes', those who regularly entered races but would never be placed for prizes were 'runners' and finally, the group of runners who may enter races occasionally were fun runners or 'joggers'.

The Consuming Running Body

Professional sport is financially supported by an array of different consumer practices that engage individuals in the sport as a participator and/or as a supporting spectator. Over the past twenty-five years sport has become increasingly linked to the media and advertising. For many sports, particular the team-based sports such as American football, soccer or football, baseball and ice hockey, there is a branded market for sports goods and services that are advertised and endorsed by sports personalities. The commodification of sport has been extended to include celebrity where sport related products are endorsed by world leading professional sports stars (Horne 2006). Major sporting events such as matches or large city marathons are also televised and sponsored by sports related brands, for example sports drinks and equipment manufacturers. Sport is part of a wider lifestyle choice that places an intrinsic link between the product, individual choice and a healthy, fit, and, successful sporting body. Individual fitness is constructed as a consumer lifestyle that requires the individual to engage in a project of the body (Featherstone 1987), and perhaps it is not unsurprising that in this context consumer culture and sporting activity have mapped together (Hargreaves 1987). The promotion of the healthy body is one that is linked to the healthy self of personal free choice and self-expression (Watson 2007). To aid the individual runner there is a plethora of running technologies available for consumption. For both men and women there is a wide variety of running clothing and equipment that is marketed as enhancing running experience, protecting/managing injury and maximising training benefits. The array of products available both aim to maintain the inner and outer body (Featherstone 1982) to both feel and look like a healthy runner. The inner body is concerned with the consumption of appropriate training regimes, nutrition and general maintenance against injury. Those activities from SES, discussed earlier, include training knowledge, dietary advice and use of sports therapists (physiotherapists, masseurs) can all contribute to the success of the visible outer body in terms of general body image and improved performance. In addition the outer body also requires the individual runner to undertake some identity work to acquire 'the look' of a runner and the mass consumption of appropriate running equipment, latest designs and technologies is driven by advertising that can be found in specialist running magazines. Smith Maguire (2002) undertook a textual analysis of fitness manuals in the US and concluded that the body of a fitness consumer was a body of consumption. This 'body of consumption' was able to calculate positive rewards for overall well-being and healthiness, to develop motivational techniques to overcome inertia and possible failure, and to undertake the physical exertion of training. The image of a runner in advertising is not just one that is thin, lean, athletic and healthy but also one that has the latest running clothing made of hi-tech wicking material, the correct shoe for their running style and terrain. There is information on dietary requirements for different distances and a range of supplements to be taken before, during and after training/race sessions. More advanced and costly technologies are available for recording individual fitness and progression storing data on time, distance and heart rate. Abbas (2004) undertook an analysis of the front cover and letters pages of a leading running magazine from 1979 to 1995 and found that the image portrayed of the successful runner was middle class. The image naturalised age and gender inequalities and promoted individual responsibility for their healthy running bodies.

While all of the discussion around sporting practices, sport and exercise science, the influence of consumerism and pursuit of health and fitness lifestyle we are still left to ponder a key questions in relation to non-elite running practices. What are the processes by which an individual, including myself, become involved in running? Are the running practices they engage in constraining or enabling, and how does running relate to wider lifestyle choices? In my autoethnography, it was these questions that I wished to consider in relation to my own reflections on my experiences.

Methods: Autoethnography

There has been a growing emergence of academic writers critically reflecting on their own autobiographical experiences to make sense of the complexities of social and political life. Critical reflection has been used by researchers in ethnographic research to make sense of research settings (May 1993), particularly those that involve particular difficulties and challenges (Lee-Treweek and Linkogle 2000), providing additional insights into the understanding of the specific focus of the research. The autoethnographic approach requires the author to engage in literary writings to clarify understanding for the reader, to engage in critical self-reflection and analysis. For Ellis (1999) autoethnography bridges the gap between the social sciences and arts; advocating a process of emotion recall to imagine being back in a social scene with both the physicality and emotions of the event. Autoethnography situates the individual writer as both the researcher subject and the researcher, to research and understand oneself. It is characterised by writing in the first person, situating the 'I' in sociological understanding (Katz Rothman 2005, 2007, Stanley 1993, 1995) through which the researcher can critically understand his/her own experiences. The 'autobiographical I' is 'inquiring and analytical' (Stanley 1993: 49). Autoethnography has been used by many academics particularly around experiences of physical and emotional pain and illness (Sparkes 1996, 2000, Ettorre 2005, 2006, forthcoming a, forthcoming b). Ettorre (2006: 153) uses autoethnography in a reflexive process to understand a recent illness where the method of 'autoethnography presents particular embodied events with people in time, their social shaping and how these can be seen as emblematic of wider cultural meanings and social trends'. The autobiographical method has also been used to consider movement and emotions (Sutton 2009, Letherby and Reynolds 2009), while autoethnography with an emphasis on emotional recall has been employed to help others to mend wounds (Ettorre forthcoming b).

My motivations for using this approach emerge as part of my future research ideas to explore the leisure or non-elite based running community. Exploring my own reflections on personal experiences would provide critical understanding that would both help inform my research and also enable sensitivity to individual differences in how we negotiate the social and political. It would allow me to clarify the concepts and emerging issues that have presented through my running body. Furthermore, it would hopefully facilitate a personal awareness of the barriers between the researcher and the researched. My autoethnography is one that focuses on both the pain and pleasure of training and participating in races. From enjoying the freedom of movement of a running body, balanced against constraints and negotiation, of moving my running body through a landscape of technologies for improving my running body and jointing a local running community.

The data for my autoethnography is drawn from my running diaries which recorded training sessions, race results and some personal comments on how I felt at the time. These diaries were kept between 1999 to 2006, a period in my 'running career' that saw a significant changes in how I choose to run moving from a causal solo jogger to joining a local running club in the UK. Detailed diary entries were kept between 2003 and 2006 as this period corresponds with a developing enthusiasm for longer distances up to and including the marathon. Prior to 1999, my last experiences of summer track running were as a teenager at school, reluctant, and always at the back running on a track disliking all aspects of the compulsory, physical education lesson. I have used the diary as the basis for remembering and re-remembering the past as an embodied narrative. Also, I have a photo album containing images of my participation in organised running events, with the images taken mostly midway and at the finish line. Depending on the specific event, there are accompanying memorabilia of medals and t-shirts. This process of revisiting textual and visual image data allows me to clarify the feelings, concepts and emerging issues that have confronted me through my running body; to critically reflect upon and to think about how my past experiences will potentially impact on my future research.

My Life and Running

It is May 2006 and I sit in my office with an open Word document ready to type a draft of my paper. Over the past three months, I have read about autoethnography, attended a mini-methods festival where the use of autoethnography was discussed by my colleague and friend, Betsy and I read some of the literature relating to the body, sociology of sport texts and feminist accounts of women and sport. My head is spinning with different ideas both about the content of this paper and the wider discussion of autoethnography in social research. Now as I come to start thinking and writing about my story, I have this fearful sense that what I have to write about is probably not that interesting to anyone but me. I also feel it is going to be hard to organise my reflections in a concise, meaningful way for the reader. Autoethnography feels a little like 'doing' English literature which was not my favourite subject at school. I then gaze out of my office window. It is a lovely sunny day. I could so easily stop at this point, get changed into my running gear and go for a run by the sea. You see running is so easy for me in comparison to academic writing. From the moment I step out of the front door, I can forget the struggles and hassles of everyday life and focus just on me, my feelings and my body.

Thinking Back in Time

Starting Out ... Summer and Autumn 1999

My story really begins in spring 1999. My mother had been diagnosed with breast cancer the year before. It had been a difficult time for her and our family. Cancer, like other serious illnesses, always brings the feeling of fear of death to families.

Working full-time and living 250 miles away from mum it was difficult to visit as much as I would have liked. I felt angry, worried and helpless as I watched her and my father deal with the endless rounds of cancer treatment and check-ups. Prior to this in 1998 I had watched my partner run the Plymouth Half marathon and I remembered feeling in awe of all of those runners, of all shapes, sizes and athletic ability who took part in this race. I distinctly remember the 'if only I could do that' thought that I quickly suppressed in my mind. 'Me and my body? Run? Never!' I recall that my participation in athletics as a child was restricted due to childhood asthma and the medical thinking of the day to minimise sporting exercise. For me, PE or physical education was not an enjoyable experience; particularly from secondary school onwards and in common with other young women I lost what little interest I had in any sporting activities. I had observed consistently that running was often used as a punishment by my PE teachers to control unruly pupils during lessons that served to heighten my personal fears of failure on the track.

While researching information on current medical breast cancer research and treatments on the internet, I found details of the Plymouth Race for Life. This is an annual women only 5km race series that is organised to raise funds for Cancer Research UK. I liked the idea of participating in this event, to do something positive in the face of all the negativity that surrounded my mother's cancer. With a group of friends, I ran the race. I enjoyed the togetherness of the run – women of all shapes, sizes and abilities. There was also a rewarding sense of having a personal challenge and of elation at crossing a finishing line. Here the finish line means accomplishment, success and feeling proud whereas at school it was a feeling of relief to simply survive the PE lesson. Afterwards I decide that I want to continue running and I am supported by my partner. I cannot really pick out any distinctive elements of running that encourage me to continue. Maybe it is the sense of doing 'something', channelling my anger about my mother... Maybe it is the fact that I am participating in a physical activity that was independent and individual, which gives me a sense of liberation and freedom. I can exercise when and where I want. While I cannot say I was particularly focussed on my overweight body, I never weighed myself back then, perhaps there was a motivation within me to lose weight, and transform myself from my 30-something-year-old, comfortable, sedentary lifestyle. At the same time, I feel a sense of guiltiness, as my mother's health deteriorated. Here I am using her illness to springboard my own improvement in physical health and well-being.

Thinking Forward to... Spring 2006

On a cold, windswept Tuesday evening I am with my friends in the car. We are laughing and half heartedly moaning about the cold weather conditions – it's about 2°C. We arrive at the running track. As usual, we warm-up before completing a session the athletic coach has planned for us; 400m at a slow marathon pace, 400m at fast 5km pace, repeated for 20 laps. We start with cold bodies, shivering until our muscles warm up. It is a heartfelt warmness that extends to my general sense of well being as we chat and share stories of our recent news. We are endurance runners and share the track with faster track athletes. I run in lycra tights and a close fitting thermal top, still slightly self-conscious that in my view I am still a 'relatively heavy and slow runner' compared to others here, but the clothes are practical and appropriate for the conditions. I have my lightweight track shoes on and my multiple lap watch. I think back to my first attempt at running faster in 2003. Although I don't especially recall giving it much thought at the time, I wore baggy leg length trousers and a cotton T-shirt back then. I was no doubt covering up my larger, heavier body. When I first started running at the track, I remember the feeling of loneliness of belonging but not belonging to this group of runners; of being the outsider. Now these women are my friends and I am happy to at last be accepted as part of the group. As we continue to chatter in the car, I allow myself a contented smile. I've come a long way in almost 6 years. New friends, new knowledge about training regimes and a smaller, fitter body. I've completed 3 marathons, over 20 half marathons and numerous 10km and 5km races and 4 dress sizes smaller. And I am still improving my race times. I love running!

Summer 2006

I am thinking about how my running has progressed over the years as I do this I flick through my training diary kept in meticulously detail on a spreadsheet. It charts my progress from my initial charity jogging body as I continued becoming a social jogging body, before joining a running club where my body became a social running body.. and finally in the last 18 months the progressing of my moving body into a competitive running body where time and speed become prominent in my diary. I feel proud of my diary as it represents a point in my life when I made time to record and acknowledge those achievements; by me and for me.

Going Back in Time to 2002. I Re-remember my First Club Evening

I arrive and am warmly greeted by smiling faces. I am asked about my running speed, I say laughing 'slow, very slow' and I am placed with a group of women who laughed and confirmed that they are the 'slow group'. They like to have a chat on the run and we get to know each other. Over the weeks and months that followed we run in different environments, urban, rural, at different times of day, sometimes very slow to chat and at other times a little faster with less talking. We all run in the club tee shirts with the club name and logo. I notice that everyone sticks to their allotted groups. The faster runners, predominately, male receive the most attention as they win prizes or are highly placed at local road races. At first I am happy to remain anonymous but over time I become angry about this, I begin to feel that the slower runners, mainly women are invisible. There are occasionally sexist, racist and homophobic comments made by a few in the club; 'I should challenge this', I think.. But no one seems bothered and when I tentatively try to approach these issues that annoy me with the women I run with they seem unwilling to discuss or see there is no issue to discuss. Of course in the world of academia, it is easier for me to say something but in 'the outside world' with local people from different backgrounds these issues are more difficult. Now I continue to flick through my training log to September 2003. The words track are listed; this was the transitional point at which I decided that I am no longer content to plod around in the slow group. I want to see if I could go faster. Emotionally I want to break out of the mould of my social jogging body that had been defined both by me and by the informal organisation of the club into well-defined running groups.

I read the training literature in magazines and on the World Wide Web about interval training, emphasised as 'essential' to improve performance. Organised weekly track sessions take place but few individuals in my club attend. The reasons given are 'too hard', 'only for the serious runners' and 'dominated by other running clubs who take themselves more seriously than we do'.

Re-remembering my First Track Session

I turn up 5 minutes early for the 18.00 hrs track session. There is no one on track-side so I sit down on the bench and wait. I look at the 400m track and think back to my school days at the summer sports day and remember how I dreaded the annual event. Almost 20 years later, I am back at a track, feeling nervous, with a sinking feeling in my stomach. 'Should I really be here?' I ask myself. A few other runners turn up, chattering and laughing amongst themselves. I am outside of this group, a stranger. They say 'hi' but not much else. It is difficult for me to start a conversation as I have serious doubts about whether I am worthy of being here. They appear to be older than me and I am reminded that this is completely different to the images of young track athletes that I see on TV. Although not young, they have lean, athletic bodies and they look like runners. I am conscious of how much bigger I am then they are. They have all the 'gear'. They have appropriate running shoes. They are wearing lycra shorts or runners shorts with well fitted wicking runners t-shirts or vests. They have proper running watches. Some have heart rate monitors that are bleeping. I still run in baggy trousers and a loose fitting cotton t-shirt to hide my flabby body. I think that they must be wondering why I am here too; I don't look or feel like a proper runner. This is the first time that I am offered advice from a UK Athletics qualified coach. I feel slightly embarrassed that he suggests some training sessions for me and seems to be saying that you can be a faster runner if you want. Yet, it is my desire is to be that faster runner. It is a wish that I want to keep as a private goal, not to be made public knowledge. I still harbour the fear of failure from school days.

At the end of the summer season formal track sessions cease as the track has no lighting facility. I now wear 'appropriate' running clothes and have bought sophisticated running watches to record my training. A small group of us decide to continue running informally using the track in darkness. We are breaking the track rules but these are happy times. My now new running friends are more 'serious' as they not only train appropriately but also eat healthy, follow professional injury prevention and recovery advice.

News of my nocturnal track training soon filters back to my running club. My altering body appearance as I start to lose a considerable amount of weight and my increase speed and endurance are obvious to all including me when I see the official race photos. I am no longer invisible. I like the contrasting photos, it feels me with pride. My race results are read out followed by the words, 'I guess that is another personal best, Carole?' It was a nice feeling but I am also feeling sadness as the distance was growing between me and the woman I was running with. 'Am I betraying the essence of their running group?' I ask myself. One women says, 'You've flown the nest' and 'Just remember that I trained you'. I can't work out if she is angry or pleased for me. I start to feel isolated and this is further reinforced when I am subjected to a very public telling off from one of the male committee members for using the track during the winter months. I find myself, no longer able to keep quiet, and uncharacteristically shout back louder, 'I am running at the track with a group of friends, without my club vest on, as a member of the public. I am not stupid and I am fully aware that I am running at my own risk'. I feel my face is red with anger. I am told that 'be it on my own head and not to come crying when I get injured'. I smile and say 'Fine', and I stubbornly resolve to continue training with my friends at track. I am ignored by everyone for the rest of the evening and run alone. I feel like I have done wrong by answering back but deep down feel that I have done right for me.

In the weeks that followed I attend club nights less regularly. Partly because they did not fit in with my marathon training schedule, partly because I felt awkward and did not want any more confrontation. Looking back now I regret the course that I took, I should have continued to attend more regularly. I start to worry that my faster running may be seen as arrogance, particular when I start to develop a niggling injury. Eventually I leave and join another club; sadness is replaced with excitement of meeting new runners. Joining the new club I do not feel the same levels of anxiety and intimidation as I join as an established runner.

And Work and Leisure Time

My changing body image starts to be noticed at work. I am surprised when people stop to ask me if I am 'okay' and 'not ill'. As I enthusiastically explain my marathon training, I receive responses. Many are supportive. They also vary but one theme remains constant – 'What damage are you doing to your knees?' 'Do you not increase your risk of having a heart attack?' Others colleagues ask, 'Do you have the right body shape to be a runner?'

As I increase my training session's time is becoming compressed. Life is becoming hectic as I try to juggle my workload which I notice increasingly I fit in around my running rather than letting work dictate. I slowly realise the amount of work that I have been doing in my out of work hours and the all consuming nature of academic work. Running has given me back that distinction of work time and 'my time'. Now that I can run faster I am able to run with my partner, sharing news about our day and the experience of the run itself. My network of friends slowly drifts as I spend more time with my running friends and less time with other friends who are mainly based within the university. Leisure time is spent talking about running and not the latest work related issues or politics. My family also become interested in my running. My mother and I talk about my running regularly and her cousin tells me, 'You know your mum is very proud of her wheezing little girl'. I feel proud and happy too at my achievements.

Discussion

In this discussion I want to consider the key themes that emerge in relation to how I became involved in running, my engagement with the different technologies of running and how they relate to gender and running together in the context of the literature. As I ran alone initially and then with others, I felt my body move between private and public spheres. Running alone, I could be in my own private world, albeit amongst the public gaze, whereas running with others involved negotiation with their whims, feelings and perceptions of me and vice versa. Improvements in my running performance particularly as I moved to a competitive running body resulted from my engagement and adoption of training knowledge and technologies. I have summarised my progression in Figure 3.2. What is represented are the changes over time that I experienced as I started running more quickly and over longer distances. Longer distances were run at a slower pace, short distances much faster. However, for all distances time performance improved.

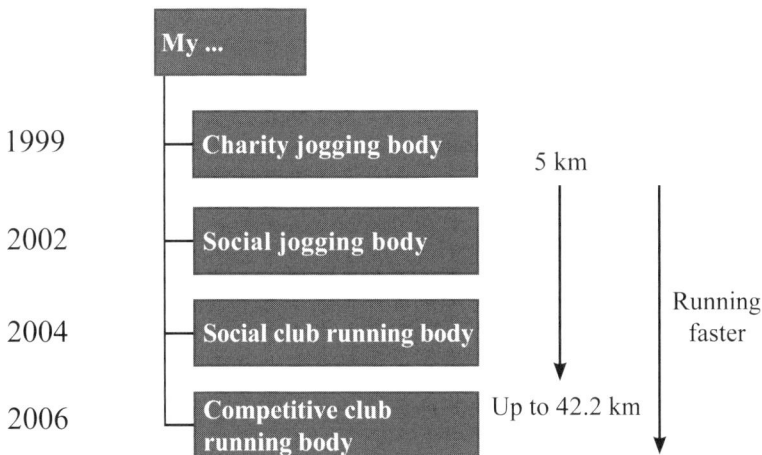

Figure 3.2   Summarising progression

The SES technologies of running situate the body as a place of regulated work, as formalised individual embodiment and modelled in part on the lifestyle of the professional, elite athlete. In a non-elite setting, I chose the degree to which I consumed these technologies within the confines of my everyday work, home and social life. As a lone runner, starting out, I gave little thought to a dedicated training regime, and yet the act of joining a club would suggest at least my understanding of training. The club training nights, while apparently gender neutral, and were in fact masculinised with the emphasis on competitive performance and improvement of the physical body. Within the club training sessions, decisions are determined by senior, predominately male club members. For me, there was a significant difference in the gender relations between my academic world and my social world; there was a greater degree of explicitness in the politics of the club and acceptance of knowing one's place. When my actions challenged this, I felt uncomfortable, lonely and these feelings were the initial trigger that led to my eventual departure.

My autoethnography has allowed me to consider how the expert knowledge of the sports sciences becomes public, everyday knowledge and language for both men and women runners. The running body is a consuming body that engages in social practices in the assimilation of technologies. Adoption of the technologies varies between individual runners depending on their particular circumstance. As my running developed the more engaged I became in the complexity of training practices designed to improve the running body and I modified these to fit my personal preferences and circumstances. The different running groups that I have belonged to represent how my acquisition and adoption of knowledge, and subsequent experiences, are situated temporally and spatially. I observed that not all women in the club follow strict training regimes; some runs were for fun and pleasure. My desire to run faster meant that I joined a different group of runners who followed the rules of sports and exercise science more rigorously. Here the importance of the social elements of engaging in a physical sporting activity is evident; as are the fun and friendships that emerged. However these are fragile relationships that within organised club sessions hinged most often on individual performance versus group collectiveness. At a personal level, my wish to improve was offset against a sense of loss of the running friends I was leaving. The unresolved tensions for me were a wish to be collegiate and run with other women while at the same time also improving my individual performance.

Joining a local running community changed the nature and way that I thought about my running body. I was no longer 'a jogging body'. I was wearing the technical clothing of the professionals. My changing body image was highly visible to both runners and non-runners, and the public gaze extended to open questioning about running as my sport and the state of my own health. Inquiries about my running were mixed with underlying fears of a risky behaviour with the potential for injury and ill-health. Reminders about the risk of injury were a powerful political tool both with the club organisation and more widely as the comments from non-runners about developing knee pain illustrate.

Conclusions

At the beginning of this chapter I stated that one of my motivations for undertaking this autoethnography was for me to gain an understanding of aspects of my own experiences and to consider these in relation to my future research plans. The importance of running with others emerges as a key theme that is negotiated against a framework of running technologies and the social and political dimensions of the social club organisation. I am currently researching the running histories and experiences of men and women runners, both club and non-club runners. The interviews are exploring the issues of training, racing, running environment and running with others. I am hoping to learn more about how others besides me 'embody a healthy running body'.

Acknowledgement

My sincere thanks to Betsy Ettorre and Imma Laitinen for their help and support in the writing of this chapter, especially sections, 'The self-regulated running body in sport, fitness and health' and 'Methods: Auto/ethnography', and for their friendship in running. Special thanks to Danny and my running friends with whom I have experienced laughter, joy and the occasional pain at different locations around the world.

References

Abbas, A. (2004). The embodiment of class, gender and age through leisure: a realist analysis of long distance running. *Leisure Studies*, 23(2): 159–75.

Bordo, S. (1990). Reading the slender body, in *Body/Politics: Women and the Discourses of Science* edited by M. Jacobus, E. Fox Keller and S. Shuttleworth. London: Routledge.

Brackenridge, C., Mutrie, N. and Choi, P. (2005). Is sport and exercise a man's game? in *Philosophy and the Sciences of Exercise, Health and Sport*, edited by N. McNamee, London: Routledge.

Bryant, J. (2005). *The London Marathon: The History of the Greatest Race on Earth*. London: Hutchinson.

Choi, P.Y.L. (2000). *Femininity and the Physically Active Woman*. London: Routledge.

Crossley, N. (2004). The circuit trainer's habitus: reflexive bodily techniques and the sociality of the workout. *Body and Society*, 1 (1): 37–70.

Deem, R. (1987). Unleisured lives: sport in the context of women's leisure, *Women's Studies International Forum*, 10(4): 423–32.

Edensor, T. (2001). Walking in the British Countryside: reflexivity, embodied practices and ways to escape, in *Bodies of Nature*, edited by P. Macnaghten and J. Urry, London: Sage Publications.

Ellis, C. (1999). Heartful ethnography, *Qualitative Health Research*. 9(5): 669–83.

Ettorre, E. (2005). Gender, older female bodies and autoethnography: finding my Feminist voice by telling my illness story, *Women's Studies International Forum*, 28: 535–46.

Ettorre, E. (2006). Making sense of my illness journey from thyrotoxicosis to health: an autoethnography, *Auto/Biography*, 14(2): 153–75.

Ettorre, E. (forthcoming a). Autoethnography: making sense of personal illness journeys, in *Handbook on Qualitative Health Research*, edited by I. Bourgeault, R. De Vries and R. Dingwall, Thousand Oaks, Sage Publications, Inc.

Ettorre, E. (forthcoming b). Nuns, dykes, drugs and gendered bodies: An autoethnography of a lesbian feminist's journey through 'good time' sociology, *Sexualities*.

Fasting, K. (1987). Sports and women's culture, *Women's Studies International Forum*, 10 (4): 423–32.

Featherstone, M. (1991). The body in consumer culture, in *The Body: Social Processes and Cultural Theory*, edited by M. Featherstone, M. Hepworth and B. Turner, London: Sage Publications.

Glassnor, B. (1989). Fitness and the postmodern self, *Journal of Health and Social Behavior*, 30: 180–91.

Hargreaves, J. (1994). The body, sport and power relations, in *Sport, Leisure and Social Relations*, edited by J. Horne, D. Jary and A. Tomlinson, Abingdon: The Sociological Review.

Hargreaves, J. (1999). The 'Women's International Sports Movement: local-global strategies and empowerment, *Women's Studies International Forum*, 22(5): 461–71.

Hirvensalo, M., Lintunen, T. and Rantanen, T. (2000). The continuity of physical activity – a retrospective and prospective study among older people, *Scandinavian Journal of Medicine and Science in Sports*, 10 (1): 37–41.

Horner, J. (2006). *Sport in Consumer Culture*. London: Palgrave Macmillan.

Katz Rothman, B. (2005). The I in sociology. *The Chronicle of Higher Education*. 51 (33): 10.

Katz Rothman, B. (2007). Writing our selves in sociology, *Methodological Innovations Online*, 2(1) http: //erdt.plymouth.ac.uk/mionline/public_html/viewarticle.php?id=40&layout=html.

Laitinen, I., Ettorre, E., and Sutton, C. (2006). Empowering depressed women: changes in 'individual' and 'social' feelings, *European Journal of Psychotherapy and Counselling*. 8(3): 305–20.

Laitinen, I., Ettorre, E., and Sutton, C. (2007). Gaining agency through healthy embodiment in groups for depressed women, *European Journal of Psychotherapy and Counselling*, 9(2): 209–26.

Lee-Treweek, G. and Linkogle, S. (eds) (2000). *Danger, Gender and Data in Qualitative Inquiry*. London: Routledge.

Letherby, G. and Reynolds, G. (2009). *Gendered Journeys, Mobile Emotions*. Farnham: Ashgate.

Lupton, D. (1995). *The Imperative of Health: Public Health and the Regulated Body*. London: Sage.

Markula, P. (1995). Firm but shapely, fit but sexy, strong but thin: the postmodern aerobicizing female bodies, *Sociology of Sport Journal,* 12: 424–53.

Markula, P. (2003). The technologies of self: sport, feminism and Foucault, *Sociology of Sport Journal,* 20: 87–107.

Markula, P. (2005). *Feminist Sport Studies: Sharing Experiences of Joy and Pain*, New York: SUNY.

Martinsen, E.W. (1994). Physical activity and depression: clinical experience, *Acta Psychiatrica Scandinavia Supplementum*, 377: 23–27.

May, T. (1993). Feelings matter: inverting the hidden equation, in *Interpreting the Field: Accounts of Ethnography*, edited by D. Hobbs and T. May, Oxford: Oxford University Press.

Monaghan, L. (1999). Creating 'the perfect body: a variable body project. *Body and Society*. 5(2–3): 267–90.

Noakes, T. (2001). *Lore of Running*. Fourth edition. Champaign IL: Human Kinetics.

Roberts, B. (2002). *Biographical Research*. Buckingham: Open University Press.

Sassatelli, R. (1999). Fitness gyms and the local organisation of experience, *Sociological Research Online* 4(3) http: //www.socresonline.org.uk/4/3/sassatelli.html.

Scraton, S. (1996). Boys muscle in where angels fear to tread – girls' sub-cultures and physical activities in *Sport, Leisure and Social Relations*, edited by J. Horne, D. Jary and A. Tomlinson, Abingdon: The Sociological Review.

Shilling, C. (1993). *The Body and Social Theory*. London: Sage Publications.

Smith Maguire, J. (2002). Body lessons: fitness publishing and the cultural production of the fitness consumer. *International Review for the Sociology of Sport*, 37 (3–4): 449–64.

Stanley, L. (1993). On auto/biography in Sociology. *Sociology,* 27(1): 41–52.

Stanley, L. (1995). *The Auto/Biographical* I: *Theory and Practice of Feminist Auto/Biography*. Manchester: Manchester University Press.

Steptoe, A., Wardle, J., Fuller, R., Holte, A., Justo, J., Sanderman, R., and Wichstrom, L. (1997). Leisure-time physical exercise: prevalence, attitudinal correlates and behavioral correlates among young Europeans from 21 countries. *Preventive Medicine,* 26: 845–54.

Sutton, C. (2009). Moving bodies in running, in *Gendered Journeys, Mobile Emotions* edited by G. Letherby and G. Reynolds. Farnham: Ashgate.

Watson, N. (2007). Culture, lifestyle and identity: constructing the health you, in *Sport and Physical Activity: The Role of Health Promotion,* edited by J. Merchant, B.L. Griffin and A. Charnock, London: Palgrave Macmillan.

PART II
Bodies and Representations

Chapter 4

The Visible Body: Health Representations in a Consumer Society

Rui Machado Gomes

Introduction

Contemporaneity (i.e. the moment we are living in) appears as a new visual regime marked by the growing power of imaging technologies – particularly those used in medicine – to access the inner body and, hence, play a constitutive role in the formation of norms on the perfectibility and changeability of the human body. The notion of body visibility was devised to highlight the body's dual nature in contemporary culture. This new visual regime brings out the true cult of the body confirming, at any given moment, that *we do have a body.* Yet, and at the same time, it also underlines the ambiguities created by excessive discourses and transparency. Thus, the use of the notion of *transparency* (Dijk 2005) interplays with body presence/absence, one of the main hallmarks of the health and well-being oriented, consumer society. Transparency comes into play as medical information and technologies show an increasing trend to support inner body examination; plus, it is validated by increasing self-observation, self-diagnosis or self-medication as a way for the layman to access body signs and effectively act inside it. *A contrario*, however, the lack of transparency is reflected in how the *fleshy body* is being progressively withdrawn from our daily life, forced as it is to undergo hygienic purification before making its appearance in public spaces and images. This chapter argues that ambivalence is one of the signs of the present day body crisis, endured side by side the image of a perfectible body.

Contemporaneity has seen the dawn of a daily life fully permeated by body crisis. The general search for a current and immediate meaning for human life is one of its main symptoms. The fear of ageing, obsession with health and fitness, maintenance and dietary rituals, the search for autonomous therapies and the spread of self-medication are in themselves indicators of an unprecedented fascination with subject self-knowledge and self-fulfilment. Meanwhile, such reflexivity, impregnated with medical and psychological knowledge – typical of late modernity – doesn't always provide the subjects with increased ability to control the situations they find themselves in. On the contrary, such reflexivity often intimidates and inhibits the subject's range of options. Wider knowledge about social life doesn't translate into greater control over the subject's destiny. This incapacity, caused by excessive reflexivity in the information era, is also a consequence of the social system's rigidity and immobility. Society appears to be immune to any change, whereas 'permanent changes' shift towards the inner individual and his/her body. The crisis of major narratives has transferred the final hope of utopian projects into each individual's body. As remarked by Bragança de Miranda (2002: 180):

> On the one hand, the 'world' has been replaced with the body, as an organising category of utopian images; on the other hand, this process develops hand in hand with the crisis of the 'body' itself. Something that should not be surprising, as the 'body' has to explode and dissipate in order to supersede the world.

We live in a time when the glamour of the body, the faithful trustee of each individual's identity, seems to be the only utopia we have been left with. And, yet, never in the past have doubts been so extreme regarding the knowledge we have of our bodies. On the one hand, we seem to believe in salvation through the body; on the other hand, we have grown deeply sceptic about the array of knowledge and technological devices made available to us to control or improve it. As a consequence of scientific and technological progress made in areas as diverse as biomedicine, genetic engineering, organ and tissue transplantation, reproduction, plastic surgery, implants or physical exercise physiology, the body was turned into the new territory where individual freedom should be exerted. Genetic engineering is not the only discipline offering us new body architecture; engineering, physics and surgery are also involved in the process of creating hybrid beings made of organic and electronic elements alike. The term, *cyborg* designates body shapes that no longer fit the 'former' notion of body as flesh. The body has gone from being nature's fixture to being progressively subject to consumer society's choices and options. Within the consumer society and in face of the current crisis of major narratives produced by ideological, political or religious entities, the body emerges as a final resource to controlling events and as a key element in identity building.

However, breakthroughs in knowledge and control over body options, seemingly within some people's reach, are not without a certain amount of scepticism. Indeed, the greater the possibility to overcome the limits imposed by the body, the greater the uncertainty about whatever remains *natural* in one's body. The anxiety for control, as much as scepticism, has shaped a cognitive and mental context favouring the evolution from medicine to techno-medicine, as a discipline increasingly dependent on sophisticated equipment to carry out both diagnosis and therapeutics. In this context, inner body imaging and simulation techniques have played a crucial role in developing a body transparency culture with obvious repercussions on how the body is presently represented.

This chapter examines body experiences as a product of medical-normative and moral discourses on the body. Understanding how body images like 'obesity' and 'slimness' are not only empirical characteristics of (un) regulated bodies, but rather the effect of discourses about bodies is the main aim of a content analysis of the media discourses in social identities construction. Social representations of the body and body practices will be studied in relationship to the impact of consumer society, examining how lifestyle magazines emphasize the importance of body image and how they create a convincing link between health and body shape. Nowadays the body seems to be gaining in both dignity and valorization, as the individual is expected to care for its good performance. Meanwhile, medicine develops a technical-scientific complex that presents predictive medicine, based upon genetic knowledge, as the perfect platform for health. Thus, the discourses about the body cannot be understood as dissociated from progress and human perfection ideology that has been leading to the progressive medicalization of society.

A documental corpus of two international magazines edited in Portugal in 2007/8 (*Men's Health* and *Happy Woman*) is used, from which 345 relevant articles concerning the body, dietary and health management are selected. We proceed to the discursive analysis using categories like metaphors, values and body images. We also look at the attribution of the social responsibility for health to the proactive citizen.

Body Transparency: From the Objective Body to the Subjective Body

The identification of the body with the *individual* who owns it is basically a modern invention. Nevertheless, the body is a long-lasting mental category, as reassured by the entire western metaphysics based on the relations between the inside and the outside, between the visible corporeal and the invisible incorporeal, or by Hobbes's reference to the political community as *body politic*. The *body* is a general assumption of the modern order, built on its legal definition as a synonym of property and freedom. In spite of that, the body as the property of an autonomous subject has also justified an increased number of interventions on its architecture, perpetrated by either its owner or others. It is from here the augmented perception of the body at risk and in crisis is derived.

The crisis of the body has also amplified its fragmentation in quite diverse directions, visible on both the objective and subjective traditions of body representation. The two main currents are deeply rooted in the Western world's intellectual tradition and both of them originated primarily in modernity and individualism. On the one hand, the realistic body, the anatomic body and the body-object has been given pride of place by the objective body tradition; on the other hand, the subjective body tradition reveals the fictionalized body, the psychological body and the body-subject. To a certain extent, we are in debt to both traditions which, although contradictory, form the common *humus* (i.e. organic basis) of the contemporary images of the body.

The first tradition is well represented in the work of anatomist Andreas Vesalius. The illustrations from Vesalius's *Corporis Fabrica*, dated 1543, unveil a mental change with numerous and meaningful consequences. The anatomist and the author of the so called Vesalius's musclemen or *écorchés* have the ambition of representing the inside of the body in an objective manner. However, the attempt to transpose natural body thickness to the two-dimension plane of a sheet of paper made it a goal that was altogether impossible to achieve. As Le Breton (1993) recalls, the artist has to be seen as part of a convention and a style. Therefore, the intention to achieve truthfulness and accuracy is really symbolically transposed to the representation of desire, death and anguish. The prints of *Corporis Fabrica* as well as those of numerous other anatomy studies up to the 18th century show tortured bodies and images of anguish and quiet horror. However, as Canguilhem pointed out, Vesalius's man remained a subject responsible for his attitudes., although the social and cultural 'tissue' of his time is still present, with all the prohibitions and the anguish inherent to the dissections and the violation of human integrity, Vesalius's anatomic observations have also introduced for the first time a perspective in which man (sic.) is methodologically separated from his body, a separation that was certainly easier than expected as the corpses dissected by Vesalius were unlawfully collected at the cemeteries and gibbets of Paris. The former insertion of man as a figure in the universe is not displayed, except for its reverse form, in the pictures of the anatomy study. Reduced to scalped skeletons, Vesalius's *écorchés* are nothing but bodies. The anatomist is thus announcing the birth of the modern body concept, by presenting a spectre of man. 'Man' is no longer himself, but rather his shadow. From this moment onwards, conditions are present for the genesis of the modern man: the ontological cleavage between body and man is now the mental horizon of a body that is self-sustaining for its own ends.

The second tradition is depicted by the images of Picasso's *monsters*. In the 1925–1932 period, Picasso produced a large number of works centred on the deformation and distortion of the human figure and body. These works were brought together under the *monsters* designation, adopted by some art historians (Caldas 1987). Paintings such as *The Dance* (1925), *The Acrobat* (1929) or *Bather With Beach Ball* (1932) reveal the deformation effect the human body has been subjected to in the first half of the century and this continued in other visual arts such as photography, sculpture, cinema, etc. The 20th century shall be remembered as an unhappy century. Early on, World War I turned the battlefields into graveyards of mutilated and limbless bodies. The war horror would repeat once again on a global scale and several times at regional ones. The objective body as seen by the 16th-century's anatomist has been replaced with the deformed body where the represented figures cannot be immediately perceived. The illusion of body transparency, provided by the enlightenment and the ontological separation between man and body, presents us with a sort of historical leftover, extended in time and leading us to believe the hypothesis of an individualized, yet identical, body. Picasso opened deep breaches in that regime of 'the identical', by rendering a representation of the human body based on deformation and illegibility. The representation of the body is no longer the mirrored image of the world but rather seen as the world's theatre. The episteme of similarity had previously given place to the episteme of representation, as demonstrated by Cervantes's *Don Quixote* or Velasquez's *Las Meninas*. The analysis made of Picasso's paintings and sculptures from the 1925–1932 periods within formalist art is impregnated with notions of violence, thus underlining the *excess* applied by Picasso to the nearly unrecognizable forms of the human body. As in other art expressions of the same period, a hysterical investment in the body appears to be present. Picasso's bodies are not defined by their shapes or their figurative representation, but rather by the deliberate act to disorganize shape as a means to access the body. The body ceases to be anything in particular, and unfolds in many simultaneous and contradictory narratives. The figures glimpsed in Picasso's paintings, or in Kertesz's photographic distortions, allow and promote the psychological projection of the human figure, leading us to attribute certain characteristics and qualities to this figure.

This subjective body, open to different interpretations, has been largely responsible for an outbreak of body-related discourses. While the 20th century may have been born as an unhappy century, it has struggled along its course to be a happy century in its closure. The happiness of the 20th century coincides to a great extent with the search for body happiness, that is, the search for the promise of an illness-free life, a body with extended longevity and an always-retrievable beauty. The 20th century opened and closed with the announcement that two rather different codes had been deciphered, either of them quite promising for future unforeseeable discoveries: the mind code and the genetic code, respectively. In 1900, Freud published *The Interpretation of Dreams*, an attempt to decipher the mental origin of some human suffering through language; 2000 has seen the discovery of the human genome with the promised ability to delve into the unfathomable universe of the causes for diseases. These two symbolic moments are highly expressive of the existing ambivalence in the century of the body. On the one hand, we relish the promise of a 'new man' with super-human capabilities; but, on the other hand, we feel ever more apprehensive in face of the great dangers caused by our interfering with Nature, including human nature.

The history of scientific medicine is made of increasingly more hybrid and efficient attempts to combine both traditions of body representation, turning the opaque content of body volume into a crystal-clear surface. To be able to see the inner matter enclosed by body surfaces has been the continuous struggle of medicine, in its pursuit to reveal the pathologic arena. Since the 16th century, with Vesalius's anatomy, medicine has tried to pinpoint pathologies inside an objective anatomic cartography detached from the patient as a person. Medicine's view over and inside the body has become a sort of exploration of new wild landscapes and power has been acquired to reveal the newly found territories. As underlined by Heidegger's concept of *aletheia* (understood as the truth of the being through unveiling), the power of revelation rewards its agents with a sacred status that is today leveraged by the ever growing scope of technosciences, especially when bodily imaging has become the core output.

The imaging of the inner body has evolved similar to medicine, in all its aspects, drawing a path from molar to molecular. Since the X-Ray was discovered by Röntgen in 1895, the opaque body has become a transparent body, through the use of prodigious medical imaging technologies. mammographies, ultrasound scans, computerized tomographies, fetal imaging and magnetic resonance have made it possible to visualize internal organs and systems. In the case of the brain, the imaging techniques evolved similarly: EEG (Electroencephalogram), PET (Positron Emission Tomography), fMRI (Functional Magnetic Resonance Imaging), SPECT (Single Photon Emission Computer Tomography) and many more. For some of them, digital simulation is a *modus operandi*; others depart from the molecular level to reconstruct molar reality, using algorithms to manipulate digital information. In any case, the mimetic realism these images are intended to attain sets off contradictory effects among both experts and laymen. Physicians tend to regard them as an amplification of their diagnosis and specialization capabilities; laymen appear to have developed greater eagerness for information in the networked society.

Information-induced anxiety makes the laymen's identity dependent on health research and data available to the general public from various information networks – Internet, television and the general and trade press. Medical knowledge is now largely accessible to the laymen, thanks to the networked society. In late modernity, the dream of social progress through knowledge was converted into the fantasy of perfect health through information.

The health versus illness issue is no longer confined to the hospital environment and the medical centres nor is it confined to the traditional doctor-patient relationship. This issue has spread to other social and commercial arenas. The promotion of health has been brought to contemporary households by TV campaigns. 'Health' is showcased in supermarkets and shopping malls; catches our eye in cosmetics advertising, is displayed in leisure sports arenas, and flows freely within cybernetic space. Nowadays, we witness the demolishing of the final frontiers, ones that have long resisted the differentiation between health production and health consumption. Today, we all appear as consumers in the great healthcare industry marketplace.

This cultural trend amplifies the risk-safety paradox, as demonstrated by the dissemination of self-diagnosis and the self-visualization practices. According to Mintel market research group (see: www.mintel.com), the self-diagnosis market is currently growing in the United Kingdom at the pace of approximately £100 million per year. The so called DIY (Do-It-Yourself) tests have broadened a quite profitable market, feeding on anxiety and uncertainty, and democratizing access to self-diagnosis devices made available by both the pharmaceutical companies and public health policies. Besides being offered osteoporosis, diabetes, cholesterol, or bowel cancer diagnosis kits, people may now go to virtual kiosks and nearby diagnosis centres to check and control their health, based on a vast array of indicators such as blood pressure, Body Mass Index, etc. Another sign of the uncertainty and anxiety market is clear in the public fascination with TV series featuring surgeons carrying out realistic procedures, documentaries displaying simulations of the blood stream, images showing the inside of internal organs and exhibitions of plastinized corpses providing a contemporary three-dimension version of the Vesalius's *muscle-men*. Magazines, radio programmes, TV thematic channels, newspapers, advertising and public medical debates disclose specialized information about nutrition and physical exercise, and put forward solutions promising physical and psychological health or body makeover. However, instead of reducing uncertainty, this complex of body-related information has turned into a source of uncertainty. This is primarily due to scientific knowledge's 'intrinsic' nature, based on assumptions of inductive and probabilistic knowledge.

Subjectivation: The Body as a Place of Discourses

In face of this, it is fair to say that our current representations of the body are the result of a complex historical process. Scientific, cultural and technical constraints contribute to shape the way in which we perceive and use the body. Mauss (1973) proposed the notion of *body techniques* to stress the social nature of body practices, a sort of variable bodily *habitus* according to social factors such as education, wealth, fashion and prestige. Mauss (1979) argues that the modern notion of person is a symbol resulting from a certain personality development, as well as a model to confer subjectivity to the individuals. This is the consequence of subjectivity technologies (Foucault 1988), leading individuals to think of themselves as the subjects of their own behaviours and capabilities. Both Mauss and Foucault deny the notion of original subjectivity as each individual's ontological essence. Subjects fail to exist when deprived of social processes, mainly those of a discursive nature that produce them as free and autonomous beings. That is precisely the meaning of the term *subjectivity technologies*: a set of ethical techniques to be imposed on one's self and whose main outputs include the very notion of subjectivity.

Within this vision, the perspective of the body as the enclosure of a unitary being should be abandoned. Instead of referring to a body-intrinsic entity, it is suggested that the 'self-identity body' may be the result of a specific body regime promoting a relationship between the body and its owner. In different terms, agency is in itself an effect, the result of self technologies invoking human beings as bodily realities. Therefore, a need is acknowledged to reflect on the historical conditions that made it possible for man (*sic*) to construe himself as a reflexive object. This self-over-the-self dominion relationship or self-knowledge has been established in quite a variety of ways. Confession, devotion, body care, and self-esteem are some of the procedures proposed or prescribed to the individuals in order to establish their identity. In any case, the self-identity body is presented as the property of a subjectivity ruling over life and death.

Today, the body seems to have been dignified and more highly valued, for it is assumed it will be well taken care of. Medicine has developed a technical and scientific complex where molecular and genetic knowledge based predictive medicine are presented as the platform for perfect health. Thus, discourses about the healthy body cannot be understood in any way other than within this ideology of human progress and perfection that has drawn society to increasing medicalization. These messages promote the myths of moral strength and will as forms of constructing contemporary subjectivities.

Moral perfection is the counterpoint of biological perfection. Yet, perfectionist ambitions conceal contradictory body practices and representations: on the one hand, overtraining (*vigorexia*) and the refuse to eat (*anorexia*) and on the other hand, 'orgiac' bodies, revelling in excessive eating (*bulimia*) and unwilling to do any physical exercise (*apathy*). The former suggest great tolerance to body pain and exhaustion. Eating disorders tend to proliferate in a cultural environment where low-calorie diets are encouraged (Bordo 1993). The latter refuse to accept body standardisation and suggest excess: excessive eating and excessive risk exposure, drifting increasingly apart from cautious behaviours, regular physical exercise and maintenance of adequate body weight. As Turner (1996) recalls, we come face to face with a swinging pendulum travelling to-and-fro between the opposite forces of Dionysius and Apollo. The cultural background of Western Christian civilization may be reasonably synthesized using the two opposing ends of orgy and fast. Orgy is rooted deeply in the Dionysian cult with its denial of rules, marginality and the protest of unprivileged social groups. Fast, in turn, is the legacy of the Apollo cult, a display of rational control, restraint and self-dominion. It is certainly not by chance that most studies carried out to analyse the effects of social and economic status on physical activity and health prevalence in different social groups show a notorious social asymmetry regarding the levels of practice and its consequences for physical capital and health (Gomes 2002).

Underlying this new healthy ideology is the rhetoric of free choice and personal autonomy. In this context, two types of discourse may be identified, with apparently contradictory values:

a. *The defence of an ascetic lifestyle*, devoted to hard working, self-denial and discipline. Conditioned by the representation of a thin and muscled body, middle and upper classes seek forms of body distinction based on the ability to live a healthy life. Resorting to self-control, enrolment in regular training and fitness programmes, often with personal trainers, they attempt to demonstrate their moral and physical superiority, as opposed to low-class groups.

b. The proliferation of practices rooted in the new prudentialism-based ethical regime (O'Malley 1992), *but also in the pleasure of body consumption*. Through sales and marketing techniques, the individual and collective anxiety about the future of each one's body is magnified, and people are encouraged to invest in improving their quality of life and health. The ethics advising lifestyle maximization, associated with the new lifestyle management technologies (what and how to eat and drink; what type of physical exercise to adopt and where to go for training; what healthcare procedures should be followed and which associated products should be taken, etc.) generates an relentless self-governance imperative.

Whatever the case may be, the effects produced by these two contradictory trends converge into the same idea of self-centring and self-dominion techniques, a phenomenon some have referred to as a return to narcissism. Narcissism may be understood as the neurotic version of a new lifestyle centred on jogging, healthy diets, weight control and physical maintenance. *Anorexia*, as an extreme version of narcissism (Turner 1996) presents some interesting elements for reflection in a sports context. Data on the prevalence of eating disorders among athletes is quite illustrative of the normative power of self-restraint techniques applied to eating habits. The American College of Sports Medicine estimates that 65 per cent of women competitors in figure skating, synchronized swimming and endurance sports suffer from eating disorders. The relationship between food, health and physical appearance is particularly important for women, especially in a society where self-representation is so highly valued. Within such a perspective, women's social value is associated with their body and is today expressed through the ideal of slimness. Being slim or *elegant* has become not only a seductive and attractive image, but also a symbol of self-control, moral integrity and high social status (Marzano-Parisoli 2001). This orthodoxy tends to produce an ascetic approach to sports and the body, and persuades a growing number of people that every individual's body can be modified and constructed to meet the intended requirements.

The Role of the New Health Brokers: A Portuguese Study and its Methodology[1]

In the 21st century western high-tech societies, the media, as new social brokers, affirm themselves as a privileged means for the transformation and dissemination of values, ideals and standards, particularly when related with body management. Relying on an average audience of 24.6 per cent of the total number of readers in the Portuguese written press (Marktest 2008), men's and women's lifestyle magazines are now in a singular position to disseminate and reinforce those values, ideals and standards.

Social representations of the body and body practices were studied in relationship to the impact of consumer society, examining how lifestyle magazines emphasize the importance of body image and how they create a convincing link between health and body shape. A documental corpus of two international magazines edited in Portugal in 2007/8 (*Men's Health* and *Happy Woman*)[2] is used, from which 345 relevant articles concerning the body, dietary management and health are selected.

---

1   Data processing and presentation in this empirical study is the responsibility of Nuno Gustavo, PhD student in *Tourism, Leisure and Culture,* University of Coimbra.

2   *MH* Magazine – issues 76 to 87. *HW* Magazine – issues 14 to 29 (except issues 20 to 22 – out of print).

The methodological work is based on a Foucauldian discourse analysis and we use categories such as metaphors, values and body images.

The two magazines were selected based on two criteria: print run and editorial style. As to print run, both magazines stand out in their respective *rankings*, with *HW* ranking first in the universe of monthly women's magazines published in Portugal. Additionally, among the existing lifestyle magazines, these are the ones showing an editorial trend that is markedly centred on body management. Data resulting from the thematic content analysis of the selected articles were statistically processed using a SPSS database and Microsoft Excel.

Reader Profile for Womens's and Men's Magazines

Women's and men's magazines have become a fixture in the daily life of about 2 million Portuguese. According to the latest data published in Marktest's Media and Advertising Yearbook (2008 edition), the public's interest in thematic women's and men's magazines runs across the entire Portuguese society, and features a whole set of particular traits.

Readers are mostly aged 18–44 years old in the case of women's magazines (81.6 per cent monthly and 75.6 per cent weekly magazines), and 18–34 for men's magazines (68.1 per cent). The readers' gender was also in line with the magazine's target group: men's magazines are predominantly read by men (76.9 per cent) while women's magazines are mainly bought by women (77.5 per cent).

Although there is a predominance of readers from the middle lower and lower classes, it is noteworthy that a public recruited in the middle class (64.8 per cent) and in the middle upper and upper classes (55.9 per cent) remains loyal to monthly published magazines. Indeed, that fact is clear in the occupational variable, where the following occupational groups stand out:

a. Top/middle management professionals – 14 per cent for men's and 15 per cent for women's monthly magazines;

b. Qualified professionals/experts – 20 per cent for men's and 7 per cent for women's monthly magazines;

c. Professionals from services, trade and administration – 16 per cent for men's and 19 per cent for women's monthly magazines;

d. Students – 25 per cent for men's and 19 per cent for women's monthly magazines.

The Media and the Body's New Social Notoriety

While in the past, family and religion were considered to be the main references available to the individual, today, self-image and self-consciousness are constructed and based on predominantly commercial references, a reflection of the social, cultural, economic and political contexts that characterize 21st-century societies. The contemporary subject is no longer an heir of traditions. Instead, the contemporary subject perceives himself as playing a determinant role in his/her own condition. In the new social regulation model, the body arises as a central element in both action and communication. That reality is expressed by tattoos used nowadays to produce identity and design the bodies of famous public figures:

> I've got tattoos with the names of the people I love best. It's my way of expressing myself, Angelina Jolie explained. (*HW*, no. 19)

In such a scenario, the body has acquired greater interest and notoriety. The *media* recognize and sustain the body's new social exposure. Out of a total 24 analysed issues, 841 articles were listed, from which 41 per cent tackled body and self-care related subjects in a range of different approaches. The average number of articles on the body subject can be set at approximately 53 per cent per issue in the case of the men's magazine and 31 per cent in women's magazine *HW*.

Set within a framework of perfectionist, naive speech and graphics where youth and the ability to manipulate the body are deemed endless and eternal, dreams, stereotypes and promises are sold. The offer is made of *quick tips to improve your life*, ranging from *three exercises to grow muscle mass in a few weeks* to *formulas to relieve stress in only 40 minutes* (*MH*, no. 85).

Sex – From Invisibility to Dominant Theme

In the group of analysed articles on the body subject, sexuality stands out, to reach an impressive 20 per cent of the sample. The most intimate parts of the body are unveiled under the form of disclosed secrets – *11 fantastic sexual secrets* (*MH*, no. 82) and unprejudiced exposure – *With no Taboos* (*HW*, no. 28), thus reshaping the form of how the body is socially seen and managed. Based on a sexual argument, men's and women's magazines reveal and teach how to manage the body physically and emotionally, presenting the body as a source of communication and attraction. In issue no. 80 of *MH*, on the *MH Sex* section, a six-page article highlights *what they [women] really think,* and promises *more and better sex as of today.*

A New Body and Health Approach for Everyone

From the sample of themes addressed by these magazines for which the body subject is a common denominator, the following subjects stand out: *physical exercise* (16 per cent), *behavioural factors* (14 per cent), *nutrition* (14 per cent), *beauty care and treatments* (14 per cent), *alternative medicines* (6 per cent), *body and mind* (6 per cent), *medical advice* (5 per cent), *health self-diagnosis* (5 per cent) and *medical surgery* (2 per cent).

In this range of themes, one can realize that the traditional players in the clinical arena are now relegated to the background. Headings as in *MH* no. 81 – *Heal yourself without seeing the doctor*- are quite common. Body management appears to have been taken over by a set of new health brokers, operating independently from the traditional healthcare players. Lifestyle magazines clearly undertake that role as they suggest *the best homemade exercises, the best health secrets for Man* (*MH*, no. 85).

New health brokers make a point in detaching themselves from the medical language. Instead, they deliver adjective-filled messages: *simple, instantaneous, fast* and *successful,* which are the notions making up a health narrative based on each subject's autonomy, efficiency and responsibility. Being a key issue, healthy nutrition and eating is repeatedly present: *eat this and never get sick* (*MH*, no. 79), *the 16 worst things you can eat* (*MH*, no. 84).

In women's magazines, the association between health, well-being and beauty is continuously linked with beauty care and treatments; the idea is created that body appearance can be changed instantaneously: *breast size boosting in 30 minutes* (*HW*, no. 29), or that a new body shape is achievable over a two-month period: *stop cellulite – get a new body in two months* (*HW*, no. 14). In turn, headlines targeting men emphasize body volume, strength and physical exercise as health signs: *more muscle in less time – only 30 minutes a day* (*MH*, no. 78) and *strong shoulders with no effort at all* (*MH*, no. 76), are a few examples of headlines aimed at building a social body image that is within everyone's reach.

Articles with numerous recipes and prescriptions, particularly, *anti-cellulite recipes* (*HW*, no. 27), plans and scripts presented under the common form of tips and hints – *1,073 new health, fitness and sex tips* (*MH*, no. 79), contribute to demystify the idea of an inaccessible body as much as to promote body condition and management through a *self-care* and *self-management* philosophy. The editorial line of *Men's Health* magazine is the expression of a self-help version focused on will power and self-care. Data from the latest scientific studies presented in a simple and understandable language is used to pass on the idea that proper body care requires some strength of will (*quit-smoking programs are not enough)* (*MH*, no. 79).

A Body Image Tailored to Consumer Societies

This type of magazine values *the latest news, the things you cannot do without, the must-haves, what's in* and *what's out,* and *tips,* thus building a relationship with the body where the economy of ephemeral well-being is constantly present. In light of these statements, *feeling well in your own body* is a concept that, additionally to being symbolic and functional, must be understood as the raw material to be shaped to external imperatives. *A 12-week plan to get your body ready for a bikini* (*HW*, no. 24) or *5 simple exercises to have this kind of body [young and muscled]* (*MH*, no. 81), are the primary assumptions of the new *Visible Body*, one that cannot be built detached from a vast set of *gadgets*, ranging from the simplest, such as clothes – *reduce thigh volume with straight fit dark-coloured trousers* (*HW*, no. 25) – to the most sophisticated ones, such as the car, *fancy, attractive, safe and comfortable,* a string of adjectives associated with the driver (*MH*, no. 78).

More than a question of looks, this is a new ideal, a new form of being in the world and living one's life. It is presented as within anyone's reach, through simple self-diagnosis and self-management processes devised to comply with certain standards and stereotypes, where aesthetic and hedonist *clichés* set the tone. Here, once again, the individual's body is seen as the key element to that materialization.

Being Self-responsible

In this new game of *Self* construction, individuals are assigned with, made aware of, and held morally responsible for the need to construct a concept of themselves, which is nothing more than the expression of how they perceive themselves in relation to the surrounding reality. The responsibility to manage one's body in a functional way has fallen short in the light of the new Self. Presently, this is also and essentially a challenge with a symbolic dimension. For instance, here is one of the challenges presented in *HW*, no. 28: *combine the season's trends with your own body features to pick your new bikini.*

The individual pursuit of health has moved forward since the healthism of the early 1970s when themes of individual effort, discipline and will came together with the deregulation of public health programs. Experts have indicated how to be healthy by means of exercise and prudent behaviour. The normalizing ethical power of the model is proposed by a rhetoric of free choice and personal autonomy. Such thinking is typical in countries which are attempting to replace old models of regulating health. These messages promote the myths of moral strength and will as a way of building the contemporaneous subjectivities.

By manipulating the body's biological nature, the body itself becomes a place of discourses, dialogues and significances, that is to say that it becomes the most elementary object in communication and identification. In this way, the passage from the biological body to the physical, psychological and self-conscious body is carried out in a reflexive way. Socially dominant stereotypes are the reference adopted, and they form and spread on the basis of a symbolic language, where the image, the signs and the visual dimension affirm themselves as the engine of the new dominant culture. Today, people live to meet challenges like *Flatten your belly forever. Do as actor Paulo Rocha* (*MH*, no. 82).

The fashionable and consumer body. Besides its scientific dimensions, the concept of health also entails relevant assertions of aesthetic, environmental and social nature. These new dimensions and interpretations of the health concept arise as: on the one hand, the reflex of the new healthist (Crawford 1980) and positivist health model, where well-being is the prime motto; and, on the other, a consequence of new discourses and novel interpretations of well-being endorsed by the new health players.

Taking the advertising indicators as a reference for different modes of health social management, an analysis of the advertising sample of the two magazines shows the following highlights: advertisements about health management-related products, particularly nutrition (e.g.: food supplements, energy supplements in the case of the men's magazine, and *light* food products in the particular case of women's magazine), and to beauty and dietary products (particularly in women's magazines). As an example, issue no. 29 of *HW* magazine had 26 per cent of pages filled with advertising (51 pages). The figure went down to 15 per cent in the case of *MH* magazine, issue no. 77 (19 pages).

Resorting to the most persuasive marketing practices, to which advertising and trademarks are faithful allies, the *media* make a massive use of images depicting the body as the central element in communication, to establish a new self-identity and self-image construction process. This would require no more than, for example, *to renew your image* using *89 style tips*. These tips, tailored to the holistic essence of the *Self*, include topics as: *personal care, travel, restaurants, engine, universe, practical fashion* and *events* (*MH*, no. 88).

In this process, magazines rely also on public figures to create common and universal language and references. This way, and by means of a reflexive dynamic, these standard ideals are set as the dominant reference, as the individual engages in the construction of his/her new *Self*. The *life of a übermodel – Gisele Bündchen* (*HW*, no. 17), the *sexy naivety of Scarlett Johansson* (*HW*, no. 23), *eat this – grow muscle – the tricks of our cover model! [Gregg Avedon]* (*MH*, no. 85) are some examples of worldwide references that help shaping the individuals' physical and symbolic *Self*.

A high-tech body perspective. As the body is established as a reference and an object of cult, the individual is now burdened with the need to make a continuous investment on his/her body, the materialization of which is so called *Self-health*. In this new vision, the individual's focus and objective as far as one's own body and health are concerned, are now the search for optimum well-being, as this will determine the individual's entire performance in all aspects of his/her life. The need for monitoring required by the *self-health* model translates into a search for information on references, mechanisms and *self-scrutiny* practices, – *don't fall victim to heart attack [...] know how your eating habits impact on your blood pressure and be on the safe side.* (*MH*, no. 80), which currently include the most sophisticated technological equipment (e.g. Heart rate or cholesterol self-measurement devices).

However, being such a new topic, the use of technology (either by invasive or non-invasive techniques) is still seen as suspicious, and therefore, the sharing of experiences by anonymous citizens who have already undergone those procedures is crucial to attest those treatments' efficiency and immediate results:

> Before going on VelaSmooth [radiofrequency treatment], I wasn't happy with my body, because I had accumulated fat, cellulite and loss of firmness. I've had 17 sessions now and I'm very happy with this treatment because results are already visible (Cláudia, 35 years-old, in *HW*, no. 19).

Resorting to new technologies favours the development of a new relationship between the visibility of the body's inside and outside. If, on the one hand, the external environment is the reference to be taken into account, resorting to technology grants one the power to manage the body, by monitoring and manipulating it on the inside. Treatments such as *endermologie* where *the client wears a specific suit and, through the operation of a machine – LPG – lumps are defragmented* restoring *skin's tonus and in-depth tissue firmness* or *radiofrequency*, a treatment in which *heat is induced to increase intercellular oxygen rate, producing a metabolic reaction of the fat cells and reducing them*, ensuring *immediate lifting effect* and *smooth firm skin* (*HW*, no. 29), are examples of the new technological arsenal managing the body from the inside, while producing the intended external effects.

Risk and Body Transparency

In recent years, the public sphere has strongly fed upon the safety-risk paradox. Safety is a symptom of bio-power which has been present ever since the 17th century. Turning death into an object of apprehension, this disciplinary power is concerned with survival, the extension of life and public hygiene protection. Now supported by new body political technologies, bio-power has been extended to the whole population in areas such as birth rate, fecundity, old age and epidemic control. Foucault uses the concept of bio-power in volume one of *The History of Sexuality*. He sets a double perspective in how power over life is seen. On the one hand, bio-power aims at maximizing the body's anatomic forces, by integrating them in efficient systems. On the other hand, bio-politics requires formulas to regulate and control diseases, mortality and longevity. In contemporary societies, this distinction between these two different poles of bio-power, referred to as discipline and regulation, respectively, has been overcome. Today, the issue of safety runs across quite diverse spheres of life, and there seems to be a consensus around key ideas of anticipation, prevention and self-responsibility for everyday life events. On the safety side, solutions are presented which promise physical and psychological health, including: magazines, radio and TV programmes, newspapers, advertising and public medical debates with more or less specialized information about how body-related risks can be mitigated. The food and agricultural industry invades all aspects of our lives, including our private life, with the wide-spread of the nutrition information labelling and its behavioural indications. On the risk side, offers are increasingly present of lifestyles encouraging alcohol and stimulants intake, leisure drugs and sedentary life. Very often, the risk is deliberately sought through adventure activities in the wild, use of motorized technologies, intense and extreme physical activities or survival contests in severe conditions.

Side by side the safety provided by the new technologies which appear to reduce fears that not long ago characterized our body existence are uncertainties as to our future risks. These are also amplified. The notion of risk becomes central in a somatized society (Turner 1992), where the notion of body preservation is highly valued in public space. The seductive promise of life with no illness and super-human longevity, has also produced menacing visions of excessive cloning or bodies incorporated by electromagnetic components. The obsession with risk presents: a sort of victory over whatever aggression may come our way. But, this is almost always haunted by the possibility of a new risk arising from newly-discovered technological solutions.

Risk presents itself in quite contradictory and paradoxical versions. On the one hand, there is an attempt to minimize risk in all areas. As a result of increasing social reflexivity, social practices of the prudential type are constantly examined and adjusted in light of the information acquired about their consequences, in such a way that *thought and action are continuously refracted one through the other* (Giddens 1992: 29). In this deeply reflexive context, bodies are subject to unprecedented risk monitoring. The health imperative is reflected also in the amount and contents of the information conveyed by the information society's networks. Insurance companies, experts and politicians introduce the idea of insurance into a growing number of areas: measurement of blood pressure, cholesterol, body mass index, sexually transmissible diseases, smoking habits, family diseases, etc. Other sets of potential risk evaluation parameters are used as forms of actuarial control or, simply, as indicators to be taken as guidelines to primary prevention policies and lay education programmes. Statistics manage to broaden the effects of those control policies. Car accident risks, occupational accidents, domestic accidents, children's accidents, stroke or cancer incidence are the object of statistical studies aimed at establishing threshold values and defining which populations are at risk, in order to anticipate and identify the most dangerous 'places', considering average values and standards. Populations as a whole are put under administrative control while, at the same time, statistics introduce individualized thought over risk and individual responsibility for its control in social reflexivity. Risk prevention and mitigation now fall under the realm of individual responsibility.

The vocabulary used by experts and by state administrators has also instilled in the most private thoughts the need to monitor and decipher one's experiences, developing a new *therapeutic sensibility* (Lipovetsky 1989). Knowledge linked with the health sciences, sexuality or physical activity has made its way into everyday routine which helps describe and provide references to one's social life. Nutrition and body weight control, the awareness of blood pressure reference values and the need to control it, cholesterol monitoring and control, moderation of sexual activity and its relation with sexually transmissible diseases, regularity and intensity of physical activity and the role it plays in health are considered to be testimonies of individual options, lifestyles and physical appearance. Under these circumstances, one's eating habits, physical activity, body monitoring and adopted sexual behaviours express a personal choice allegedly expected to constitute one's narrative. Therefore, illness has also become associated with one's insufficient ability to take good care of him/herself. Not doing any exercise, not being able to quit smoking, not eating in an adequate and moderate way are perceived as moral and volitional deficits and hold each individual responsible for his/her own well-being. Ill people are more frequently blamed for their condition (Shilling 1993): failure to actively monitor one's health is often deemed as a deviation (Crawford 1980) and obesity is almost always explained by a lack of will.

The search for and the escape from death are the faces of a society coping with the crisis of major narratives and the loss of meaning. The other side of risk is communitarism, the protection of traditional cultural references, the fight against social and individual precariousness. As individuals become more fearful of ageing and death, they tend to take good care of proper body functioning. The notion of a healthy body also reveals an eagerness to control body image: workout and controlled eating habits cannot be dissociated from the efforts to recover body control. Well-being and health are the linguistic operators used to justify free time spent in physical activities, and provide the grounds for using physical condition and appearance as one of the worker's productive force. Marx's compulsion of work interplays with Baudrillard's compulsion of consumption. In the past, the worker struggled to use his/her free time in a manner as different as possible from his/her working time. Contemporaneity has witnessed the dawn of a daily time totally contaminated by the general reproduction of human life. Health self-management has brought the subject to the need of managing the economy of his own body.

The Contamination of the Other and the Transparency of Different Bodies: Final Comments

The recent focus on health is largely supported by the metaphor of body *contamination*. The body is now subject to a vast range of aggressions and contaminations that may be caused by pollution, contagion or sexually transmissible diseases. This has brought along the spread of new images of the 'subjects' subjectivity', such as increased monitoring of the biological effects of what we eat, sunbathing, intake of air and water, or the sexual intercourse one enters into. Simultaneously, susceptibility and aversion to body decay increases. Sick people, the elderly and all of those who show body marks of physical decay are excluded or ignored under the trivialization of urban interaction. They become transparent to others. The same kind of voiding is present in the picture offered by advertising, by the cinema and by the inflated use of body photography in the public scene:

> The growing interest for magazines with photo illustrations (especially in those areas where the body was the dominant theme) has made body images a constant centre of interest in everyday life. People got used to having photographs of half naked (although idealised) bodies around the house, on their dining tables or on their bedside tables: young, tanned, smiling and vigorous bodies, embodying a promise of health, wealth and happiness as long as they are properly taken care of, obviously, with the right products (Ewing 1999).

However, under the shameless exposure of intimacy, advertising has at the same time pushed aside the *fleshy* signs of man. Anything that conjures up the organ-made body is banned from sight in leisure industries. Ageing, fatigue, sweat, wrinkles and all the signs of time passing are put away, out of the social actors' sight. Alternatively, those same signs are shamelessly shown in humorous contexts. The threshold of aversion to the decaying body is altered in the new visual regime. Displaying the body seems to imply also the responsibility to do so in accordance with certain dominant physical standards of appearance. Through the body, the subject is judged for his social and professional performance. Success is dependant on the subject's ability to shape his body in line with new emerging requirements. The advertising campaign of *Clinique Formule Homme* is a good example of the relationship between body appearance, identity and performance:

> Man thinks about himself (that's not new), he also thinks about his skin (something he doesn't want people to know about). Times have changed: those times are long gone. Just like a suffragist, man discovers, affirms and claims his identity as he looks at the bathroom mirror. He finally dares to speak aloud of whatever he used to do silently, when he secretly used his wife's cream, her mask or her exfoliating scrub. Virility is no longer an obstacle, man changed criteria and he has also adopted new icons in terms of looks. Today, clean is good, from head to toe. Being successful means, more than anything else, feeling good in your skin.

The rituals linked with body transparency are also visible in the attempt to eliminate from sight everything that emanates from the body. There is a promise to clean away anything that may stain one's appearance, to have us decontaminated from whatever may prevent wealth, to scrub away everything that drags us away from happiness. After surgery, the true identity is reborn. The body arises as a place of redemption and judgement of how successful one has been; men's skin is today seen as a symbolic sign and an erotic value. Just like women became entitled to muscles and virility, so have men become entitled to *skin-deep* sensibility. In many professions, the vital reproduction time

> is indeed a second shift of productive work, and is filled with jogging, gym, massages, workout, etc. (Santos 1994).

The individuals' will to dominate their own body and whatever flows in it has been present, to a greater or lesser extent, throughout history. Changes in body ideal and health-related moral values are associated with illness-induced anxiety and, especially, anxiety caused by the presence of the *dangerous others* and the risk of being contaminated with their diseases (Gilman 1988, 1995). The body, through its visual traits, exposes the identity of the subject in relation to 'himself', but also in relation to the society and the group he wants to be recognized in. Determining what is identical and excluding what is different is part of an historical process by which identity and alterity have consistently been constructed. The deviator may be the foreigner, who comes from beyond the borders, but he can also be the insane, the criminal, the ill person or the aberration for whom special areas are defined intended to confine them as much as make them noticeable. The asylum, the hospital and the prison, as disciplinary spaces, are a part of this power-knowledge complex and play a didactic role. Just as diabolic images were used in the Middle Ages, body images used in advertising establish what is to be feared and rejected, and are seen as a warning of what human *nature* shouldn't be. This was the role of the disciplinary spaces that helped construct the notions of insanity, illness and delinquency. Contemporary control societies have replaced the confinement of disciplinary spaces with an appealing operation put in place by the media, with a view to typifying and dividing human activities into allowed and illicit, public and private, individual and collective, producing a simultaneously individualizing and totalizing power. Present day control societies have shaken the disciplinary boundaries based on public/private differentiation, and made them permeable and subject to inter-contamination. Between maximum intimacy involving the private exploration of sensations, and maximum public exposure where the individual is compelled to reveal him/herself, a new notion of public space is emerging, tainted with slight traces of incivility and dissolution of public roles (Lipovetsky 1989, Sennett 2002).

Indifference towards the moral standards ruling other people's life comes hand in hand with maximum exposure of each one's body, emotions and feelings, even if it takes place in new protected architectural or symbolic spaces. That is the case of the new body leisure activities based on a particular therapeutic sensibility. Certain physical activities are highly illustrative of the modern obsession with the self, expressed in one's desire for self-knowledge and knowledge of one's own limits, as well as for the intimate revelation of the true authentic being. Activities such as body expression, yoga, tai-chi, bio-energy or relaxation techniques became a space where the psychological body takes over the objective body. Bringing the body into existence for one's self and re-conquering body innerness are the staging grounds where one's self representations are produced today. More than narcissistic representations, which they unquestionably are, the new representations express a normative narcissism, because self-knowledge technologies have managed to replicate restrictions imposed by the new body brokers within everyone's innermost sphere. In a system personalised by this *movement of consciousness*, where everyone is the ultimate one responsible for his/her condition, the individual seems to be left with the sole goals of improving his/her body's reliability, remaining young and being actively committed to self-preservation.

References

Anders, G. (2002). *L'Obsolescence de L'Homme.* Ivrea: L'Encyclopédie des Nuisances.

Andrieu, B. (2004). *A Nova Filosofia do Corpo.* Lisboa: Instituto Piaget.

Balandier, G. (1988). *Le Désordre.* Paris: Fayard.

Baudrillard, J. (1976). *L'Échange Symbolique et la Mort.* Paris: Gallimard.

Bordo, S. (1993). *Unbearable Weight.* Berkeley: University of California Press.

Brown, P. (1989). *The Body and the Society: Men, Women and Sexual Renunciation in Early Christianity.* Columbia, NY: Columbia University Press.

Caldas, M.C. (1987). *A figura e o corpo.* Lisboa: Imprensa Nacional-Casa da Moeda.

Crawford, R. (1980). Healthism and the medicalization of everyday life. *International Journal of Health Services*, 10: 365–88.

Deleuze, G. (1998). *Foucault* (2nd ed). Lisboa: Vega.

Dijk, J.V. (2005). *The Transparent Body. A Cultural Analysis of MedicalImaging.* Seattle and London: University of Washington Press.

Foucault, M. (1975). *Surveiller et Punir.* Paris: Gallimard.

Foucault, M. (1988). Technologies of the self, in *Technologies of the Self,* edited by L.H. Martin, H. Gutman and P.H. Hutton. London: Tavistock, 16–49.

Giddens, A. (1992). *As consequências da modernidade.* Oeiras: Celta.

Gilman, S.L. (1995). *Health and Illness: Images of Difference.* London: Reaction Books.

Gomes, R. (2003). A cultura de consumo do corpo contemporâneo e a queda da Educação

Física escolar. Reflexões pouco óbvias, in *O Desporto para Além do Óbvio.* Lisboa: IDP, 87–99.

Gomes, R. (2004). Dilemas e Paradojas del Autogobierno del Cuerpo, *Apunts*, 78, 33–40.

Gomes, R. (2005a). Novos corpos para novas personagens. Ensaio sobre a 'manutenção da forma' e o 'cuidado de si'. *Boletim da Sociedade Portuguesa de Educação Física,* 30/31, 151–62.

Gomes, R. (2005b). Young bodies identities in leisure. A critical approach. *World Leisure Journal*, 47(3): 54–60.

Gomes, R. (2005c). O corpo como lugar de lazer, in *Os lugares do Lazer*, edited by R. Gomes. Lisboa: Instituto de Desporto de Portugal, 105–21.

Hardman, K. (2000). Ameaças à Educação Física. Ameaças ao Desporto para Todos? *Boletim da da Sociedade Portuguesa de Educação Física,* 19/20, 11–35.

Kerckove, D. (1997). *A Pele da Cultura.* Lisboa: Relógio d'Água.

Le Breton, D. (1993). *La Chair à Vif.* Paris: Métailié.

Le Breton, D. (2000). *Passions du Risque.* Paris: Métailié.

Lipovetsky, G. (1989). *A Era do vazio.* Lisboa: Relógio d'Água.

Mauss, M. (1973). Techniques of the body. *Economy and Society,* 2(1), 70–88.

Mauss, M. (1979). The category of the person, in *Psychology and Sociology: Essays,* by M. Mauss. London: Routledge and Kegan Paul, 57–94.

O'Malley, P. (1992). Risk, power and crime prevention. *Economy and Society*, 21, 252–75.

Marzano-Parisoli, M.M. (2001). The contemporary construction of a perfect body image: bodybuilding, exercise addiction, and eating disorders, *Quest*, 53. 216–30.

Miranda, J.A.B. (2002). *Teoria da cultura*. Lisboa: Edições Século XXI.

Mirzoeff, N. (1995). *Bodyscape. Art, Modernity and the Ideal Figure*. London: Routledge.

Rojek, C. (1999). *Decentring Leisure* (3rd ed). London: Sage.

Shlling, C. (1993). *The Body and Social Theory*. London: Sage.

Turner, B. (1992). *Regulating Bodies. Essays in Medical Sociology*. London: Routledge.

Turner, B. (1996). *The Body and Society* (2nd ed). London: Sage.

Chapter 5

The Internet and Medicalization: Reshaping the Global Body and Illness

Peter Conrad and Ashley Rondini[1]

Sociologists have studied medicalization for more than three decades, especially in North America (Zola 1972, Conrad and Schneider 1992, Conrad 2007). By medicalization we mean defining and/or treating a social problem or human condition as a medical problem. This includes a range of conditions including attention deficit hyperactivity disorder (ADHD), alcoholism, anorexia, post traumatic stress disorder (PTSD), premenstrual syndrome (PMS), menopause, social anxiety disorder, and obesity, among many others (see Conrad 2007). One manifestation of this has been the expansion of diagnoses in the Diagnostic and Statistical Manual (DSM) of the American Psychiatric Association; the number of diagnostic categories grew from 106 in DSM-1 in 1952 to 297 diagnoses in DSM-IV in 1994 (Mayes and Horwitz 2005). Over the past decade, medicalization scholars have noted that the 'engines of medicalization' have shifted from the medical profession and social movements to biotechnology, managed care, and consumers (Conrad 2005). It has long been noted that medicalization can be bi-directional, including demedicalization and new medicalization. Despite the important cases of demedicalization (e.g. homosexuality and masturbation), there is strong evidence that medicalization has been expanding, with a considerable concern about 'over-medicalization'.

In recent years, the Internet has become a vehicle for promoting or criticizing medicalized approaches to human problems. The global reach of the Internet has expanded medicalization debates to a more worldwide scale. This chapter examines two cases of 'problems' of the body that have utilized the Internet to promote their views and state their claims; one of the cases is seeking a form of demedicalization while the other is making claims for medicalization. The first case consists of what have been called 'pro-ana' websites, which began in the US, promoting the view that anorexia is a legitimate way of life rather than an illness. Here we see the emergence of an international 'counter narrative' to the medical views that are available worldwide. The second case is what Carl Eliott has depicted as 'wannabe amputees'; these are individuals who communicate with one another on websites and discuss how they wish to obtain their amputee status.

1   Acknowledgements: Our thanks to Bekah Richards and Samantha Cornell for sharing some valuable background research for this chapter.

Recently, they have increasingly desired to have their disorder recognized as a medical problem, Body Integrity Identity Disorder or BIID.

Coming of the Internet

The browser enabled worldwide web began in the 1990s. The Internet has grown enormously in the past fifteen years, as have the number of users. The number of Internet users keeps growing, with roughly 360 million users in 2000 and an estimated 1.5 billion users in 2007 (http: //www.internetworldstats.com/stats. htm). The greatest penetration of usage is of course in the developed world, but China has pulled ahead of the US as the largest number of Internet users (Barboza 2008). According to recent statistics, North America has roughly 250 million Internet users. Sophisticated search engines, like Google, make accessing relevant information quick and simple. Virtually everything about the Internet is growing or increasing. The Internet revolution has affected health information and communication as well; nearly 100 million Americans regularly access the Internet for health information, with most focusing on specific diseases (see Conrad and Stults 2010). The Internet has become a global marketplace for health related information.

One of the most interesting and widespread aspects concerning health on the Internet are the thousands of interactive or participatory websites, bulletin boards, discussion groups, social network groups and other forums for virtually any illness or disorder one could imagine. These often become online communities, where many members participate regularly while some just visit occasionally and others 'lurk', by reading the posts without actively contributing. While the Internet has helped individuals become more active consumers, it has also transformed them into *producers* of knowledge. In this Web 2.0 (more interactive) era, individuals now have the ability to construct their own websites, 'home pages' or develop blogs about their health issues, transforming them from consumers of health information to producers of health information and care (Hardey 1999). The Internet is truly an interactive marketplace of communication about specific illnesses as well as discussions about health and treatments. Thus the Internet has become a repository of lay knowledge, as well as a medium for promoting alternative and challenging perspectives about particular problems and disorders. It has become a place where lay viewpoints exist alongside professional perspectives, at times supporting, questioning, or challenging medical knowledge.

There are now thousands of electronic support groups (ESGs) available online. Prior to the Internet, illness was a private affair for most people. Now, given the virtual online worlds, illness can be more of a shared and public experience. As Barker notes, 'the process of understanding one's embodied distress has been transformed from an essentially private affair between doctor and patient to an increasingly public accomplishment among sufferers in cyberspace' (Barker 2008: 21). On occasion these interactive Internet groups (or sets of web-based groups) develop distinctive and challenging perspectives to the dominant medical view. In the cases we examine here, one web group is seeking demedicalization while the other is seeking greater medicalization. By examining these here, we hope to develop some insight into the role of the Internet in increasing or reducing categories of medicalized conditions.

Pro-Ana Websites: Anorexia is a Lifestyle Choice, not a Disease

The dominant perspective on anorexia is that it is an eating disorder and a psychiatric illness marked by extremely low body weight, body image distortion, and an obsessive fear of gaining weight. Anorectics control their body weight by extremely limiting their food intake, excessive exercise, or diet pills or diuretics. Bulimia is a related eating disorder characterized by binge eating and subsequent purging. Contrasting and challenging medical definitions, so-called pro-ana websites and online communities present a view that rejects the medical perspective and offers an alternative stance on extreme dieting and thinness.

'Pro-ana' and 'pro-mia' websites and online discussion boards emerged on the Internet in the late 1990s. 'Ana' and 'Mia' are the community's nicknames for 'anorexia' and 'bulimia', respectively, and the early forums advocated for an understanding of eating disorders that was not negatively slanted. For simplicity sake we will refer to them all as pro-ana websites here. Internet websites for anorexics provide a forum that enables individuals living with an eating disorder to share experiences. Pro-ana websites, however, go beyond merely creating a forum for interaction and discussion but also developing a community with a strong point-of-view about anorexia. They attempt to present a 'positive' and non-medicalized view of anorexia. Individuals with eating disorders who participated in these communities could recontextualize and reframe their own understandings of anorexia and bulimia within an online sub-cultural framework that counters dominant medical paradigms. (McLorb and Taub 1987, Pascoe and Boero 2009) Some websites self-consciously see themselves as part of a pro-ana movement, selling pro-ana and pro-mia identity bracelets (Miah and Rich 2008).

It is difficult to reconstruct the content of the original pro-ana sites now, since the sites became very controversial (i.e. they were accused of proselytizing young girls to become anorexic) and many have been shut down or reconfigured in response to negative publicity. Similarly, a number of the interactive forums currently on pro-ana websites or social networking web pages now have become more restrictive requiring administrator approval, limiting access to 'outsiders.' Current 'pro-ana/pro-mia' websites reference the original sites as 'first wave Pro-Ana', from the current offerings of 'second wave-' or even 'third wave' pro-ana spaces. Our interest here is primarily in the early and pioneering pro-ana websites, with some reflection on the evolution of the more recent sites.

One of the hallmarks of the early pro-ana websites was the clear assertion that anorexia was *not* a disease, but rather a 'lifestyle choice' which should be respected as a matter of individual autonomy concerning one's body. Pro-ana sites actively rejected the medical label; some stating directly, 'Anorexia is a lifestyle not a disease.' The 'lifestyle choice' assertion squarely contradicted the dominant medical view that saw anorexic behavior and bodies as distinct pathology, by advocating for the demedicalization of extreme ultra thin bodies and extreme dieting and exercise. Articulations of collective identity and 'community' were centered around adherence to this doctrine of anorexia as lifestyle, and pro-ana as the movement which advocates the celebration of this lifestyle (Boero and Pascoe 2009). Implicit here is both resistance to medicalized definitions of what it means to be anorexic, as well as a movement toward a positive, idealistic view of anorexic eating and bodies. In a sense the attempt was to normalize, destigmatize, and, at times, valorize anorexia. As one site posits,

> If people are allowed to smoke, drink, box, and do other things that may harm themselves just as much or even worse than anorexia, and the media and people allow commercials and websites that encourage such destructive behaviors, why not Pro-Ana? (http: //www.freewebs.com/thinnest/whynotproana.htm)

Many of these sites displayed galleries of photos labeled 'Thinspiration', or 'Thinspo', which includes pictures and montages of incredibly thin, even emaciated looking, people, reinforcing a cultural ideal of extreme thinness. These include celebrities, advertisements from magazines, and images from members of the website community. These photos were both meant to be a form of positive inspiration for thinness and a graphic depiction of the 'normalness' of extreme thin. While 'Thinspo' photos were displayed to celebrate the idealization of this body type, 'reverse trigger' galleries depicted photographs of extremely obese people in an effort to remind viewers of what they should desire to avoid. Early pro-ana sites demonstrated contempt for body fat, and inadvertently, for individuals who had obese bodies. Obesity was juxtaposed with anorexia and framed as the 'real' health risk to be wary of; the two were constructed as polar opposites; fat was unhealthy and unattractive and thin was ideal and beautiful. In this sense, thinness (and, in this case, extreme thinness) was thereby framed as a more 'natural' body state, as was demonstrated by 'inspirational quotes' on the sites such as the following:

> One day I will be thin enough. Just the bones, no disfiguring flesh. Just the pure clear shape of me, bones. That is what we all are, what we're made up of and everything else is just storage, deposit, waste. Strip it away, use it up...In the body, as in sculpture, perfection is attained not when there is nothing left to add, but when there is nothing left to take away. (http: //www.freewebs.com/thinnest/.htm)

The notion that anorexia is a medical condition from which one should 'recover' was anathema to the core principles around which these original pro-ana communities advocated. Early pro-ana sites, then, were not usually a space wherein 'recovery' from anorexia was characterized as a desirable outcome. The medical view saw anorectics as deviant, while early pro-ana sites inverted this ideology by claiming that anorexic bodies are in fact 'ideal', 'pure', and 'natural', citing 'common-sense' understandings of hegemonic beauty standards as evidence to this claim. Consistent with this desire to reject the dominant medical discourse regarding anorexia, these sites also offered advice regarding how to undermine the unwanted imposition of medical interventions in one's anorexic 'lifestyle'. This included 'tips' about how to avoid detection of weight loss, such as, 'Wear nail polish to hide the discoloring in your nails from lack of nutrients' ('Big n' quick 257 tips'), or use 'fishing weights' to fool one's parents or doctors about actual body weight.

In contrast to these sites, a number of slightly different sites emerged after 2005 at least partly the result of the negative publicity and repression of the original pro-ana sites. The creators of the new pro-ana sites, in an attempt to differentiate themselves from what they called the first wave of the pro-ana 'movement,' developed second wave sites that were markedly different from earlier ones. These sites often had warnings like; 'Pro-Ana Nation does not encourage distorted eating or reinforce ideals of physical perfection. Anorexia is not a lifestyle choice, but a serous mental disorder.' It is likely these warnings reflect an attempt to protect the website from the kinds of pressure and harassment that closed down most first wave websites. While these new sites still supported demedicalization of anorexia, they did it in a less challenging and more subtle fashion. These new sites were still lifestyle-oriented, but they now included spaces wherein the discussion of recovery could take place, albeit in a value-neutral way. These sites neither rejected nor promoted recovery, but instead acknowledged the desire to pursue recovery as one possibility within an anorexic community. As one site, Blue Dragonfly announced:

> We do not promote disordered eating or the mentality that causes it, but we won't attack you if you have not recovered yet, or if you don't ever plan to recover, or if you are in limbo between the two. Already recovered? Come on in... (http: //blue-dragonfly.org/)

Many of these sites now contained advice about how to safely be an anorexic, sometimes even citing the principle of 'harm reduction.' Harm reduction is a public health term for strategies that reduce harmful effects that may result as a consequence of certain forms of deviant behavior. This is a common in the world of addiction and drugs, especially in Europe. Examples include developing needle exchange programs to reduction HIV infection risk or offering medical heroin maintenance to reduce the criminal behavior necessary to maintain one's drug habit (see Inciardi and Harrison 2000). While these websites didn't cite harm reduction, in a sense they offered advice about how to be a better anorexic. They gave advice about how to be safe with anorexia, e.g. to survive on minimal calories, get enough calcium, or to bulimics 'drink a ton of water when binging.' Such advice can contribute to demedicalization by helping individuals manage their disorder better and avoiding the perception of an acute need for medical treatment. At the same time, there is evidence of a collective distrust towards recovery programs and treatments administered by medical institutions and mental health practitioners (also referred to as 'the pros') who were not themselves anorexic. This was illustrated by a number of allusions to the ways that 'the pros' treated anorexics, juxtaposed with the ways that the online communities regarded 'their own' members. Help from the former was seen as inherently dehumanizing, stigmatizing, and generally suspect, while support from the latter was characterized as loving, non-judgmental, and genuine. One example of this kind of differentiation from the website 'House of Thin' (http: //www.houseofthin.com/entrance/mission.php) is found below:

> What we do is make a safe place for others to come to and be themselves. Some say we promote the eating disorder, but again, not true. We do say that there is no shame in being eating disordered, the only bad thing is what causes the eating disorder. That is how pro-ana is different. The pro-recovery sites make you feel like trash for having an eating disorder and make you feel like you are in competition to recover and no matter how well you're doing with it, it's not as good as everyone else who go around preaching the gospel of recovery and making you feel even worse. On pro-ana sites, you will recover when you are ready for it and at your own pace.

The conclusion that these contrasts would seem to point to is that participants in the pro-ana online communities are making an authenticity claim to the 'real' knowledge and understanding of their experiences. This dynamic is mirrored in the findings of Pascoe and Boero (2009: 17), in their analysis of pro-ana and pro-mia discussion forums, as they note, '...knowledge is used to establish authenticity'. These claims of access to 'real' (i.e. first hand) knowledge are constructed in opposition to the views of those who espouse medicalized understandings of anorexia as a disease that invariably constitutes an immediate need for treatment and eradication.

The second-wave pro-ana sites reflect an ambivalent relationship with medicalization. On the one hand, diagnostic criteria is effectively cut and pasted from medical texts to describe the effects of eating disorders on the body, while moving away from the fervent 'lifestyle' language of the first wave sites. On the other hand, these criteria are listed as 'signs' rather than 'symptoms' of eating disorders, and the notion of extreme dieting and thinness as deviant is still contested. These sites resist explanatory frameworks for disordered eating which are focused on individual level pathology. In contrast to their first wave predecessors, these sites attribute responsibility for the 'problem' of eating disorders to a variety of contextual factors which can damage individuals' self esteem, including society, family structure, the media, and so on. In contrast to first-wave pro-ana sites, second wave sites do not depict loathing for, or rejection of, either body fat, or fat bodies. Rather, the sites claiming to be part of the 'evolution' of pro-ana introduce what could be called a politic of more universal body-acceptance. While earlier sites rejected the stigma associated with anorexia by positing that anorexic bodies were ideal, with obesity as the enemy, later sites espoused a more inclusive ideological stance, whereby it is asserted that *no individual*—neither the extremely thin anorexic nor the extremely obese—should be stigmatized, or discriminated against for any kind of body type. This shift is also significant to medicalization in that contrasting anorexic bodies to obese bodies was previously used as a mechanism through which the former were idealized and the latter were held up as the 'real' deviant bodies vis a vis their apparent 'unhealthiness'. The rhetoric of second wave pro-ana sites recognized potential harm but still rejected medical diagnoses and treatments. In a sense, these sites now extolled a form of body acceptance rather than a pathological model of deviant bodies.

The medical profession and the eating disorders treatment community continue to oppose the pro-ana sites, arguing that they encourage severe dieting and eating disorders, discourage people from seeking necessary treatment, and normalize dangerous anorexic behaviors. The 'eating disorder treatment establishment' and related anorexia and eating disorder organizations view the pro-ana sites with distain and have done what they can to challenge and contradict the Pro-Ana message and, when possible, work to close down the websites.

While the first wave pro-ana groups were seeking a demedicalization of anorexia by challenging medical categories and treatments, the second wave groups, while still committed to demedicalization, do it more by advising how to live safely as an anorectic (harm reduction) and with a broader acceptance of a range of body sizes and shapes. While there is still 'thinspiration' here it is less shrill and exclusive, although still affirmed as beautiful.

Wannabes: Amputees by Choice

In the December 2000 issue of *The Atlantic* magazine Carl Elliott published an article 'A new way to be mad.' In this article Elliott described individuals who, while normally able-bodied, had long-standing and firmly held belief they should be amputees. Paradoxically, they feel their body is incomplete with their four limbs and the desire for amputation can become a central feature of their lives or even an obsession. As one individual noted:

> It has been precisely in these last years that the desire has gotten so strong, so strong that I can no longer control it but I am completely controlled by it. (quoted in Elliott 2003: 221).

Another individual typified these feelings when he said 'two legs made him incomplete' and, paradoxically, amputation would make him whole (First 2004: 2).

Many of these individuals become obsessed with finding a way to become an amputee, even by doing great damage to their limbs with shotguns, chain saws, dry ice or putting their legs in the way of an oncoming train, in an attempt to create a situation where they would receive an amputation. While most recognize that there are currently no doctors who will amputate a healthy limb, some still search for surgeons who would be willing to undertake amputation surgery. One Scottish surgeon, Dr. Robert Smith, performed surgery on two individuals in 1997, but the negative medical reaction to these procedures was so strong he quickly discontinued this practice. As of now no doctors are willing to perform amputations on healthy limbs (Bayne and Levy 2005). To the best of our knowledge, the Elliott article was the first time individuals with these unusual proclivities had received such public exposure.

For the most part, the body location of the desired amputation is quite specific; e.g., the left leg two inches above the knee. These individuals say very explicitly that this specific amputation is what they seek and without it their body will not feel whole. Over the years, various clinicians have described this disorder and called it by various names: Apotemnophilia, Amputee Identity Disorder, Amputee by Choice, Body Dysmorphic Disorder, or Body Integrity Identity Disorder. Despite the proliferation of names, none of these names has become an 'official' medical diagnosis, but rather remain descriptors of individuals who strongly desire limb amputation. There are variations in emphasis: one of these terms assume a connection with sexuality (Apotemnophilia), body identity (Amputee Identity Disorder, Body Dysmorphic Disorder) or that this is a chosen state (Amputees by Choice). For the purposes of our analysis we will use the indigenous term wannabes (as in wannabe an amputee), a term individuals have come to use to describe themselves, since it doesn't assume any disorder or medical etiology.

Many wannabes keep their amputation desires secret from families, partners and friends. They recognize that others would see these wishes as unusual or even bizarre. But for many years, these wannabes have been connecting with one another through Internet list serves, discussion sites, blogs, and websites. What might seem like a strange or even idiosyncratic desire—to have a healthy limb amputated—to most people, now had a medium where others with the same desires could contact and communicate with each other. Elliott reports one list serve with 3,200 subscribers (2003: 209), and there are now numerous websites and discussion groups where wannabes and others can share information, get support and, as we will see, promote their condition as a medical disorder in need of medical treatment.

Michael First, a psychiatrist at Columbia University, has conducted the most developed research on wannabes (First 2004). He has interviewed 52 individuals who were self-identifed as desiring the amputation of a limb. Sixty-five percent were recruited from Internet sites; seventeen percent (n=9) of these had an arm or leg amputated, two-thirds using high risk self-inflicted techniques with the other third engaging surgeons in the amputation. The most common explanation for desiring an amputation (85 percent of the sample) was a mismatch between the individual's anatomy and their true identity as an amputee. Overwhelmingly, the individuals focused on a specific limb they wished to have amputated. First found that none of his interviewees were delusional, and that although some had sought treatment for their desires, neither psychotherapy nor medications had reduced the intensity of their of their desire for amputation. These respondents who had been able to secure the amputation reported feeling better than ever, more whole and complete. First (2004: 1) concluded that this an 'extremely unusual clinically distinct condition characterized by a lifelong desire to have an amputation of a particular limb.' He compares it to Gender Identity Disorder and suggests the name as Body Identity Integrity Disorder (BIID). First (2004: 9) notes this *could* be a medical clinical disorder:

> If additional research replicates and expands this study's results, could a case be made to include this condition in future DSMs, on the grounds that, although rare, it is a distinct condition associated with distress, impairment and risk of death (e.g., due to botched amputation)...

First was the editor for DSM-IV, so he speaks with authority about the potential of BIID to be included in the next DSM. However, First has also been quoted as saying that people with BIID arc basically normal.

> They have families. They have all kinds of jobs, doctors, lawyers, and professors. They are not screwed up apart from this. You could spend the evening with them and not have the slightest clue (Quoted in Henig 2005).

There are numerous websites created by and for wannabes providing a medium for connection and information. Given the rarity and potentially stigmatized nature of their desires, the Internet presents a unique venue for wannabe interaction. Without these sites, an individual might well believe he or she was the only one that harbored the desire to be an amputee. But with the Internet, there are now communities of wannabes that can communicate with each other, exchange information and give one another support. In a real sense these sites have been able to unite individuals who had previously felt alienated or alone. As one man noted:

> For a long time I thought I was alone in the world with this bizarre wish. I collected information about amputation and amputees and and several time I threw it all away. I wanted this wish to go away... Although [eventually] I knew there were others I had no idea how to get in touch with them. Or where to turn for help....Later on I learned the potential of the Internet. Most information was on devotees (people sexually attracted to amputees) but I also found some concerning wannabes. The quality of information varied a lot...Finally I had mustered enough courage to contact other wannabes and I have not regretted If for a fraction of a moment. It was a great relief as well as a bit scary finding out how similar the experiences were despite the dissimilarities in personalities...

> This [experience on the Internet] has made me feel much better about myself. (http: //www.geocities.com/starstranger_2000/)

These Internet websites and discussion group provide social support, a collective legitimation for the longings for amputation, a forum to search for doctors who will help them, and discussion of 'safer' ways to achieve self-amputation. There has been some concern that these sites might lead to more risky attempts at self-amputation, but others have suggested that the information on the sites and the quest for medicalization provides the potential for harm reduction (Berger et al. 2005).

In recent years, there has been more discussion on the wannabe websites about the 'disorder', the potential for treatment (surgery), and especially advocacy among some parts of the community for the inclusion of BIID in the next edition of the DSM (which will be published in 2012). It is common to hear comparisons to 'transsexual' or 'transgendered' individuals; that they are 'trapped in the wrong body,' are mismatched with their body and self-identity, and that medical treatment is available to treat an individual's difficulties and suffering. Individuals with diagnoses such as 'Gender Dysphoria' and 'Gender Identity Disorder', can receive 'treatment' in terms of sex reassignment surgery, so why not wannabes (who are now are beginning to refer to themselves with a related designation, 'transabled')? If BIID could be included in the next DSM, this would make those with the disorder eligible for reimbursement by health insurance. This of course brackets the question of whether there would be surgeons who would be willing to perform amputations on a healthy leg, hand or arm. As one site explains:

> And if BIID does become a recognized mental illness, then we are more likely to be accepted by the medical community. just as transsexuals started to see accepted avenues of treatment when their condition was accepted as a mental illness, we believe that it will take us being formally labeled as mentally ill before we see treatment options open to us. And we don't necessarily mean to have a 'cure' for BIID (BIID-Info.org).

Another site echoes the view that BIID is a mental illness and that is OK:

> There are those people who are transabled that will argue thatBIID is not a mental illness. I think part of that reaction is dueto the generally negative view of society over mental illnesses.For me, I don't care about being labeled with a mental illness, oneway or the other. If it takes BIID 'achieving' mental illness status,and be included (sic) in the next edition of the DSM for us to have doorsopening on avenues of treatment that fit our needs, then I embracethe idea that I have a mental illness. For me it's a means toward anend. But this is also a reality. It is something that affects my mental health (Transabled.org).

While not all wannabes/transabled individuals believe that the acceptance of BIID as a medical diagnosis in the DSM-V would be a key to treatment and acceptance, many do. For those who do advocate the medicalization of persistent desires for amputation do so with the hope for greater acceptance of their condition, especially by the medical community, and the firm belief that the only kind of treatment would be some kind of body realignment surgery that would essentially be an amputation. If BIID were accepted it could be argued that surgical amputation was a safe form of harm reduction compared to the highly dangerous attempts at self-amputation and could affect an example of patient autonomy (Bayne and Levy 2005: 79–82). Several researchers and advocates alike believe that medicalized amputation would have therapeutic affects on the obsessions and mental health of the individual (First 2004, Bayne and Levy 2005, Furth and Smith 2002). This raises the question about what kind of status is voluntary disability would have under the Americans with Disability Act and other entitlements for people with disabilities.

Leaving aside whether persistent desires for amputation and the related identity discomforts should be defined as BIID and included in the DSM, it is very clear that many of the wannabe websites and their participants are using the Internet sites in part to actively advocate for the medicalization of Body Identity Integrity Disorder as a medical/psychiatric illness which merits medical intervention

Concluding Remarks

Pro-ana and wannabe websites have become active vehicles for sharing information, creating community, and advocating particular positions. With the pro-ana sites the overall message is that anorexia is an acceptable (sometimes even valorous) condition and that medical interventions may not be necessary because anorexia is not an illness. The wannabes, on the other hand, aspire to both legitimation and medical recognition, especially those who advocate for the inclusion of BIID in the DSM. Thus one group is pursuing a strategy of non-medicalization if not always demedicalization, while the other seeks medicalization and what they perceive to be its benefits. While these websites act as a 'refuge' for these socially defined deviants, in a real sense each of these groups is also something of a fledgling social movement, promoting their vision of reform. It is interesting that each web-based movement extols that acceptance of their position would be a way of reducing harmful or risky aspects of living with the condition (one by medicalizing, the other as part of demedicalizing).

The Internet shapes the formation and strategies of each group. It is our belief that wannabes would not (indeed probably could not) have a collective presence without the Internet. Given the rarity of the condition, its invisibility, and the potential stigma from revealing one's desires publicly, the accessibility, anonymity, and wide reach of the Internet are critical to the creation of wannabes as any kind of community or activist group. This raises the question when does an idiosyncratic desire become a social movement? Anorexics are both more common since anorexia is not rare among adolescent girls (the National Institute for Mental Health estimates that up to 3.7 percent of females suffer from anorexia, while up to 4.2 percent suffer from bulimia) and more visible, since anorexia actually affects the body in ways others can see. So anorexics could probably find each other in real life if they so desired. What makes the pro-ana sites unique is that they have become a locale where numerous anorexics can virtually gather and share and develop strategies that either reinforce anorexia as a valorous condition or provide a venue where girls can coach each other about how to become a better anorexic, sharing anorexic strategies for maintaining their condition. In short, pro-ana sites allow for the development of a counter narrative of anorexia challenging the dominant medical treatment narrative. In each case, the Internet is critical to the formation and sustenance of the group's ideology and purpose.

Participating in these website groups can profoundly impact individuals as well. While it seems doubtful that individuals are recruited to the disorders by these websites, those inclined toward the obsession with thinness or with becoming an amputee are certainly likely to be attracted to the sites, especially in a world that would stigmatize or attempt to alter their desires. At first wannabes may be completely confused by their desires, and anorexics, while recognizing their desire in more common cultural terms, try to hide their desires from family and others who they believe would disapprove. The existence of a community of individuals with similar desires and outlook on the Internet is very attractive to the individuals and reassuring that there are others like them out there. Hearing about others' experiences and exposure to the viewpoints on the websites may alter participants own experience of their condition (First 2004: 9). Using Ian Hacking's (1995) conception of 'looping' effect, the perspectives promoted on these websites create material for participants to construct or modify their identities and shift or reinforce their take on medical views of their condition. In short, individuals' participation in the websites creates the possibility of new identities about themselves and their bodies.

What makes these websites and related online communities so intriguing is that they become nascent social movements as they promote alternative perspectives to the standard medical viewpoints of their condition. The Internet has a global reach and is expanding rapidly, so whatever happens online can resonate throughout the world. Whether these web groups become a significant force and harbinger for change in the medicalization-demedicalization process, or whether they will be relegated to an interesting footnote in social and medical history is yet to be determined.

References

Bayne, T. and Levy, N. (2005). Amputees by choice: body integrity identity disorder and the ethics of amputation. *Journal of Applied Philosophy*, 22: 75–86.

Barboza, D. (2008). China passes US in number of internet users. *NY Times*, July 26 (http: //www.nytimes.com/2008/07/26/business/worldbusiness/26internet.html)

Barker, K. (2008). Electronic support groups, patient-consumers, and medicalization: the case of contested illness. *Journal of Health and Social Behavior.* 49: 20–36.

Berger, B.D., J.A. Liebermann, G. Larson, L. Alverno, and C.L. Tsao. (2005). Nonpsychotic, nonparaphillic self-amputation and the Internet. *Comprehensive Psychiatry,* 46: 380–83.

Conrad, P. (2005). The shifting engines of medicalization. *Journal of Health and Social Behavior,* 46: 3–14.

Conrad, P. (2007). The medicalization of society: on the transformation of human conditions into treatable disorders. Baltimore: Johns Hopkins University Press.

Conrad, P. and J.W. Schneider. (1992). *Deviance and Medicalization: From Badness to Sickness*, expanded edition. Philadelphia: Temple University Press.

Conrad, P. and C. Stults, (2010). The Internet and the experience of illness, in *The Handbook of Medical Sociology, Sixth Edition.* Nashville, TN: Vanderbilt University Press.

Elliott, C. (2000). A new way to be mad. *The Atlantic Monthly.* December. p. 72–84.

Elliot, C. (2003). *Better than Well: American Medicine Meets the American Dream.* New York: Norton.

First, M.B. (2004). Desire for amputation of a limb: paraphilia, psychosis, or new type of identity disorder. *Psychological Medicine* 34: 1–10.

Furth, G. and R. Smith. (2002). *Amputee Identity Disorder: Information, Questions, Answers and Recommendations about Self-Demand Amputation.* Indianapolis, IN: 1st Books.

Hacking, I. (1999). *The Social Construction of What?* Cambridge, MA: Harvard University Press.

Hardey, M. (1999). Doctor in the house: the Internet as a source of lay health knowledge and the challenge to expertise. *Sociology of Health and Illness.* 21 (6): 820–35.

Henig, R.M. (2005). At war with their bodies, they seek to sever limbs. *NY Times*, March 22. http: //www.nytimes.com/2005/03/22/health/psychology/22ampu.html?_r=1&pagewanted=print&position=).

Hesse-Biber, S. (1996). *Am I Thin Enough Yet?: The Cult of Thinness and the Commercialization of Identity.* New York: Oxford University Press.

Inciardi, J.A. and L.D. Harrison. (2000). *Harm Reduction: National and International Perspectives.* Thousand Oaks, CA: Sage Publishing.

Mayes, R. and A.V. Horwitz. (2005). DSM-III and the revolution in the classification of mental illness. *Journal of the History of the Behavioral Sciences* 41: 249–67.

McLorg, P.A. and D.E. Taub. (1987). Anorexia nervosa and bulimia: the development of deviant identities. *Deviant Behavior,* 8: 177–89.

Miah, A. and Rich, E. (2008). *The Medicalization of Cyberspace.* London and New York: Routledge.

National Institutes of Mental Health. 2008. http: //www.nimh.nih.gov/health/publications/the-numbers-count-mental-disorders-in-america/index.shtml#Eating.

Pascoe, C.J. and N. Boero. (2009). Anas, *Mias, and Wannas: Authenticity and Embodiment in Pro-Anorexia Discussion Groups.* unpublished manuscript.

Zola, I.K. (1972). Medicine as an institution of social control. *Sociological Review* 20: 487–504.

Chapter 6

The Ageing Body: From Bio-Medical Fatalism to Understanding Gender and Biographical Sensitivity

Jason L. Powell

The significance of the ageing body is important for the discipline of gerontology. For example, illness can limit the functioning of the body and this can have psychological, political and social consequences. Recent debates on 'healthy ageing' (Gilleard and Higgs 2001) is conceptualized in terms of body maintenance and such activities form a central feature of consumer societies (Featherstone and Wernick 1995). At the same time, biomedical models of ageing have devised the means to foster intellectual respectability to a range of 'scientific' ideas about the body. The bio-medical model suggests it can reconstruct the biology of bodies through plastic surgery; it can interfere with genetic structures; and it can move internal organs from one body to another. There is an irony: the more we know about bodies and the more were are able to control, intervene and modify them, the more uncertain we become as to what 'the body' actually is. The boundaries between the physical body and consumer society are becoming increasingly blurred. In this context, the body represents an important issue for gerontology in particular and social science disciplines in general. The chapter addresses the question as to how the biological ageing body acquires meaning, and also how the meaningful body itself, relates to such signifying processes and social efforts as to understand gender and the ageing body. In particular, we assess the relevance of the ageing body, and ageing identity for pointing toward a Feminist theory that can be defined as interconnecting gender and ageing. To add insights to gendered ageing, the chapter will conclude arguing for a biography of ageing. Part of the context for realizing the potential of biography is its dissection of meaning, not as fixed, but as fluid as found in the context of everyday life. Biography provides a significant contribution to un-locking an understanding of what is means to be a human person situated within and across the lifecourse. Biography can be used to reveal critical consciousness, understanding of personal identity and social meanings.

Despite this, there are ambivalent representations of the ageing body in western culture. There has long been an occidental tendency, in matters of ageing and old age, to reduce the social dimension of ageing to a fixed set of life 'stages' which are said to determine the experience of old age. Accordingly, being old would primarily be a private experience of social adaptation to inevitable physical and mental decline and of preparation for death. This of course was the main viewpoint of disengagement theory which suggested that people of retirement age should adapt themselves for the ultimate disengagement of death. This was not only a dominant functionalist narrative in American gerontology, but also such arguments played a key positional role in shaping negative societal representations of ageing.

The representations of what it is to be old have been shown to structure the ways in which individuals and social groups alike recognize old age in others and in themselves. In their content analysis of retirement magazines, Featherstone and Hepworth (1993) suggest that the types of images of old people presented in specialist magazines are consonant with attempts at focusing on the positive side of being old. This is usually linked to the 'Third Age', those in early retirement and the continuation of a full round of leisure and other activities. The message here is that there now exist opportunities for consumption. Betty Friedan (1993) argues that consumer culture promotes a concern of 'active ageing' and then exploits it. Morris (1998) agrees, asserting that consumer culture is pre-occupied with perfect bodies, spread through glamorized representations of advertising. The visual image is increasingly dominant in western culture. Thus, consumer society reinforces and creates negative language and images of later life. There seems to be an inverse relationship between images of old age and the participation in social life (Bytheway 1993). Further, Morris (1998) suggests that consumer culture emphases youthfulness as the ultimate aspiration of social identity – 'the body beautiful' – it is increasingly marginalizing the identities of older people in later life.

Literary evidence of the sudden realization that old age has caught up with the young self is plentiful – see for instance Bytheway's (1993) account of Bernard and Mary Berenson's encounters with their aged bodies or J.B. Priestley's description of the sudden realization that he had become old. The visible physical manifestations of senescence therefore constitute a disguise that conceals the real, unchanged, self (Featherstone and Hepworth 1993). Bytheway and Johnson (1998) assert that we need a well-constituted image of what old looks like before we could recognize the signs in our own images.

Social gerontologists can study persons of a certain age, but their reality seldom reflects that of the subjects they study when their bodies are ignored, because becoming, and being, old are embodied processes. In those parts of the bio-medical establishment where care is most emphasized, rather than regimen and control, particularly in nursing, there seems to be a deeper focus on the provision of care based on a rigorous emphasis on the patient's subjective experience (Benner 1995). In these patient care contexts, substantial attention has been devoted to the ethical implications of various disease definitions. Specifically, the discussion also focuses on how language shapes the response to illness, and to how disease definitions and paradigmatic models impact communication between health professionals and patients (Rosenberg and Golden 1992). Significant work on social understanding of disability has demonstrated how the *lived body* is experienced in altered form and how taken for granted routines are disrupted, invoking new action recipes (Toombs 1995). Nonconventional healing practices have also been examined. In this context, embodiment and the actor's subjective orientation reflexively interrelate with cultural imagery and discourse to transfigure the self (Csordas 1997). Even emotions are best analysed as interpretive processes embedded within experiential contexts (May and Powell 2008). Hence, simultaneously, becoming, and being, old are about the corporeality of being old, the embodiment experience of holding on to physical/mental integrity and reasonable health (Baltes and Carsterson 1996).

Yet it has only been in the past two decades has there been any sustained attempt to fuse together postmodern concerns about ageing bodies in order to foster a deeper understanding of ageing identity (Gubrium and Holstein 1995). Gubrium (1992) has investigated how ageing is constituted in the consciousness of persons. The struggle for meaning when accompanied by chronic pain may be facilitated or impaired by constructs that permit the smoother processing of the experiences. Biggs (1999) makes the point that postmodern ideas of embodiment encourages care-givers of older people to gain empathic appreciation of their clients' lifeworlds and enhanced affiliation with them through the use of biographical narratives that highlight their individuality and humanity. It is therefore important to focus on the construction of identity that is imposed upon the discourses of exteriority and interiority that impinge upon the body.

Bio-medicine and the 'Truth' Stories about Bodies

In this discussion the biomedical model is understood to have four components. 1) The mind and body are essentially different and medicine is restricted to considerations related to the body. 2) The body can be understood as analogous to a machine. 3) Medical answers are thought to be more reliable when they are founded on the basic sciences. 4) And thus biophysical answers are preferred to all others (Longino and Murphy 1995). This model is reductionistic and by focusing almost entirely on the body, it ignores the person that animates the body, and the lifeworld that contextualizes the person.

The bio-medical model has dominated the perceptions of old age in gerontology. As Powell and Longino (2002) pointed out, the medicalization of old age is not an objective scientific process, but rather a series of policy struggles at local, national and international levels. These struggles to define the nature of ageing are between several *provinces of meaning* such as old and potentially old people, their network of informal care-givers, the helping professionals of different types, entrepreneurs from family run care homes through to pharmaceutical companies of global reach, and finally the institutions of the state and the organization and distribution of resources through policy spaces (Biggs and Powell 2001).

Michel Foucault (1977) has shown important insights for gerontological theorizing. He attempts to analyse the extent to which institutional medicine objectifies the 'sick' body, once it has been medicalized. For Foucault (1977) the body is not natural but created and reproduced through discourse. Foucault maps out how medical power became a disciplinary strategy which extended 'control over minutiae of the conditions of life and conduct' (Cousins and Hussain 1984: 146) of individual bodies. Arguably, the medical profession became an institution in which the advice and expertise of professionals was geared to articulating 'truths' about bodies (Armstrong 1983). Medical domination through observation and scientific discourses objectified 'sick' bodies as 'diagnoses began to be made of normality and abnormality and of the appropriate procedures to achieve the norm' (Smart 1985: 43). In this way examining the body of older people was central to the development of power relationships in social situations:

> The examination is at the center of the procedures that constitute the individual as effect and object of power, as effect and object of knowledge. It is the examination which by combining hierarchical surveillance and normalizing judgement, assures the great disciplinary functions of distribution and classification (Smart 1985: 49).

Arthur Frank (1990: 135–6) has suggested that the medical model occupies a privileged position in contemporary culture and society:

> Medicine does occupy a paramount place among those institutions and practices by which the body is conceptualized, represented and responded to. At present our capacity to experience the body directly, or theorize it indirectly, is inextricably medicalized.

The way in which biomedical models of ageing have interacted with older people is a subtle aspect of control and power (Katz 1996). This interaction legitimizes the search within the individual body, for signs, for example, that s/he 'requires' forms of surveillance and processes of medicalization (Powell and Biggs 2000). This legitimation permeates an intervention into older people's lives, because professional practices of surveillance are said to befit older people – because of the discourse of pathological ageing (Powell and Biggs 2000). Biomedicine, hence, constructs the identities of older people as objects of power and knowledge:

> This form of power applies itself to immediate everyday life which categorises the individual, marks him by his own individuality, attaches him to his own identity, imposes a law of truth on him which he must recognise and which others have to recognise in him. It is a form of power which makes individuals subjects (Foucault 1982: 212).

Unfortunately, the medical model perceived old age, in particular, as related to physical, psychological and biological problems of the 'body' (Longino and Powell 2009). Such 'problems' of the ageing body were tied to narrow individualistic explanations such as that ageing bodies 'decay' and 'deteriorate'. In western culture, therefore, the ageing body has been perceived as the 'bottom line' – subject to relentless growth and decay and 'body betrayals' (Biggs and Powell 2001). Insofar as there is a history of ageing, there is also a history of medical discourses of power which have attempted to 'colonize' narratives that would understand the body (Powell, Biggs and Wahidin 2006). According to Katz (1996), the effects of the decline analogy can be seen in the hegemonic dominance of medico-technical solutions to the 'problems' of ageing that bear on the 'body'. As Biggs and Powell (2001: 95) point out:

> This has led to a skewing of gerontological theorizing and research towards geriatric medicine and the relative failure of more broadly based social and life-course approaches to impinge upon thinking about old age.

The dominance of the medical model and its understanding of the ageing body has colonized definitions of old age. However, there is also ambivalence. It has also sought to re-invent itself as the 'saviour' of ageing via the bio-technological advancements that foster re-construction of the 'body' and to prevent the ageing process (Twigg 2004). It appears:

> established and emerging master narratives of biological decline on the one hand and consumer agelessness on the other co-exist, talking to different populations and promoting contradictory, yet interrelated, narratives by which to age. They are contradictory in their relation to notions of autonomy, independence and dependency on others, yet linked through the importance of techniques for maintenance, either via medicalised bodily control or through the adoption of 'golden-age' lifestyles (Biggs and Powell 2001, 97).

The medical model also has tended to disembody older patients by ignoring their 'lived bodies.' Research by Twigg (2004) indicates that medical discourses of power play a key interventionist role in societal relations and in the management of social arrangements. That is, medical 'experts' pursue a daunting power to classify, which has serious consequences for the reproduction of knowledge. The power to classify also serves to maintain power relations (Powell and Biggs 2000).

Schrag also (1980: 252) powerfully illustrates that the medical model provides a:

> subtle and erosive process [to individual identity]. Almost every agency of education, social welfare and mental health talks the seductive language of prevention, diagnosis and treatment; and almost every client is held hostage to

an exchange which trades momentary comfort and institutional peace for an indefinite future of maintenance and control.

'Lived bodies' play not only a crucial part in the identity formation of older people via medical discourses but also, of equal importance, in the social constructions and representations of the body between older men and women. While the naturalization of the body has been pointed out and contested its 'objective' stance via the appropriation of social constructivist insights, gender is a key identity variable identified and evaluated, a dividing practice between men and women. Gender, therefore, is important and significant for the further gerontological study of ageing, identity, and embodiment.

Gender and the Ageing Body

Feminism has focused on the ways women's bodies were controlled and dominated within patriarchy. A series of social institutions – medicine, the law and family – were implicated in the control of women through the control of their bodies. According to Twigg (2000) feminism drew our attention as to how women are represented in culture as more embodied than men, as representing the body itself.

The 'body' within social gerontology pays insufficient attention to the ways in which gendered bodies have always enjoyed varying degrees of absence or presence in old age – in the guise of 'female corporeality' and 'male embodiment' (Gittens 1997). Indeed, there are discursive strategies whereby 'the body' and 'the social' are dissociated in the first place. In this framework, woman is saturated with, while man is divested of, corporeality. Older women have higher rates of chronic illnesses than do men, and their bodies outlast those of men (Estes 2001). In clinical settings, in old age, women outnumber men in nearly all waiting rooms (Moody 2001). Yet she is divested while he is invested with sociality. The absent women in social gerontology were the women in the body excluded from the social. It is male bodies that animate the social – they appear for a fleeting moment, only to disappear immediately, in the space between 'corporeality' and 'sociality'. Thus, it is not simply a case of recuperating bodies into the social, but of excavating the gendered discourses whereby gendered bodies are differently inscribed into and out of the social in the first place. As a needed qualification, Harper (1997: 169), reminds us that because women are always embodied and men are not, 'men become embodied as they age' through the experience of the experiential and constructed body.' So the gap between women and men may narrow, in some ways, as they age.

Indeed, Feminists have underlined the limits of Cartesian thought which considered the subject as disembodied and, above all, a-sexual (Braidotti 1994). In the representation of the female body, the dichotomy between body and mind has been used to emphasize sexual difference. On the one hand, we have masculinity which is defined in relation to the mind and the 'logos,' while the feminine is defined in relation to the body and its procreative functions, an essentialist construction, par excellence (Twigg 2000). As Adrienne Rich (1976: 184) reminds us, women have had to deconstruct the patriarchal stereotype which links the female body with its procreative function: 'I am really asking whether women cannot begin, at last, to think through the body, to connect what has been so cruelly disorganized.

Rich stresses that women have to overcome the damning dichotomy between soul and body, in order to re-appropriate their bodies and to create a female subject, in which the two entities are complementary. Contrary to andro-centric and Euro-centric philosophical tradition, feminist philosophical studies have emphasized that the body is a symbolic construct, located in a specific historical and cultural context: in other words its conceptualization can no longer ignore the close nexus between sex, class and race (Blaikie 1999). Women often find themselves defined as 'the other' (the residual category).

Contemporary cultural representations of ageing focus on the body because this provides the clearest evidence of the historical inequality between gender differentiation: the body of women is inscribed with oppressive ideological mystifications (Friedan 1993, Sontag 1991). Western literature and iconography are full of anthropomorphic discursive representations of old age as a woman with 'grey hair', 'withered', 'faded', 'pale and wan face', 'foul and obscene' (Friedan 1993). The old woman becomes a symbol of 'evil' and an allegory of time which completely corrupts everything. In Portrait of an Old Woman by Giorgione (1508–1510), the devastation impressed on the curved figure, balding with few teeth and deep lines on her face, her eyes pervaded by sadness, acts as a reminder of the transience of beauty. It provides a terrible warning of what is to come, hence the scroll laid on one of her hands reads: 'with time' (Greenblatt 1980).

The notion of 'intertextuality' can be used as it is a mechanism by which the social world is fabricated and this explains why cultural 'ideologies' continually perpetuate perceptions of ageing and gender. Postmodern perspectives can facilitate an understanding of how older people can intertextually re-construct cultural narratives to explain their representations of identity and self-identity. Such a strategy involves a challenge to the homogeneity of the social category 'elderly' as an embodiment of the 'times up' medical narrative. When the issue of social identity in later life is analysed Foucault's (1977) contention seems powerful in articulating that there has been a growth in the localities of power and knowledge that seek to inscribe physical and social bodies with discourses of normality and self-government. In the search for a stable identity not dominated by both professional and cultural discourses of power, older people must 'achieve' it through 'ontological reflexivity' (Giddens 1991). Accordingly, the self-identity needs to be consciously constructed and maintained. The ageing self has a new pathway to follow, stepping outside dominant discourses of medical and patriarchal reason, to include a process of safety, self-exploration, self-struggle and self-discovery, it is anything but given. This allows the inner and outer space to reflect on the self but more specifically a 'biography of the self'.

Towards a Biographically Sensitive Approach?

The notion of biography is central to gendered older people's meanings and experiences of mind and body relevant to the lifecourse. Older women make their own biographical histories across the lifecourse. From earliest age to old age, individuals create biographical narratives to create a sense of coherence and self-identity (Biggs 1999). The social worlds that older people create are put together by categorized experiences. Categories take on an existence of their own for interpreting and constructing meaning. The interior mental processes of individuals and their self-identities dynamically collide and interact with social forces to produce and reproduce the forms of experience.

Alfred Schutz's notion of 'biographical work' (Starr 1983) is the means of embracing this dynamic interplay of subjective and objective social processes. By tracing an individual's life career trajectory over the lifecourse, the concept of biography allows us to document the development of their unique configuration of personal powers, skills and emotional-cognitive capacities as they emerge out of the interplay of social involvements and constraints. This is because biography refers to the comparative development of variable powers between older people, while tracing specific individual's experiential trajectories of across the lifecourse and the unique social configurations in which they are enmeshed.

One could apply this example just as well to the other end of the lifecourse; old age. According to Encandela, when we look at ageing and the social construction of 'pain' we can see the use of a postmodern perspective. Encandela (1997) investigated the interrelationship of ageing and trauma and found it was constituted in the consciousness of members and helping agents. The struggle for meaning accompanied by chronic pain may be facilitated or constrained by the availability of constructs that permit the processing of the experiences. Members of cultures that stock recipes for skillfully managing pain may well be more likely than others to construct beneficial interpretations in the face of these challenges (Encandela 1997). Postmodern gerontology in this content encourages the professionals who work in the field of pain management with older people to gain an empathic appreciation of their clients' lifeworlds and enhanced affiliation with them through the use of biographical narratives that highlight their individuality and subjective sense of self (Biggs 1999).

Subjective experience, in this sense, is an amalgam of several, often seemingly diverse, sensitivities and operations. Settersten (1999) suggests that the study of the lifecourse teaches us that it is open to historical contingency. Distinctive changes for older people cannot be understood without reference to biographical contexts. At the same time, Settersten (1999) claims that there has been scarce study of inter and intra cohort variation in the ways that socio-historical circumstances relate to particular lives. Members of cohort groups react in unpredictable ways to historical contexts. The timing into expectable social roles can influence the ways in which they are experienced and alter expectable role entrances and exits in life zones such as work and employment. Similarly, sub-groups of individuals may hold basic values of their generational cohort but hold a different outlook to their larger cohort; a process of 'self-identity'. To understand the ageing self in such terms enables us to appreciate the power and control dimensions of human conduct as they apply to individual self-identity of older people and how they are linked to the social world. Because older people vary in terms of their biographically produced personal powers and capacities across age and gendered cohorts it is important to recognize how these feed into, and in turn are influenced by, other social domains such as 'situated activity' or the arena of interpersonal relations and social settings, gender and contextual resources and as such are reproduced social positions, relations and discourses.

Conclusion

It would seem that the ageing body is yet another mode of embodied subjectivity for gerontologists to unravel. The re-territorialization of the ageing body by society, and paradigmatically by social gerontology, is a strategy, which parallels the denial of subjectivity within the main traditions of scientific medical and social practice. The concept of the 'body' itself may take on particular sets of gendered meanings for older people, both men and women, whose subjectivity of identity formation conflicts with the objectified scientific definition. In terms of the latter, the explanatory frameworks derived from bio-medicine help to reinforce stereotypes that late life is synonymous with and indeed caused by being old. Medical narratives of the body, far from totalizing knowledge about bodies, obscure the social construction of identity and practice. The body like parchment is written upon, inscribed by variables such as gender, age, sexual orientation and ethnicity and by a series of inscriptions, which are dependent on types of spaces and places. We have questioned gender with ageing in highlighting how gendered and ageist discourses serve to confine and define, old bodies. What has been attempted to bring to the fore, are the different ways medical and gendered knowledge of ageing are socially constructed in western society that animate opportunities for biographical development. To realize biography, is to re-cast gerontology around a more reflexive framework, a movement in social science that illuminates an understanding of the relationship between states of individual consciousness and social life. As an approach within social gerontology, postmodernism seeks to reveal how human ageing awareness is implicated in the production of social action, social situations and social worlds. Postmodern ideas asks of us to note the misleading substantiality of social products and to avoid the pitfalls of reification. It is inadequate for gerontologists to view older people only as 'objects'. Older people are 'subjects' with sentient experience and as such, we should focus on the investigation of social products as humanly meaningful acts. The 'meaning contexts' applied by the social gerontologist explicates the points of view of older actors based on gender and ageing. It also expresses their lifeworld. A reflexive gerontology strives to reveal how older men and older women construe themselves, all the while recognizing that they themselves are actors construing their subjects and themselves.

References

Armstrong, D. (1983). *The Political Anatomy of the Body*, Cambridge: CUP.

Arney, W. and Bergen, B. (1984). *Medicine and the Management of Living*, Chicago, IL: University of Chicago Press.

Baltes, M. and Carstensen, L. (1996). The process of successful ageing, *Ageing and Society*, 16, 397–422.

Benner, P. (1995). Interpretive phenomenology: embodiment, caring and ethics in health and illness. Sage: Thousand Oaks, California.

Biggs, S. (1999). *The Mature Imagination*. Buckingham: OUP.

Biggs, S. and Powell, J. (1999). Surveillance and elder abuse: the rationalities and technologies of community care, *Journal of Contemporary Health*, 4(1), 43–49.

Biggs, S. and Powell, J. (2001). A Foucauldian analysis of old age and the power of social welfare, *Journal of Ageing and Social Policy*, 12(2), 93–112.

Blaikie, A. (1999). *Ageing and Popular Culture*. Cambridge: Cambridge University Press.

Bytheway, B. (1993). Ageing and biography: the letters of Bernard and Mary Berenson, *Sociology*, 27(1), 153–65.

Bytheway, B. and Johnson, J. (1998). The sight of age. S. Nettleton and J. Watson (eds), *The Body in Everyday Life*. London: Routledge.

Braidotti, R. (1994). Nomadic subjects. embodiment and sexual difference in contemporary feminist theory. New York: Columbia U.P.

Calasanti, T.M. (1996). Incorporating diversity: Meaning, levels of research, and implications for theory. *The Gerontologist*, 36, 2, 147–56.

Cassel, E.J. (1991). *The Nature of Suffering and the Goals of Medicine*. New York: Oxford.

Cavan, R.S., Burgess, E.W., Havighurst, R.J. and Goldhamer, H. (1949). *Personal Adjustment in Old Age*. Chicago: Science Research Associates.

Cottrell, L.S., Jr. (1942). The life adjustment of the individual to his age and sex roles. *American Sociological Review*, 7, 617–20.

Cousins, M. and Hussain, A. (1984). *Michel Foucault*. London: Macmillan.

Dannefer, D. (1988). Differential gerontology and the stratified life course: conceptual and methodological issues. G. Maddox and P. Lawton (eds), *Varieties of Ageing, Annual Review of Gerontology and Geriatrics*, 3–36.

Derrida, J. (1978). *Writing and Difference*. Chicago: University of Chicago Press.

Dowd, J.J. (1980). *Stratification Among the Aged*. Monterrey, CA: Brooks/Cole Publishing Co.

Elder, G.H., Jr. (2001). Life course, in Maddox, G.L. (ed.) *The Encyclopedia of Ageing*, Third Edition. New York: Springer Publishing Co., 593–96.

Encandela, J. (1997). Social construction of pain and ageing: individual artfulness within interpretive structures. *Symbolic Interaction* 20: 251–73.

Featherstone, M. and Hepworth, M. (1993). Images in ageing, in Bond, J. and Coleman, P. (eds) *Ageing in Society*. London: Sage.

Featherstone, M. and Wernick, A. (1995). *Images of Ageing*. London: Routledge.

Fish, S. (1989). *Doing What Comes Naturally*. Durham, NC: Duke University Press.

Foucault, M. (1977). *Discipline and Punish*. London: Tavistock.

Frank, A.W. (1990). Bringing bodies back, in: *A Decade Review, Theory, Culture and Society*, 7, 1, 131–62.

Frank, A.W. (1996). *The Wounded Storyteller: Body, Illness and Ethics*. Chicago: University of Chicago Press.

Frank, A.W. (1998). Stories of illness as care of the self: a Foucauldian dialogue, *Health*, 2, 3, 329–48.

Freund, P. (1988). Bringing society into the body: understanding socialized human nature, *Theory and Society*, 17: 839–64.

Freund, P. and McGuire, M.B. (1991). *Health, Illness, and the Social Body: A Critical Sociology*. Englewood Cliffs, NJ: Prentice Hall.

Friedan, B. (1993). *The Fountain of Age*. London: Cape Books.

Gilleard, C. and Higgs, P. (2001). *Cultures of Ageing*. London: Prentice Hall.

Giddens, A. (1991). *Modernity and Self-Identity*. Cambridge: Polity Press.

Gittens, C. (1997). *The Persuit of Beauty*. London, NPG.

Greenblatt, S. (1980). *Renaissance Self-Fashioning: From More to Shakespeare*. Chicago: Chicago University Press.

Grosz, E. (1994). *Volitile Bodies*. Bloomington, IN: Indiana University Press.

Gubrium, J.F. (1992). *Out of Control: Family Therapy and Domestic Disorder*. Thousand Oaks, CA: Sage.

Haraway, D. (1991). *Simians, Cyborgs and Women*. London: Free Association Books.

Katz, S. (1996). *Disciplining Old Age: The Formation of Gerontological Knowledge*. Charlottesville: University of Virginia.

Katz, S. (1999). Busy bodies: activity, ageing and the management of everyday life, *Journal of Ageing Studies*, 14(2), 135–52.

Harper, S. (1997). Constructing later life/constructing the body: some thoughts from feminist theory. A. Jamieson, S. Harper and C. Victor (eds), *Critical Approaches to Ageing and later life*. Buckingham: Open University Press, 160–71.

Laslett, P. (1991). *A Fresh Map of Life: The Emergence of the Third Age*. Cambridge: MA: Harvard University Press.

Longino, C.F., Jr. (1995). Pressure from our ageing population will broaden our understanding of medicine. *Academic Medicine*, 72 (10), 841–47.

Longino, C.F., Jr. (2000). Beyond the body: An emerging medical paradigm. A.M. Warnes, L. Warren, and M. Noland (eds), *Care Services for Later Life: Transformations and Critiques*. London: Jessica Kingsley Publishers.

Longino, C.F., Jr. and Murphy, J.W. (1995). *The Old Age Challenge to the Biomedical Model: Paradigm Strain and Health Policy*. Amityville, NY: Baywood Press.

Lyotard, J. (1984). *The Postmodern Condition*. Minneapolis: University of Minnesota Press.

Manheimer, R.J. (1995). *The Second Middle Age*. Washington, DC: Invisible Ink Press.

May, T. and Williams, M. (2002). *Knowing the Social World*. Milton Keynes: OUP.

May, T. and Powell, J. (2008). *Situating Social Theory*, Milton Keynes: McGraw Hill.

McAdams, D. (1993). *The Stories We Live By*. New York: Morrow.

Miller, J. (1993). *The Passion of Michel Foucault*, New York: Simon and Schuster.

Moody, H. (1998). *Ageing, Concepts and Controversies*. Thousand Oaks: Pie Forge Press, Sage.

Morris, D.B. (1998). *Illness and Culture in the Postmodern Age*. London: University of California Press.

Murphy, J.W. and Longino, C.F., Jr. (1997). Reason, the lifeworld, and appropriate intervention. *Journal of Applied Gerontology*, 16 (2), 149–51.

Neugarten, B.L. (1974). Age groups in American society and the rise of the young-old. *Annals of the American Academy of Political and Social Sciences*, 415, 187–98.

Oberg, P. and Tornstam, L. (1999). Body images among men and women of different ages. *Ageing and Society*, 19, 645–58.

Phillipson, C. (1998). *Reconstructing Old Age*. London: Sage.

Powell, J. (1998). *Us and Them: Connecting Foucauldian and Political Economy insights to understanding Ageing Bodies*, paper presented to British Sociological Association's Annual Conference, University of Edinburgh.

Powell, J. (2000). The importance of a 'critical' sociology of old age, *Social Science Paper Publisher*, 3(1), 1–5.

Powell, J. and Biggs, S. (2000). Manageing old age: the disciplinary web of power, surveillance and normalisation, *Journal of Ageing and Identity*, 5(1), 3–13.

Powell, J. and Biggs, S. (2002). Bio-ethics and technologies of the self: Understanding ageing. *Journal of Medical Humanities*

Rich, A. (1976). *Of Woman Born: Motherhood as Experience and Institution*. New York: Dell Publishing.

Ritzer, G. (2004). *The Globalization of Nothing*. Thousand Oaks, CA: Pine Forge Press.

Ritzer, G. (2007). *The McDonalization of Society*. Thousand Oaks, CA: Pine Forge Press

Rosenberg, C. and Golden, J. (eds) (1992). *Framing Disease: Studies in Cultural History*. New Brunswick, NJ: Rutgers University Press.

Scarfe, G. (1993). *Scarface*. London: Sinclaire-Stevenson.

Schrag, P. (1980). *Mind Control*. New York: Marion Bowyars.

Settersten, R. (1999). *Lives in Place and Time. The Problems and Promises of Developmental Science*. Amityville, New York: Baywood

Shehan, L. (cd.) (1999). *Through the Eyes of the Child: Revisioning Children as Active Agents of Family Life*. Greenwich: JAI Press.

Shilling, C. (1993). *The Body and Social Theory*. London: Sage.

Sibeon, R. (2004). *Rethinking Social Theory*, Sage: London.

Starr, J.M. (1983). 'Toward a Social Phenomenology of Ageing: Studying the Self Process in Biographical Work', *International Journal of Ageing and Human Development*, 16, 4, 255–70.

Smart, B. (1985). *Michel Foucault*. London: Tavistock.

Sontag, S. (1991). *Illness as Metaphor and AIDS and its Metaphors*. London: Penguin.

Toombs, S. (1995). The lived experience of disability. *Human Studies* 18: 9–23.

Treas, J. (1995). Older Americans in the 1990s and beyond. *Population Bulletin*, 50 (2), 2–46.

Treas, J. and Longino, C.F., Jr. (1997). Demography of ageing in the United States. K. Ferraro (ed.), *Gerontology: Perspectives and Issues*. New York: Springer.

Tulle-Winton, E. (1999). Growing old and resistance: towards a new cultural economy of old age? *Ageing and Society*, 19, 281–99.

Twigg, J. (2000). Social policy and the body, in G. Lewis, S. Gewirtz and J. Clarke (eds), *Rethinking Social Policy*, London: Sage.

Wahidin, A. and Powell, J. (2001). The loss of ageing identity: Social theory, old age and the power of special hospitals, *Journal of Ageing and Identity*, 6, 1, 31–49.

PART III
Abject Bodies

Chapter 7

'Where the Excess Grows': Demarcating 'Normal' and 'Pathologically' Obese Bodies

Shirlene Badger

Obesity is a public disease, both in discourse and in physical expression. Despite complex understandings across disciplines as to the causation of obesity, the obese body is commonly seen to be somewhat self-evident revolving around a simple equation of input and output. Beyond discussions of causation, descriptions of the obese body hold an increasingly significant political, public health, scientific and personal power. How actors engage with this description varies from the moral and self-evident, to scientific curiosity, through to personal experience. That is to say, the multiplicity of norms that can be attributed to the obese body to define some parts as normal and other parts as beyond normalcy cross a broad range of public and private structures and experiences.

In this chapter I draw on data collected as part of an ethnographic study that crosses the various locales and experiential perspectives of actors in a 'genetics of obesity' study. My research involves observation within and recruiting through a genetic research team to explore the impact of undergoing investigation for a genetic cause for obesity in severely obese children and their families. While, my research specifically seeks to explore the obese body within genetics of obesity research, it will be clear that the obese child or adult must cross and navigate an ever increasing array of terrains and care pathways of which recruitment to a genetics study is unsurprisingly perhaps, only one, of many layers. To illustrate this, I will focus on the stories of bodies of children and the roles they play within different contexts, evoking realities and categorisations both surreal and mundane. I provide a series of snapshots from across my ethnographic engagements and I plot them amid two stories: the fictional story of *Charlie and the Chocolate Factory* and the political story of a child who acted as a 'poster girl' for the obesity epidemic in Britain. As such, these act as moments that highlight the *situation* of the classificatory act of obesity and more importantly, the political and fictional moments act as further evidence of the generalisability and assumed knowing-ness that is inferred on the fat body. They highlight themes of moral identity and how particular bodies are seen to threaten the 'natural' order of things. Drawn together, they allow me to begin to tell about obesity (see Mol 2002: 53). Perhaps I can illustrate how bodies move between different categorisations according to the specificities of context by recounting the ethnographic moment from my research that I have come to refer to as *The Bridget Jones moment.*

The Bridget Jones Moment: Distorting Categorisations of Time and Identity

It was my second visit to Samantha and her family. Near the end of a long day that had involved interviews with her two daughters aged 12 and 8 and a family visit (including interview) with the girls paternal grandparents, Samantha, her daughters and I were all in the living room chatting and drawing, having afternoon tea against the background noise from the music MTV channel on television. It had been a day full of moving accounts of bullying and hospital encounters, followed by rather different interpretations of fat by the grandparents. In a joint interview with a rather slim tall grandfather and his much bigger wife, I had been told of their open affection for each other: of Ron's view that 'once you've been with a big woman there's no going back', of the sexuality of fat bums and the intimacy of their relationship where fat was not pathologised but was celebrated, where their granddaughter Nerali 'fitted' both in physical expression and their future hopes for her. In the next moment Geri Halliwell's cover of the song *It's Raining Men* came on the MTV channel and the volume was immediately turned up. Samantha, her daughters and I started dancing around the room singing with Geri: 'It's raining men, Hallelujah! It's raining men, Amen ... God bless Mother Nature, She's a natural (sic) woman too...'[1] The song had been used in the sound track to the first *Bridget Jones' Diary* movie. The movie is a dramatisation of the book by Helen Fielding where thirty-something Bridget records her life and modern preoccupation with her weight, alcohol, cigarette and food consumption alongside the complications of trying to be a modern independent woman desperate for a boyfriend. There is a moment in the movie when Bridget Jones is dressing for a date and she systematically goes through her selection of underwear, famously choosing the unattractive 'big knickers' that work their magic refining the figure under clothing. The scene of Bridget holding up the 'big knickers' flashed onto the television between shots of Geri singing. At this moment, Samantha's youngest daughter Juliette yells out 'Ha! Nerali wears knickers that big doesn't she Mum!' Nerali quickly retorts: 'No I don't, I wear knickers my own age size now don't I Mum?' More singing: 'It's raining men!' In a momentary culmination of the interviews of that day with grandparents and granddaughters and talk of family relationships and expectations, the concluding credit clips from the movie flashed through my mind. Bridget Jones eventual boyfriend is Mark Darcy and his parents are interviewed about the news that Bridget and Mark are together. In the movie, Mr Darcy responds using language and sentiment not too dissimilar to Ron earlier in the day. He says: 'Oh Marvellous, marvellous! Yes. Nice, healthy, well-built girl. Can't be doing with a girl who's just skin and bone. I like a woman with a backside you can park your bike in and rest a pint on. Hmm.'

---

1   While the original lyrics to the song are 'She's a single woman too', the prominent chorus from the family members during this moment was 'She's a natural woman too'.

For me, this moment, in both real and surreal ways, merges both fiction and reality to highlight the various categorisations of the body that can be enacted at a given time. I began to see what could happen when the classifications of human time as measured through a child body meet what could be classified as a disease of space. Generationally speaking, distinctly normalised and valued views of the larger body and of the potential normal life narrative for a grand-daughters body clashed with the current preoccupations of the modern body project. For the grandparents, there was nothing *ab*-normal about Neralis' body. However in the context of her peers, the schoolyard and her sister, the measures of normal were somewhat differently applied. The most everyday expression of this throughout my research was how the model of normal human development and a mundane example of a variation on Quetelet's 'average man' is captured in the size = age assumptions of children's clothing. In this ethnographic moment, big underwear served as a signal of weight out of context on the one hand, and potential sexuality on the other. These mundane measures of normality serve an interesting ordering function in society. In this research, the talk of time and its passing is frequently measured by children's bodies alongside and in comparison with other children. It is captured in the cry of parents that their child's growth seems boundless and 'when will it stop?' It is also captured in the temporal distortion of clothing where produced according to the above mentioned age = size equation.

Knowing Through Fictional Worlds

Roald Dahl's story *Charlie and the Chocolate Factory* is a popular children's novel that has been adapted into theatrical productions and movies, most recently starring Johnny Depp as the bizarre owner of the Chocolate Factory – Willy Wonka. The story revolves around the announcement that Willy Wonka has hidden five golden tickets in chocolate bars shipped throughout the world for sale. The finder of a golden ticket will 'win' a visit to Willy Wonka's chocolate factory. With the final ticket discovered by Charlie (the only child depicted as deserving of the find), Willy Wonka opens his gates to the group of 'winners' and their accompanying adult family members. Through each themed moment a child eliminates themselves, firstly from the tour and secondly, we find out, from the ultimate reward of the chocolate factory itself. Each elimination occurs by virtue of the expression of a moral mark on the child; whether that be the over indulgence of Veruca Salt, the consumerist addictions of Mike Teavee or the greed of Augustus Gloop so evident in his 'enormity'. As each child's flaw brings about their own downfall, their exit is accompanied by the singing of those exotic little people that inhabit and staff the chocolate factory – the Oompa-Loompa's. Their songs tell of the obvious distaste and intolerance for 'selfish brat's' and 'greedy nincompoops' and the quite awful endings they inevitably cause for themselves. According to the narrator, it is only the innocent and generous Charlie who is not immune to the fearsome implications of the Oompa Loompas' songs and whose story continues.

Where children's bodies are represented, they seem to serve a particular ordering function in society. Stories, whether they take the form of fairytales, legends, fables, political discourses or personal narratives, act as reminders of the boundaries within which social action occurs (Plummer 1995; see also Christensen, James and Jenks 2001). Bettleheim has noted that:

> Fairy tales, unlike any other form of literature, direct the child to discover his (*sic*) identity and calling ... Fairy tales intimate that a rewarding, good life is within one's reach despite adversity-but only if one does not shy away from the hazardous struggles without which one can never achieve true identity...The stories also warn that those who are too timorous and narrow-minded to risk themselves in finding themselves must settle down to a humdrum existence if an even worse fate does not befall them (1976: 24).

In Dahl's world, parents and children are either good or bad. Distinguishing between these virtues is easy because those who are bad visibly embody their vices. For example, Augustus is greedy, eats all the time and is fat. Juxtapose this against the small-ness of the 'good' characters – Charlie and Willy Wonka: Charlie is pitied by the crowds gathered outside the factory for his visible frailty and poverty and Willy Wonka's 'loneliness' and lack of family is similarly captured in descriptions of his smallness and squirrel-like actions. As a moral tale a number of deeply embedded tropes are evoked through the bodies of specific children and their virtues. There is a clear narration of the moves of good behaviour against bad and reward against punishment that despite specificity imply a generalisability to other children. Goodman (1978: 105) has argued that '[f]ictional worlds are metaphors for real worlds, metaphors that may themselves become literal descriptions. Fictional worlds make, unmake, and remake real worlds in ...ways that may be recognised as real'.

The Spectacle of Childhood Obesity

Through various media we are increasingly seeing the spectacular display and representation of fat bodies, especially those belonging to children. Reality television shows such as *Fat Camp* or *Can Fat Teens Hunt?* follow a group of children or teenagers who are said to be embarking 'on a journey that could save their lives'. Other documentaries follow a single child like eight-year-old *Connor McCreaddie* or the *34 Stone Teenager* providing spectacular representations of a body that fills the screen, enormous in the mundane tasks of walking or finding a seat on the bus.

This increasing fascination with the fat pre-adult body runs parallel with a renewed portrayal of children with rare deforming disorders. In the British media we have seen documentaries in recent times about the Peruvian case of the Mermaid girl, the story of Lakshmi, the little Indian girl born with four arms and four legs and named after the four armed Indian deity, or the Indonesian boy with a tumour for a face. Such spectacular displays of course have a long history in both their clinical and social forms. Michel Foucault (1963) has written extensively on the clinical 'gaze' and the development of modern clinical experiences. Indeed, in the case of the genetics of obesity team I studied, the role of the image was an inherent method for displaying the self-evidence of biological error and of the expertise of various team members to identify causative syndromes. Kemp and Wallace (2000) have outlined a history of the spectacular and its' various representations from fine-art anatomical drawings and dissections through to modern imaging technologies. The fascination with abnormal appearances for the public and indeed medical imagination has been well documented by the developmental biologist Leroi (2003). He highlights the extremes of human mutation in order to explain how we become what we are, reflecting a long held belief that somehow the physical evidence of the body tells us something about the inner (*cf.* Featherstone et al. 2005).

Many of the family members in this study recounted moments when they felt that their size was read as a moral mark on their identity, specifically where others were believed over them. For example, Glenda and Nerali recounted incidences at school:

Glenda: Like this girl in class one day, I'll always remember it, she called me a fat ugly cow and she put me over the teachers desk and the teacher weren't there and I don't know if you remember the skulls that we used to have well she was hitting me over the head with it and it was my mate actually who came and dragged her off and we all had to go to the head mistress and we was all going to get caned for it and she was going to get away with it because she came off worse because my mate hit her and I said 'No look here' I said 'it didn't happen like this' and they said 'well she's given us a different story' and I said 'well who are you going to believe?' and they believed her. When you're big it isn't just being fat – they don't believe – that they don't believe it isn't your fault, they believe it is your fault. But anything else you tell them they don't believe you anyway.

Nerali: One of the teachers shouted at me because she wouldn't like listen they never told the kids to stop. Bullying. Calling me names and wouldn't let me join them and going to. There was this one girl and she was called Erin and the teachers thought she couldn't do nothing wrong cos her Mum worked in the school and she thought she were everything … I didn't like her at all. This one time, this other girl and Erin we were supposed to go on this trip out to the museum and I bought this river thing and Caragh said that I'd stolen it from her so my head teacher said to me, 'Well if its Caragh's I'm taking it off you. Anyway, Caragh says its hers and you're not allowed to have it cos its Caraghs' and she said she was going to phone the police because if it was Caragh's then it would have her fingerprints on it and if it was mine she said it would have my

fingerprints on it and she wouldn't give it back, she gave it to Caragh. It made
me feel unwanted, horrible.

The learned association between the visibly excessive body and moral traits
is deeply pervasive. There is increasing empirical evidence that suggests that
discrimination of fat adults as lazy and incompetent in current Western societies
(Puhl and Brownell 2001), is also expressed from early childhood toward fat
children (Latner and Stunkard 2003). In *Charlie and the Chocolate Factory* when
Augustus Gloop is spotted drinking from the chocolate river, Willy Wonka shouts
urging him to stop: 'You will dirty my river'. The ability of the moral mark to
pervade, indeed infect other objects and characters has been repeatedly referred to
in literatures on fat (see Murray 2005). In an interesting study, Klaczynski (2008)
has shown how children believe and operate as if obesity is contagious and how
contact with objects or people so infected is avoided. Hence, the body is a visible
sign that can be read.

Embodying the tensions outlined so far in this chapter, the body of the child
(especially the child monster) is also believed to carry some sort of diagnostic
power that tells us something about society. The proliferation of 'fat stories' relies
on a certain need to tell and a need to consume (*cf* Plummer 1995). The need to
tell the modern personal story becomes a means by which an explanation can be
built to describe what is going on and who one is in the scheme of things. During
my own research, I became aware of the various resources that participants relied
on to construct their stories and explain their (parents and children) appearance
in a medical space as opposed to another space such as the diet clinic or the gym.
Sometimes the stories told the progression through all logical spaces to this point.
Many expressed that they had never had the opportunity to tell anyone 'the whole
story' and that in the telling they experienced a firming of the boundaries of their
identity.

The consumption of fat stories poses interesting questions. For example Lucy
Mangan (2007) who writes a blog on the *Guardian.co.uk* website talks of the TV
reality show *Can Fat Teens Hunt?* She writes:

> Sometimes there is a title so brilliantly appalling, or appallingly brilliant, that
> it exerts a hypnotic fascination. Though one's rational mind fights against the
> urge, the primitive, reptile brain, which alas is the part that controls the hand that
> controls the remote control, is helpless before it.

Another online review of the same show reported:

> TV is the theatre of cruelty. Most programmes seem to be about misery or, the
> impending misery of people…I realised this during *Can Fat Teens Hunt?* when I
> agreed with my girlfriend who flatly stated 'We'll have to watch this every week
> you understand.. I want to see these people break..'. Instead of being appalled, I
> agreed wholeheartedly (Gimmers 2007).

The gothic fascination with those liminal bodies that transgress the boundaries of the 'natural' or of the modern 'body project' (Shilling, 1993) is revealed in the idea of 'breaking the body' – of pushing those bodies to their limits until they 'crack'. In a similar vein to that which Plummer (1995: 49) describes about the proliferation of modern sexual stories, a major pattern is discernable in the telling and consuming of fat stories: these are the stories of suffering, surviving and overcoming.[2] As Plummer notes, this is a particular story telling form of our time.

Who does this Body Belong to? A Case Study of Responsibility

Early on in my data collection period, a particular media and political moment immediately exposed the central questions of this research. The death of a three-year-old girl from obesity related causes became 'the poster girl' for a political report and media furore that seemed both a public and private altercation of the adult conundrum 'How did we come to be who we are?' that has been expressed by Henrietta Moore (2004: 736). At this time, I had spent two days observing other members of the girl's family in the clinical research facility at the hospital during which nothing was said of the loss of a sister or daughter. Any grief expressed was on the part of staff who both enjoyed the childlike qualities that were perfectly performed against staff suggestions of a backdrop of relative economic disadvantage. With great degrees of patience in-between tests, I was taught to play the Playstation game *Snowboarder*: the essential goal being that somehow I produce a higher score than the medical staff. The children drew pictures, were cheeky to the nurses, and asked inquisitive questions to the extent that I frequently overheard nurses comment to each other 'They're such nice children' or 'They're so good'. These observations preface the story I am about to tell of the House of Commons Health Committee's Report on Obesity (2004) as an attempt to recognise the criticism that the sociology of childhood has relied heavily on descriptions and the analysis of the socially constructed child. While critical social constructionism undoubtedly challenges the dualisms of modernity and asks under what conditions and how is the child produced, it also privileges discourse over materiality (Prout 2005: 63). In the remainder of this chapter I want to follow Wallace (1994) who in exploring the issues raised by the child 'everywhere in representation' (294) asks: 'Are there significant points of coincidence between discourses of 'the child' and the lives of children?' (Wallace 1994: 298).

---

2   See Monaghan (2006, 2007) for the ways that fat and morality are narrated in regards masculinity and Throsby (2007) for the importance of stories in accounts about gastric bypass surgery.

The House of Commons Health Select Committee Report on Obesity 2004

During May 2004, I had noted during fieldwork that those academics and practitioners I was coming into contact with had some sort of mental note of expectation that a report from the Health Select Committee's Inquiry into Obesity was due to be released. This would be the resulting document from a much-publicised enquiry launched in 2003. Conducted by one of those investigative committees comprising members of all political parties equipped with the task to inform and justify policy decisions confronted in the House of Commons,[3] the publicity surrounding the Report claimed widespread evidence collection through visits to the USA, Brussels, Finland and Denmark in order to glean from best practice. In contrast I encountered many ambivalent murmurs as to the level and routes in which evidence had been sought, with some specialists in the field making it clear that they had not given evidence or had made written submissions but not been invited to provide supporting evidence. Thus, the validity and impact of the report was not held high in expectations or in regards implementation. Perhaps this was not peculiar to obesity or to this report, nor was it a matter of simple disciplinary positioning and ownership of the field. Rather, it was situated within a wider discontent with such political outputs in the UK at the time as was borne out in responses to the delays and eventual release of a similarly timed government white paper on public health and the jostling between John Reid (then Secretary of State for Health) and Tessa Jowell (then Secretary of State for Culture).

The Report was due for official publication on May 27th 2004. A press release issued on 26th May and embargoed until publication, highlighted rising rates of obesity, potential health consequences, the need to increase physical activity and a focus on preventing obesity in children. At about 6.30am on the morning before the official release, in between the sports news and statements by Colin Powell regarding the political status of American troops in Iraq, Roger Harrabin told the BBC Radio 4 *Today* programme of key points in the contents of 'a late draft'. He told presenter John Humphrys 'It is very strong meat. It starts with a reference to a case at the Royal London Hospital where an obese child died of heart failure aged just three. Now that's a rare case but it is, they say, a portent of things to come.'

The focus on 'premature loss of life' was made explicit in the first paragraph of the introduction. The future scenario of obesity soon surpassing 'smoking as the greatest cause of premature loss of life' was situated firmly within the borders of the British nation. National statistical evidence was given to qualify the use of the descriptor 'epidemic' to 'what has happened'. It also situated the problem as being population wide and hence, beyond personal BMI scores with the potential to impact on structures relied on by citizens and representing the health of the nation. 'It (obesity) will bring levels of sickness that will put enormous strains on the health service, perhaps even making a publicly funded health service

---

3   See http: //www.parliament.uk/parliamentary_committees/health_committee.cfm.

unsustainable' (HOC 2004: 7). But it is the second paragraph that prompted many of the resulting media headlines and on which this case study will focus.

> 2. Dr Sheila McKenzie, a consultant at the Royal London Hospital which recently opened an obesity service for children, offered a powerful insight into the crisis posed to the nation's health. Despite only being in existence for three years, her service had an eleven-month waiting list. Over the last two years, she had witnessed a child of three dying from heart failure where extreme obesity was a contributory factor. Four of the children in the care of her unit were being managed at home with non-invasive ventilatory assistance for sleep apnoea: as she put it, 'in other words, they are choking on their own fat' (HOC 2004: 7).[4]

Predictably perhaps, the dying 'child of three' became the reference point and marker for both the report and the obesity crisis in England. A member of the committee, Dr Taylor, reported: 'We had a lot of evidence throughout the Inquiry that obesity in children is a huge huge increasing problem. As it is children we have to get at more than anybody else, it was felt that this was a way of emphasising the danger for children' (Boseley et al. 2004: 4). Thus, the death of a child became some sort of modern moral fairy tale. Although the child was never named or pictured, many reports suggested a knowingness of the child. This was reflected in conversations I later had with people about the case where they would state 'Oh yes, I remember the pictures of her.' It is perhaps useful to stress that there were no pictures and no naming of the girl or her family. Generally speaking, pictures of fat people in newspaper reports tend to be headless with a focus on the torso and from below in a manner referred to as 'headless fatties' (Cooper 2007). The three-year-old body was evoked discursively in an attempt to evoke public recognition of a pathological threat. A single child became the vector of national destinies touching both the individual and the family and representing the risk inherent in every body as illustrated in the following excerpt: '[t]heir report into obesity, published last

---

4   The original evidence referred to in this paragraph was submitted as a brief letter from Dr Sheila MacKenzie for the Childhood Obesity Service, Royal London Hospital and also bore the names of Dr Nigel Meadows (Consultant Paediatrician in Children's Nutrition) Sophie Aubrey (Children's Dietician) Kat Blakely (Clinical Psychologist) Dr Siobhan Carr (Consultant Respiratory Paediatrician) and Alison Franklin (Children's Nurse for Sleep Disordered Breathing). It is the second paragraph in the letter that is cited in the Report. It reads: 'My role is to identify medical problems associated with obesity. In the last two years one child at the age of three has died of heart failure secondary to extreme obesity. Four other children also with severe obesity are managed at home with non-invasive ventilatory assistance because they have severe obstructive sleep apnoea (OSA) because of their obesity. In other words they are being choked by their fat. Were we able to study all severely obese children, I'm confident that we would identify many more children with OSA. In addition, many of these children have abnormally high insulin levels, a prelude to Type II diabetes.'

week, paints a picture of a Britain so gluttonous that we are choking on our own fat' (*The Sunday Telegraph* 2004: 2).

Newspaper articles following the release of the Report played on the sensationalist introduction with headlines such as 'Choking our children on their fat, 'Fat and dead at 3' and 'Now obesity kills child aged three'. The flurry of media activity developed a culpability argument not just of national interest but of particular parental responsibility. One journalist wrote: 'When a three-year-old girl who weighs 40 kilograms dies of heart failure brought on by obesity, you know her parents are guilty of gross child abuse' (Devine 2004). Similarly, in a letter to the editor of the Evening Times (Glasgow) on May 31 2004, Agnes Barton of Scotstoun wrote: 'Surely her parents, despite their grief, should be charged with child abuse … If people treated animals in such a manner they would find themselves before the courts'. While the family remained anonymous, the culpability argument directed toward the parents flourished. Almost two weeks later a 'corrective' story emerged reporting interviews with Professor Stephen O'Rahilly and Dr Sadaf Farooqi. Prior to her death the Cambridge GOOS team had identified a mutation in the leptin appetite pathway. They were quoted as saying:

> When a child is exposed on the front page of The Sun as the poster child for the obesity problem it seemed to us rather cruel that this was being presented as an example of how parents were stuffing their children. It seemed a terrible indictment on the parents when we knew there was a genetic defect in this child and we knew 100 per cent that was the cause of her obesity (O'Rahilly quoted in Laurance 2004: 19).

> The death has become part of the discussion about what children eat when in fact it was the result of something else entirely ... We are mixing up children's weight issues with distinct medical problems ... It is an incontrovertible fact that a genetic defect was the cause of this child's problem (Farooqi quoted in Laurance 2004: 19).

Following these corrective statements, media excerpts talked about 'apologetic science' or referred to the genetic condition as Prader Willi Syndrome including interviews with parents of children with Prader Willi Syndrome. Further incorrect statements within 'corrective' reports concluded that 'siblings of the girl who died are understood to be of normal weight, indicating that the fault did not lie with the parents' (Laurence 2004: 19). The response from the Chairman of the Committee Dr David Hinchcliffe was:

> What's really annoyed me about this is that the two people who were quoted on the Today programme appear to have drawn conclusions about our report from the tabloid treatment of part of our report. They don't appear to have read the report. When you've got a consultant pediatrician in a unit dealing with serious obesity saying that she's got children choking on their own fat, quite frankly it

is pretty serious stuff. Had we not referred to her letter, which we do respecting in its entirety they way she put this, I think we would have been accused of suppressing some very important evidence ... My suspicion is that there is more than a whiff of medical politics between the two groups of doctors concerned (Hinchcliffe quoted in Boseley et al. 2004).

In this sense, the three year old thus became a symbol of both medical/scientific and political disputes over legitimacy in regards evidence. The body of the child that had previously been evidence of a threat to the nation, became further victim and scapegoat in the adult world of political pollution. Headers in the Report reflect these ideas of obesity and pollution further. The heading *Obesity: Gluttony or Sloth?* caused both Stephen O'Rahilly and Sadaf Farooqi to respond:

'What a disgusting way to talk about a medical condition,' she says. 'If someone has a tumor in their throat you wouldn't say, I hope, that they were choking on their own dirt or something' (Farooqi cited in O'Neill 2004).

Imagine that someone had written a report 'Cervical cancer – promiscuity or poor hygiene?' People would be outraged. These are sick people, yet they are being vilified (O'Rahilly in Parry 2004: 6).

Here I wish to acknowledge that while the Report clearly belongs to a specific political genre of outputs, and subscription to, and participation in the process bears a level of consent and awareness of this, it could be argued that the intentionalities with which the evidence was given and then used could bear a mark of dissidence between the paediatrician and the committee. It is often the case that when paediatricians are quoted in the media there is strong emotion expressed. The regular workplace confrontation with tragedy could arguably produce a particularly extreme view of the world. While there is a great deal to unpack in this political and public story, I wish to limit further discussion to elaborate on the idea of the dangerous liminal space occupied by the body of this girl (although never visually represented). Her death dominates the story and is taken up to pose questions of the natural and the social, of human and animal, of public and private and of being and becoming in the question of how does a child of three die of obesity? Most strikingly is the re-discovery of the threat of child mortality in a western society.

The Re-discovery of Child Mortality

Some commentators have suggested that the most striking part of the Report is that which reads: 'This will be the first generation in which children die before their parents as a consequence of obesity'. For many, obesity is a 'soft' threat to health as it is overcome by the management of the social body and bears no real pathological threat to life as a disease that kills. Like earlier threats to infant mortality such as diarrhoea, obesity is a disease entity in classification, but in medical theory the dominant view is that it is a symptom of disease. In this section I want to explore the re-entry of the Victorian threat of death in discourses about children and the redistribution of the causes of death and illness in this context. As such, I am influenced by the work of Scheper-Hughes (1992) and Das (1997), whose ethnographies on suffering and everyday violence may, at first glance, seem removed from the topic of childhood obesity in Britain. I use these references, not to make light of the human suffering of those impoverished communities that the ethnographies above write of, but rather, to illuminate the various ways that certain discourses are being inscribed on the bulging bodies of children and how those children get gobbled up in these stories.

The death of a child in much of the Western world is not something that we would expect or consider normal. In fact the only way an encounter between death and infancy or childhood enters our worlds is generally through some tragedy – whether that be incurable illness, accident or criminal activity. However, it was not so long ago (and remains in many countries in which people live on the margins) that infant death was considered a mundane inescapable fact of nature or simply a biological function ensuring the survival of the fittest (*cf* Wright 1988). In short, infant death was historically treated as part of the 'natural order' of things. Both Armstrong and Wright have provided fascinating analyses of the discovery or 'invention' of child mortality and of the move to no longer see the infant as ' one of death's natural habitats, but rather as a terrain in which death was an obscene intrusion' (Wright 1988: 306). They map the development of a certain type of moralisation about child rearing as it came to be replaced by fundamental medical and hence, a resolvable policy problem. This involved the development of birth and death records based on medical classifications. But perhaps more pertinent for this discussion, that two of the greatest killers for children (diarrhoea and malnutrition) were not regarded as paediatric illnesses and, as mentioned above, were believed to be trivial. Thus many of the deaths recorded during this time bore no distinction between the young or old and were categorised under 'diseases of growth, nutrition and decay' (Armstrong 1986: 221).

It is ironic then to consider that when infant and child mortality have come to signify an important indicator of a nation's general status and well-being, that obesity (a pseudo-signifier of wealth historically) comes to feature as the new or 'modern' child mortality. For many of us in the world, as Scheper-Hughes puts it, 'the dialectic between fertility and mortality has lost its edge and is buried in the back of consciousness. For most Europeans and North Americans each birth signifies new life, not the threat of premature death' (1992: 273). And while this remains true for childbirth statistics, obesity is being put on the political agenda as a threat to childhood, where an extreme example of one child becomes the potential path for a nation branded as 'loving their children to death'. The further irony is contained within a juxtaposition of two seemingly contradictory epidemiological profiles: that infant mortality is connected with diseases of malnutrition and 'wasting' and the current threat of premature loss of life is from obesity. Juxtaposed yet again, against frequent discussion of an aging population, the threat of premature death from obesity seems to defy the current improvements in standards of living that have produced this longevity. Against a backdrop of epidemics of infectious diseases such as measles, smallpox and pneumonia – we have obesity. Scheper-Hughes talks of the modernisation of child mortality in Brazil and highlights its uneven distribution and containment to one strata of society. Furthermore, she talks about an 'old' and 'new' pattern of child mortality where the 'old' diseases are controlled by immunisation only to be replaced by the 'new' killers related to bottle feeding. She says that in Brazil 'under the new childhood mortality pattern, death comes to children at an even earlier age' (1992: 280). Babies, importantly, come to be described as born into a power struggle. Poor infants are already disadvantaged in the womb and are born 'already thirsty and starving'. Whereas 'the babies of the rich were described as coming into the world fat and fair and 'greedy' for life ....fat, resilient babies were described as having *forca*, an innate charismatic power and strength' (Scheper-Hughes 1992: 315–16). Interestingly in western and developed societies, obesity has been problematised in terms of power and class issues. It is a signal of lower socio-economic status within supposed meritocratic and egalitarian societies (see Sobal and Stunkard 1989). Furthermore, the childhood mortality threatened by obesity seems to pose a boundless age limit: the risk level compounded with age.

The high rates of obesity in childhood in the Western world bear echoes of the explanations we have heard account for demographic transitions in the past. These rely on discourses of economic and social underdevelopment and so pose fundamental questions about taken-for-granted assumptions about social order. Berger and Luckmann (1971) have argued that death is the ultimate marginal situation. They argue that:

> death also posits the most terrifying threat to the taken-for-granted realities of everyday life. The integration of death within the paramount reality of social existence is, therefore, of the greatest importance for any institutional order. This legitimation of death is, consequently, one of the most important fruits of symbolic universes (Berger and Luckmann 1971: 119).

Within this research, the threat of premature death was never far from the narratives of identity work that family members told me. For example, Kelly talks of her fears as a 17 year old. She talks about her desire for gastric bypass surgery as being beyond a desire for a reconstructed body – this was a need that was based on life and death:

> *Kelly*: Yeah I just want to have the operation really bad. I don't want to wait for it. I just want it to happen. I've never wanted something so much in my life. It's the only thing that I want. But I'm worried I need it. I want it as well but I need it more than I want it. Because I'm scared by it. Whether I'm going to be like twenty or so and I'm going to have a heart attack or something. But I can't play

like football or anything like my friends because I get out of breath so much. And I don't like eating in front of people because they're like 'Oh she's eating. Look at her she's going to put on more weight'.

Similarly, Carol talked about the potential threat of obesity to her 12 year old son's life:

Carol: It's not only that you're fat, it's the fact of the other illness that come with that, with the obesity related um.

SB So that concerns you?

Carol: Yeah definitely. I worry to death about the weight on Dean um. I know his heart takes a lot of his weight but some days I go through and I sit and think God, I'm frightened to death I'm going to get a phone call about a pain in his chest or something'. I don't know. I'm really frightened for him.

The spectacle of parents burying their children has, throughout history, symbolised a challenge to the natural order of things. In this sense, the three year old held up as an example of the impending epidemic in Britain becomes an image-laden metaphor. The confrontation with death evokes a number of cultural codes in order to reflect the liminal space of both specificity and generalisability across generations. Perhaps I can explain this further by contrasting this with the encounter 17-year-old Joel had with discourses of mortality and obesity:

Joel: I keep trying to lose weight because, something, I mean there was a bloke I was reading about in the paper yesterday. There was a guy in the paper I was reading about yesterday and he's trying to lose weight. He's about 18 stone and he's about my age and he wants to lose weight because his father dropped dead of a heart attack at 45 and he weighed 28 stone. So I thought to myself, that ain't giving me long to live like that. I mean if I only live to be 45 that's not very good. Not today. But I know it will happen because your body just can't stand it.

SB: It must be quite a scarey thought.

Joel: Oh yeah. I keep thinking to myself I'll be retired when I'm 60 and my Dad said yesterday 'if you make it'. I've got to lose some weight.

SB: Just a hard think to think about though isn't it?

Joel: Yeah I work in the cemetery and I see a lot of things you know. We had one when my Dad first started there when I was quite young and I remember him saying about it when he come home. This woman she was so heavy they had to lower her coffin into the grave with a digger. I mean, I'm 27 stone, four of my mates tried to pick me up in the wheelbarrow at college and they couldn't. So like they said if you fall over we can't help you. We can't pick you up and carry you. That's part of the problem – if anything ever did happen to me, they'd need a crane to get me out the house.

This is an extraordinary account of all the things that particular family members in this study live with and hold within their consciousness. In this excerpt Joel has seen and participated in burials. He remembers the spectacle of the burial of an extremely obese local woman. He considers his own death and burial. The spectacle of childhood obesity and the spectacle of burial culminate in Joel's account to reveal much more than a challenge to the natural order of things. Although Joel is a young adult and in that sense falls beyond the categorisation of confronting child mortality as it is commonly categorised, the threat of premature loss of life through obesity related causes was of great concern for him as it was for many others in this study. Firstly, it is interesting to note that the story Joel read of the death of a 45-year-old man from obesity related causes did not receive as much mainstream media attention as the death of the three year old. Secondly, if we consider the following quote from Das, we are confronted by the performance of death and its associated rituals that distinguish between a good death and a bad death. She says:

> In a sense, every death, except that of a very old person, introduces disorder in personal and social life. But in the flow of everyday life this is understood to be caused by events beyond the control of the living community. Indeed, one of the underlying tensions of mourning rituals is to absolve the living of responsibility for the death that has occurred. A common refrain in the mourning laments is to say that the ostensible cause of the death (for instance a particular disease) is only the pretext for death to do its appointed job (Das 1997: 81–2).

The performance of mourning rituals, whether that be the burial as Joel indicates, or the very public witnessing to the death of the three year old, serve to articulate what sort of death this is in social terms. What is interesting is that in these two stories of deaths, obesity as a cause of death does not seem to serve as an appropriate categorisation to either absolve the living or normalise the death. The mourning wail is transformed into a moral tale of spectacle. The stories of these deaths highlight questions not only of causation, and of the impact of illness, but also of what does it mean to be human and at what stage does illness signal a degeneracy of identity (*cf* Lawton 2000)?

Discussion

In this chapter I have highlighted some of the dualities that the child body has come to represent and embody and that the sociology of medicine has exposed. I have explored a selection of moments in which the child body enacts these categorisations and yet challenges them. In using the fictional and political tales I attempt to illustrate the very potent moral tales and discourses that the child body embodies when it comes to beliefs within a general population. As we saw, a story of *a* child is quickly able to enter the imagination as representing a generalised view of reality and a potential for *all* actors. In this sense we can see how the body of a child can become the vector of, indeed embody, a range of moral messages.

I have moved through a vast literary, narrative, theoretical and analytical landscape in this chapter and I am fully aware that it raises a good deal of issues about which a great deal could be said. Much of the data I have collected is extreme and I have taken much care to try not to exaggerate this. But, in some moments there is a sense of unreality about the narrations family members provide. In a similar way that Bowker and Star (1999: 178) mobilise two classic texts around tuberculosis, time and hospitalisation and describe how on the arrival at Mann's Magic Mountain 'everything that was normal appears to change, and the whole place seems macabre and oddly humorous', we find that in the case of children's bodies and obesity, the flows of time and 'the insides and outsides of people become mixed up in almost monstrous ways' (p. 185). The movement between inside and outside and between various contexts for the families in my research comes to occupy a surreal landscape where the story may seem at once comical in its extremity, and for others deeply tragic. Where the child body measures time and the passage along the line of normal human development, disruptions to this are monstrous. Following Mary Douglas (1966) I have endeavoured to show the importance of acknowledging the public categories of which a body is a part or representative. The public categories of child as being and becoming are confounded further by the visible expression of obesity and the ways in which fat can be normalised (again within different contexts) or presented as an anomaly.

In this chapter we have seen that the obesity 'epidemic' resides in single children, in individual bodies. It is made alarming and public by the examples of these bodies in governmental inquiries and made knowable by the pervasive moral characters attributed to the fictional comparative caricatures of Charlie against Augustus. While knowledge of the general, be that obesity or childhood, is arguably valuable in its ordering function for morals and politics, it also clearly delineates and 'brackets' subjects and actions. Interestingly, if we are to believe the hype and subscribe to views about the primacy of the gene and concepts such as geneticisation, then surely we would have expected to see a great deal more media attention given to the death of the three year old in light of her genetic diagnosis. Attributing the child's obesity to a genetic cause instead closed down all discussions of morality (apart from political morality) and the hopes placed in medical science. Perhaps this indicates even more that there is something about children, and indeed obesity, that occupies an 'in-between' space (Bhabha 1994), or borderland of complexity.

References

Armstrong, D. (1986). The invention of child mortality. *Sociology of Health and Illness* 8(3): 211–32.

Barton, A. (2004). Letter to the Editor *Evening Times (Glasgow),* May 31 2004.

Berger, P. and Luckmann, T. (1971). *The Social Construction of Reality.* Harmondsworth: Penguin.

Bettelheim, B. (1976). *The Uses of Enchantment: The Meaning and Importance of Fairy Tales.* London: Penguin.

Bhabha, H. (1994). *The Location of Culture.* London: Routledge.

Boseley, S., Bowcott, O., Watt, N. (2004). Doctors irate over report on child's death. *The Guardian*, June 10 2004.

Bowker, G. and Star, S.L. (1999). *Sorting Things Out: Classification and Its Consequences.* Cambridge, MA: MIT Press.

Christensen, P., James, A. and C. Jenks. (2001). 'All we needed to do was blow the whistle': Children's embodiment of time, in (eds) Cunningham-Burley, S. and Backett-Milburn, K. *Exploring the Body.* Basingstoke: Palgrave.

Cooper, C. (2007). *Headless Fatties.* Available online http: //www.charlottecooper. net/docs/fat/headless_fatties.htm.

Dahl, R. (1967). *Charlie and the Chocolate Factory.* London: Penguin Books.

Das, V. (1997). Language and body: transactions in the construction of pain, in Kleinman, A. Das, V. and M. Lock (eds) *Social Suffering.* Berkeley: University of California Press.

de Certeau, M. (1984). *The Practice of Everyday Life.* London: University of California Press.

Devine, M. (2004). Dying for another snack. *Sydney Morning Herald*, May 30, 2004.

Douglas, M. (1966). *Purity and Danger: An Analysis of Concepts of Pollution and Taboo.* London: Routledge.

Featherstone, K., Atkinson, P., Pilz, D., Clarke, A. and J. Latimer. (2005). Dysmorphology and the spectacle of the clinic. *Sociology of Health and Illness* 27(5): 551–74.

Foucault, M. (1963/1989). *The Birth of the Clinic.* London: Routledge.

Gimmers, M. (2007). *TV Review – Can Fat Teens Hunt? BBC Three, Monday, 9pm.* http: //www.tvscoop.tv/2007/11/set_the_video_c_35.html.

Goodman, N. (1978). *Ways of Worldmaking.* Sussex: Harvester.

HOC (2004). Health Select Committee Report *Obesity.* London: The Stationary Office.

Kemp, M. and Wallace, M. (2000). *Spectacular Bodies: the Art and Science of the Human Body from Leonardo to Now.* Berkeley: University of California Press.

Klaczynski, P.A. (2008). There's something about obesity: Culture, contagion, rationality and children's responses to drinks 'created' by obese children. *Journal of Experimental Child Psychology*, 99(1): 58–74.

Latner, J.D. and Stunkard, A.J. (2003). Getting worse: The stigmatization of obese children. *Obesity Research*, 11(3): 452–56.

Laurance, J. (2004). 'Poster child' for obesity died of gene abnormality. *The Independent*, 10 June 2004.

Lawton, J. (2000). *The Dying Process: Patients' Experiences of Palliative Care*. London: Routledge.

Leroi, A. (2003). *Mutants: On the Form, Varieties and Errors of the Human Body*. London: Harper Perennial.

Mangan, L. (2007). *Cable Girl: Can Fat Teens Hunt?* http: //blogs.guardian.co.uk/ tv/2007/11/cable_girl_can_fat_teens_hunt.html.

Mol, A. (2002). *The Body Multiple: Ontology in Medical Practice*. London: Duke University Press.

Monaghan, L. (2006). Weighty words: Expanding and embodying the accounts framework. *Social Theory and Health*, 4: 128–67.

Monaghan, L. (2007). Body Mass Index, masculinities and moral worth: Men's critical understandings of 'appropriate' weight-for-height. *Sociology of Health & Illness*, 26(4): 584–609.

Moore, H. (2004). On being young, *Anthropological Quarterly* 77(4): 735–46.

Murray, S. (2005). (Un/be)coming out? Rethinking fat politics. *Social Semiotics*, 15(20): 153–63.

O'Neill, B. (2004). Choking on the facts. *Spiked-Online*, 7 June 2004.

Parry, V. (2004). Bottom line on obesity. *The Guardian*, 17 June 2004.

Plummer, K. (1995). *Telling Sexual Stories: Power, Change and Social Worlds*. London: Routledge.

Prout, A. (2005). *The Future of Childhood: Towards the Interdisciplinary Study of Childhood*. London: Routledge Falmer.

Puhl, R. and Brownell, K.D. (2001). Bias, discrimination and obesity. *Obesity Research*, 9(12): 788–805.

Scheper-Hughes, N. (1992). *Death Without Weeping: The Violence of Everyday Life in Brazil*. Berkeley: University of California Press.

Shilling, C. (1993). *The Body and Social Theory*. London: Sage Publications.

Sobal, J. and Stunkard, A.J. (1989). Socioeconomic status and obesity: a review of the literature. *Psychological Bulletin*, 105(2): 260–75.

The Sunday Telegraph (2004). Britain so gluttonous. May 30, 2004.

Throsby, K. (2007). 'How could you let yourself get like that?': Stories of the origins of obesity in accounts of weight loss surgery. *Social Science & Medicine*, 65: 1561–71.

Wallace, J, (1994). De-scribing the water babies: the child in post-colonial theory, in Tiffin, C. and Lawson, A. (eds) *De-Scribing Empire*. London: Routledge.

Wright, P. (1988). Babyhood: the social construction of infant care as a medical problem in England in the years around 1900, in Lock, M. and Gordon, D. (eds) *Biomedicine Examined*. Dordrecht: Kluwer.

Chapter 8
Bodies, Drugs and Reproductive Regimes

Elizabeth Ettorre

Inscribing Disorder on Pregnant Drug Using Bodies: Cyborg Trumps Biopower?

Over the past decades indeed centuries, scientific and biomedical discourses on the body have become rooted in contemporary culture while bodies have become more flexible, ambiguous and 'socially produced' (Lorber and Moore 2007). As social scientists position bodies centrally in their approaches to society and culture (Martin 1992, Turner 1996, Frank 1995, Shilling 2005, Featherstone 1982, Davis 1997, Bordo 1993a; 1993b), natural scientists and biomedical experts continue to persist with creating techniques to alter the boundaries of these bodies and endeavour to close up the spaces between them. Often times, this has meant that social issues and cultural problems are not only allowed but also forced to emigrate to our bodies. At times, the troubling social and cultural issue of drug use emigrates in this way alongside the drug addict as a 'transgressive figure unable to speak his/her own truth' (Keane 2005: 91). In effect, we have all become unwittingly members of a captive audience to the cultural spectacle of drug use. Of course for drug using women this spectacle has damaging consequences.

Until recently, accounts of women offered in the drugs field have been uncritical and ahistorical. A systematic enquiry into this issue must highlight key individual and social factors which offer full accounts of the day-to-day experiences of women drug users. We need to be able to explain comprehensibly the structural roots of power and for women, the issue of power whether cultural, social, political or economic is most important. In contemporary theory, power is a contested concept. However, with regards embodiment theory, power has a specific pivotal point: the body is the product of power relationships. Turner (1996: 63) contends that an excursion into these sorts of power issues can be considered a materialist enquiry: this material body as an object of power is produced in order to be controlled, acknowledged and reproduced. For Turner, power manifests itself through bodily disciplines or technologies of the self and regulatory regimes targeting particular bodies as well as entire populations. Since the Enlightenment, the embodied subject has been the focal point of practices and techniques of rational scientific domination. According to Foucault, this body has been at the core of productive control that marks the command of discourse in modernity and the concurrent sexualization and medicalization of the body in a new power configuration, biopower (Braidotti 1994: 58).

Modernity is the era of biopower – of constant normativity. Biopower is about the power of normativity over living organisms; the force producing and normalizing bodies to serve prevailing relations of dominance and subordination and total control over human living matter (Braidoti 1994: 58). In this era, the body has not only exploded into a network of social practices but also imploded into a fetishized and obsessive object of care and concern (Braidotti 2002: 229). In this complex process, the body, constructed by biopower, is many layered and situated over multiple and opposing factors. Clearly, bodies are encircled by many disciplinary regimes and strategies of attention in a relentless, incessant endeavour to normalize them.

On the other hand, contemporary power may be seen to work by networking, communication redesigns and multiple interconnections rather than normalized heterogeneity (Braidotti 2002: 242). Donna Haraway (1991: 155) argues that in our fast moving technological and scientized societies, techno-bodies or cyborgs emerge as a type of political identity, resistance or antagonist consciousness. This identity accentuates issues of race, gender, sexual and class difference within a broad remit for survival and social justice (Braidotti 2002: 243). This is because this cyborg identity is embodied by those refused stable race, sex and/or class membership who have proficiency in reading 'webs of power' (Haraway 1991: 155).

If the body is not already always there to be constructed by discourses nor its existence permanently postponed behind the meaning imposed by discourse (Shilling 2003: 70), the body can be envisaged as Haraway's cyborg – embedded and embodied, seeking for connections and expressions in a non-gendered and non-ethnocentric perspective (Braidotti 2002: 243). In this sense, the cyborg trumps the body confronting biopower because the cyborg is not subject to biopolitics, rather it replicates politics. The cyborg is crucial to confronting the 'informatics of domination', these frightening new networks of a world system of production, reproduction and communication (Haraway 1991: 161–3). The cyborg is a kind of disassembled and reassembled, postmodern collective and personal self – a self, which Haraway argues, feminists must code.

Whether or not we embraces Haraway's cyborg, her ideas are instructive. They teach us that women's position is deeply related to their assimilation or manipulation in this global system. Thus, for feminists, that bodies really do matter in this assimilation or manipulation is about recognizing that beliefs in, discourses about and tools of modern technologies impose and embody novel social relations for women on a global scale. Most importantly, the drug field can not escape this type of coding, that is to say, technologies and scientific discourses about drugs and drug use can be tools for imposed, compulsory meanings and continued exploitation on the basis of race, gender and class. While drug users will be pressed into constant normativity, those with ability to read 'webs of power' may champion their own survival and social justice and exhibit forms of 'resistance consciousness'.

This chapter examines the intersections between the biological and social dimensions of gender and health with special reference to bodies, drugs and reproduction. Thus, I turn attention to a type of embodiment that is on offer to drug using women – the reproducing body. In this chapter, I aim to trace the cultural representations of pregnancy and drug use with regards to our 'bodily obsessed' society, examine the regulatory regime of reproduction with special reference to pregnancy and drugs and look closely at the 'real' material sites or gendered bodies upon which the chaos and disorder of drug use are inscribed.

Given the above, I discuss five inter-related issues related to drug reproducing bodies. First, I look at what is meant by reproductive regimes. Second, I look at reproductive bodies, both drug using and non-drug using, within 'the somatic society'. Third, I look at how 'normal' or 'deviant' and non-drug using or drug using pregnant bodies become visible and indeed visualised through the 'scopic drive', a characteristic of this somatic society. Fourth, related to the somatic society with its scopic drive is the regulatory regime of reproduction which I explore with regards its disciplinary practices directed towards drug using pregnant bodies. Last, I present and analyse ideas on women, drugs and pregnancy and look specifically at pregnant drug using bodies as 'material sites' related to the notion, 'disordered body'. Here, the idea of resistance to the dominant ideology of reproduction emerges.

My assumption in this chapter is that the pregnant drug using body is constructed as a deviant body, a discursive construct which is separated from other female bodies and deciphered by experts as being immoral, inferior, disgusting and 'out of order'. This process generates a controlling response and has devastating intended and unintended consequences for these gendered, drug using bodies.

Defining Reproductive Regimes: The Governance of Pregnant Bodies

Similar to gender (Lorber 1994), reproduction as a component of culture is exhibiting signs of a social institution. As reproduction ascends as a social institution, it develops into a system of governance further surrounded by attendant regulatory regimes, focused on the replication of bodies which must exemplify completeness, health, well being, individual and social potential and the future welfare of society (Ettorre 2002). Reproduction is socially organized around a set of values, norms, activities and social relations that symbolize notions of able-bodiness, human survival, progress and individual promise. At the same time, reproductive bodies, especially female reproductive bodies, become more valorized than ever before through reproductive regimes and the surveillance of their pregnant wombs in and through biomedicine.

There is an array of practices guiding pregnant bodies as they are gathered together in a systematic way under the flag of reproduction. The symbol of reproduction as an emergent social institution (and regulatory regime) is the pregnant body; the body of a woman producing a baby, as well as the chemicals, hormones, eggs, cells, genes, blood, fetal tissues – all gathered, drawn, scraped, tested, examined, and at times, discarded within reproductive medicine. Women are reproductive containers and science's (mis)representation of the female body shapes our whole understanding of how reproduction 'works', has been and continues to be gendered throughout the life course from conception onwards. An assortment of disciplinary strategies (i.e. biomedical knowledge, technologies, public health discourses, etc.) attends to the pregnant body to construct and normalize it. This process is carried out under the supposedly munificent gaze of the physician. Here, reproductive regimes exist as systems and processes structured around regulating reproductive bodies whether pregnant or not. They include the complex methods of governance linking, submerging and sometimes fusing women's reproductive bodies with assortments of medical technologies and biomedical discourses, defining what are 'normal' and 'deviant' pregnant bodies as well as 'tried and tested' procedures.

For the purposes of this chapter, the term reproductive regimes affirms the sociality of reproduction; directs attention to governmentality through which pregnant women play an active role in their own pregnancies; highlights power dynamics, the organized practices (mentalities, rationalities, and techniques) through which pregnant women are governed; establishes material bodies; recognizes the 'conflictual' nature of reproduction and makes links with both micro and macro levels.

Drugs, Reproductive Bodies and the Somatic Society

Reproduction is an important aspect of social and cultural corporeality in the somatic society defined by Turner (1992: 12–13) 'as a social system in which the body, as simultaneously constraint and resistance, is the principle field of cultural and political activity – a system which is structured around regulating bodies'. For Turner, the body in the somatic society becomes the dominant means by which the crises and tensions of societies are thematized. The body makes available the material for our political ruminations as we learn that our cultures are obsessed with bodies.

For example, experts frequently ask the questions: How do bodies move?; What do bodies consume?; How do bodies get sick?; How do bodies stay healthy?; How healthy or how sick are bodies?; What do bodies look like?; How do bodies differ from the 'norm'?; What is the body 'norm'?; What colours or race are bodies?; How do bodies appear?; When?, How? and With whom do bodies have sex or not have sex?; How old or young are bodies?; How do bodies change?; What do bodies ingest?; Do bodies decorate or mark themselves?; How do bodies die?; etc. These sorts of questions are asked in the somatic society with one overriding aim – to regulate and control bodies. In this way, the clout of staking cultural and political claims through the body rests on the assumption that bodies like property are real material objects whose dispositions are of great concern to society as a whole (Urla and Terry 1995: 6). The feminist adage, 'the personal is political' rings true today, given that material, gendered bodies are political targets and extend our feminist ontological and political concerns to cultures of resistance. Furthermore, it is important to note that from a feminist point of view an inherently political agenda includes an intense interest in the 'effects that new paradigms of thought have upon material bodies' (Shildrick and Price 1998: 15). For me, some of these new paradigms relate to the discourse and application of biomedicine.

In the somatic society, women's bodies and specifically, their prenatal, reproductive spaces or wombs became construed over time as the battlefield for the social body's survival (Stormer 2000: 118). These reproductive bodies become the substance of our ideological reflections on human life in a world of risk, insecurity and disorder. In the 19th century, women's reproductive organs began to coincide with colonial nation states' perception that their material landscapes were apparently lacking sufficient White populations (Stormer 2000: 118). Today, the White majority's heterosexual, able-bodied, young, female wombs perform a functional role by normalizing prenatal space in a society obsessed with regulating reproductive bodies. In the contemporary drugs field, when poor, pregnant, African-American women produce 'crack babies' (Humphries 1999) or 'infant addicts', these deviant bodies are able to connect institutionalized racism and sexism to biological reproduction, while being increasingly targeted and oppressed in the battleground for the social body's 'war against drugs'.

The biopolitics and concerns of somatic society revolve around controlling reproduction (rather than increasing production) and regulating the spaces between bodies – to monitor the interfaces between bodies, societies and culture as well as to legislate the tensions between habitus (i.e. life world of actors or cultural codes) and the body (Turner 1992: 12). Turner contends that we want to close up bodies by promoting safe sex, using clean needles, etc. In this context, the pregnant drug user becomes a visible feature, if not potent symbol of the somatic society. A 'using woman' (Campbell 2000) exposes how the personal and public problem of 'drug addiction' during pregnancy reflects simultaneously embodied desires for an unfettered womb and an open ingesting body as well as the cultural need for bodily restriction, control and regulation. Of course, her race, class and age will govern both the formulation of her desires and the way culture controls these seemingly 'uncontrollable' desires.

In the somatic society, treating women as mere uterine environments that can be invaded or punished involves the kind of blaming the victim mentality that can only seem proper when one completely ignores the complex social conditions surrounding prenatal harm to future persons (Callahan and Knight 1992: 235). Blaming pregnant drug users is all about wanting to close up these 'deviant' female bodies and regulate them physically and psychologically, while, at the same time denying that self-surveillance within the context of a desire for a positive fetal outcome (Irwin 1995) may exist for many, if not all of these women. From a feminist point of view, a series of significant suspicions are raised in this context, given that the disciplinary power of the drug treatment system often operates to adjust these pregnant drug users to dominant gender, race and class structures as well as depoliticizes and individualizes their situations (Young 1994: 33–4). One can rightly ask, 'Who really benefits from this type of drug treatment system? Surely, it is not pregnant women. Related to this issue of benefiting from treatment, previous research (Pursley-Crotteau and Stern 1996) has shown that pregnant women in treatment who are going through the developmental process of achieving a 'maternal identity', found that their psychological and biological needs often conflicted with the treatment philosophy that was offered to them.

As implied above, the ideal body in the somatic society is a conforming body not a deviant one. Thus, a drug using body, particularly a female pregnant one, falls short of this conforming body ideal. In general, the pregnant body is constructed both as a docile subject, submitting to invasive medical scrutiny and as an active agent, responsible for optimizing fetal health (Lee and Jackson 2002: 126). On the other hand, for the pregnant drug using body, her docility and active agency appear as questionable, if not vigorously denied by society. This denial may be one reason why attempts are made in the drug treatment system to give pregnant drug users treatment priority (Arfken et al. 2002, Carter 2002, Curet and Hsi 2002, Nishimoto and Roberts 2001, Greberman and Jasinski 2001, Rosenbaum and Irwin 2000): these women are constructed as being wild, out of control bodies. This cultural denial of these women's agency and normality implies that their bodies as well as their fetuses are worthless.

Ironically in the somatic society, bodies become more conforming, compliant or obedient when they become healthier and less ill as well as more ill and less healthy. Either way, they are drawn into some form of self and cultural governance. Both conceptions, health and illness, are culturally and socially constructed and all cultures have known disciplinary practices and regulatory regimes surrounding the notions, health and illness. That the notions, health and illness, can be embodied and furthermore, are able to be translated into notions of 'good' or 'bad' and 'normal' or 'deviant' bodies, reflects the fact that morality is deeply embedded in the discourses of health, wellbeing and disease. Of course, a similar process is visible with regards the discourse of drugs use, as drug using bodies are constructed as 'bad'/'deviant' bodies. Drug users are perceived as socially, physically and mentally diseased individuals. Given that the somatic society is concerned with regulating reproductive bodies as a fundamental activity of social, cultural and political life, women's drug using bodies are centrally located and become represented as 'bad'/'deviant'/'diseased' bodies in need of, regulation, restraint and control.

Becoming Visible: Visualization Through the Scopic Drive

The disciplinary practices and regulatory regimes surrounding health and illness in the somatic society can be seen to mirror those surrounding the drugs discourse. These practices and regimes vary from culture to culture according to how ill or healthy, 'good' or 'bad' and 'normal' or 'deviant' bodies become visible and, as we shall see, are visualized. Importantly, these practices and regimes differ according to the extent and range of the scopic drive (Braidotti 1994: 64) in science and medicine. The scopic drive is a powerful cultural force which categorizes 'normal' or 'deviant' bodies and achieves biomedical aims by making embodied subjects observable and comprehensible according to the ideology of scientific representation. Here, it is interesting to consider what addiction specialists refer to as the molecular basis of addiction (de Belleroche 2002) when pleasure centres and reinforcement centres in neurons as well as adaptive responses to cell signalling are visualized. These scientific representations disembody the drug user (e.g. her body is absent), while at the same time expose how troublesome addictions can be represented visually on a cellular level. This unique process involves the commodification of the scopic and the triumph of vision over all other senses (Braidotti 2002: 246). In effect, for the biomedical expert, seeing is believing. Braidotti (2002: 246) is concerned with this vision centred approach to thought, knowledge and science, characterized by this scopic drive which turns visualization into a crucial form of governance. This indomitable, scopic drive not only breaks the connection between seeing and the mind but also denies embodiment, by visualising what's in bodies through seeing technologies or strategies such as ultrasound, MRI scanners, high power microscopes, or more traditional pictorial representation of cellular processes.

In our era, we experience the omnipresence of the visual – visualization has been turned into the ultimate form of control. The triumph of this scopic drive or what I call, 'disembodied vision', is that it is a clear gesture of science's epistemological domination and control to make visible the invisible and to visualize the secrets of nature (Braidotti 1994: 64). Pregnant bodies may be the objects of medical scrutiny and surveillance as what's in their wombs become more visible, but these bodies are also sources of discomfort and disgust in popular culture (Stabile 1994: 84).

Furthermore, it is difficult to conceptualize pregnant embodiment given that there are striking taboos surrounding representations of the pregnant body in visual culture (Tyler 2001: 74). Nevertheless, visualization can be an important means of controlling pregnant drug users in a variety of settings – on the street dealing or buying, with her partner, at home, in work, in treatment, in prison, etc. If and when her pregnancy is visible, she is likely to be more vulnerable to the vagaries of her social situation.

While cultural representations of pregnant women depict this body as vulnerable and in need of protection, by using drugs, pregnant women are perceived as consciously abandoning that sort of protection and putting their bodies and fetuses in jeopardy. The pregnant drug user is the embodiment of risk. A pregnant drug user is viewed as doubly disgusting – she is pregnant and she consumes drugs. In this context, whether sick or healthy; drug using or non-drug using; 'good' or 'bad'; male, female, transgendered or intersexed; Black, brown, White or coloured; etc. bodies scrutinized by the scopic drive are inevitable merely experimental objects. Here, there is an assumed transparency of bodies. For pregnant drug users, this assumed transparency means that 'seeing' into her womb or visualizing her embodiment reveals not only fetal but also social damage.

Side by side the scopic drive generated by science and medicine is a powerful desire to classify all forms of deviance, situate them in biology and guard them in wider cultural and social spaces. Urla and Terry (1995: 1) contend that since the 19th century, the somatic territorializing of deviance has been part and parcel of a larger effort to organize social relations according to categories denoting health versus pathology, normality versus abnormality and national security versus social danger. Moreover, deviance, translated into the early 21st century, has become 'embodied' – a matter of somatic essence facilitated by moral discourses surrounding addiction and other bodily anomalies (Urla and Terry 1995: 2). Urla and Terry argue that as a result of these complex cultural embodied processes, bodies have become marked and social relations organized in terms of deviant and conforming bodies. Crucially, pressing social issues and cultural concerns are being displaced onto the body.

However, before cultural conceptions of normal or abnormal, conformity or non-conformity and health or pathology can be made, there needs to exist a collection of bodies upon which these categories can be inscribed. In particular, the unique process of inscribing bodies as 'healthy' or 'diseased', 'good' or 'bad', 'ordered' or 'disordered' and 'lovely' or 'monstrous', etc. is performed by authoritative discourses and scientific practices, targeting bodies. A whole series of discourses and practices shape the drug using body as somatically different from the non-drug using body. When a fetus is added to this equation, the moral character of the pregnant female body is put into question. She is viewed not only as behaviourally aberrant but also as social disruptive by the very fact that she uses drugs while pregnant. As we have seen, she embodies disgust both by being pregnant and consuming illegal drugs. More importantly, the cultural fear is that by embodying disgust, she will reproduce something disgusting – a fetus – which will be ghastly, deformed or less than normal.

Mixing Drugs with the Regulatory Regime of Reproduction

All bodies must confront the bodily task of reproduction upon which society sets certain cultural requirements. In this context, Turner (1996: 109) contends that for every society there is strict disciplinary regime and bodily order which means that society is compelled to reproduce its members. The discipline of Western, urbanized civilization with its neo-liberal ideology is one requiring that most, if not all citizens reproduce. In terms of procreation and replicating bodies, medical and other experts' disembodied visions of these bodies have had a major impact on contemporary notions of reproduction. Consistently, the future embodied products of these procreative gendered bodies have taken priority over the process of reproduction (Newman 1996).

While drug use in pregnancy holds the interest of clinicians and public health officials alike (Markovic et al. 2000), this type of drug use tends to produce a punishment response (Young 1999) as well as scapegoating policies which are not conducive to the well-being of the pregnant user (Paone and Alpern 1998). In this area, moral panics are often generated relating to society's perceptions regarding the race, class (Duster 1970: 20–21) and gender of those who are using drugs. It is a shame that empathy is lacking in these cultural responses, as previous research (Fiorentine, Nakashima and Anglin 1999) suggests that women drug users, particularly those in treatment, respond favourably to an empathic environment.

In order to best contextualize the notion of embodiment and to understand the conditions and experiences of embodiment *vis a vis* living, reproducing, female drug using bodies, we need to be cognizant of whole series of complex cultural practices and moral discourses which target these pregnant bodies. If we return to the ideas of Braidotti (1994: 80), we see that within a logocentric economy and phallocentric discursive order, there is a traditional association of women with monstrosity. In this context, Braidotti uses the image of a pregnant body to provide clarity. For example, a woman's body can change shape in pregnancy and childbearing. The pregnant body defies the notion of fixed bodily form – visible, recognizable, clear and distinct shapes as that which marks the contours of the body (Braidotti 1994: 80). What's more, the pregnant body is 'morphologically dubious'; the fact that this female body can change shape so drastically is 'troublesome' within the context of the logocentric economy within which to see (as we have seen earlier) is the primary act of knowledge (Braidotti 1994: 80).

On a similar ontological level, Longhurst (2001: 81) contends that pregnant embodiment disrupts dualistic thinking given that expectant women go through a bodily process that transgresses the boundaries between inside and outside, self and other, one and two, mother and fetus, subject and object. Furthermore, when occupying public space, pregnant bodies are to be dreaded not trusted, given that they threaten to break their boundaries, to spill or to leak (Longhurst 2001: 82). When drugs are placed within this cultural mix, pregnant drug users not only upset dualistic thinking but also represent leaky bodies who endow dangerous substances with mystical properties (Sedgwick 1993: 132). Taking these magical or mind-altering supplements (i.e. drugs) is seen to operate corrosively on the self and thus, imply a lack of moral fiber. The pregnant drug using body is not only the abject or monstrous body who threatens to leak but also the 'bad' body whose leakiness contaminates the rational, public world of the logocentric economy. This body infects or contaminates the intimate, private spaces related to inside and outside, self and other and mother and fetus.

If we look at the social and cultural processes, marking the boundaries between 'good' and 'bad' bodies, we see some of the cultural components of the scientific, legal and medical orthodoxies which shape these reproductive female bodies as abnormal bodies. Within the regulatory regime of reproduction, we need to envisage the reproductive body and more specifically, the drug using, reproductive body as the end-product of a whole system of cultural relations. Drug use in pregnancy is heavily stigmatized and can be legally punishable (Goldstein et al. 2000: 356). Indeed, coercive and punitive sanctions can be imposed on pregnant or post pregnant female bodies. These measures may include: incarceration to prevent damage or further damage to a fetus or invoking criminal sanctions such as being charged with reckless homicide; criminal mistreatment of a child; reckless endangerment, child abuse and child neglect (DeVille and Kopeland 1998: 239–40). While pointing out that many women will be punished for behaviour that results in no harm to the newborn, these authors (DeVille and Kopeland 1998: 251) rightly ask, 'In what other context does society punish individuals criminally with potential imprisonment merely for creating a risk of harm?' Furthermore, to get pregnant women into treatment other criminal and civil approaches may involve treatment in lieu of prosecution, involuntary civil commitment, removing child custody and denial of public benefits (Nishimoto and Roberts 2001: 162).

These types of harsh disciplinary practices are not just about the surveillance of pregnant bodies within the institution of reproduction. They are also about the cultural imperative impelling women to perform 'correctly' or 'normatively' their pregnant bodies in the regulatory regime of reproduction. We know that one basic requirement of this regime is that reproducers, especially female ones should be free from any and all substances viewed as harmful, addictive or mind altering. This requirement is linked to the cultural expectation which is part of a more general, fairly recent trend towards increasingly severe 'rules of pregnancy' (Oaks 2001: 19). These new 'rules of pregnancy' are derived from the medical professions' changing knowledge on fetal health and furthermore, results in a visible biomedical policing of pregnant women's lifestyles (Paone and Alperen 1998).

While Oaks (2001) looks specifically at pregnancy through the lens of women smokers, we are able to recognize similar 'rules of pregnancy' or stringent disciplinary practices operating for women drug users. For example, Oaks (2001: 19) contends that the discovery over the years that women's reproductive biology (Read bodies) fails to protect the fetus has strengthened the idea that women's behaviour while pregnant must be regulated and supervized by health professionals as well as by each pregnant women herself. But, of course, the 'pregnant addict' is viewed as incapable of regulating her own health and behaviour. For her, 'rules of pregnancy' usually mean the experience of stigma and discrimination in relation to not only her drug use but also her race, gender, and socioeconomic status (Abercrombie and Booth 1997). In this context, all pregnant bodies are directed by physicians and scientific experts to play out their reproductive roles in biomedically approved ways, as these bodies are pushed into the service of 'doing pregnancy' the correct way. The fact that a pregnant woman is a subject situated within a labouring body with her own point of view (Sbisa 1996) tends to be minimized by clinicians within the institution of reproduction. Any woman's choice to take drugs is seen not only to pollute her reproducing body but also to be regarded by others as unnatural, deviant, selfish or evil (Lewis 2002: 40).

Bordo (1993a: 93) contends that in contemporary society women's reproductive rights are being fought over as well as their status as subjects within cultural arrangements which, for better or worse, the safeguarding of the 'real' subject, the foetus, is central. In an attempt to understand why the cultural idiom of reproduction has such credible social power, we are able to see important, sometimes not so visible, social processes and disciplinary practices being played out. This is especially true when we attempt to envisage this cultural idiom through the lens of drug use. In this context, Murphy and Rosenbaum (1999: 1) note that when people believe the hand that rocks the cradle would rather be taking drugs, various constituencies unite in moral outrage and condemnation – for women, drug use is viewed as the antithesis of responsible behaviour and good health during pregnancy.

Pregnancy, Drugs and the Disordered Body

At its core, the regulatory regime of reproduction privileges an individualistic, mechanistic view of the pregnant female body with the result that the full importance of the cultural and biological processes of reproduction is lost for many of these women. Of course, this view, modelled on the workings of an inorganic object is not new in medicine, science and culture. Within this sort of paradigm, the body is ministered to as a machine and it is the doctor, the mechanic, who repairs it (Martin 1992). It is interesting to note that conceptions formulated within 'the body as machine' perspective facilitate the maintenance of gender prejudices rather than gender impartiality (Mahowald 1994). Indeed, the science of biomedicine is embedded in gendered social practices and like all gendered social practices (Lorber 1997: 3), these are able to transform bodies.

While drug use may alter the bodies of those who use drugs (see de Belleroche 2002), pregnant drug users are affected in particular by scientific research on reproduction and childbirth in which gendered practices and norms are embedded. Scientific research helps to establish, manage and perpetuate the 'rules of pregnancy' which affect all pregnant women, drug using or not. Bertin (1995: 384) contends that certain tendencies are entrenched in this type of scientific research and these include an overstatement of women's biological and behavioural responsibility for the well-being of the next generation; an underestimation of the importance of paternal biological and behavioural factors for the well-being of the next generation and the use of scientific maxims to reinforce social behavioural norms, particularly the definition of appropriate behaviour.

Pregnant drug users feel the brunt of these tendencies and usually experience an acute sense of how 'bad' they 'do pregnancy'. While women drug users are generally pathologized (Haller, Miles and Dawson 2002, Jainchill, Hawke and Yagelka 2000) and viewed as scientifically disordered, pregnant drug users tend to become the objects of disgust in contemporary culture. Disgust is seen to take over these material sites (e.g. pregnant drug using bodies) as 'objects'. Disgust is a type of all-encompassing affective, embodiment. Disgust is the very designation of badness that society assumes is inherent in these bodies (Ahmed 2004: 84).

Here, scientific research and social disgust fuel the cultural and at times, self-imposition of badness, shame or guilt (Murphy and Rosenbaum 1999: 69) for these drug using women. Furthermore, if and when these women give birth and their drug use is extended to motherhood, some researchers believe that their irresponsible, embodied choices reflect 'the chaotic values of the mother's behaviour regarding the needs of the child' (Stocco, Calafat and Mendes 2000: 15). In the end, a pregnant drug user is viewed as being in a no win situation bodily, emotionally, relationally and culturally.

Linking the pregnant drug using body to the discourse of scientific research, I want to look briefly at Bordo's (1993a) critique of biomedicine in an attempt to further elucidate disordered embodiment. Bordo (1993a: 67) contends that the body of the subject in the medical model is the passive tablet on which 'disorder' is inscribed and deciphering that inscription is the working domain of the medical expert who alone can unlock the secrets of this disordered body. These notions suggest that the injunction on activity and focus on disorder may have special effects on pregnant women who experience all sorts of gendering practices when masculinist science re-conceptualizes reproduction as a technological rather than natural process.

Within the regulatory regime of reproduction, governed by these scientists and biomedical experts, pregnant women are encouraged to treat their bodies as passive instruments of new emergent technologies (Bordo 1993a: 86). For pregnant drug users, it would be disastrous if they treated their bodies as 'passive instruments'. As pregnant users, they need, in order to survive and 'do a successful pregnancy', a type of active embodiment which may involve choosing strategies for reducing drug related harm such as switching to 'safer' drugs; counteracting drug use by taking vitamins and other remedies; altering their drug using lifestyles by forcing oneself to sleep or moving from drug using neighbourhoods and in some instances, seeking prenatal care (Rosenbaum and Irwin 2000).

Regardless of these survival strategies for pregnant drug users, recent developments in biomedicine shape new values for the standards of reproduction – values to which all pregnant women even pregnant drug users are told they must conform. In this context, for the feminist theorist, the disordered body, like all gendered bodies, is engaged in a process of making meaning, of 'labour on the body' (Bordo 1993a: 67). Here, the notion of reproduction as a valuable, material site of embodied experience for all women emerges. Nonetheless, we must work hard and labour so that feminine ontology of the female body is privileged, especially when we are looking at a specific form of reproductive embodiment that presents opportunities for resistance, for making meanings that oppose or evade the dominant ideology (Bordo 1993b: 193).

From this feminist standpoint, drug use during pregnancy is under no circumstances purely selfish, self-indulgent, irresponsible or bad, under no circumstances purely a fall from grace or embodiment of evil. Nor is being pregnant while using drugs facilitated by cultural images of 'crack whores' or 'pregnant addicts'. Drug use during pregnancy is not 'behaviour derived from immorality rather than from illness' (Paone and Alperen 1998: 101) nor a licence for doctors to treat pregnant users harshly (Boyd 1999: 66). Rather drug use during pregnancy may be an attempt to embody particular cultural values and norms and to construct a gendered, expectant body that will speak for itself in a consequential and powerful way. For example, these pregnant drug users may use drugs to cope with the strains of family life (Raine 2001) or to increase their sense of authority or control over their difficult situations (Taylor 1993). For pregnant women, drugs can be used as a resource or a survival strategy to help them endure the problems they face as women drug users and victims of abuse (Sales and Murphy 2000: 709) or to make their lives more manageable and inclusive of a little, if not some leisure.

Sales and Murphy's (2000) research revealed that drugs were used by pregnant women to relieve pain, to create a sense of control or to prevent partner violence and abuse. Other research demonstrated that worries or fears about the welfare of others were important for these women, especially their concerns for the welfare of their children (Copeland 1998: 333, Baker and Carson 1999). Obviously, the cultural belief that presumes these pregnant women are uncaring and totally irresponsible is erroneous. Women drug users are not merely 'victims' of their circumstances but by using drugs may be attempting to cope with a range of issues in their lives in which drug use forms part of a coping strategy (Malloch 2004: 388). Nevertheless, in order to manage their status as pregnant drug users, women need to navigate a safe passage through a series of perceived risks such as losing custody of their children, causing fetal damage or being severely stigmatized in public settings (Irwin 1995: 635). Here, pregnant drug using bodies are capable of being employed as a conduit for the expression of a variety of at times conflicting concerns, desires and predicaments, existing in society. Within this type of viewpoint, illuminating drug use in pregnancy does not necessitate expert knowledge. Rather, what is needed is attentiveness to the myriad strata of cultural representations that are embedded in this type of gendered, 'disordered body' or 'deviant body'.

For example, ideas surrounding pregnancy in contemporary society are spurred on by the surveillance practices of biomedical experts and materialize as resistance to autonomous motherhood (De Gama 1993). Furthermore, beneath the compelling cultural apprehension of drug addicted babies and the development of public health programmes designed for the special needs of certain populations especially minority women who are or would like to be pregnant (Balsamo 1999: 241) lies a basic animosity and resistance to women's self governance (Campbell 1999: 917).

This cultural animosity reveals the problematic and politicized nature of human reproduction and the fact that whether pregnant drug users bring their babies to term or have an abortion, they are unable to experience any form of normality in and through the biomedical discourse. Inevitably, female drug users will bear the three stigmata of being immoral, sexually indiscrete and inadequate caregivers –

stigmata which become even more punitive when women are seen to abuse drugs during pregnancy and perpetuated by unprofessional behaviour and pejorative attitudes of health care providers (Carter 2002: 302). It is important to note here that negative social responses to pregnant drug users such as stigmatization and imputing legal liability may impact disproportionately on racialized women and women of low economic status (Goldstein et al. 2000: 364–5). Here, there is a sense of urgency for treaters to be aware of the emotional, psychological, economic and social impacts of these issues and to try to actively engage *all women drug users* in caring environments (Curet and Hsi 2002). The above type of negative expert response exists side by side controlled scientific reproduction (Spallone and Steinberg 1987: 15) which not only fragments the meaning of motherhood (Hill Collins 1999: 279) but also brings both the physician and the pregnant woman into a system of normative surveillance which for pregnant drug users means that the dominant narrative is one of maternal excess and fetal victimization (Balsamo 1999: 243).

In conclusion, this chapter has demonstrated that the cultural workings of reproduction, drugs and the gendered body expose the long-standing feminist unease that the medicalization of reproduction, pregnancy and childbirth has more often than not been against the interests of pregnant women, making them objects of medical care rather than subjects with agency and rational decision making powers. Compound this situation with using drugs and we can rightly say that, 'All hell breaks loose'. In the above discussions, I have outlined how cultural representations of pregnant drug users in the somatic society and within the regulatory regime of reproduction become 'eye food' for biomedical experts in their visualization of these disembodied/deviant female subjects. I have attempted to weave together the notions pregnant drug use, somatic society, drug use, scopic drive, disgust and disordered bodies in order to demonstrate their symbolic relationship in popular culture.

As a feminist theorist, I have wanted to make meaning and labour on the drug using reproducing body in order to further demonstrate how an embodiment approach is able to illuminate some of the complexities of pregnant drug users' intractable, social situation. The very act of using drugs during pregnancy is confounding the dominant discourse on drugs and reproduction. For pregnant users, there may be power and pleasure (see Ettorre 2007a, 2007b) in this type of embodied cultural work. Resisting normalization may produce some benefits. At the very least, their disordered bodies are resisting the grip of the regulatory regime of reproduction on their 'deviant' bodies and attempting to give those experts employing the all pervasive scopic drive a proper black eye.

References

Abercrombie, P.D. and Booth, K.M. (1997). Prevalence of human immunodeficiency virus infection and drug use in pregnant women: a critical review of the literature, *Journal of Women's Health,* 6, 2: 163–87.

Ahmed, S. (2004). *The Cultural Politics of Emotions.* New York: Routledge.

Arfken C.L., Borisova, N., Klein, C., di Menza, S. and Schuster, C.R. (2002). Women are less likely to be admitted to substance abuse treatment within 30 days of assessment, *Journal of Psychoactive Drugs,* 34(1): 33–8.

Baker, P.L. and Carson, A. (1999). 'I take care of my kids': mothering practices of substance-abusing women, *Gender and Society,* 13, 3: 347–63.

Balsamo, A. (1999). Public Pregnancies and cultural narratives of surveillance, in A.E. Clarke and V.L. Olsen (eds) *Revisioning Women, Health and Healing: Feminist, Cultural and Technoscience Perspectives,* New York and London: Routledge, pp. 231–53.

Bertin, J. (1995). Regulating reproduction, in J. Callahan (ed.) *Reproduction, Ethics and the Law,* Bloomingtom: Indiana University Press, pp. 380–97.

Bordo, S. (1993a). *Unbearable Weight: Feminism, Western Culture and the Body,* Berkeley: University of California Press.

Bordo, S. (1993b). Feminism, Foucault and the politics of the body, in C. Ramazanoglu, *Up against Foucault: Explorations of Some Tensions between Foucault and Feminism,* London: Routledge, pp. 179–202.

Boyd, S.C. (1999). *Mothers and Illicit Drugs.* Toronto: University of Toronto Press.

Braidotti, R. (1994). *Nomadic Subjects: Embodiment and Sexual Difference in Contemporary Feminist Theory.* New York: Columbia University Press.

Braidotti, R. (2002). *Metamorphoses: Towards a Materialist Theory of Becoming.* Cambridge: Polity Press.

Callahan, J.C. and Knight, J.W. (1992). Women, fetuses, medicine and the law, in H.B. Holmes and L.M. Purdy (eds) *Feminist Perspectives in Medical Ethics,* Bloomington: Indiana University Press, pp. 224–39.

Campbell, N. (1999). Regulating maternal instinct: governing mentalities of late twentieth century us illicit drug policy, *SIGNS: Journal of Women in Culture and Society,* 24(4), 895–923.

Campbell, N. (2000). *Using Women: Gender, Drug Policy and Social Justice,* New York: Routledge.

Carter, C.S. (2002). Prenatal care for women who are addicted: Implications for gender-sensitive practice, *Affilia: Journal of Women and Social Work,* 17, 3: 299–313.

Copeland, J. (1998). A qualitative study of self-managed change in substance dependence among women, *Contemporary Drug Problems,* 25, 2: 321–45.

Curet, L. and Hsi, A. (2002). Drug abuse during pregnancy, *Clinical Obstetrics and Gynecology,* 45,1: 73–88.

Davis, K. (1997). Embody-ing theory: beyond modernist and postmodernist readings of the body, in K. Davis (ed.) *Embodied Practices: Feminist Perspectives on the Body*, London: Sage Publications, Ltd., pp. 1–23.

deBelleroche, J. (2002). Molecular basis of addiction, in W. Caan and J. de Belleroche (eds) *Drink, Drugs and Dependence: From Science to Clinical Practice*, London: Routledge, pp. 123–33.

DeGama, K, (1993). A Brave new world? Rights, discourse and the politics of reproductive autonomy, *Journal of Law and Society*, 20: 114–30.

Deville, K.A. and Kopelman, L.M. (1998). Moral and social issues regarding pregnant women who use and abuse drugs, *Obstetrics and Gynecology Clini North America*, 25(1): pp. 237–54.

Duster, T. (1970). *The Legislation of Morality: Laws, Drugs and Moral Judgment*, New York: Free Press.

Ettorre, E. (2002). *Reproductive Genetics, Gender and the Body*, London: Routledge.

Ettorre, E. (2007a). Women, drugs and popular culture: is there a need for a feminist embodiment perspective?, in P. Manning (ed.) *Drugs and Popular Culture: Drugs, Identity, Media and Culture in the 21st Century*, Cullompton, Devon: Willan Publishing.

Ettorre, E. (2007b). *Revisioning Women and Drug Use: Gender, Power and the Body*, Houndmills: Palgrave Macmillan.

Featherstone, M. (1982). The body in consumer culture, in M. Featherstone, M. Hepworth and B. Turner (eds) *The Body: Social Process and Cultural Theory*, London: Sage Publications, pp. 170–96.

Fiorentine, R., Nakashima, J. and Anglin, M.D. (1999). Client engagement in drug treatment, *Journal of Substance Abuse Treatment*, 17, 3: 199–206.

Frank, A. (1995). *The Wounded Storyteller: Body, Illness and Ethics*, Chicago: University of Chicago Press.

Goldstein, R.B., Mcavay, G.J., Nunes, E.V. and Weissman, M.M. (2000). Maternal life history versus gestation-focused assessment of prenatal exposure to substances of abuse, *Journal of Substance Abuse*, 11, 4: 355–68.

Greberman, S.B. and Jasinski, D. (2001). Comparison of drug treatment histories of single and multiple drug abusers in detox, *Addictive Behaviors*, 26, 2: 285–88.

Haller, D.L., Miles, D.R. and Dawson, K.S. (2002). Psychopathology influences treatment retention among drug-dependent women, *Journal of Substance Abuse Treatment*, 23, 4: 431–6.

Haraway, D. (1991). *Simians, Cyborgs, and Women: The Reinvention of Nature*. New York: Routledge.

Hill Collins, P. (1999). Will the 'real' mother please stand up?: The logic of eugenics and American national family planning, in A.E. Clarke and V.L. Olsen (eds) *Revisioning Women, Health and Healing: Feminist, Cultural and Technoscience Perspectives*, New York and London: Routledge, pp. 266–82.

Humphries, D. (1999). *Crack Moms*. Columbus: Ohio State University Press.

Irwin, K. (1995). Ideology, pregnancy and drugs: differences between crack-cocaine, heroine and methamphetamine users, *Contemporary Drug Problems* 22: 613–37.

Jainchill, N., Hawke, J. and Yagelka, J. (2000). Gender, psychopathology, and patterns of homelessness among clients in shelter-based TCs, *American Journal of Drug and Alcohol Abuse*, 26, 4: 553–67.

Keane, H. (2005). Addiction and the Bioethics of Difference, in M. Shildrick and R. Mykitiuk (eds) *Ethics of the Body: Postconventional Challenges.* London: The MIT Press, pp. 91–112.

Lee, E. and Jackson, E. (2002). The pregnant body, in M. Evans and E. Lee (eds) *Real Bodies: A Sociological Introduction.* Houndmills: Palgrave, pp. 115–32.

Lewis, S. (2002). Concepts of motherhood, in H. Klee, M. Jackson and S. Lewis (eds), *Drug Misuse and Motherhood.* London: Routledge, pp. 32–44.

Longhurst, R. (2001). Breaking corporeal boundaries: pregnant bodies in public places, in R. Holliday and J. Hassard (eds) *Contested Bodies.* London: Routledge, pp. 81–94.

Lorber, J. (1994). *Paradoxes of Gender.* New York: Yale University Press.

Lorber, J. (1997). *Gender and the Social Construction of Illness.* London: Sage Publications.

Lorber, J. and Moore, L.J. (2007). *Gendered Bodies: Feminist Perspectives.* Los Angeles: Roxbury Publishing Company.

Mahowald, M.B. (1994). Reproductive genetics and gender justice, in K. Rothenberg and E.J. Thomson (eds) *Women and Prenatal Testing: Facing the Challenges of Genetic Testing.* Columbus, Ohio: Ohio State University Press, pp. 67–87.

Malloch, M.S. (2004). Not fragrant at all: criminal justice responses to 'risky' women', *Critical Social Policy*, 24, 3: 385–405.

Markovic, N., Ness, R.B., Cefilli, D., Grisso, J.A., Stahmer, S. and Shaw, L.M. (2000). Substance use measures among women in early pregnancy, *Americal Journal of Obstetrics and Gynecology*, 183, 3: 627–32.

Martin, E. (1992). *The Woman in the Body: A Cultural Analysis of Reproduction.* Boston: Beacon Press.

Murphy, S. and Rosenbaum, M. (1999). *Pregnant Women on Drugs: Combating Stereotypes and Stigma.* New Brunswick, New Jersey: Rutgers University Press.

Newman, K. (1996). *Fetal Positions: Individualsim, Science, Visuality.* Stanford: Stanford University Press.

Nishimoto, R.H. and Roberts, A.C. (2001). Coercion and drug treatment for postpartum women, *American Journal of Drug and Alcohol Abuse*, 27, 1: 161–81.

Oaks, L. (2001). *Smoking and Pregnancy: The Politics of Fetal Protection.* New Brusnwick, New Jersey: Rutgers University Press.

Paone, D. and Alperen, J. (1998). Pregnancy policing: policy of harm, *International Journal of Drug Policy,* 9, 2: 101–108.

Pursley-Crotteau, S. and Stern, P.N. (1996). Creating a new life: dimensions of temperance in perinatal cocaine crack users, *Qualitative Health Research*, 6, 3: 350–67.

Raine, P. (2001). *Women's Perspectives on Drugs and Alcohol: The Vicious Circle*. Aldershot: Ashgate.

Rosenbaum, M. and Irwin, K. (2000). Pregnancy, drugs, and harm reduction, in J.A. Inciardi and L.D. Harrison (eds) *Harm Reduction: National and International Perspectives*. Thousand Oaks, California: Sage, pp. 89–109.

Sales, P. and Murphy, S. (2000). Surviving violence: pregnancy and drug use, *Journal of Drug Issues*, 30, 4: 695–724.

Sbisa, M. (1996). The feminine subject and female body in discourse about childbirth, *European Journal of Women's Studies*, 3, 4: 363–76.

Sedgwick, E. (1994). *Tendencies*. London: Routledge.

Shildrick, M. and Price, J. (1998). Vital signs: texts, bodies and biomedicine, in M. Shildrick and J. Price (eds) *Vital Signs: Feminist Reconfigurations of the Bio/logical Body*, Edinburgh: Edinburgh University Press, pp. 1–17.

Shilling, C. (2003). *The Body and Social Theory* (Second edition). London: Sage Publications.

Shilling, C. (2005). *The Body in Culture, Technology and Society*. London: Sage Publications.

Spallone, P. and Steinberg, D.L. (1987). Introduction, in P. Spallone and D.L. Steinberg (eds) *Made to Order: The Myth of Reproductive and Genetic Engineering*. Oxford and New York: Pergamon Press.

Stocco, P., Calafat, A. and Mendes, F. (2000). Preface, *Women Drug Abuse in Europe: Gender Identity*, in Stocco, P., Llopis-llacer, J.J., DeFazio, L., Calafat, A. and Mendes, F. (eds) Palma de Mallorca: IREFREA.

Stormer, N. (2000). Prenatal space, *SIGNS: Journal of Women in Culture and Society*, 26, 1: 109–44.

Taylor, A. (1993). *Women Drug Users: An Ethnography of a Female Injecting Community*. Oxford: Clarendon Press.

Turner, B. (1992). *Regulating Bodies: Essays in Medical Sociology*. London: Routledge.

Turner, B. (1996). *The Body and Society* (Second edition). London: Sage Publications Ltd.

Tyler, I. (2001). Skin-tight: celebrity, pregnancy and subjectivity, in S. Ahmed and J. Stacey (eds) *Thinking through the Skin*, London: Routledge, pp. 69–83.

Urla, J. and Terry, J. (1995). Introduction: mapping embodied deviance, in Terry, J. and Urla, J. (eds) *Deviant Bodies: Critical Perspectives on Difference in Science and Popular Cultures*, Bloomington, Indiana: Indiana University Press, pp. 1–18.

Young, I.M. (1994). Punishment, treatment, empowerment: three approaches to policy for pregnant addicts, *Feminist Studies*, 20, 1: 33–57.

Index

Parallel Programming with C# and .NET

Fundamentals of Concurrency and Asynchrony Behind Fast-Paced Applications

Vaskaran Sarcar

Foreword by Naga Santhosh Reddy Vootukuri

Apress®

Parallel Programming with C# and .NET: Fundamentals of Concurrency and Asynchrony Behind Fast-Paced Applications

Vaskaran Sarcar
Near Garia Station, Post: Garia
Kuntala Furniture, 2nd Floor
Kolkata, West Bengal, India

ISBN-13 (pbk): 979-8-8688-0487-8   ISBN-13 (electronic): 979-8-8688-0488-5
https://doi.org/10.1007/979-8-8688-0488-5

Managing Director, Apress Media LLC: Welmoed Spahr
Acquisitions Editor: Smriti Srivastava
Development Editor: Laura Berendson
Coordinating Editor: Kripa Joseph

Cover designed by eStudioCalamar

Cover image designed by Freepik (www.freepik.com)

Distributed to the book trade worldwide by Apress Media, LLC, 1 New York Plaza, New York, NY 10004, U.S.A. Phone 1-800-SPRINGER, fax (201) 348-4505, e-mail orders-ny@springer-sbm.com, or visit www.springeronline.com. Apress Media, LLC is a California LLC and the sole member (owner) is Springer Science + Business Media Finance Inc (SSBM Finance Inc). SSBM Finance Inc is a **Delaware** corporation.

For information on translations, please e-mail booktranslations@springernature.com; for reprint, paperback, or audio rights, please e-mail bookpermissions@springernature.com.

Apress titles may be purchased in bulk for academic, corporate, or promotional use. eBook versions and licenses are also available for most titles. For more information, reference our Print and eBook Bulk Sales web page at http://www.apress.com/bulk-sales.

Any source code or other supplementary material referenced by the author in this book is available to readers on GitHub (https://github.com/Apress/Parallel-Programming-with-CSharp-and-.NET). For more detailed information, please visit https://www.apress.com/gp/services/source-code.

If disposing of this product, please recycle the paper

To those who are often labeled as "workaholics," "introverted," or "antisocial," only because they forget the world while coding.

Table of Contents

About the Author

Vaskaran Sarcar obtained his master's of engineering from Jadavpur University, Kolkata (India), and his master's of computer applications from Vidyasagar University, Midnapore (India). He was a National Gate Scholar (2007–2009) and has more than 12 years of experience in education and the IT industry. He devoted his early years (2005–2007) to the teaching profession at various engineering colleges, and later he joined HP India PPS R&D Hub in Bangalore. He worked there for more than 10 years and became a senior software engineer and team lead. After that, he decided to follow his passion and is now an independent full-time author.

You can find his books at `https://amazon.com/author/vaskaran_sarcar` and find him on LinkedIn at `www.linkedin.com/in/vaskaransarcar`.

About the Technical Reviewer

Naga Santhosh Reddy Vootukuri is a senior software engineering manager at Microsoft, specializing in cloud computing and artificial intelligence. With a distinguished career spanning 16 years across India, China, and the United States, Naga has amassed a wealth of experience in distributed systems, microservices, and large-scale infrastructure management building cloud and intelligent systems.

At Microsoft, Naga leads the Azure SQL Database team, driving initiatives to optimize SQL deployment processes for millions of databases worldwide. His leadership was pivotal in the development of Master Data Services (MDS), a critical component of Microsoft's SQL enterprise solutions, which saw a significant increase in customer adoption under his stewardship.

Naga has authored and published numerous research articles in peer-reviewed and indexed journals. He is a senior member of IEEE, teaches workshops on AI, and writes technical articles as a Core MVB member at DZone, engaging with millions of active readers. You can read his articles at `https://dzone.com/authors/sunnynagavo`. He also serves as an editorial board member for a highly reputed science journal (SCI), where he reviews research articles on cloud computing and AI, further solidifying his influence in the academic and professional spheres.

Beyond his corporate roles, Naga actively contributes to the tech community by speaking at events, reviewing books for Apress, and actively helping people in forums like the Microsoft Tech Community. His commitment to advancing technology is underscored by his recent role as a judge for the Globee Awards, where he evaluated and recognized innovations in the industry. He also served as a judge for the Microsoft AI hackathon, with more than 10,000 developers participating.

Throughout his career, Naga has demonstrated exceptional leadership and technical prowess, evident in his mentorship on ADP List and his key role in conducting more than 100+ interviews to recruit top talent for Microsoft. You can contact him at `https://adplist.org/mentors/sunny`.

In summary, Naga embodies a blend of technical expertise, leadership excellence, and community engagement, making profound contributions to both Microsoft and the broader tech industry. His dedication to innovation and mentorship continues to inspire professionals and shape the future of technology globally.

Acknowledgments

First, I thank the Almighty. I sincerely believe that with His blessings only I could complete this book. I also extend my deepest gratitude and thanks to the following:

- **Naga Santhosh Reddy Vootukuri:** He is the technical reviewer of this book, located in a different country, and works in a different time zone. Despite these factors, whenever I was in need, he provided support. He answered all my queries through phone calls, WhatsApp, and emails. Thank you one more time.

- **Smriti, Laura, Celestin, and the Apress team:** I sincerely thank each of you for giving me another opportunity to work with you and with Apress.

- **Nirmal, Kim Wimpsett, Selvakumar and Pushparaj:** Thanks to each of you for your exceptional support in beautifying my work. Your efforts are extraordinary.

Finally, I thank those people from the online C# developer community, .NET developer community, and Stack Overflow community who have shared their knowledge in various forms. In fact, I thank everyone who directly or indirectly contributed to this work.

Foreword

Mastering a programming language is much like an artist perfecting their craft; it demands dedication, practice, and the right tools. In the realm of modern computing, where efficiency and speed are paramount, parallel programming stands as a cornerstone. In fact, parallel programming is like conducting an orchestra—each thread must play its part perfectly, or you end up with chaos instead of harmony. This book, *Parallel Programming with C# and .NET*, is an indispensable guide for anyone looking to harness the full power of parallel computing, ensuring their applications are both fast and scalable.

Vaskaran Sarcar, an esteemed author, is known for his ability to explain complex ideas clearly. He is passionate, well-informed, skilled, and very knowledgeable in this area. His systematic approach and curiosity have earned him respect in the programming community. I've seen Vaskaran tackle tough problems with focused determination, consistently finding elegant solutions that showcase his analytical skills and dedication.

Parallel Programming with C# and .NET focuses sharply on the complex world of parallel computing. Each chapter breaks down different techniques step-by-step, starting with basic concepts explained in a simple manner. It includes practical sample programs and quizzes to reinforce your understanding. This structured approach simplifies learning and ensures you can apply these concepts effectively. This pedagogical style ensures that readers not only grasp fundamental concepts but also retain them effectively.

FOREWORD

In today's tech landscape, performance and efficiency are crucial. C# has grown beyond its Windows origins, now used in diverse environments like Mac and Linux, thanks to Microsoft's open-source culture. This book provides advanced knowledge to help developers fully utilize C#'s capabilities, crafting efficient solutions optimized for various platforms.

I am confident that *Parallel Programming with C# and .NET* will accelerate many developers' learning so they become proficient in parallel computing in record time. Vaskaran's exemplary work establishes a solid foundation for understanding and utilizing advanced language features, paving the way for creating robust software.

Developers will gain clarity on complex concepts and rely on this book as their essential resource for mastering parallel computing challenges. Happy coding!

Naga Santhosh Reddy Vootukuri
Senior Software Engineering Manager
Microsoft, Azure SQL Server
(Cloud + AI division)

Introduction

Modern-day software is highly responsive and scalable. As a result, support for parallel computation is an essential part of it. Undoubtedly this is an advanced concept, and the solutions are not straightforward. Many developers have been burned (and are still burning) by them.

In addition, parallel programming is a vast topic that requires many different considerations. You may also note that many patterns used in the past to deal with asynchronous and parallel programming are not recommended now. This book tries to simplify the concept using modern C# features and libraries that Microsoft recommends. Welcome to your journey through *Parallel Programming with C# and .NET: Fundamentals of the Concurrency and Asynchrony Behind Fast-Paced Applications*.

C# is a powerful programming language, well-accepted in the programming world, that can help you make a wide range of applications. Throughout C# development, supportive features and libraries have been developed to support parallel programming. This is one of the primary reasons that it is continuously growing and always in high demand. So, it is not a surprise that existing and upcoming developers (for example, college students and programming lovers) want to use C# for parallel programming.

Many developers try to learn parallel programming in the shortest possible time frame. Trying to learn something as quickly as possible is laudable, but do you know the problem? We are living in a world that offers you lots of materials, advertisements, and quick fixes to capture your attention. We human beings love to daydream. So, they take advantage of this behavior and start claiming that you can learn everything in a day, a week, or a month. Is this true? Ask yourself and you'll get the answer.

Malcolm Gladwell in his book *Outliers* (Little, Brown, and Company) talked about the 10,000-hour rule. This rule says that the key to achieving world-class expertise in any skill is, to a large extent, a matter of practicing the correct way for a total of about 10,000 hours. So, you can probably see that even though we may claim that we know something very well, we actually probably know very little. Learning is a continuous process, with no end.

Then should we stop learning? Definitely, the answer is no. What should we do then? We can follow an *effective learning* process that teaches you how to learn quickly to serve the need. This is where I like to remind you about the Pareto principle, or 80-20 rule. This rule simply states that 80% of outcomes come from 20% of all causes. This is useful in programming too. When you truly learn the fundamental and most important aspects of parallel programming, that is when you can use it effectively to improve your code. Most importantly, your confidence level will rise, and you won't be afraid to experiment more. This book is for those who acknowledge these facts.

How Is the Book Organized?

This book helps you to understand the core principles of parallel programming using six chapters with plenty of supportive materials. To give you an idea how each chapter is organized, the following list talks about the contents of the book:

- Chapter 1 starts with an overview of the Task Parallel Library (TPL) and discusses tasks. These topics are the foundation for the upcoming chapters. Chapter 2 discusses special scenarios such as handling exceptions and cancellations. Chapter 3 discusses synchronization techniques and concurrent collections. Chapter 4 discusses the `Parallel` class, which helps you experiment with parallel loops to speed up computations. Chapter 5 discusses Parallel LINQ (PLINQ). Chapter 6 discusses simplifying asynchronous programming using the `async` and `await` keywords. Finally, the appendix provides you with some extra materials that are not discussed in the previous chapters.

- I have always enjoyed learning when analyzing case studies, asking questions, and performing exercises. So, throughout this book, you will see interesting program code, "Q&A Sessions," and exercises. By analyzing these Q&As and doing the exercises, you can verify your progress. As mentioned, these are presented to make your learning easier and more enjoyable, but most importantly, they will make you confident as a developer.

- Each question in these "Q&A Sessions" is marked with **Q<chapter#>.<question#>**. For example, Q5.3 means question 3 from Chapter 5. At the end of the chapter, you'll see some exercises. You can use them to evaluate your progress. Each question in these exercises is marked with **E<chapter#>.<question#>**. For example, E6.2 means exercise 2 from Chapter 6.

- You can download all the source code for the book from the publisher's website.

Prerequisite Knowledge

I expect you to be very familiar with C#. In fact, knowing about some of the advanced concepts like delegates and lambda expressions can accelerate your learning. So, I assume that you know how to compile or run a C# application in Visual Studio. This book does not invest time in basic topics, such as how to install Visual Studio on your system, how to write a "Hello World" program in C#, and so forth. In short, the target readers of this book are those who want to make the most of C# by harnessing the power of both object-oriented programming (OOP) and functional programming (FP).

Who This Book Is For

You will get the most from this book if you can answer "yes" to the following questions:

- Are you familiar with .NET, C#, and basic object-oriented concepts such as polymorphism, inheritance, abstraction, and encapsulation?

- Are you familiar with some of the advanced concepts in C# such as delegates, lambda expressions, and generics?

- Do you know how to set up your coding environment?

- Are you interested in knowing how the modern-day constructs of C# can help you in parallel programming?

You will probably struggle with this book if you can answer "yes" to any of the following questions:

- Are you looking for a C# tutorial or reference book?

- Are you not ready to experiment with parallel programming using a programming language other than C#?

- Do you dislike Windows, Visual Studio, and/or .NET or want to learn parallel programming without them?

Useful Software

These are the important tools that I used for this book:

- All the programs were tested with C# 12 and .NET 8. In this context, it is useful to know that nowadays the C# language version is automatically selected based on your project's target framework so that you can always get the highest compatible version by default. In the latest versions, Visual Studio doesn't support the UI to change the value, but you can change it by editing the `.csproj` file.

- As per the new rule, C# 12 is supported only on .NET 8 and newer versions. C# 11 is supported only on .NET 7 and newer versions. C# 10 is supported only on .NET 6 and newer versions. If you are interested in learning more about the C# language versioning, you can refer to `https://docs.microsoft.com/en-us/dotnet/csharp/language-reference/configure-language-version`.

- During the development of this book, software updates kept coming and I also kept updating. When I finished my initial draft, I had the latest edition of Visual Studio Community 2022 (64-bit, version 17.8.5).

- The good news for you is that this community edition is free. If you do not use the Windows operating system, you can use Visual Studio Code, which is also a source-code editor developed by Microsoft that runs on Windows, macOS, and Linux operating systems.

This multiplatform integrated development environment (IDE) is also free. However, I recommend that you check the license and privacy statement as well because this statement may change in the future.

Author's Note: I have tested my code only on Visual Studio. At the time of this writing, Visual Studio 2022 for Mac is scheduled for retirement on August 31, 2024. To learn more about this, you can refer to `https://learn.microsoft.com/en-us/visualstudio/mac/what-happened-to-vs-for-mac?view=vsmac-2022`.

Guidelines for Using This Book

Here are some suggestions so that you can get the most out of this book:

- This book suits you best if you are familiar with some advanced features in C# such as delegates and lambda expressions. If not, please read about those topics before you start reading this book.

- I organized the chapters in a manner that can help you understand parallel programming. For example, if you directly start using the `async` and `await` keywords in your programs, you may miss many other concepts that actually caused them to appear in C# in a later version. This is why I believe you should read the chapters sequentially. Another reason for this suggestion is that some useful topics may have already been discussed in a previous chapter, and I have not repeated those discussions in the later chapters.

- The programs in this book should give you the expected output in the upcoming versions of C#/Visual Studio. Though I believe that these results should not vary in other environments, you know the nature of software: it is naughty. So, I recommend that if you want to see the same output, you should mimic the same environment that I am using.

- You can download and install the Visual Studio IDE from `https://visualstudio.microsoft.com/downloads/`. You are expected to get the screen shown in Figure FM-1.

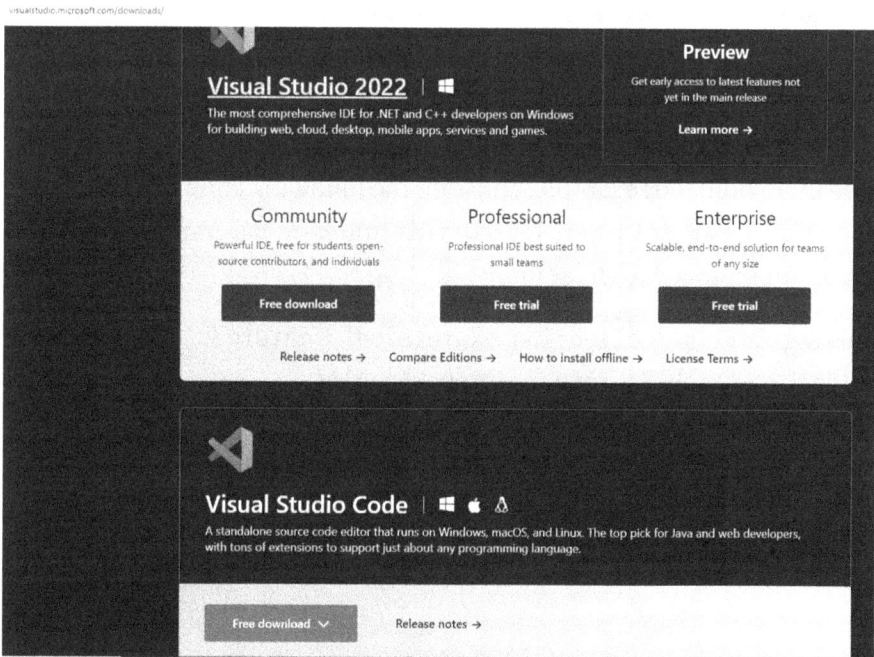

Figure FM-1. *Download screen for Visual Studio 2022 and Visual Studio Code*

> **Note** At the time of this writing, this link works fine, and the information is correct. However, the link and policies may change in the future. The same comment applies to all the mentioned links in this book.

Conventions Used in This Book

In many places, I give you links to Microsoft's documentation. Why? For me, the creators of the products are the authenticated source of information to describe a feature.

In addition, to draw your attention to some places in the code, I have made them bold. For example, consider the following code fragment (taken from Chapter 1 where I discuss continuation tasks and want to draw your attention to a particular line):

```
// Using C#12's "Collection expression" feature
var task3 = Task.Factory.ContinueWhenAll(
  [task1, task2],
  tasks =>
  {
    WriteLine("Arranging dinner.");
  }
);
```

Final Words

You are an intelligent person. You have chosen a topic that can assist you throughout your career. As you learn and review these concepts, I suggest you write your own code; only then will you master this area. There is no shortcut for this.

Do you know the ancient story of Euclid and Ptolemy, ruler of Egypt? Euclid's approach to mathematics was based on logical reasoning and rigorous proofs, and Ptolemy asked Euclid if there was an easier way to learn mathematics. Euclid's reply to the ruler? "There is no royal road to geometry."

Though you are not studying geometry, the essence of this reply applies here. You must study these concepts and code. Do not give up when you face challenges. They are the indicators that you are growing better.

Errata: I have tried my best to ensure the accuracy of the content. However, mistakes can happen. So, I plan to maintain "errata," and if required, I will make some updates/announcements there. You can visit the online link: `https://github.com/Apress/Parallel-Programming-with-CSharp-and-.NET` to receive any important corrections or updates.

An appeal: You probably understand that good-quality work takes many days and months (even years!) to complete. Many authors like me invest most of their time in writing and heavily depend on it. You can encourage and help these authors by preventing piracy. If you come across any illegal copies of our works in any form on the Internet, I would be grateful if you would provide me or the Apress team with the location using the following link: `https://www.apress.com/gp/services/rights-permission/piracy`.

Share your feedback: I believe that this book is designed for you in such a way that you will develop a keen knowledge of parallel programming using C# and .NET. If you value the effort, I request you provide your valuable feedback on the Amazon review page or any other platform you like.

CHAPTER 1

Understanding Tasks

Modern-day life is full of work. Consider those working mothers who need to complete a lot of housework before they go to the office. You may see them performing all these activities asynchronously. For example, they start preparing breakfast, and they come back from the kitchen to prepare the kids for school. Then they go back to the kitchen to check the status of the food only to leave the kitchen to start preparing themselves for the office. You can see that with this approach, when they start a task, they do not wait for that task to complete; instead, they start the next task and then go back to check the status of the previous task. This process continues until all these tasks are finished. Psychologists who vote for doing one task at a time may not like this approach, but at the same time, we cannot ignore that this is how people do things. The programming world tries to mimic real-world scenarios. Throughout this book, we will explore those possibilities using C# and .NET.

Stepping into Parallel Development

You are probably familiar with synchronous method calls where you see that the caller method is blocked until the callee method finishes its execution. To illustrate, consider the following code segment:

```
// Some code before
int temp = RetrieveSomeValue(); // Line 1
int result = Process(temp);// Line 2
// Some code after
```

© Vaskaran Sarcar 2024
V. Sarcar, *Parallel Programming with C# and .NET*,
https://doi.org/10.1007/979-8-8688-0488-5_1

If you exercise this code in a single-threaded environment, you cannot execute line 2 before you get the temp value in line 1. Why? Calling the RetrieveSomeValue method blocks the thread until the method finishes its execution. We are probably all familiar with this type of coding. In fact, we often exercise typical .NET calls that are blocking.

However, it is not a good idea to always rely on the blocking calls. For example, consider the situation when you trigger a method that attempts to download a large file. While the download is in progress, if you cannot do any other work, that is a problem for sure. What is the solution? You guessed it: you will opt for a multithreading environment and opt for asynchronous operations.

You may also notice that computing machines are becoming faster by the day. The role of multicore CPUs is inevitable. So, regardless of the programming languages, developers will want to take advantage of them. This is why parallel programming is becoming an essential technique for developing powerful software that is highly responsive.

Parallel programming is interesting as well as challenging. Undoubtedly it is hard, but in the past it was harder. In those days, developers had the following options:

- Creating and using threads directly

- Using the ThreadPool class

- Using event-based asynchrony

- Using the AsyncResult pattern

- Using the callback methods

These are not the recommended approaches now. I'd like to start the discussion with tasks that make up the foundation of the Task Parallel Library (TPL). Why? Once .NET Framework 4 was released, Microsoft stated the following (see https://learn.microsoft.com/en-us/dotnet/standard/parallel-programming/task-based-asynchronous-programming):

TPL is the preferred API for writing multithreaded, asynchronous, and parallel code in .NET

Note   It is also interesting to know that behind the scenes, tasks are queued to the ThreadPool class, which determines and adjusts the number of threads. The ThreadPool class follows some algorithms to control the load balancing to gain maximum throughput.

Introduction to the Task Parallel Library

Why is the TPL important? As mentioned, handling concurrent programs and adding parallelism to an application are challenging tasks. Undoubtedly, these are advanced concepts of programming. The TPL aims to make them easy for you by providing a set of public types and APIs. You can find them in the following namespaces:

- System.Threading
- System.Threading.Tasks

Author's Note: Developers often refer to the Parallel class with the task parallelism constructs as the TPL. You'll learn about the Parallel class in Chapter 4. However, at this stage, you do not need to worry about them. You'll learn about these constructs one at a time.

How Does the TPL Help?

Microsoft's documentation states the following (see `https://learn.` `microsoft.com/en-us/dotnet/standard/parallel-programming/task-` `parallel-library-tpl`):

> *The purpose of the TPL is to make developers more productive by simplifying the process of adding parallelism and concurrency to applications.*

These are some of the useful scenarios for the TPL:

- Managing a multithreaded environment efficiently
- Scaling the concurrency level
- Providing support for task cancellations
- Managing state
- Partitioning your work

You can easily guess that we are going to cover all these scenarios. For now, it will be sufficient for you to understand that the TPL simplifies the multithreading scenarios and helps you write high-performance code without worrying about the nitty-gritty of threading or other low-level details.

The Concept of Tasks

What are tasks? Microsoft states the following (see `https://learn.` `microsoft.com/en-us/dotnet/standard/parallel-programming/task-` `based-asynchronous-programming`):

> *The Task Parallel Library (TPL) is based on the concept of a task, which represents an asynchronous operation. In some ways, a task resembles a thread or ThreadPool work item but at a higher level of abstraction. The term task parallelism refers to one or more independent tasks running concurrently.*

A *task* is a code block that represents a unit of work. You use tasks to inform the scheduler that this code block can execute on a separate thread while the main thread of execution continues. For example, consider the following code segment:

```
static void PrintNumbers()
{
    WriteLine("Starts executing the task1.");
    // Doing Some work
    Thread.Sleep(5);
    WriteLine("The task1 is finished.");
}
```

This can be a unit of work, and we can execute it on a separate thread. Some common examples of tasks include the following:

- Perform a calculation and display the result.

- Compute a value with/without a supplied input.

- Ask for a network resource.

- Check the health of a website, for example, pinging a website.

Creating and Executing a Task

You can create and execute tasks in different ways. Let me show you a sample code segment that creates and starts executing the task:

```
Task task1=new Task(PrintNumbers);
task1.Start();
```

From C# 9 onward, you can use target-typed new expressions. So, the previous code can be further simplified as follows:

```
Task task1=new (PrintNumbers);
task1.Start();
```

Basically, you create a task by providing a delegate that encapsulates the intended code. This delegate can be expressed as a named delegate, an anonymous method, or a lambda expression. This is why I present in the following task example, I encapsulate the necessary code inside a lambda expression:

```
Task task1 = new(
    () =>
    {
        WriteLine("Starts executing the task1.");
        // Simulating a delay
        Thread.Sleep(1);
        WriteLine("The task1 is finished.");
    }
);
```

Now I can start this task as follows:

```
task1.Start();
```

Note   I have introduced the delay using the Thread.Sleep method. Later, you'll also see me using Task.Delay in a similar context, particularly when I discuss asynchronous programming in more depth in Chapter 6.

The Alternative Approaches

I told you that you can create and execute tasks in different ways. Here I present you with two more approaches.

Approach 2: You can create and execute a task in a single operation using Task.Run method as follows:

```
Task task2 = Task.Run(
    () =>
    {
        WriteLine("Starts executing the task2.");
        // Simulating a delay
        Thread.Sleep(1);
        WriteLine("The task2 is completed.");
    }
);
```

Alternative 3: You can also create and execute tasks in a single operation using TaskFactory.StartNew method. The following code segment demonstrates the usage:

```
Task task3 =Task.Factory.StartNew(
    () =>
    {
        WriteLine("Starts executing the task3.");
        // Simulating a delay
        Thread.Sleep(1);
        WriteLine("The task3 is completed.");
    }
);
```

You can choose the approach that suits you best.

> **Note**   The previous approaches that **explicitly** creates and execute tasks. There are other approaches as well. For example, you can **implicitly** create and execute tasks using **Parallel.Invoke** method. In addition, **TaskCompletionSource<TResult>** class also helps you create specialized tasks that are suitable for particular scenarios. However, let us learn the concepts one at a time. The code examples and exercises in this book use all these methods to create and execute tasks to make you familiar with them.

Demonstration 1

The following program demonstrates the creation and execution of three different tasks on three different threads. Here are two notable characteristics:

- You'll see three different approaches for task creation and execution that I just discussed.

- In addition, this example also includes the following lines to ensure that these tasks finish their job before the console mode application ends.

```
task1.Wait();
task2.Wait();
task3.Wait();
```

Let's see the complete program now.

POINT TO REMEMBER

From .NET 6 onwards, you may notice the presence of implicit global directives for new C# projects. This helps you use the types in these namespaces without specifying the fully qualified names or manually adding a "using directive." You can learn more about this at https://learn.microsoft.com/en-us/dotnet/core/project-sdk/overview#implicit-using-directives.

For the C# projects in this book, I did not change the default settings. As a result, you will not see me mentioning the following namespaces that were available by default:

```
System
System.Collections.Generic
System.IO
System.Linq
System.Net.Http
System.Threading
System.Threading.Tasks
```

```csharp
using static System.Console;

WriteLine("The main thread starts executing.");

// Approach-1
Task task1 = new(
    () =>
    {
        WriteLine("Task-1 starts.");
        for (int i = 100; i < 105; i++)
        {
            Write($"Task-1 prints {i}\t");
            // Simulating a delay
```

9

```
                Thread.Sleep(1);
        }
        WriteLine("Task-1 is completed.");
    }
);
// Starting the task
task1.Start();

// Approach-2
Task task2 = Task.Run(
    () =>
    {
        WriteLine("Task-2 starts.");
        for (int i = 210; i < 215; i++)
        {
            Write($"Task-2 prints {i}\t");
            // Simulating a delay
            Thread.Sleep(1);
        }
        WriteLine("Task-2 is completed.");
    }
);

// Approach-3
Task task3 = Task.Factory.StartNew(
    () =>
    {
        WriteLine("Task-3 starts.");
        for (int i = 320; i < 325; i++)
        {
            Write($"Task-3 prints {i}\t");
            // Simulating a delay
            Thread.Sleep(1);
```

```
        }
        WriteLine("Task-3 is completed.");
    }
);

WriteLine($"The main thread is doing some other work...");
Thread.Sleep(10);

WriteLine($"Main thread is completed.");
task1.Wait();
task2.Wait();
task3.Wait();
```

Output

Here is some sample output (the output may vary on your system).
You can see that there is a nice mixture of output from all the different
threads/tasks.

```
The main thread starts executing.
The main thread is doing some other work...
Task-2 starts.
Task-2 prints 210       Task-1 starts.
Task-2 prints 100       Task-3 starts.
Task-3 prints 320       Task-2 prints 211       Task-2 prints
212       Task-3 prints 321       Task-1 prints 101       Task-3
prints 322       Task-1 prints 102       Task-2 prints
213       Task-2 prints 214       Task-1 prints 103       Task-3
prints 323       Main thread is completed.
Task-3 prints 324       Task-1 prints 104       Task-2 is
completed.
Task-1 is completed.
Task-3 is completed.
```

Q&A Session

Q1.1 What are the benefits of using tasks over threads?

Here are some common benefits:

- The tasks are relatively lightweight. They will help you achieve **fine-grained parallelism**.

- Later you'll see that by using the built-in API for tasks, you can easily exercise useful operations such as waiting, cancellations, continuations, custom scheduling, or robust exception handling. So, when you opt for tasks instead of threads, you'll have **more programmatic control**.

Q1.2 To create and execute tasks, you have shown me the use of the Run, Start, and StartNew methods. How can I decide which one is best for me?

If you see the method definitions in Visual Studio, you will see the following.

The Start method starts System.Threading.Tasks.Task, scheduling it for execution to the specified System.Threading.Tasks.TaskScheduler. The Run method queues the specified work to run on the thread pool and returns a System.Threading.Tasks.Task object that represents that work. This is a lightweight alternative to the StartNew method. It helps you start a task with the default values. This indicates that the Run method uses the default task scheduler, regardless of a task scheduler that is associated with the current thread. This is why Microsoft provides the following suggestions (see https://learn.microsoft.com/en-us/dotnet/standard/parallel-programming/task-based-asynchronous-programming):

- The Run methods are the preferred way to create and start tasks when more control over the creation and scheduling of the task isn't needed.

Microsoft further says that you can use the StartNew() method for the following situations:

- Creation and scheduling don't have to be separated, and you require additional task creation options or the use of a specific scheduler.

- You need to pass an additional state into the task that you can retrieve through its Task.AsyncState property.

POINT TO NOTE

Shortly, you'll learn about child tasks (or nested tasks). You'll learn that by using TaskCreationOptions.AttachedToParent, you can attach a child task to the parent task (if the parent task allows this activity). This option is available in some of the overloads of the StartNew method. Here is such an overload:

```
public Task StartNew(
 Action action,
 CancellationToken cancellationToken,
 TaskCreationOptions creationOptions,
 TaskScheduler scheduler)
  {
    // Some code
  }
And you can use it as follows:
var printHelloTask = Task.Factory.StartNew(
    () =>
    {
      WriteLine("Hello!");
```

```
    },
    CancellationToken.None,
    TaskCreationOptions.AttachedToParent,
    TaskScheduler.Default
);
```

But, in case you use the Run method, a similar option is not available for you.

Passing and Returning Values

In this section, I'll discuss how you can pass values to a task or get back a computed value from a task.

Passing Values into Tasks

Let's start the discussion on passing values into tasks. Consider the following code:

```
static void PrintNumbers(int limit)
{
    for (int i = 0; i < limit; i++)
    {
        Write($"PrintNumbers prints {i}\n");
        // Doing remaining things, if any
        Thread.Sleep(1);
    }
}
```

If you want to execute this method on a separate thread, you need to pass a valid argument for the limit parameter from the calling thread. How can you do that? You can use the following lines of codes:

```
var task1 = new Task(() => PrintNumbers(10));
task1.Start();
```

Alternatively, you can use the following line:

```
var task2=Task.Factory.StartNew(() => PrintNumbers(10));
```

or the following line:

```
var task3 = Task.Run(() => PrintNumbers(10));
```

Notice that in either case, you pass the lambda expression:

```
() => PrintNumbers(10)
```

What does this indicate? This lambda does not take any argument, but I pass the required argument explicitly.

Let's investigate an alternative approach. At the time of this writing, the Task class has the constructors in Figure 1-1.

```
public class Task : IAsyncResult, IDisposable
{
    public Task(Action action);
    public Task(Action action, CancellationToken cancellationToken);
    public Task(Action action, TaskCreationOptions creationOptions);
    public Task(Action<object?> action, object? state);
    public Task(Action action, CancellationToken cancellationToken, TaskCreationOptions creationOptions);
    public Task(Action<object?> action, object? state, CancellationToken cancellationToken);
    public Task(Action<object?> action, object? state, TaskCreationOptions creationOptions);
    public Task(Action<object?> action, object? state, CancellationToken cancellationToken, TaskCreationOpt
```

Figure 1-1. *The overloaded versions of the Task constructors*

Notice the constructor that is highlighted:

```
public Task(Action<object?> action, object? state);
```

In the same way, you can investigate the StartNew method too. At the time of this writing, the StartNew method has 16 overloads in the TaskFactory class, and one of them is as follows:

```
public Task StartNew(Action<object?> action, object? state)
{
  // Remaining code not shown
}
```

The previous two code segments give you the idea that you can pass an object argument to them. So, let me introduce another function called PrintNumbersVersion2 that takes an object parameter and does a similar thing. It is as follows:

```
static void PrintNumbersVersion2(object? state)
{
    int limit = Convert.ToInt32(state);
    for (int i = 0; i < limit; i++)
    {
        Write($"PrintNumbers prints {i}\n");
        // Doing remaining things, if any
        Thread.Sleep(1);
    }
}
```

This time you can write the following:

```
var task3 = new Task(PrintNumbersVersion2,10);
task3.Start();
```

Or the following:

```
var task4 = Task.Factory.StartNew(PrintNumbersVersion2,10);
```

You have now seen five different approaches while passing a state so far. Let's summarize them:

```
// Approach-1:
var task1 = new Task(() => PrintNumbers(10));
task1.Start();

// Approach-2:
var task2=Task.Factory.StartNew(() => PrintNumbers(10));
```

```
// Approach-3:
var task3 = Task.Run(() => PrintNumbers(10));

// Approach-4:
var task4 = new Task(PrintNumbersVersion2,10);
task4.Start();

// Approach-5:
var task5 = Task.Factory.StartNew(PrintNumbersVersion2,10);
```

You can see that in each approach, I passed an int. But, notice that in the last two cases, the target method (PrintNumbersVersion2) expected an object. As a result, these two approaches suffer from the impact of boxing and unboxing. On the contrary, they look cleaner compared to approaches 1, 2, or 3. In the end, it is up to you how you want to organize it.

Note   You can download the project Demo_PassingValues to experience the different approaches that you have seen up until now.

Returning Values from Tasks

When you execute a task, you may need to access the final value. In such cases, you need to use the generic version of the Task class and the Result property. Here is a sample:

```
var task1 = Task<int>.Factory.StartNew(() => 100);
var result = task1.Result;
WriteLine(result);
```

However, Visual Studio will help you recognize that the type argument can be inferred, and as a result, you can further simplify this code as follows:

```
var task1 = Task.Factory.StartNew(() => 100);
var result = task1.Result;
WriteLine(result);
```

Similarly, given the following method:

```
static int Add(int number1, int number2) => number1 + number2;
```

you can write the following:

```
var task2 = Task.Factory.StartNew(() => Add(5, 7));
var result2 = task2.Result;
WriteLine(result2);
```

Let's see a complete program where you deal with some tasks, pass some values into them, and finally retrieve the computed result.

Demonstration 2

In the following demonstration, I create two tasks where the first task calculates the factorial of an integer (5) and the second task adds two integers (25 and 17). Once these tasks are finished, I retrieve the computed results and display them in the console window. Let's see the complete program now.

Note   I could use `Task.Run` in this demonstration as well. However, from Chapter 2 onward, I'll use `Task.Run` heavily in this book. Before that, I am intentionally showing a few demonstrations using `Task.Factory.StartNew` in this chapter. It is because I want you to be familiar with both of them.

```
using static System.Console;

WriteLine("Passing and returning values by executing tasks.");
static string CalculateFactorial(int number)
{
    int temp = Enumerable
                .Range(1, number)
                .Aggregate((x, y) => x * y);
    return $"The factorial of {number} is {temp}";
}

static int Add(int number1, int number2) => number1 + number2;

var task1 = Task.Factory.StartNew(() => CalculateFactorial(5));
var task2 = Task.Factory.StartNew(() => Add(25, 17));

var result1 = task1.Result;
WriteLine(result1);
var result2 = task2.Result;
WriteLine($"The sum of 25 and 17 is {result2}");
WriteLine($"The main thread is completed.");
```

Output

Here is the output:

```
Passing and returning values by executing tasks.
The factorial of 5 is 120
The sum of 25 and 17 is 42
The main thread is completed.
```

Q&A Session

Q1.3 I can see that in the previous demonstration, you did not use the lines `task1.Wait();` and `task2.Wait();`. Was this intentional?

When you want to get a result from a task, you need to wait until the task finishes its execution. It means you need to invoke a blocking operation. Using the `Result` property, I did the same: I blocked the calling thread until those tasks were finished. As a result, I did not need to use the line `task1.Wait()` or `task2.Wait()` separately.

Continuation Tasks

Suppose there are two tasks called Task-A and Task-B. If you want to start executing Task-B only after Task-A, you'd probably like to use callbacks. But the TPL makes it easy. It provides the functionality through a continuation task, which is just an asynchronous task. The idea is the same: once an antecedent task finishes, it invokes the next task that you want to continue. **In our example, Task-A is the antecedent task, and Task-B is the continuation task.**

You understand that continuation is just chaining tasks. This is helpful when you want to pass data (or, execute some logic) from an antecedent to the continuation task. The TPL provides many built-in supports in this context.

- You can invoke a single as well as multiple continuation tasks.

- You can control the continuation. For example, if there are three tasks, called Task-A, Task-B, and Task-C, you can decide that Task-C should continue only after both Task-A and Task-B finish their executions. Alternatively, you may decide that Task-C should not wait for both Task-A and Task-B; instead, it should continue when any of them finish the execution.

- You can pass data as well as exceptions to the continuation task.

- You can also cancel a continuation task if you want. This is often useful during an emergency or when you find a typical bug that keeps occurring during the execution of an application.

Simple Continuation

Assume that a person wants to invite his friends for dinner. At a high level, let's divide the overall activity into three different tasks as follows:

1. Order food.

2. Invite friends.

3. Arrange dinner.

Let's start with a simple continuation scenario where the host decides to do these steps in order, with ordering food at the beginning. Then he invites his friends, and finally, he arranges the dinner. Since the process starts with ordering food, you will see the following task at the beginning:

```
var task1 =
 Task.Factory.StartNew(() => WriteLine("Ordering food."));
```

Since the task of invitation comes after ordering food, this time you'll notice the use of the ContinueWith method. This method creates a continuation that executes when the target task is completed. At the time of this writing, there are 20 overloads of this method. In this example, I use the simplest version of ContinueWith that accepts an Action<Task> as the parameter. This is why you will see the following code:

```
var task2 =
 task1.ContinueWith((t) => WriteLine("Inviting friends."));
```

Similarly, since arranging dinner comes after the second task (task2) finishes, you will see the following code:

```
var task3=
 task2.ContinueWith((t) => WriteLine("Arranging dinner."));
```

Finally, to show you the output messages, I'll wait for the final task (task3) to finish. This is why you will notice the following line at the end of the program:

```
task3.Wait();
```

Demonstration 3

Here is the complete demonstration:

```
using static System.Console;

var task1 =
 Task.Factory.StartNew(() => WriteLine("Ordering food."));
var task2 =
 task1.ContinueWith((t) => WriteLine("Inviting friends."));
var task3=
 task2.ContinueWith((t) => WriteLine("Arranging dinner."));
task3.Wait();
```

Output

Here is the output:

```
Ordering food.
Inviting friends.
Arranging dinner.
```

Specialized Continuation

In the previous demonstration, task3 followed task2, which in turn, followed task1. This flow guaranteed that task3 could not be completed before task1. However, if task2 runs independently and does not follow task1, there is no guarantee that task3 will be completed after task1 (it is because task3 follows task2 but not task1). So, if you want to confirm that task3 should always continue only after the completion of other tasks, you need to have more control over the continuation process. Let's examine this type of specialized continuation with some case studies.

Case Study 1

Let's assume you want to confirm that task3 executes when both task1 and task2 complete their executions. In this case, you'll see me using the ContinueWhenAll method. As usual, there are many overloads of this method. I am about to use the following one that accepts two parameters. This method has the following form:

```
public Task ContinueWhenAll<TAntecedentResult>
(
  Task<TAntecedentResult>[] tasks,
  Action<Task<TAntecedentResult>[]> continuationAction
)
{
  // Method body not shown
}
```

Here, the first parameter accepts an array of antecedent tasks (which means that these need to be finished before you continue), and the next parameter is for the Action delegate that will execute when all tasks in the array have been completed.

This is why you'll see the following line that indicates that task1 and task2 must be completed before you start a continuation task:

```
var task3 = Task.Factory.ContinueWhenAll(
    new [] { task1, task2 },
    tasks =>
    {
        WriteLine("Arranging dinner.");
    }
);
```

Demonstration 4

Let's see the complete program now:

```
var task1 = Task.Factory.StartNew(() => WriteLine("Ordering food."));
var task2 = Task.Factory.StartNew(() => WriteLine("Inviting
 friends."));

var task3 = Task.Factory.ContinueWhenAll(
    new [] { task1, task2 },
    tasks =>
    {
        WriteLine("Arranging dinner.");
    }
);

task3.Wait();
```

Output

Here is some possible output where food is ordered at the beginning:

```
Ordering food.
Inviting friends.
Arranging dinner.
```

Here is some other possible output where the invitation is done at the beginning:

```
Inviting friends.
Ordering food.
Arranging dinner.
```

Analysis

In every case, you can see that dinner has been arranged only after the task of ordering food is completed and the invitations are done.

POINT TO REMEMBER

You may note that the "Collection expressions" feature in C# 12 allows us to rewrite task3 as follows (notice the change in bold for your reference):

```
// Using C#12's "Collection expression" feature
var task3 = Task.Factory.ContinueWhenAll(
    [task1, task2],
    tasks =>
    {
        WriteLine("Arranging dinner.");
    }
);
```

Q&A Session

Q1.4 I can see that you did not use the lambda parameter tasks in the following code:

```
tasks =>
{
    WriteLine("Arranging dinner.");
}
```

This indicates that you could omit the parameter. Is this correct?

Nice observation. I was forced to use this parameter to get support from the built-in construct. If you do not use the parameter in this place, you'll see the following error:

```
CS1593 Delegate 'Action<Task[]>' does not take 0 arguments
```

But this parameter is useful when you want to analyze the individual tasks that were finished before. For example, see the following program:

```
#region For Q&A session
var task1 = Task.Factory.StartNew(() => "Ordering food.");
var task2 = Task.Factory.StartNew(() => "Inviting friends.");
var task3 = Task.Factory.ContinueWhenAll(
    new Task<string>[] { task1, task2 },
    //new [] { task1, task2 }, // Ok too
    // [task1,task2], // C#12 onwards
    tasks =>
    {
        foreach (var task in tasks)
        {
            WriteLine(task.Result);
        }
        WriteLine("Arranging dinner.");
    }
    );
task3.Wait();
#endregion
```

This code can produce the following output:

```
Ordering food.
Inviting friends.
Arranging dinner.
```

Author's Note: The C# compiler can also infer the type Task<string>, as shown in the commented code. From C# 12 onward, you can further simplify the code, which is also shown in the commented line.

Note   You can download the project Demo4_Specialized Continuation from the Apress website to test Demonstration 4 and the Q&A.

Case Study 2

Let's analyze one more case study where you continue a task (say, task3) if any one of the previous tasks (say task1 or task2) completes the execution. In this case, you can use ContinueWhenAny (instead of ContinueWhenAll). For example, you can replace ContinueWhenAll with ContinueWhenAny in the previous code, and you will get any of the following outputs:

Possible Output 1:

```
Ordering food.
Arranging dinner.
```

Possible Output 2:

```
Inviting friends.
Arranging dinner.
```

Possible Output 3:

```
Ordering food.
Inviting friends.
Arranging dinner.
```

Possible Output 4:

```
Inviting friends.
Ordering food.
Arranging dinner.
```

Nowadays computers are very fast. As a result, you may not see the possible case 1 or possible case 2. So, to demonstrate the working mechanism of ContinueWhenAny, let me simulate some delay inside task1 and task2. I assume ordering food can be faster than inviting friends. So, I introduce Thread.Sleep(10) inside task1 and Thread.Sleep(100) inside task2.

Demonstration 5

Let's see the complete program now:

```
using static System.Console;

var task1 = Task.Factory.StartNew(
    () =>
    {
        Thread.Sleep(10);
        WriteLine("Ordering food.");
    }
    );
var task2 = Task.Factory.StartNew(
    () =>
    {
        Thread.Sleep(100);
        WriteLine("Inviting friends.");
    }
    );
```

```
var task3 = Task.Factory.ContinueWhenAny(
    new[] { task1, task2 },
   // [task1, task2], // C#12 onwards
    tasks =>
    {
        WriteLine("Arranging dinner.");
    }
    );

task3.Wait();
```

Output

This time the probability of getting the following output is very high:

```
Ordering food.
Arranging dinner.
```

Author's Note: I hope that you now understand the concept of task continuations. I suggest you exercise a program where you check the result of an antecedent task before you continue a new task. I leave this as an exercise for you.

Nested Tasks

The following code creates two Task instances, called parent and child. Notice that the child task is created inside the parent task.

```
using static System.Console;
var parent = Task.Factory.StartNew(
    () =>
    {
```

```
        WriteLine("The parent task has started.");
        var child = Task.Factory.StartNew(
            () =>
            {
                WriteLine("The child task has started.");
                // Forcing some delay
                Thread.Sleep(1000);
                WriteLine("The child task has finished.");
            });
        WriteLine("The parent task has finished now.");
    }
);
parent.Wait();
```

Here is some possible output once you run this program:

```
The parent task has started.
The parent task has finished now.
The child task has started.
```

Notice that this output does not reflect whether the child task is finished. Why? In the following documentation, Microsoft provides the following information (see https://learn.microsoft.com/en-us/dotnet/standard/ parallel-programming/attached-and-detached-child-tasks):

A child task (or nested task) is a System.Threading.Tasks.Task instance that is created in the user delegate of another task, which is known as the parent task. A child task can be either detached or attached. A detached child task is a task that executes independently of its parent. An attached child task is a nested task that is created with the TaskCreationOptions. AttachedToParent option whose parent does not explicitly or by default prohibit it from being attached. A task may create any number of attached and detached child tasks, limited only by system resources.

Using TaskCreationOptions

The previous information is self-explanatory. You understand that in the previous code, the main thread waits for the parent task to finish, but it does not wait for the child task. To create the parent-child relationship, we need to attach the child task to the parent. Now the question is: how can we create such a relationship? See the following program that demonstrates how to use an overloaded version of the StartNew method to accept the following argument: TaskCreationOptions.AttachedToParent.

Demonstration 6

Here is a sample program with the key changes in bold:

```
using static System.Console;
var parent =
    Task.Factory.StartNew(
    () =>
    {
        WriteLine("The parent task has started.");
        var child = Task.Factory.StartNew(
            () =>
            {
                WriteLine("The child task has started.");
                // Forcing some delay
                Thread.Sleep(1000);
                WriteLine("The child task has finished.");
            },TaskCreationOptions.AttachedToParent);
        WriteLine("The parent task has finished now.");
    }
);
parent.Wait();
```

Output

Run this program and notice the output. You can see that this time the child task completed its execution too:

```
The parent task has started.
The parent task has finished now.
The child task has started.
The child task has finished.
```

Q&A Session

Q1.5 In this demonstration, you have written this:

```
parent.Wait();
```

This means you are not waiting for the child task to finish. As a result, there is no guarantee that the output will reflect whether the child task has finished. Is this a correct understanding?

No. Microsoft has designed the architecture in such a way that if you create a parent-child relationship, waiting on the parent task forces you to wait for the child task to complete.

Q1.6 At the beginning of this section, when the child task was not attached to the parent, I saw that the output did not reflect whether the child task completed its execution. You explained the scenario saying that in that code segment, you waited only for the parent task but not for the child task. So, if I replace the line parent.Wait(); with Task.WaitAll(parent, child);, I can see whether the child task finishes its execution. Am I right?

No. In that code sample, the child task was nested. So, it was not in the scope. So, your proposed code will cause the following compile-time error:

```
CS0103 The name 'child' does not exist in the current context
```

Using TaskContinuationOptions

You have already seen a demonstration where a parent task waits for a child task to finish. Also, I have printed a message in the console saying that the child task has finished. But there is a better way to check whether the task was completed properly. For example, if you want to verify the status of the child task, you can introduce another task that will continue after the child task as follows:

```
var statusChecker = child.ContinueWith(
 task =>
 {
  WriteLine($"Task id {task.Id}'s status is {task.Status}.");
 }, TaskContinuationOptions.AttachedToParent);
```

In this case, I use an overloaded version of the ContinueWith method where the first parameter accepts an Action<Task> and the next parameter indicates the **option for when the continuation is scheduled and how it behaves.** Figure 1-2 shows the various continuation options in Visual Studio.

```
namespace System.Threading.Tasks
{
    public enum TaskContinuationOptions
    {
        None = 0,
        PreferFairness = 1,
        LongRunning = 2,
        AttachedToParent = 4,
        DenyChildAttach = 8,
        HideScheduler = 16,
        LazyCancellation = 32,
        RunContinuationsAsynchronously = 64,
        NotOnRanToCompletion = 65536,
        NotOnFaulted = 131072,
        OnlyOnCanceled = 196608,
        NotOnCanceled = 262144,
        OnlyOnFaulted = 327680,
        OnlyOnRanToCompletion = 393216,
        ExecuteSynchronously = 524288
    }
}
```

Figure 1-2. *The members of TaskContinuationOptions*

If you expand these options, you can see more detail in them. For example, I can expand `AttachedToParent` to get the information shown in Figure 1-3.

```
// Summary:
//     Specifies that the continuation, if it is a child task, is attached to a parent
//     in the task hierarchy. The continuation can be a child task only if its antecedent
//     is also a child task. By default, a child task (that is, an inner task created
//     by an outer task) executes independently of its parent. You can use the System.Threading
//     option so that the parent and child tasks are synchronized. Note that if a parent
//     task is configured with the System.Threading.Tasks.TaskCreationOptions.DenyChildAttach
//     option, the System.Threading.Tasks.TaskCreationOptions.AttachedToParent option
//     in the child task has no effect, and the child task will execute as a detached
//     child task. For more information, see Attached and Detached Child Tasks.
AttachedToParent = 4,
```

Figure 1-3. *The detail of AttachedToParent in TaskContinuationOptions*

Demonstration 7

Let's see an implementation. The following program is a modified version of the previous demonstration where we verify the status of the child task using the Status property. Notice the key changes in bold.

Note   You can see that I have used Task.CurrentId to get the ID of the task that is currently executing. You can use the same for debugging purposes in a parallel environment.

```
using static System.Console;

var parent = Task.Factory.StartNew(
    () =>
    {
        WriteLine($"The parent task[id:{Task.CurrentId}] has
          started.");
        var child = Task.Factory.StartNew(
            () =>
            {
                WriteLine($"The child task[id:
                {Task.CurrentId}] has started.");
                Thread.Sleep(1000);
                WriteLine("The child task has finished.");
            }, TaskCreationOptions.AttachedToParent);

        var statusChecker = child.ContinueWith(
            task =>
            {
                WriteLine($"Task id {task.Id}'s status is
```

```
            {task.Status}.");
        },
        TaskContinuationOptions.AttachedToParent);

    WriteLine("The parent task has finished now.");
    }
);

parent.Wait();
```

Output

Here is some sample output with the important changes in bold:

```
The parent task[id:9] has started.
The parent task has finished now.
The child task[id:10] has started.
The child task has finished.
Task id 10's status is RanToCompletion.
```

Analysis

The life cycle of a Task instance passes through various stages. The status property is used to verify the current state. On investigation, you'll see that TaskStatus is an enum type and has many members. Figure 1-4 the members in Visual Studio.

```
namespace System.Threading.Tasks
{
    public enum TaskStatus
    {
        Created = 0,
        WaitingForActivation = 1,
        WaitingToRun = 2,
        Running = 3,
        WaitingForChildrenToComplete = 4,
        RanToCompletion = 5,
        Canceled = 6,
        Faulted = 7
    }
}
```

Figure 1-4. *Different possible states of a Task instance*

In a concurrent environment, it is possible that by the time you receive the value of a task status, the status has changed. The interesting point is that once a state is reached, it does not go back to a previous state. For example, once a task reaches a final state, it cannot go back to the Created state. Interestingly, there are three possible final states as follows:

- RanToCompletion
- Canceled
- Faulted

As per their names, these states have their usual meaning. For example, RanToCompletion indicates that the task was completed successfully. Similarly, Faulted indicates the task completed due to an unhandled exception. I assume that I need not mention that Canceled indicates that a task was canceled, which can occur due to various reasons such as user intervention, timeouts, or any other application logic. I'll discuss cancellations and exceptions in the next chapter.

Now you understand that in the previous output, the task (which had ID 10) was completed successfully.

Q&A Session

Q1.7 In the previous output, I see the IDs of the parent task and the child task are 9 and 10, respectively. It looks like many other tasks were also running. Is this correct?

Yes, I ran this code in Visual Studio 2022 with the default settings in the debug configuration where the hot reload was enabled. I asked the same question at https://stackoverflow.com/questions/77726578/vs2022-versus-vs2019-how-why-are-the-additional-tasks-being-created and received the answer. If you run the same code in the release configuration (or disable the "hot reload" setting), you can see the following output:

```
The parent task[id:1] has started.
The parent task has finished now.
The child task[id:2] has started.
The child task has finished.
Task id 2's status is RanToCompletion.
```

Author's Note: To choose your preferred configuration, you can follow these steps: **right-click the Solution Explorer, select Configuration Properties and Configuration, and then choose Debug or Release configuration.**

POINT TO REMEMBER

I often execute my programs in debug mode. So, to get the lower task IDs such as 1, 2, 3, and so forth in the output, I often run those programs with the "hot reload" setting disabled.

Q1.8 In your example, the child task was completed successfully. But you told me that the final state of a task can be different. For example, a child task can encounter an exception or someone can cancel it while it is running. How can you handle these scenarios?

You can use separate branches to handle different scenarios. Since I have not discussed task cancellation and exception handling yet, I showed you an example that could be completed easily. Once you learn about handling those special scenarios in Chapter 2, the following program will be easy for you to understand. For now, you can concentrate on the following code that demonstrates two possible cases where a child task can finish successfully if a user does not press C immediately (more specifically, within five seconds once the child task starts). Otherwise, it will be canceled. This is why you'll see the following two branches:

```
var successHandler = child.ContinueWith(
    task =>
    {
        WriteLine($"Task id: {task.Id} finished successfully");
    },
    TaskContinuationOptions.AttachedToParent |
    TaskContinuationOptions.OnlyOnRanToCompletion);

var cancelHandler = child.ContinueWith(
    task =>
    {
        WriteLine($"Task id:{task.Id} was canceled.");
    },
    TaskContinuationOptions.AttachedToParent |
    TaskContinuationOptions.OnlyOnCanceled);
```

Demonstration 8

I have included this program to answer your question only. Since I have not discussed cancellations yet, you may not understand all the lines in this program. For now, you can focus on the two branches where one branch handles the successful completion of a child task and the other branch handles the cancellation of the child task. Still, if you find it difficult to understand, you can come back here after you learn how to cancel a task (discussed in Chapter 2).

Here is the complete program:

```
using static System.Console;

var tokenSource = new CancellationTokenSource();
var token = tokenSource.Token;

var parent = Task.Factory.StartNew(
    () =>
    {
        WriteLine("The parent task has started.");
        var child = Task.Factory.StartNew(
            () =>
            {
                WriteLine($"The child task[id:
                  {Task.CurrentId}] has started.");
                Thread.Sleep(5000);
                token.ThrowIfCancellationRequested();
                WriteLine("The child task has finished.");
            },
            token,
            TaskCreationOptions.AttachedToParent,
            TaskScheduler.Default
        );
```

```
    var successHandler = child.ContinueWith(
        task =>
        {
            WriteLine($"Task id: {task.Id} finished
            successfully.");
        },
        TaskContinuationOptions.AttachedToParent |
        TaskContinuationOptions.OnlyOnRanToCompletion);

    var cancelHandler = child.ContinueWith(
        task =>
        {
            WriteLine($"Task id: {task.Id} was canceled.");
        },
        TaskContinuationOptions.AttachedToParent |
        TaskContinuationOptions.OnlyOnCanceled);

    WriteLine("The parent task has finished now.");
    }
);

WriteLine("Press 'c' immediately to cancel the child task.");
char ch = ReadKey().KeyChar;
if (ch == 'c')
{
    WriteLine("\nTask cancellation requested.");
    tokenSource.Cancel();
}
parent.Wait();
```

Output

Here is the sample output when a user does not cancel the task:

```
Press 'c' immediately to cancel the child task.
The parent task has started.
The parent task has finished now.
The child task[id:2] has started.
The child task has finished.
Task id: 2 finished successfully.
```

Here is another sample output when the user raised a request to cancel the child task:

```
Press 'c' immediately to cancel the child task.
The parent task has started.
The parent task has finished now.
The child task[id:2] has started.
c
Task cancellation requested.
Task id: 2 was canceled.
```

Discussion of Waiting

When you execute a task and analyze the outcome, you must wait for the task to finish. Now the question is: how can you wait? There are different built-in constructs for this, and by using any of them, you can design your application. In this chapter, you have already seen me using some of those constructs.

In this section, I will show you the need to "wait," and I will discuss some useful methods to implement this idea.

Note   Waiting for a task literally blocks the current thread. So, in a parallel execution environment, you must be careful before implementing the idea.

Why Do We Wait?

First, let's understand why you need a waiting mechanism. The following demonstration will give you an idea.

Demonstration 9

Here is a program that runs two simple tasks. Let's execute the following program and analyze some of the possible outputs:

```
using static System.Console;

WriteLine("The main thread starts.");

var task1 = Task.Run(
    () =>
    {
        WriteLine("Task1 starts.");
        WriteLine("Task1 ends.");
    }
);

var task2 = Task.Run(
    () =>
    {
        WriteLine("Task2 starts.");
```

```
        WriteLine("Task2 ends.");
    }
);
WriteLine("The end of main.");
```

Output

Here are two possible outputs.

Output 1:

```
The main thread starts.
The end of main.
```

Output 2:

```
The main thread starts.
The end of main.
Task1 starts.
```

Analysis

These outputs reflect the following characteristics:

- The main thread ends before task1 and task2 finish their executions.

- None of these outputs reflects whether task1 or task2 completes their job.

How Do We Wait?

To see the final status of these tasks, you may need to wait. How can you do that? There are different approaches. Let me show you some of them in the following section.

Using Sleep

One of the simplest solutions is to block the main thread until the other tasks are finished. Here is a sample where I block the main thread for 1,000 milliseconds:

```
// The previous code is the same
Thread.Sleep(1000);
WriteLine("The end of main.");
```

This one line of additional code increases the probability of seeing some output that reflects that task1 and task2 complete their executions before the control leaves the main thread. Here is some possible output:

```
The main method starts.
Task2 starts.
Task1 starts.
Task1 ends.
Task2 ends.
The end of main.
```

The advantage of using this approach is obvious. We can see that when the main thread sleeps, the other tasks could execute their jobs. This indicates that during sleep, the scheduler can schedule other tasks.

On the contrary, this approach has an obvious problem: you may block the thread unnecessarily for some additional time. For example, I can see the same output on my computer if I block the main thread for 500 milliseconds or less. **However, the problem is that since we cannot predict the exact time for these tasks to be completed, I need to block it for a reasonable amount of time.** Still, if any of these tasks take more time to complete due to some other factors, you may not see any of the task's completion messages in the final output. This is a problem for sure!

We do not want unnecessary waiting. At the same time, we do not want to miss any key information. From this point of view, this is an inefficient approach. In fact, the situation can be worse if you work on an application that tries to block the UI. This is why relying on the Sleep method may not always be a good idea.

Using Delay

If you replace the Thread.Sleep methods with Task.Delay methods, you may see similar output. For example, in the previous code, let me replace the statement Thread.Sleep(1000); with Task.Delay(1000); and run the program again. Again, my computer shows different possible outputs, and one of them is as follows:

```
The main thread starts.
Task1 starts.
Task1 ends.
The end of main.
Task2 starts.
Task2 ends.
```

This output reflects that task1 and task2 completed their jobs. However, notice that the calling thread was not blocked this time. So, you see the line The end of main. before the line Task2 starts.

In fact, Visual Studio says that when you use the Delay method, the call is not awaited and the calling thread can continue before the call is completed (see the message shown in Figure 1-5).

```
 5        var task1 = Task.Run(
 6            () =>
 7            {
 8                WriteLine("Task1 starts.");
 9                // Simulating some delay
10                //Thread.Sleep(1000);
11                Task.Delay(1000);
12                WriteLine("Task1 ends.");
13            }
14        );
15
```

9 %   ⊗ 0   ▲ 1   ↑   ↓   ✦ ▾

rror List

Entire Solution   ▾   ⊗ 0 Errors   ▲ 2 Warnings   ⓘ 0 of 3 Messages

Code   Description

▷ ▲ CS4014   Because this call is not awaited, execution of the current method
             continues before the call is completed. Consider applying the 'await'
             operator to the result of the call.

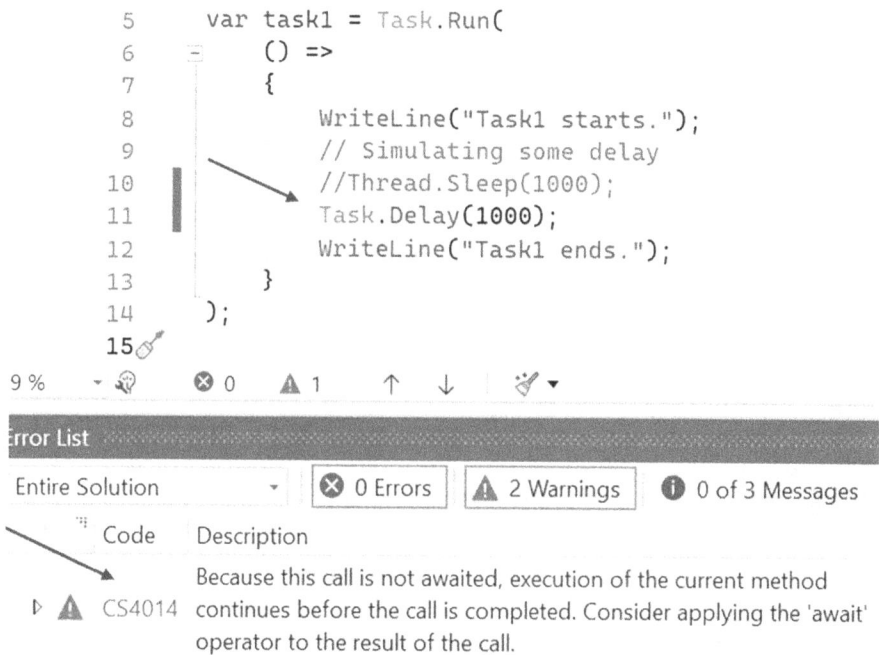

Figure 1-5. *Visual Studio confirms that the call is not awaited*

This gives you a clue that you should use Sleep for the synchronous pauses whereas you should prefer the Delay method for nonblocking delays. In this book, you'll also see me using the Delay method in many demonstrations (particularly, in Chapter 6 when I'll use the async and await keywords in my programs). The reason is that Task.Delay is more suitable in asynchronous programming. While answering the question Q1.12 in the Q&A Session, I'll compare the Sleep method and the Delay method in more detail.

Note   Using the async and await keywords simplifies asynchronous programming. They are explained in Chapter 6. You do not need to worry about them now.

Using ReadKey()

Sometimes you will see the presence of ReadKey(), Read(), or ReadLine() in a program. The basic idea of using these methods is to block control of execution until the user provides the required input. For example, you can wait for task1 and task2 to finish, and then you can press a key from the keyboard to get the final output. Here is some sample code:

```
// The previous code is the same
ReadKey();
WriteLine("The end of main");
```

Using Wait

Earlier you saw that by using the Result property, I blocked the calling thread until the specified tasks were finished. This means I was waiting for those tasks to be completed. It is not necessary in every scenario to analyze the outcome of task execution. In fact, a task may not return a value at all. So, let's search for alternatives for the waiting techniques.

First, let me remind you about the Wait method that you have seen already. When invoking the Wait method on a Task instance, you can wait for it to complete. Here is a sample where I call Wait on task1 and task2 separately:

```
// The previous code is the same
task1.Wait();
task2.Wait();
WriteLine("The end of main.");
```

Here is some sample output after this change:

```
The main thread starts.
Task2 starts.
Task2 ends.
```

```
Task1 starts.
Task1 ends.
The end of main.
```

Using WaitAll

Instead of waiting for the individual tasks to be completed, you can wait for a group of tasks. In such cases, you use the WaitAll method and provide the task objects for which you want to wait as parameters. Here is a sample:

```
// The previous code is the same
Task.WaitAll(task1, task2);
WriteLine("The end of main.");
```

This change can also produce an output that reflects both tasks finished their execution.

Note   You can download the project Demo9_DiscussionOnWaiting from the Apress website to run and validate all these program segments on your computer.

Using WaitAny

Suppose there are multiple tasks, but you'd like to wait for any of them to complete. In such cases, you use the WaitAny method as follows:

```
// The previous code is the same
Task.WaitAny(task1, task2);
WriteLine("The end of main.");
```

To show you the effect of this change, let me introduce a small delay in task2 as follows:

```
var task2 = Task.Run(
    () =>
    {
        WriteLine("Task2 starts.");
        // A small delay is introduced here
        Thread.Sleep(10);
        WriteLine("Task2 ends.");
    }
);
```

Run the program now. From these outputs, you will see that the main thread completes when at least one of these tasks finishes its execution. Here I have included some samples that show by the time the main thread finished, task1 completed its execution, but task2 could not do that.

Output-1:

```
The main thread starts.
Task1 starts.
Task1 ends.
The end of main.
Task2 starts.
```

Output-2:

```
The main thread starts.
Task1 starts.
Task1 ends.
The end of main.
```

POINTS TO NOTE

Remember the following points:

- You may see different output on your computer.

- These methods have various overloads. For example, at the time of this writing, the Wait method has six different overloads. Using these overloaded versions, you can provide a maximum duration to wait, a CancellationToken instance, or both of them to monitor while waiting.

Using WhenAny

Notice the previous outputs once again. You can see that the line The end of main. came after task1 finished its execution. If you execute the program repeatedly, you'll never see that the mentioned line appears before any of these tasks finish the execution. That is because, **in the case of** WaitAny, **the calling thread is blocked until any of those tasks finishes the execution.** Interestingly, there is another method, called WhenAny, that does not block the calling thread.

Consider the following code where I replace WaitAny with WhenAny:

```
// The previous code is the same
Task.WhenAny(task1, task2);
WriteLine("The end of main.");
```

Here is some sample output where you can see that the main thread completes before task1 and task2:

```
The main thread starts.
Task1 starts.
The end of main.
Task1 ends.
Task2 starts.
```

To make the concept clearer, let me apply some modifications to the existing program as follows:

```
// The previous code is the same
var task=Task.WhenAny(task1, task2);
WriteLine("The end of main.");
WriteLine($"Task1's ID: {task1.Id} Task2's ID: {task2.Id}");
WriteLine($"Completed task id: {task.Result.Id}");
```

Run this modified program now. The following output confirms that the use of WhenAny does not block the calling thread. This is why I include a possible output to show you that the line The end of main. appeared before task1 or task2 finished their executions. Here is some sample output:

```
The main thread starts.
The end of main.
Task1's ID: 1 Task2's ID: 2
Task1 starts.
Task1 ends.
Completed task ID: 1
Task2 starts.
```

Note   You can download the project Demo10_ DiscussingWaitAnyAndWhenAny from the Apress website to run and validate the new program segments on your computer.

Waiting for Cancellation

There will be situations when you need to be prepared for possible cancellations of tasks. In those cases, you need to have a cancellation token. Since the topic is important as well as big, I will discuss it in the next chapter.

Q&A Session

Q1.9 In some articles, I see the usage of `Thread.SpinWait` instead of `Thread.Sleep`. How do they differ?

The `SpinWait` method is useful for implementing locks but not for ordinary applications. When you use spin waiting, the scheduler does not pass the control to some other task, which means it avoids context switching. The documentation at `https://learn.microsoft.com/en-us/dotnet/api/system.threading.thread.spinwait?view=net-7.0` states the following:

> *In the rare case where it is advantageous to avoid a context switch, such as when you know that a state change is imminent, make a call to the SpinWait method in your loop. The code SpinWait executes is designed to prevent problems that can occur on computers with multiple processors. For example, on computers with multiple Intel processors employing Hyper-Threading technology, SpinWait prevents processor starvation in certain situations.*

Note   .NET Framework classes such as `Monitor` and `ReaderWriterLock` internally use the `SpinWait` method. Still, instead of using this method directly, Microsoft recommends that you use the built-in synchronization classes to serve your purpose. (I discuss different synchronization techniques in Chapter 3 and Appendix A.) I also recommend not using this method for one typical reason: `SpinWait` accepts an integer argument that represents the number of iterations for the CPU loop to be performed. As a result, the waiting time depends on the processor's speed.

It is useful to note that you can use the SpinUntil method as well. At the time of this writing, there are three overloaded versions of this method.

```
SpinUntil(Func<Boolean>)
SpinUntil(Func<Boolean>, Int32)
SpinUntil(Func<Boolean>, TimeSpan)
```

Let me show you how to use the simplest version that spins until the specified condition is fulfilled. Here is an example where I wait until task1 completes its execution properly:

```
// Previous code is the same.
SpinWait.SpinUntil(() => task1.Status == TaskStatus.RanToCompletion);
WriteLine("The end of main.");
```

Here is some possible output after this change is made to this program:

```
The main thread starts.
Task2 starts.
Task1 starts.
Task1 ends.
The end of main.
```

Note that this time the output shows that task1 completes the execution, but it does not reflect whether task2 completes the execution. So, the key takeaway is that there are different ways of waiting. You can use the one that is more convenient for you.

POINT TO NOTE

I am mentioning only those methods that will be sufficient for you to understand the rest of this book. As said before, these methods have various overloaded versions as well.

Q1.10 "These methods have various overloaded versions as well." How can I know about them?

You can follow any of the traditional approaches. For example, you can use Visual Studio's intelligence or read Microsoft's documentation to learn about them. For example, Figure 1-6 shows that the Sleep method has two overloaded versions and the first one accepts an int parameter.

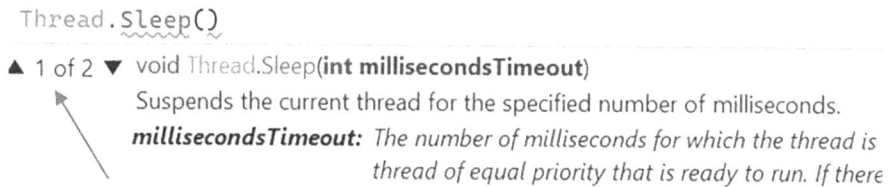

Thread.Sleep()

▲ 1 of 2 ▼   void Thread.Sleep(**int millisecondsTimeout**)
Suspends the current thread for the specified number of milliseconds.
millisecondsTimeout: *The number of milliseconds for which the thread is*
thread of equal priority that is ready to run. If there

Figure 1-6. *The Sleep method has two overloaded versions*

Q1.11 Can you give me an example where you'd use WhenAny or WaitAny. Between these two methods, which one would you like to use?

Suppose you are working with two different tasks and each task works with different URLs. Let's further assume that each URL can help you test the current health of a website. You understand that any of these links will be sufficient to check the current status of a website. So, your program can execute the tasks and continue as soon as you get the data. In such a case, you can use WhenAny or WaitAny.

Unless there are sufficient reasons, I'll opt for WhenAny in such a case, because it is nonblocking. This is because if a task waits to get a notification from a set of tasks where none can be completed due to some unpredictable circumstances, the use of WaitAny can cause a deadlock as well.

Q1.12 Between Thread.Sleep and Task.Delay, which one do you prefer?

The Sleep method suspends the calling thread, which may not be ideal in every scenario. The problem was already discussed, so I won't discuss it here. However, for a simple demonstration, this method is handy; so, I used it in other demonstrations as well. Once you complete this book, I assume that you'll have a fair idea of how asynchronous programming works in a parallel execution environment. In most cases, you'll want to use the Delay method. The obvious reason for this is that invoking the Delay method does not cause the calling thread to be blocked. This is why the use of the Delay method can help you build a more responsive UI.

Once you're familiar with async/await programming, you'll learn that you can write something like the following: await Task.Delay(1000); however, you cannot write something like await Task.Sleep(10);.

While using the Delay method, you can also assign it to a task and await at a later point in time as follows:

```
Task task= Task.Delay(1000);
// Do something here
await task;
```

You should also note that the Delay method has various overloads, and many of them accept CancellationToken as a parameter (this is discussed in the next chapter). Using this parameter, you can avoid aborting the thread and terminate it nicely.

Exercises

Check your understanding by attempting the following exercises.

POINT TO REMEMBER

As mentioned, for all code examples, the "Implicit Global Usings" was enabled in Visual Studio. This is why you won't see me mentioning the following namespaces that are available by default:

```
System
System.Collections.Generic
System.IO
System.Linq
System.Net.Http
System.Threading
System.Threading.Tasks
```

The same comment applies to all the exercises in this book.

E1.1 Can you predict the output of the following program?

```
using static System.Console;

Task printHelloTask = new (
    () => WriteLine("Hello!")
);
WriteLine("End.");
```

E1.2 Can you predict the output of the following program?

```
using static System.Console;

Task printHelloTask = new(
    () => WriteLine("Hello!")
);
printHelloTask.Start();
WriteLine("End.");
```

E1.3 Can you predict the output of the following program?

```
using static System.Console;
var saySomething = (string msg = "Hello") => msg;

var printHelloTask = Task.Factory.StartNew(
    () =>
    {
        Thread.Sleep(1000);
        WriteLine(saySomething());
    }
);
printHelloTask.Wait();
WriteLine("End.");
```

E1.4 Can you predict the output of the following program?

```
using static System.Console;

var calculate = Task.Run(() => GetTotal(5));
WriteLine(calculate.Result);
WriteLine("End.");

static int GetTotal(int count)
{
    int total = 0;
```

```
    for (int i = 1; i <= count; i++)
    {
        total += i*2;
    }
    return total;
}
```

E1.5 Starting with C# 12, we can define a primary constructor as a part of the class declaration. Here is an example:

```
class Employee( string name,int id)
{
    private string _name=name;
    private int _id = id;
    public override string ToString()
    {
        return $"Name:{_name} Id:{_id}";
    }
}
```

You can create an instance of the Employee class as follows:

```
Employee emp = new("Bob", 1);
```

Now assume that there are two tasks where the first task will create an Employee instance. The second task will follow the first task and perform the following steps: first, it will verify whether the first task completes the process successfully. In addition, it will print the current date and time. Can you write a program fulfilling the criteria? (You do not need to handle exceptions or cancellations for this exercise.)

E1.6 Consider two websites such as www.google.com and www.yahoo.com. You may know that a hostname can be associated with multiple IP addresses. Can you write a program that involves multiple tasks where one task prints the IP addresses associated with the hostnames and another task pings these websites and displays the result? (Assume that your computer is already connected to the Internet. In addition, you do not need to handle exceptions or cancellations for this exercise.)

E1.7 Can you predict the output of the following program?

```
using static System.Console;

var helloTask = Task.Run(() =>
{
    WriteLine("Hello reader!");
    var aboutTask = Task.Factory.StartNew(() =>
    {
        Task.Delay(1000);
        WriteLine("How are you?");
    }, TaskCreationOptions.AttachedToParent);
});

helloTask.Wait();
```

E1.8 State **True/False:**

    i)   There are three possible final states of a task: RanToCompletion, Canceled, and Faulted.

    ii)   When you create a child task inside a parent task, it is detached by default.

    iii)   A parent task always waits for its child task to finish.

    iv)   Waiting for a task completion blocks the calling thread.

    v)   The WaitAny method blocks the calling thread, but the WhenAny method does not block the calling thread.

Summary

This chapter gave you a quick overview of task programming. The discussion started by introducing you to the TPL and described various aspects of task creation and execution. It also described different approaches to implementing a waiting mechanism for task completion.

In brief, it answered the following questions:

- What is a task, and how can you create a task?

- How can you pass values into tasks and return a value from a task?

- How can you implement simple task continuation as well as a conditional continuation mechanism?

- How can you create branches to employ a conditional continuation mechanism?

- How can you check the status of the current task?

- How can you employ a waiting mechanism to ensure a task finishes its execution before the application ends?

Solutions to Exercises

Here is a sample solution set for the exercises in this chapter.

E1.1

The program will output the following:

End.

Notice that you have created the task but you have not started this task.

E1.2

The program can show more than one possible output. You may think that it will print the following:

```
Hello!
End.
```

But, notice that you did not wait for the task to finish its execution. So, you may see End. before you see Hello.

```
End.
Hello!
```

It is also possible that in the output, you see End. only if the task takes some extra time to start. To examine this, you can run the following code in which by introducing some delay inside the task, I increase the probability of finishing the main thread early:

```
using static System.Console;

Task printHelloTask = new(
    () =>
    {
        Thread.Sleep(1000);
        WriteLine("Hello!");

    }
);
printHelloTask.Start();
WriteLine("End.");
```

E1.3

C# 12 allows you to define default values for parameters on lambda expressions. So, the code will compile without any issues. As a result, this time the output is also predictable because the main thread must wait for the task to finish. So, you will see the following output:

```
Hello!
End.
```

E1.4

You will see the following output:

```
30
End.
[Clue: 1*2+2*2+3*2+4*2+5*2=30]
```

E1.5

Here is a sample program based on the features that you learned in this chapter:

```
using static System.Console;

var createEmp = Task.Factory.StartNew(
    () =>
        {
            Employee emp = new("Bob", 1);
            WriteLine($"Created an employee with {emp}");
        }
    )
```

```
    .ContinueWith(
      task =>
      {
          WriteLine($"Was the previous task completed?
           {task.IsCompletedSuccessfully}");
          WriteLine($"Current time:{DateTime.Now}");
      }
    );
createEmp.Wait();

class Employee( string name,int id)
{
    private string _name=name;
    private int _id = id;
    public override string ToString()
    {
        return $"Name: {_name} Id: {_id}";
    }
}
```

Here is some sample output:

```
Created an employee with Name: Bob Id: 1
Was the previous task completed? True
Current time:12/24/2023 12:06:25 PM
```

E1.6

Here is a sample program that fulfills the criteria:

```
using System.Net;
using System.Net.NetworkInformation;
using static System.Console;

List<string> websites = ["www.google.com", "www.yahoo.com"];
```

```
// Same as:
// List<string> websites = new() {
// "www.google.com", "www.yahoo.com" };

var task1= Task.Run(()=>PrintHostNameAndIPs(websites));
var task2 = Task.Run(() => PingAll(websites));

Task.WaitAll(task1, task2);

void PrintHostNameAndIPs(List<string> urls)
{
    urls.ForEach(url =>
    {
        IPAddress[] ips = Dns.GetHostAddresses(url);
        WriteLine($"{url}'s IP addresses are:");
        ips.ToList().ForEach(WriteLine);
        WriteLine("--------------");

    });
}

void PingAll(List<string> urls)
{
    urls
    .Select(PingSite)
    .ToList()
    .ForEach(url => WriteLine($"{url.Address} ping
     status: {url.Status} "));
}

static PingReply PingSite(string url)
{
    return new Ping().Send(url);
}
```

Here is some sample output:

```
www.google.com's IP addresses are:
2404:6800:4009:826::2004
142.250.183.196
--------------
www.yahoo.com's IP addresses are:
2406:8600:f040:1fa::3000
2406:8600:f040:1fa::2000
27.123.43.204
27.123.43.205
--------------
2404:6800:4009:826::2004 ping status: Success
2406:8600:f040:1fa::3000 ping status: Success
```

POINT TO REMEMBER

I have used the "Collection expressions" feature that was introduced in C# 12. This feature allows you to create a list as follows:

```
List<string> websites = ["www.google.com", "www.yahoo.com"];
```

This line of code is equivalent to the following:

```
List<string> websites = new()
{
  "www.google.com",
  "www.yahoo.com"
};
```

Additional Note

The shown program looks more functional and less object-oriented. If you are biased toward OOP, you can consider the following alternative solution with the key changes in bold:

```
using System.Net;
using System.Net.NetworkInformation;
using static System.Console;

List<string> websites = ["www.google.com", "www.yahoo.com"];

var task1 = Task.Run(() => PrintHostNameAndIPsOOP(websites));
var task2 = Task.Run(() => PingAllOOP(websites));

Task.WaitAll(task1, task2);

void PrintHostNameAndIPsOOP(List<string> urls)
{
    foreach (string url in urls)
    {
        IPAddress[] ips = Dns.GetHostAddresses(url);
        WriteLine($"{url}'s IP addresses are:");
        foreach (IPAddress ip in ips)
        {
            WriteLine(ip);
        }
        WriteLine("-------------");
    }
}

void PingAllOOP(List<string> urls)
{

    List<PingReply> pingReplies = new();
```

```
    foreach (string url in urls)
    {
        pingReplies.Add(PingSite(url));
    }
    foreach (PingReply reply in pingReplies)
    {
        WriteLine($"{reply.Address} ping status:
        {reply.Status}");
    }
}
static PingReply PingSite(string url)
{
    return new Ping().Send(url);
}
```

E1.7

On my computer, this program shows the following output:

```
Hello reader!
```

This is because the application terminated before aboutTask finishes its execution. Using the ReadKey or ReadLine() method you can hold the control until you see the following output:

```
Hello reader!
How are you?
```

You may wonder about this. Notice that I have used the Run method, but not the StartNew method. Implement the following change (shown in bold):

```
var helloTask = Task.Factory.StartNew(() =>
{
    WriteLine("Hello reader!");
    var aboutTask = Task.Factory.StartNew(() =>
    {
        Task.Delay(1000);
        WriteLine("How are you?");
    }, TaskCreationOptions.AttachedToParent);
});
helloTask.Wait();
```

You can expect to see the following output:

```
Hello reader!
How are you?
```

In this context, I also suggest you see the online documentation that states the following (see https://learn.microsoft.com/en-us/dotnet/api/system.threading.tasks.taskfactory.startnew?view=net-8.0):

> *Starting with the .NET Framework 4.5, you can use the Task. Run(Action) method as a quick way to call StartNew(Action) with default parameters. Note, however, that there is a difference in behavior between the two methods regarding : Task.Run(Action) by default does not allow child tasks started with the TaskCreationOptions.AttachedToParent option to attach to the current Task instance, whereas StartNew(Action) does.*

E1.8

The answers are as follows:

i) There are three possible final states of a task-
    RanToCompletion, Canceled, and Faulted. [**True**]

ii) When you create a child task inside a parent task, it
     is detached by default.[**True**]

iii) A parent task always waits for its child task to
      finish. [**False**]

      [**Clue**: In the case of an attached child task, the
      statement is true; but for a detached child task, it
      is false.]

iv) Waiting for a task completion blocks the calling
     thread. [**True**]

v) The WaitAny method blocks the calling thread,
    but the WhenAny method does not block the calling
    thread. [**True**]

CHAPTER 2

Handling Special Scenarios

In Chapter 1, you learned about various aspects of tasks including continuation tasks and nested tasks. In this chapter, I'll continue the discussion of task programming, but this time the focus will be handling special scenarios such as exceptions and cancellations. Let's get started.

Introduction to Exceptions

In a multithreaded environment, handling exceptions can be tricky. The reason is obvious: different tasks may throw different exceptions. Since you are reading about the advanced concepts of programming, I assume you are familiar with the fundamentals of exceptions and how to handle them in a C# project, so I will not discuss the basics in this book. Instead, I'll focus on possible exceptional scenarios when you program with tasks in a multithreaded environment.

Understanding the Challenge

Let's start with a simple class, called Product. This class has a method, called CheckUser, to identify whether a user is a valid user. For simplicity,

© Vaskaran Sarcar 2024
V. Sarcar, *Parallel Programming with C# and .NET*,
https://doi.org/10.1007/979-8-8688-0488-5_2

let's assume the following characteristic: **Each valid user ID starts with u. Otherwise, the CheckUser method throws an instance of UnauthorizedAccessException.**

Demonstration 1

Now let me hack the system to create this exception and handle it inside a try-catch block. Here is a sample demonstration:

```
using static System.Console;

WriteLine("Exception handling demo.");

try
{
    var validateUser = Product.CheckUser("abc");
    WriteLine(validateUser);
}

catch (Exception e)
{
    WriteLine($"Caught error: {e.Message}");
}

class Product
{
    /// <summary>
    /// This method throws an exception when the user ID does
    /// not start with 'u'
    /// </summary>
    /// <param name="userId"> The user ID</param>
    /// <returns>Confirming the valid user</returns>
    /// <exception cref="UnauthorizedAccessException"> The
    /// exception is thrown when the <paramref
    /// name="userId" is an invalid ID </exception>
```

```
public static string CheckUser(string userId)
{
    string msg;
    if (userId.StartsWith("u"))
    {
        msg = $"{userId} is a valid user";
    }
    else
    {
        throw new UnauthorizedAccessException($"Id:
          {userId} is invalid.");

    }
    return msg;
}
}
```

Output

There is no surprise that upon executing this program, you'll see the following output:

```
Exception handling demo.
Caught error: Id: abc is invalid.
```

You are probably familiar with this type of program and there is nothing new up to this point.

POINT TO NOTE

Visual Studio can still display this exception if you want. For example, in Visual Studio's Exception Settings (Ctrl+Alt+E), if you want your program to break when a particular exception is thrown, you can enable the checkbox for that particular exception. For example, I have the settings shown in Figure 2-1 for the common language runtime exceptions.

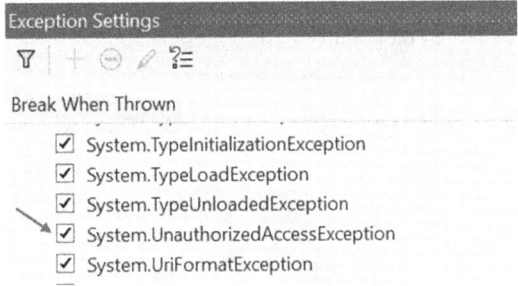

Figure 2-1. *Exception Settings for Common Language Runtime exceptions in Visual Studio*

While executing the program, you will see the exception shown in Figure 2-2.

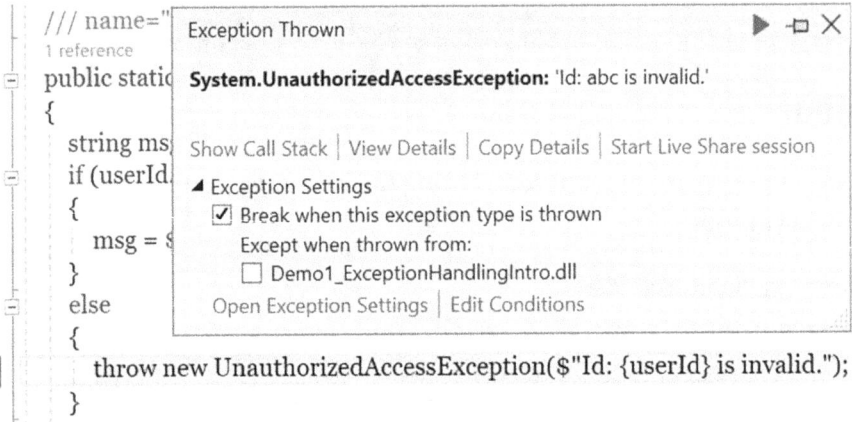

Figure 2-2. *Visual Studio displays the UnauthorizedAccessException while the program was running*

Note that the program has not crashed yet; you can click the Continue button to resume the execution.

Demonstration 2

Now change the program a little bit and analyze the situation again. This time, let's invoke the CheckUser method through a task that is created inside the main thread, as shown in the following program:

```
using static System.Console;

WriteLine("Exception handling demo.");

try
{
  var validateUser = Task.Run(() => Product.CheckUser("abc"));
  WriteLine("End");
}

catch (Exception e)
{
    WriteLine($"Caught error: {e.Message}");
}

// The Product class is the same. It is not shown to avoid
// repetition.
```

Output

Upon executing this program, you may see the following output:

```
Exception handling demo.
End
```

You can see that this time the output does not show anything about the exception. **Why does this happen?** Notice that this time the main thread did not encounter the exception; it was encountered by the task called validateUser that was created by this main thread. However, an unobserved exception can cause problems at a later stage. So, you may be interested in watching all the exceptions and decide to handle them as per the priority. **This is an important note for you to remember.**

POINT TO NOTE

I'd like to remind you that many developers like to use `Task.Run` instead of `Task.Factory.StartNew`. I also belong to that category. So, from this time onward, I'll be using `Task.Run` much more compared to `Task.Factory.StartNew`. In this context, you may want to revisit Q&A 1.2 in Chapter 1. In the end, it's up to you, so choose the approach that you prefer. Once you finish Chapter 6 of this book, you can read an online post comparing these approaches at `https://devblogs.microsoft.com/pfxteam/task-run-vs-task-factory-startnew/`. Though the article was written a while ago, but it is still useful.

Retrieving the Error Details

How can I show you information about the exception? An obvious way is to handle the exception inside the task itself. For example, I can replace the following line:

```
var validateUser = Task.Run(() => Product.CheckUser("abc"));
```

with something like the following:

```
var validateUser = Task.Run(
    () =>
    {
        string msg = string.Empty;
        try { msg = Product.CheckUser("abc"); }
        catch (Exception e)
        {
            WriteLine($"Caught error inside the task:
```

```
            {e.Message}");
        }
        return msg;
    });
```

However, you understand that inside the main thread, we can launch many tasks, and if we code like this, there will be a lot of code duplication.

So, let's search for alternative approaches. Interestingly, in the main thread, if you use WriteLine(validateUser.Result); or validateUser.Wait(); inside a try block, you can observe the exceptions. Let's see the next program.

Demonstration 3

Here is a sample demonstration where I use the statement validateUser.Wait(); inside the try block as follows:

```
// Previous code as it is

try
{
  //Product.CheckUser("abc");
  var validateUser = Task.Run(() => Product.CheckUser("abc"));
  validateUser.Wait();
  WriteLine("End");
}
// There is no change in the remaining code as well
```

Output

Once you execute the program again, you will see the following output:

```
Exception handling demo.
Caught error: One or more errors occurred. ('abc' is an
 invalid user.)
```

The output depicts that abc is an invalid user and it was the key information that I wanted to display. If you put a breakpoint inside the catch block as shown in Figure 2-3 and debug this code, you can see the values shown.

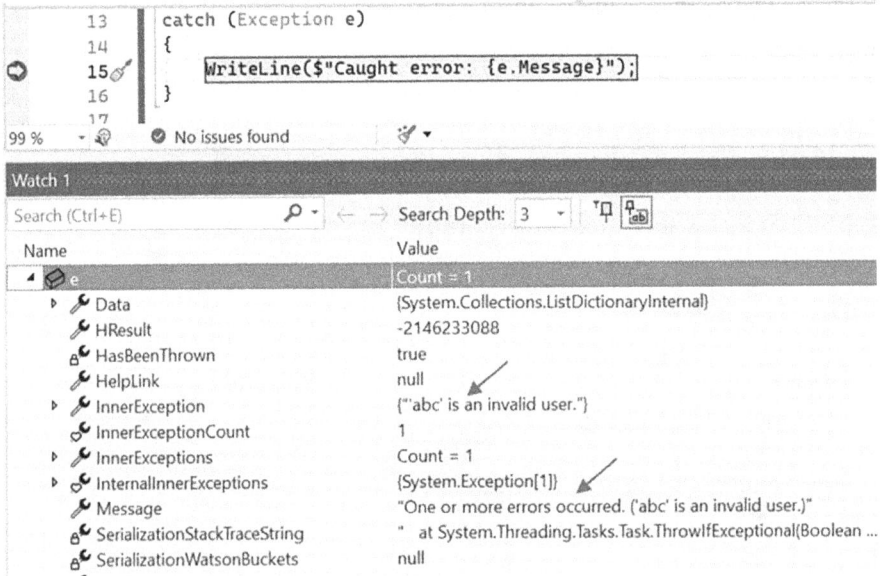

Figure 2-3. *A partial snapshot from Visual Studio that shows an InnnerException*

You can see that "'abc' is an invalid user." is an InnerException. For a situation like this, we can simply pass through the inner exceptions and display the error detail.

Q&A Session

Q2.1 In the previous output I can see that "'abc' is an invalid user." was wrapped as an InnerException. Is there any specific reason for this?

Good question. It is because the program caught the
AggregateException exception. To see this, you can slightly modify the
catch block as follows:

```
catch (Exception e)
{
    WriteLine($"Caught error: {e.Message}");
    WriteLine($"Exception name: {e.GetType().Name}");
}
```

If you execute the application again, you will see the following output:

```
Exception handling demo.
Caught error: One or more errors occurred. ('abc' is an
 invalid user.)
Exception name: AggregateException
```

Now the question is, what is an AggregateException? Do not worry!
You will get familiar with it in the following section.

Consider Using AggregateException

When you consider exception handling, we try to identify the potential
error locations and place the try-catch (or try-catch-finally) block
accordingly. There should be no confusion about this. However, in the
case of task programming, exception handling is a challenging task. This
is because, during the running state of an application, different tasks can
throw different exceptions at various levels. You have also seen that if you
are not careful enough, some of the exceptions can go unnoticed as well.
And this is an obvious problem because any exception can cause a system
to move into an inconsistent state. So, the question is, how can we handle
exceptions in task programming?

There are indeed different approaches, but the first thing that you
should note is that in the System namespace, there is a class called

AggregateException that inherits from the Exception class. Instead of using any other exception class, you should prefer this class. This class is specially designed to handle the exception handling scenarios when you deal with tasks. Microsoft states the following (see https://learn. microsoft.com/en-us/dotnet/standard/parallel-programming/ exception-handling-task-parallel-library):

> *To propagate all the exceptions back to the calling thread, the Task infrastructure wraps them in an AggregateException instance. The AggregateException exception has an InnerExceptions property that can be enumerated to examine all the original exceptions that were thrown, and handle (or not handle) each one individually.*

This is why you will see that AggregateException is used heavily in the development code to consolidate multiple failures/errors in concurrent environments, particularly, when we use Task Parallel Library (TPL) and/ or Parallel LINQ(PLINQ). This is why next time onward you will see me using AggregateException inside the catch block as well.

Note   PLINQ is discussed in Chapter 5.

Exception Management

How should we handle exceptions? Different programming model follows different strategies. For example, if you follow object-oriented programming (OOP), you'd like to use try, catch, and finally blocks. However, these are typically absent in functional programming (FP). In my other book *Introducing Functional Programming Using C#*, I had a detailed discussion on this topic. For now, we do not need to investigate those details. Instead, let's simplify the overall strategies by putting them into the following categories:

- Handling possible exceptions in a single location

- Handling possible exceptions in multiple locations

Handling Exceptions in a Single Location

In this section let's consider the first category, i.e., how to handle the possible exceptions in one place.

Demonstration 4

Here is the complete program where I simulate the exceptional situations using some simple code. In this program, in addition to the Product class, you will see another class called Database. This class contains a method called StoreData that can throw an InsufficientMemoryException when a user tries to store more than 500 MB data. Here is the sample code for this:

```
class Database
{
    /// <summary>
    /// This method throws an exception when
    /// requested size is greater than 500MB
    /// </summary>
    /// <param name="sizeInMB"> The requested size for
    ///  allocation in MB</param>
    /// <returns> Confirming the storage</returns>
    /// <exception cref="InsufficientMemoryException"> The
    ///  exception is thrown when the <paramref
    /// name="sizeInMB" is greater than 500 </exception>
    public static string StoreData(int sizeInMB)
```

```
    {
        string allocation;
        if (sizeInMB > 500)
        {
            throw new InsufficientMemoryException($"Cannot
                store {sizeInMB} MB data.");
        }
        else
        {
            // Some code for allocation
            allocation = $"{sizeInMB} is allocated";
        }
        return allocation;
    }
}
```

Now I create two different tasks inside the main thread and simulate the code in a way that both tasks encounter exceptions. As discussed in the previous section, it will be sufficient for you to pass through the inner exceptions and display the error details. Go through the complete program now:

```
using static System.Console;
WriteLine("Exception handling demo.");

try
{
    var task1 = Task.Run(() => Product.CheckUser("abc"));
    var task2 = Task.Run(() => Database.StoreData(501));
    Task.WaitAll(task1, task2);
}
catch (AggregateException ae)
{
```

```
    foreach (Exception e in ae.InnerExceptions)
    {
        WriteLine($"Caught error: {e.Message}");
    }
}
// The Product class and the Database classes are not shown
// to avoid repetition.
```

Output

Here is some sample output from this program:

```
Exception handling demo.
Caught error: Id: abc is invalid.
Caught error: Cannot store 501 MB data.
```

Alternative Approaches

You have seen a simple approach to handling exceptions. Now let me show you two more approaches that can be used in a similar context.

Alternative Approach 1

Notice the previous catch block. You can see that I used ae.InnerExceptions to display the errors in the output. Here is an alternative version where **I flatten the inner instances and then start traversing the exceptions** as follows:

```
catch (AggregateException ae)
{
    // Alternative approach-1
    var exceptions = ae.Flatten().InnerExceptions;
    foreach (Exception e in exceptions)
    {
```

```
        WriteLine($"Caught error: {e.Message}");
    }
}
```

Alternative Approach 2

In the AggregateException class, you can see a method called Handle that has the following form:

```
public void Handle(Func<Exception, bool> predicate)
{
 // The method body is not shown
}
```

Using this method, you can invoke a handler on each exception contained in an AggregateException. For example, let's replace the foreach loop inside the catch block in Demonstration 4 with a new block of code as follows (I have shown all the different approaches that we have discussed so far using code comments for easy comparison):

```
catch (AggregateException ae)
{
    //// Initial approach
    // foreach (Exception e in ae.InnerExceptions)
    // {
    //      WriteLine($"Caught error: {e.Message}");
    // }

    //// Alternative approach-1
    // var exceptions = ae.Flatten().InnerExceptions;
    // foreach (Exception e in exceptions)
    // {
```

```
//      WriteLine($"Caught error: {e.Message}");
//}

// Alternative approach-2
ae.Handle(e =>
{
    WriteLine($"Caught error: {e.Message}");
    return true;
});
}
```

If you execute the program now, you will see the same output.

Q&A Session

Q2.2 I can see that you have thrown two different exceptions from two different tasks. If both tasks throw the same type of exception, how can I distinguish them?

This is easy. You can associate the task IDs with the exception's Source property. For example, if you replace the following lines:

```
throw new UnauthorizedAccessException($"Id: {userId} is
 invalid.");
throw new InsufficientMemoryException($"Cannot store {sizeInMB}
MB data.");
```

with the following lines in the previous program:

```
throw new UnauthorizedAccessException($"Id: {userId} is
 invalid."){ Source = Task.CurrentId.ToString() };
throw new InsufficientMemoryException($"Cannot store {sizeInMB}
 MB data.") { Source = Task.CurrentId.ToString() };
```

and modify the catch block as follows:

```
catch (AggregateException ae)
{
    ae.Handle(e =>
    {
        WriteLine($"Caught error: {e.Message}
         Source: {e.Source}");
        return true;
    });
}
```

then you can get output like the following:

```
Exception handling demo.
Caught error: Id: abc is invalid. Source: 1
Caught error: Cannot store 501 MB data. Source: 2
```

Similarly, **if multiple tasks throw the same exception**, you can set the Source property to identify the source of the error.

Demonstration 5

Here is a complete program to illustrate the idea:

```
WriteLine("Q&A on exception handling.");
try
{
    var task1 = Task.Run(
        () => throw new InsufficientMemoryException($"Cannot
            store 500 MB data."){ Source = "task1" });
    var task2 = Task.Run(
        () => throw new InsufficientMemoryException($"Cannot
            store 500 MB data."){ Source = "task2" });
```

```
    Task.WaitAll(task1, task2);
}
catch (AggregateException ae)
{
    ae.Handle(e =>
    {
        WriteLine($"Caught error: {e.Message} [From
         {e.Source}]");
        return true;
    });
}
```

Output

Here is the sample output:

```
Q&A on exception handling.
Caught error: Cannot store 500 MB data. [From task1]
Caught error: Cannot store 500 MB data. [From task2]
```

Handling Exceptions in Multiple Locations

I assume that you have gotten the idea of how to handle multiple exceptions. This is OK and probably the most common approach. Next, I will show you a mechanism where you can handle one part of the aggregate exception in one place and the remaining part in another place. More specifically, you propagate this remaining part of the exception up to the hierarchy and handle it there. There is a reason for this: I want you to show the effectiveness of the Handle method.

First, see the following code. This code fragment indicates that you catch the probable set of exceptions but handle only one of them: InsufficientMemoryException.

```
// Some code before
catch (AggregateException ae)
{
 ae.Handle(
    e =>
    {
      if (e is InsufficientMemoryException)
      {
        WriteLine($"Caught error: {e.Message}");
        return true;
      }
      else
      {
        return false;
      }
    });
}
```

By returning true, you indicate that this particular exception is handled. More specifically, this code fragment says that you like to handle only the InsufficientMemoryException but no other exceptions in this location.

Demonstration 6

For example, in the upcoming program, the main thread calls the InvokeTasks method that, in turn, creates and runs three new tasks as follows:

```
var task1 = Task.Run(() => Product.CheckUser("abc"));
var task2 = Task.Run(() => Database.StoreData(501));
var task3 = Task.Run( () => throw new DllNotFoundException
   ("the dll is missing!"));
```

The first two tasks are already shown in the previous demonstration. You know that these tasks will raise exceptions. *The third task, named task3, is added for the sake of discussion so that you do not assume that you need to handle an equal number of tasks in each location.*

You'll see that I catch all the possible sets of exceptions inside InvokeTasks but handle only one of them: InsufficientMemory Exception. As a result, the remaining exceptions will be passed up to the calling hierarchy. So, I have handled them inside the Main method aka main thread. Let's go through the complete program now.

Note   I remind you that I have heavily used top-level statements and enabled implicit using statements for the C# projects in this book. These features came in C# 9.0 and C# 10.0, respectively. This is why you do not see a method named Main in this program.

```csharp
using static System.Console;
WriteLine("Exception handling demo.");
try
{
    InvokeTasks();
}
catch (AggregateException ae)
{
    ae.Handle(e =>
    {
        WriteLine($"Caught error inside Main(): {e.Message}");
        return true;
    });
}
```

```csharp
static void InvokeTasks()
{
    try
    {
        var task1 = Task.Run(() => Product.CheckUser("abc"));
        var task2 = Task.Run(() => Database.StoreData(501));
        var task3 = Task.Run(() => throw new
            DllNotFoundException("the dll is missing!"));
        Task.WaitAll(task1, task2, task3);
    }
    catch (AggregateException ae)
    {
        // Handling only InsufficientMemoryException, others
        // will be propagated up to the hierarchy
        ae.Handle(
            e =>
            {
                if (e is InsufficientMemoryException)
                {
                    WriteLine($"Caught error inside
                      InvokeTasks(): {e.Message}");
                    return true;
                }
                else
                {
                    return false;
                }
            });
    }
}
```

```
// There was no change inside the "Product" class and the
// "Database" class. So, they are not shown again to avoid
// repetitions.
```

Note   You can download the project Demo6_HandlingExceptions Separately from the Apress website to see and execute the complete program.

Output

Here is some sample output from this program:

```
Exception handling demo.
Caught error inside InvokeTasks(): Cannot store 501 MB data.
Caught error inside Main(): Id: abc is invalid.
Caught error inside Main(): the dll is missing!
```

Final Suggestion

I hope you have gotten an idea of how to handle exceptions in a parallel execution environment. I'd like to share one final thought with you: if you do not handle exceptions within tasks, you should try to handle them as close as possible to those places where you wait for the task completion and/or retrieve the result of the task invocation.

Understanding Cancellations

If you want to open a fixed deposit (FD) in India, banks give you two options: callable FD and non-callable FD. Usually, the interest rates for non-callable FDs are slightly higher than their counterpart. This is because you are not allowed to cancel the FD and withdraw the amount before the specified date. But you know that in a crisis, a customer may need to cancel the FD. So, if the customer does not have sufficient backup, he may opt for a callable FD. Similar situations are observed in programming as well. You may need to work with several tasks, and while those tasks are running, you may need to cancel one or more of them due to various reasons. Some of the examples include terminating a long-running process or releasing a critical resource. This is why you may like to work with cancellable tasks. Let's see how to cancel a task.

Different Ways of Cancellation

To support possible cancellations, this time onward you'll see me using cancellation tokens. To generate such a token, you need the instances of the CancellationTokenSource and CancellationToken. You may see the following lines of code in this context:

```
CancellationTokenSource tokenSource = new();
CancellationToken token = tokenSource.Token;
```

Obviously, using the var keyword, you can see a slight variation as follows:

```
var tokenSource = new CancellationTokenSource();
var token = tokenSource.Token;
```

Next, you pass this token to the intended task. Earlier, you saw (in Figure 1-1 in Chapter 1) that the Task constructor has several overloaded versions. Some of them accept a CancellationToken instance as a method parameter. Here is an example:

```
public Task(Action action, CancellationToken cancellationToken);
```

The StartNew method of the TaskFactory class has the overloaded versions as well, and some of them also accept a CancellationToken instance as a method parameter. Here is an example:

```
public Task StartNew(Action action, CancellationToken
  cancellationToken);
```

Similarly, the Run method of the Task class has similar overloads.

These constructs give you a clue on how to pass a CancellationToken instance to a task. Shortly, you'll see me using the following version:

```
public static Task Run(Action action, CancellationToken
  cancellationToken)
```

In the upcoming demonstration, I created a task that can keep printing the numbers from 0 to 99. Nowadays computer processors are very fast. So, this task can finish its execution very fast. To prevent this, I impose a short sleep after it prints a number. I also opt for the support for cancellation while it executes. So, I create a CancellationToken instance, called token, and pass it as follows:

```
var printTask=Task.Run
    (
      () =>
      {
          // A loop that runs 100 times
          for (int i = 0; i < 100 ; i++)
          {
              // Some other code is skipped here
              WriteLine($"{i}");
              // Imposing the sleep to make some delay
              Thread.Sleep(500);
          }
      }, token
    );
```

However, you must remember the following guidelines from Microsoft (see https://learn.microsoft.com/en-us/dotnet/standard/parallel-programming/how-to-cancel-a-task-and-its-children):

> *The calling thread does not forcibly end the task; it only signals that cancellation is requested. If the task is already running, it is up to the user delegate to notice the request and respond appropriately.*

Note   This prior message indicates that it is possible that by the time a calling thread raises a cancellation request, the running task finishes its execution. So, if you want to cancel a running task, you should raise the cancellation request as soon as possible.

Let me show you some cancellation techniques.

Initial Approach

In the first approach, you can use an if condition to evaluate whether the cancellation request is raised. If so, you can do something before you cancel the task. For example, you can introduce a message saying that this task is going to cancel itself (and clean up the resources, if required), and then you can put a break or return statement. Probably, most of us are aware of this kind of "soft exit" mechanism. Let me show you an example.

Demonstration 7

The following demonstration shows you a sample where I added a new code block in the previous code segment and made it bold for your reference:

```
using static System.Console;

WriteLine("Simple cancellation demonstration.");
```

```
var tokenSource = new CancellationTokenSource();
var token = tokenSource.Token;

var printTask = Task.Run
 (
   () =>
   {
       // A loop that runs 100 times
       for (int i = 0; i < 100; i++)
       {
           if (token.IsCancellationRequested)
           {
               WriteLine("Cancelling the print activity.");
               // Do some cleanups, if required
               return;
           }
           WriteLine($"{i}");
           // Imposing the sleep to make some delay
           Thread.Sleep(500);
       }
   }, token
);

WriteLine("Enter c to cancel the task.");
char ch = ReadKey().KeyChar;
if (ch.Equals('c'))
{
    WriteLine("\nTask cancellation requested.");
    tokenSource.Cancel();
}
// Wait till the task finishes the execution
while (!printTask.IsCompleted) { }
```

```
WriteLine($"The final status of printTask is: {printTask.Status}");
WriteLine("End of the main thread.");
```

POINT TO NOTE

This program uses the following line:

```
while (!someTask.IsCompleted) { }
```

Microsoft suggests you avoid this kind of polling in the production code as it is very inefficient (see https://learn.microsoft.com/en-us/dotnet/standard/parallel-programming/exception-handling-task-parallel-library). So, a better solution can be made with printTask.Wait();. But if I use the Wait() method, I need to guard the possible exceptions using try-catch blocks. To avoid this, I have used this line of code in this program and the next few demonstrations because I wanted to focus purely on cancellations, instead of mixing it up with exceptions.

Output

Here is some sample output:

```
Simple cancellation demonstration.
Enter c to cancel the task.
0
1
2
c
Task cancellation requested.
Cancelling the print activity.
The final status of printTask is: RanToCompletion
End of the main thread.
```

Q&A Session

Q2.3 In the previous demonstration, you canceled the task, but in the output, the final status of the task was displayed as `RanToCompletion`, instead of `Canceled`. Is this a bug?

No. Let's see what Microsoft says about it. The online documentation states the following (see `https://learn.microsoft.com/en-us/dotnet/standard/parallel-programming/task-cancellation`):

In the Task classes, cancellation involves cooperation between the user delegate, which represents a cancelable operation, and the code that requested the cancellation. A successful cancellation involves the requesting code calling the `CancellationTokenSource.Cancel` method and the user delegate terminating the operation in a timely manner. You can terminate the operation by using one of these options:

- By returning from the delegate. In many scenarios, this option is sufficient. However, a task instance that's canceled in this way transitions to the `TaskStatus.RanToCompletion` state, not to the `TaskStatus.Canceled` state.

- By throwing an `OperationCanceledException` and passing it the token on which cancellation was requested. The preferred way to perform this is to use the `ThrowIfCancellationRequested` method. A task that's canceled in this way transitions to the `Canceled` state, which the calling code can use to verify that the task responded to its cancellation request.

The first bullet point is easy to understand and justifies the final status of `printTask` in Demonstration 7. In the next section, I'll show you the other approach where you will notice that the final status is `Canceled`.

Alternative Approach

Let's see the alternative ways of cancellations as well. In a similar context, developers often like to throw an OperationCanceledException exception as follows:

```
if (token.IsCancellationRequested)
  {
      WriteLine("Cancelling the print activity.");
      throw new OperationCanceledException(token);
  }
```

Demonstration 8

It is time for another demonstration. You can update the task definition in Demonstration 7 as follows:

```
var printTask = Task.Run
  (
    () =>
    {
        // A loop that runs 100 times
        for (int i = 0; i < 100; i++)
        {
            // Approach-1
            // if (token.IsCancellationRequested)
            // {
            //      WriteLine("Cancelling the print activity.");
            //      // Do some cleanups, if required
            //      return;
            // }
```

```
        // Approach-2
        if (token.IsCancellationRequested)
        {
            WriteLine("Cancelling the print activity.");
            // Do some cleanups, if required
            throw new OperationCanceledException(token);
        }

        WriteLine($"{i}");
        // Imposing the sleep to make some delay
        Thread.Sleep(500);
    }
  }, token
);
```

Now execute the program again.

Output

Here is a sample output. Notice that in Demonstration 7, the final status of the task was RanToCompletion, but in this demonstration, it appears as Canceled.

```
Simple cancellation demonstration.
Enter c to cancel the task.
0
1
2
c
Task cancellation requested.
Cancelling the print activity.
The final status of printTask is: Canceled
End of the main thread.
```

Shortening the Code

Microsoft says that the ThrowIfCancellationRequested method is the functional equivalent of the following lines (see https://learn.microsoft.com/en-us/dotnet/api/system.threading.cancellationtoken.throwifcancellationrequested?view=net-8.0):

```
if (token.IsCancellationRequested)
    throw new OperationCanceledException(token);
```

This implies that you can use the ThrowIfCancellationRequested method for the following two things:

- You can check whether a cancellation request is raised.

- You can throw the OperationCanceledException exception when such a request is raised.

This is why you can shorten the code as follows:

```
var printTask = Task.Run
 (
  () =>
  {
      // A loop that runs 100 times
      for (int i = 0; i < 100; i++)
      {
          // Approach-3
          token.ThrowIfCancellationRequested();
          WriteLine($"{i}");
          // Imposing the sleep to make some delay
          Thread.Sleep(500);
      }
  }, token
 );
```

This is a common and widely used approach. Normally, I prefer to use this approach. If you like to do some cleanups before this call, you can write something like the following as well:

```
if (token.IsCancellationRequested)
{
    // Do some cleanups, if required
    token.ThrowIfCancellationRequested();
}
```

Q&A Session

Q2.4 In Demonstration 7, you simply did a soft exit and got the final task status as `RanToCompletion`, whereas in Demonstration 8, the final task status was canceled. I understand that this is a design decision, but I'd like to know your thoughts on them.

Normally, I'd like to follow the approach that is shown in Demonstration 8. This is because in an enterprise application, we normally deal with several tasks, and we often need to understand the log/output. In those cases, I can go through the log to understand which task was canceled. But if you simply exit from the method without doing anything, there is no such record left for you.

One Final Note

At the time of this writing, the `OperationCanceledException` class has 7 overloaded constructors that may take 0, 1 or 2 parameters. You can use them to initialize a new instance of `OperationCanceledException` as per your needs. Here I include some of them for your reference:

- `OperationCanceledException(CancellationToken)`:
  Initializes a new instance with a cancellation token.
  (You have already seen this in Demonstration 8).

- `OperationCanceledException(String)`: Initializes a new instance with a specified error message.

- `OperationCanceledException()`: Initializes a new instance with the system-supplied error message.

See that you can avoid passing a `CancellationToken` instance to initialize a new instance of `OperationCanceledException` Or, you can instantiate it with a different token. In such cases, you get the final status as `Faulted` (instead of `Canceled`).

To experiment with this, let's create a new token, say `token2`, and update the `if` block in Demonstration 8 as follows:

```
// Approach-2
if (token.IsCancellationRequested)
{
  WriteLine("Cancelling the print activity.");
  // Do some cleanups, if required
  throw new OperationCanceledException(token2);
}
```

Execute the program again. Notice that the final status appears as `Faulted`, but not `Canceled`. Here is a sample for you:

```
Simple cancellation demonstration.
Enter c to cancel the task.
0
1
2
3
c
Task cancellation requested.
Cancelling the print activity.
The final status of printTask is: Faulted
End of the main thread.
```

Q&A Session

Q2.5 Why does the output show the final status Faulted instead of Canceled?

This is a design decision. The documentation states the following (https://learn.microsoft.com/en-us/dotnet/standard/parallel-programming/task-cancellation):

> If the token's IsCancellationRequested property returns false or if the exception's token doesn't match the Task's token, the OperationCanceledException is treated like a normal exception, causing the Task to transition to the Faulted state. The presence of other exceptions will also cause the Task to transition to the Faulted state.

Monitoring Task Cancellation

Have you noticed the output of Demonstration 7 and Demonstration 8? In both cases, you saw the following line: Cancelling the print activity.. I used this line to monitor the canceled task before the cancellation operation. Interestingly, there are alternatives. Let's see some of them.

Using Register

You can subscribe to an event notification. For example, in the following code, I register a delegate that will be called when the token is canceled:

```
token.Register(
    () =>
    {
        WriteLine("Cancelling the print activity.
        [Using event subscription]");
        // Do something else, if you want
    }
);
```

Using WaitHandle.WaitOne

Let me show you one more approach that is relatively complicated compared to the previous one. However, this will also give you an idea about how to monitor task cancellation. The documentation describes WaitHandle's WaitOne method as follows (see https://learn. microsoft.com/en-us/dotnet/api/system.threading.waithandle. waitone?view=net-8.0):

> *Blocks the current thread until the current WaitHandle receives a signal.*

The WaitOne method has many overloads. In the upcoming demonstration, I'll show you the simplest form that does not require you to pass any argument. The basic idea is that the current thread will consider a token and wait until someone cancels it. As soon as someone invokes the cancellation, the blocking function call will be released. This is why I can launch another task from the calling thread as follows:

```
Task.Run(
    () =>
    {
        token.WaitHandle.WaitOne();
        WriteLine("Cancelling the print activity.
         [Using WaitHandle]");
        // Do something else, if you want
    }
);
```

Notice that it is similar to subscribing to an event notification, because here also you wait for the cancellation to occur. This is why I have written a similar statement in this code block.

Demonstration 9

It is time for another demonstration where I show you two approaches to monitor the cancellation operation. Notice the key changes in bold:

```
using static System.Console;

WriteLine("Monitoring the cancellation operation.");

var tokenSource = new CancellationTokenSource();
var token = tokenSource.Token;

token.Register(
    () =>
    {
        WriteLine("Cancelling the print activity.[Using event
         subscription]");
        // Do something else, if you want
    }
  );

var printTask = Task.Run
 (
  () =>
  {
      // A loop that runs 100 times
      for (int i = 0; i < 100; i++)
      {
          // Approach-3
          token.ThrowIfCancellationRequested();
          WriteLine($"{i}");
          // Imposing the sleep to make some delay
          Thread.Sleep(500);
      }
```

```csharp
    }, token
);
Task.Run(
    () =>
    {
        token.WaitHandle.WaitOne();
        WriteLine("Cancelling the print activity.[Using
          WaitHandle]");
        // Do something else, if you want
    }
);
WriteLine("Enter c to cancel the task.");
char ch = ReadKey().KeyChar;
if (ch.Equals('c'))
{
    WriteLine("\nTask cancellation requested.");
    tokenSource.Cancel();
}
// Wait till the task finishes the execution
while (!printTask.IsCompleted) { }
WriteLine($"The final status of printTask is: {printTask.Status}");
WriteLine("End of the main thread.");
```

Output

Here is some sample output. Notice the changes in bold.

```
Monitoring the cancellation operation.
Enter c to cancel the task.
0
```

```
1
2
c
Task cancellation requested.
Cancelling the print activity.[Using WaitHandle]
Cancelling the print activity.[Using event subscription]
The final status of printTask is: Canceled
End of the main thread.
```

Cancelling Child Tasks

I assume you understand task cancellations now. I'd like to remind you that Demonstration 8 in Chapter 1 showed you how to cancel a child task to answer Q1.8. That is why I won't repeat the discussion here.

Q&A Session

Q2.6 I understand that to provide support for cancellation, I need to create a CancellationTokenSource instance and get a token from it. However, I may need to support several cancellation strategies in a program. How can I implement the concept?

Good question. You may need to work with several tokens. The upcoming demonstration will give you the idea.

Managing Multiple Cancellation Tokens

An application can indeed be canceled due to various reasons. In such a case, you can use multiple tokens and provide the necessary logic. In this context, you can use the CreateLinkedTokenSource method. Let's see an example.

In the following demonstration, you'll see two different tokens as follows:

```
var normalCancellation = new CancellationTokenSource();
var tokenNormal = normalCancellation.Token;

var unexpectedCancellation = new CancellationTokenSource();
var tokenUnexpected = unexpectedCancellation.Token;
```

Once the tokens are created, I pass them to the CreateLinkedTokenSource method as follows:

```
var compositeToken = CancellationTokenSource.
 CreateLinkedTokenSource(tokenNormal,tokenUnexpected);
```

The idea is that you can cause a cancellation using either normalCancellation or unexpectedCancellation.

You may note that the CreateLinkedTokenSource method has different overloads, and you can pass more tokens if required. Remember that the core idea is the same: you can cancel any of these tokens to make the final task status Canceled.

Demonstration 10

In the following program, a user can trigger a normal cancellation. But you can also observe an unexpected/emergency cancellation as well. To mimic an emergency cancellation, I rely on a generated random number. If the number is 5, the unexpected cancellation will be triggered. Here is the complete program to demonstrate the idea:

```
using static System.Console;

WriteLine("Monitoring the cancellation operation.");

var normalCancellation = new CancellationTokenSource();
var tokenNormal = normalCancellation.Token;

var unexpectedCancellation = new CancellationTokenSource();
```

```
var tokenUnexpected = unexpectedCancellation.Token;

tokenNormal.Register(
    () =>
    {
        WriteLine(" Processing a normal cancellation.");
        // Do something else, if you want
    }
  );

tokenUnexpected.Register(
    () =>
    {
        WriteLine(" Processing an unexpected cancellation.");
        // Do something else, if you want
    }
  );

var compositeToken = CancellationTokenSource.CreateLinkedTokenSource(
 tokenNormal,
 tokenUnexpected
);

var printTask = Task.Run
 (
  () =>
  {
      // A loop that runs 100 times
      for (int i = 0; i < 100; i++)
      {
          compositeToken.Token.ThrowIfCancellationRequested();
          WriteLine($"{i}");
```

```
        // Imposing sleep to make some delay
        Thread.Sleep(500);
    }
}, compositeToken.Token
);

int random = new Random().Next(1, 6);
// A dummy logic to mimic an emergency cancellation
if (random == 5)
    unexpectedCancellation.Cancel();
else
{
    WriteLine("Enter 'c' for a normal cancellation ");
    char ch = ReadKey().KeyChar;
    if (ch.Equals('c'))
    {
        WriteLine("\nTask cancellation requested.");
        normalCancellation.Cancel();
    }
}

// Wait till the task finishes the execution
while (!printTask.IsCompleted) { }
WriteLine($"The final status of printTask is: {printTask.Status}");
WriteLine("End of the main thread.");
```

Output

Here is some sample output after a user presses C to mimic a normal cancellation:

```
Monitoring the cancellation operation.
Enter 'c' for a normal cancellation
```

```
0
1
2
c
Task cancellation requested.
 Processing a normal cancellation.
The final status of printTask is: Canceled
End of the main thread.
```

Here is some more sample output when an emergency cancellation was triggered:

```
Monitoring the cancellation operation.
0
 Processing an unexpected cancellation.
The final status of printTask is: Canceled
End of the main thread.
```

Microsoft's Note for Visual Studio Users

If you are a Visual Studio user and write programs that deal with multiple cancellation requests, I want you to remember the following note from Microsoft (see `https://learn.microsoft.com/en-us/dotnet/standard/threading/how-to-listen-for-multiple-cancellation-requests`):

> *When "Just My Code" is enabled, Visual Studio in some cases will break on the line that throws the exception and display an error message that says "exception not handled by user code." This error is benign. You can press F5 to continue from it.*

It keeps saying the following:

> *To prevent Visual Studio from breaking on the first error, just uncheck the "Just My Code" checkbox under Tools, Options, Debugging, General.*

Organizing Exceptions and Cancellations

In Chapter 1, you learned that there are three possible final states of a task: RanToCompletion, Canceled, and Faulted. In this chapter, you learned about cancellations and exceptions (particularly, we talked about AggregateException and OperationCanceledException). However, up until now, I discussed exceptions and cancellations in separate sections. This is why typical try-catch blocks were absent when I discussed cancellations. But typical software must be prepared for exceptions and cancellations. So, it is time to consolidate all this knowledge in a single place. Let's analyze some case studies.

Case Study 1: Using Wait()

The following program simulates a money transfer process. It also shows the progress status in the output. To simplify everything, let's assume that a money transfer takes five seconds. So, after every second, I increase the progress status by 20%.

In the upcoming program, there is a try block followed by two catch blocks. Why? Instead of catching all exceptions in a single catch block, I'd like to use separate catch blocks to handle the possible scenarios of exceptions and cancellations. One of these catch blocks handles AggregateException, and another catch block handles OperationCanceledException.

Demonstration 11

Here is the complete program:

```
using static System.Console;
WriteLine("Handling cancellations and exceptions.");
CancellationTokenSource cts = new();
CancellationToken token = cts.Token;
```

```
var transferMoney = Task.Run(
 () =>
 {
     WriteLine($"Initiating the money transfer.");
     int progressBar = 0;
     WriteLine("Press c to cancel within 5 sec.");
     // Assuming the task will take 5 seconds.
     // So, after every second, we'll increase
     // the progress by 20%
     for (int i = 0; i < 5; i++)
     {
         token.ThrowIfCancellationRequested();
         Thread.Sleep(1000);
         progressBar += 20;
         WriteLine($"Progress:{progressBar}%");
     }
     return "The money transfer is completed.";
 }, token);

var input = ReadKey().KeyChar;
if (input.Equals('c'))
{
    WriteLine("\nCancellation is requested.");
    cts.Cancel();
}
try
{
    transferMoney.Wait();
}
catch (AggregateException ae)
{
    ae.Handle(e =>
    {
```

```
        WriteLine($"Caught error:   {e.Message}");
        return true;
    });
}

catch (OperationCanceledException oce)
{
    WriteLine($"Caught error due to cancellation: {oce.Message}");
}

if (transferMoney.Status == TaskStatus.RanToCompletion)
{
    WriteLine(transferMoney.Result);
}

WriteLine($"Current status: {transferMoney.Status}");
WriteLine("Thank you, visit again!");
```

Output

Let me show you some possible outputs. Notice the important lines in bold in these outputs.

Case 1: In this case, you do not cancel the task. Here is some sample output:

```
Handling cancellations and exceptions.
Initiating the money transfer.
Press c to cancel within 5 sec.
Progress:20%
Progress:40%
Progress:60%
Progress:80%
Progress:100%
The money transfer is completed.
Current status: RanToCompletion
Thank you, visit again!
```

Case 2: Here is some sample output from the program when you try to cancel the task:

```
Handling cancellations and exceptions.
Initiating the money transfer.
Press c to cancel within 5 sec.
Progress:20%
Progress:40%
Progress:60%
c
Cancellation is requested.
Progress:80%
Caught error:   A task was canceled.
Current status: Canceled
Thank you, visit again!
```

Case Study 2: Using Wait(token)

Let's replace the try block in the previous program with the following one:

```
// There is no change in the previous code
try
{
    //transferMoney.Wait();
    transferMoney.Wait(token);
// There is no change in the remaining code
```

Let's execute this modified program and analyze the previous cases again. *First, if you do not cancel the task, you will not observe any change in the output. However, if you initiate a cancellation, there are some differences.* Let me show you some sample output:

```
Handling cancellations and exceptions.
Initiating the money transfer.
```

```
Press c to cancel within 5 sec.
Progress:20%
Progress:40%
Progress:60%
c
Cancellation is requested.
Caught error due to cancellation: The operation was canceled.
Current status: Running
Thank you, visit again!
```

You can see that this time the catch block for AggregateException could not catch OperationCanceledException; this is why I used two different catch blocks in this program.

Q&A Session

Q2.7 Why does the previous output show the final status Running instead of Canceled?

The Wait(token) differs from Wait(). In the case of Wait(token), the wait terminates if a cancellation token is canceled before the task is completed. In this case, the main thread exited early. So, to see the final status of the task as Canceled, you can introduce the following code (shown in bold) in the following location:

```
// There is no change in the previous code.
```

```
// Wait till the task finishes the execution
while (!transferMoney.IsCompleted) { }
WriteLine($"Current status:{transferMoney.Status}");
```

```
// There is no change in the remaining code.
```

Here is some sample output after this change:

```
Handling cancellations and exceptions.
Initiating the money transfer.
Press c to cancel within 5 sec.
Progress:20%
Progress:40%
Progress:60%
c
Cancellation is requested.
Caught error due to cancellation: The operation was canceled.
Progress:80%
```
Payment processing status: Canceled
```
Thank you, visit again!
```

POINT TO NOTE

When you examine this in detail, you'll see that Wait() can throw
only AggregateException, whereas Wait(CancellationToken
cancellationToken) is cancellable and can raise OperationCanceled
Exception. If interested, you can see a discussion of this topic at https://
stackoverflow.com/questions/77833724/why-the-catch-block-
of-aggregateexception-was-not-sufficient-to-handle-cancell
at/77833858#77833858.

Handling I/O-Bound Tasks

In addition to running the essential tasks, sometimes you'll want to run
an additional task to monitor the overall activity. At a later stage, you
may provide a choice: whether the user likes to retrieve the details of the
activity. In a traditional scenario, a user supplies some specific input(s) to

know the details. You may think that this is a common activity. Wait! There is something more to add: since it purely depends on the user's choice, you would like to run this additional task without blocking the current thread. Can you design such an application? The following section will show you an implementation strategy.

Using TaskCompletionSource

You can consider using the `TaskCompletionSource<TResult>` class to implement the idea. Using it you can a create task out of any operation that will be completed in the future. Microsoft describes this class as follows (see `https://learn.microsoft.com/en-us/dotnet/api/system.threading.tasks.taskcompletionsource-1?view=net-8.0`):

> *Represents the producer side of a Task<TResult> unbound to a delegate, providing access to the consumer side through the Task property.*

More specifically, behind the scenes, using this class, you get a "slave" task that you can manually drive when the operation finishes (or faults). It can be ideal for such a type of I/O-bound work where you reap all the benefits of using a task without blocking the calling thread.

Now the question is: how do you use this class? First, you need to instantiate it. Once you instantiate this class, you will get some built-in methods that can serve your purpose. Figure 2-4 shows the details of this class in Visual Studio.

```
 using System.Collections.Generic;

-namespace System.Threading.Tasks
 {
      public class TaskCompletionSource<TResult>
      {
          public TaskCompletionSource();
          public TaskCompletionSource(object? state);
          public TaskCompletionSource(TaskCreationOptions creationOptions);
          public TaskCompletionSource(object? state, TaskCreationOptions creationOptions);

          public Task<TResult> Task { get; }

          public void SetCanceled();
          public void SetCanceled(CancellationToken cancellationToken);
          public void SetException(IEnumerable<Exception> exceptions);
          public void SetException(Exception exception);
          public void SetResult(TResult result);
          public bool TrySetCanceled();
          public bool TrySetCanceled(CancellationToken cancellationToken);
          public bool TrySetException(IEnumerable<Exception> exceptions);
          public bool TrySetException(Exception exception);
          public bool TrySetResult(TResult result);
      }
 }
```

Figure 2-4. *The TaskCompletionSource class details*

Before you see the code examples, I suggest that you note the following points:

- Figure 2-4 confirms that the method names start either with Set or with TrySet. The first category returns void, and the second category returns bool.

- When you call any of these methods, the task moves into any of the final states: RanToCompletion, Faulted, or Canceled.

- You should call the first category (i.e., where the method names start with the word Set) exactly once; otherwise, you'll see exceptions.

To illustrate the previous bullet point, let me give you an example: in the upcoming program, there is a custom class called Job. I created an instance of it, called job, and used it in the task definition as follows (notice that the SetResult method is called exactly once):

```
var backgroundTask = Task.Run(
    () =>
    {
        // Some other codes before this line are not shown
        // to focus on the main point of discussion
        // taskCompletionSource.SetResult(job);
        // The following line will cause an exception now
        // taskCompletionSource.SetResult(job);

    });
```

Now if you uncomment the commented-out line in the previous code and wait for this task to finish (for example, using the line backgroundTask.Wait();), you will see the following exception in the final output:

```
Unhandled exception. System.AggregateException: One or more
errors occurred. (An attempt was made to transition a task to a
final state when it had already completed.)
// The remaining details are not shown
```

To avoid this kind of error, I prefer to use the TrySetResult method instead of the SetResult method. The reason is obvious: it returns a Boolean, i.e., either true or false.

Note   In the Demo12_UsingTaskCompletionSource project, I kept the erroneous code block as commented code for your experimentation/ reference. You can download it from the Apress website.

Demonstration 12

To understand the following demonstration, go through the following points:

- There is a Job class in this program. To create an instance of it, I pass a job identification number and the name of the executor. Passing the executor's name was optional for me.

- At the beginning of the program, I created an instance of the TaskCompletionSource<Job> class, called taskCompletionSource. As a result, I can use its Task property in a later stage.

- The user of this application can get the details of the created Job instance by entering the character y to get the details. In such a case, the result will be collected through a task called backgroundTask that completes taskCompletionSource.Task.

- If the user enters any other character, the program completes execution without showing the job details.

Let's see the complete program now:

```
using static System.Console;

TaskCompletionSource<Job> taskCompletionSource = new();
Task<Job> collectInfoTask = taskCompletionSource.Task;

WriteLine($"Starts processing a job.");
Job job = new(1)
{
    Executor = "Roy"
};
```

```csharp
// Do something else if required

// Starting a background task that will complete
// taskCompletionSource.Task
var backgroundTask = Task.Run(
() =>
{
WriteLine(" Monitoring the activity before setting the result.");
 // Imposing some forced delay before setting the
 // result to mimic real-world
 Thread.Sleep(3000);
 bool setResultStatus= taskcompletionSource.TrySetResult(job);
});

// Imposing a forced delay so that the background task can
// start running before executing the rest of the code
Thread.Sleep(1000);

WriteLine("Press 'y' to get the details.");
var input = ReadKey();
if (input.KeyChar == 'y')
{
  WriteLine(collectInfoTask.Result);
  // Same as:
  // WriteLine(taskCompletionSource.Task.Result);
}
WriteLine("\nThank you!");

internal class Job
{
    public int JobNumber { get; init; }
    public string Executor { get; set; }
```

```
    public Job(int jobNumber, string executor = "Anonymous")
    {
        JobNumber = jobNumber;
        Executor = executor;
    }
    public override string ToString() =>
      $"\n{Executor} executed the job number {JobNumber}";
}
```

Output

Here is some sample output:

Case-1(The user opt for the detail):

```
Starts processing a job.
 Monitoring the activity before setting the result.
Press 'y' to get the details.
y
```
Roy executed the job number 1

```
Thank you!
```

Case-2(The user does not opt for the detail):
```
Starts processing a job.
 Monitoring the activity before setting the result.
Press 'y' to get the details.
```
n
```
Thank you!
```

Q&A Session

Q2.8 I can see that you have used a property and a constructor to instantiate a Job instance. Is there any specific reason behind this design?

Yes. You can indeed opt for any of them. But notice that I have used the init accessor in this example. About this accessor, Microsoft says the following (see https://learn.microsoft.com/en-us/dotnet/csharp/language-reference/keywords/init):

> *In C# 9 and later, the init keyword defines an accessor method in a property or indexer. An init-only setter assigns a value to the property or the indexer element only during object construction. This enforces immutability, so that once the object is initialized, it can't be changed again.*

This is why the job number cannot be changed in this program, but its executor can be reassigned. Fixing the job number for a particular job, I promote immutability. In a multithread environment, promoting immutability is a good idea.

Q2.9 How does immutability fit into a multithreaded programming environment?

Immutable types are thread-safe. They prevent nasty bugs from implicit dependencies, destructive updates, and state mutations. Therefore, in a multithreaded environment, they make your programming life easy.

In addition, immutable types can help you avoid side effects and temporal coupling as well. Indeed, I am not focusing on functional programming in this book. So, for the simple demonstrations, I do not care about them. I simply wanted you to keep these notes in your mind using this program.

Exercises

Check your understanding by attempting the following exercises:

REMINDER

As said before for Chapter 1's exercises, for all code examples, the Implicit Global Usings setting was enabled in Visual Studio. This is why you will not see me mentioning some other namespaces that were available by default. You can safely assume that all other necessary namespaces are available for these code segments. The same comment applies to all exercises in this book as well.

E2.1 If you execute the following code, can you predict the output?

```
using static System.Console;
WriteLine("Exercise 2.1");

try
{
    int b = 0;
    Task<int> value = Task.Run(() => 10 /b);
}
catch (Exception e)
{
    WriteLine($"Caught error: {e.Message}");
}
WriteLine("End");
```

E2.2 If you execute the following code, can you predict the output?

```
using static System.Console;
WriteLine("Exercise 2.2");
try
```

```
{
    int b = 0;
    Task<int> value = Task.Run(() => 10 / b);
    WriteLine(value.Result);
}
catch (Exception e)
{
    WriteLine($"Encountered with {e.GetType()}");
}
WriteLine("End");
```

E2.3 If you execute the following code, can you predict the output?

```
using static System.Console;
WriteLine("Exercise 2.3");

try
{
    var task1 = Task.Run(
      () => throw new InvalidDataException("invalid data"));
    var task2 = Task.Factory.StartNew(
      () => throw new OutOfMemoryException("insufficient
            memory"));
    Task.WaitAll(task1, task2);
}
catch (AggregateException ae)
{
    foreach (Exception e in ae.InnerExceptions)
    {
        WriteLine($"Caught error: {e.Message}");
    }
}
```

E2.4 If you execute the following code, can you predict the output?

```
using static System.Console;
WriteLine("Exercise 2.4");

try
{
    var task1 = Task.Run( () => throw new
     InvalidDataException("invalid data"));
    var task2 = Task.Run(() => throw new
     OutOfMemoryException("insufficient  memory"));
    task1.Wait();
    task2.Wait();
    WriteLine("End");
}
catch (AggregateException ae)
{
    ae.Handle(e =>
        {
            if (e is InvalidDataException |
                e is OutOfMemoryException )
            {
                WriteLine($"Caught error: {e.Message}");
                return true;
            }
            return false;
        }
    );
}
```

E2.5 If you execute the following code, can you predict the output?

```
using static System.Console;
WriteLine("Exercise 2.5 and Exercise 2.6");
```

```
try
{
    DoSomething();
}
catch (AggregateException ae)
{
    ae.Handle(
        e =>
        {
            WriteLine($"Caught inside main: {e.Message}");
            return true;
        }
    );
}
static void DoSomething()
{
    try
    {
      var task1 = Task.Run(() => throw new
      InvalidDataException("invalid data"));
      var task2 = Task.Run(() => throw new
      OutOfMemoryException("insufficient memory"));
        // For Exercise 2.5
        Task.WaitAll(task1, task2);
        // For Exercise 2.6
        // task1.Wait();
        // task2.Wait();
    }
    catch (AggregateException ae)
    {
        ae.Handle(
            e =>
```

```
            {
                if (e is InvalidDataException)
                {
                    WriteLine($"Caught inside DoSomething:
                     {e.Message}");
                    return true;
                }
                else
                {
                    return false;
                }
            }
        );
    }
}
```

E2.6 Predict the output when you replace the following line:

```
Task.WaitAll(task1, task2);
```

with the following lines in the previous program:

```
task1.Wait();
task2.Wait();
```

E2.7 If you execute the following code, can you predict the output?

```
using static System.Console;
WriteLine("Exercise 2.7");

try
{
    var task1 = Task.Run(() => throw new
     InvalidOperationException("invalid operation"));
    var task2 = Task.Run(() => throw new
     OutOfMemoryException("insufficient  memory"));
```

```
    Task.WaitAny(task1, task2);
    WriteLine("End");
}
catch (AggregateException ae)
{
    ae.Handle(e =>
    {
        if (e is InvalidOperationException |
            e is OutOfMemoryException
        )
        {
            WriteLine($"Caught error: {e.Message}");
            return true;
        }
        return false;
    }
    );
}
```

E2.8 If you execute the following code, can you predict the output?

```
using static System.Console;
WriteLine("Exercise 2.8");

try
{
    var someTask = Task.Run(() => throw new
     InvalidOperationException("invalid operation")
     { Source = "Task1"});
    // Allowing some time so that task can get up and running
    while (someTask.Status != TaskStatus.Running)
    {
        Thread.Sleep(10);
    }
```

```
    // Waiting for the state change now
    while (someTask.Status == TaskStatus.Running)
    {
        Thread.Sleep(10);
    }
    WriteLine($"SomeTask's status: {someTask.Status}");
    WriteLine("The application ends here.");
}
catch (AggregateException ae)
{
    ae.Handle(e =>
    {
        if (e is InvalidOperationException )
        {
            WriteLine($"Caught error: {e.Message} Source=
            {e.Source}");
            return true;
        }
        return false;
    }
    );
}
```

E2.9 If you execute the following code, can you predict the output?

```
using static System.Console;

var tokenSource = new CancellationTokenSource();
var token = tokenSource.Token;
var printTask = Task.Run
 (
  () =>
```

```
    {
        int i = 0;
        while (i != 10)
        {
            if (token.IsCancellationRequested)
            {
                WriteLine("Cancelling the print activity.");
                return;
            }
            // Do some work, if required.
            Thread.Sleep(1000);
            i++;
        }
    }, token
);

Thread.Sleep(500);
WriteLine("Task cancellation initiated.");
tokenSource.Cancel();
// Wait till the task finishes the execution
while (!printTask.IsCompleted) { }
WriteLine($"The final status of printTask is: {printTask.Status}");
WriteLine("End of the main thread.");
```

E2.10 In the previous exercise, if you replace the following code segment:

```
if (token.IsCancellationRequested)
{
    WriteLine("Cancelling the print activity.");
    return;
}
```

with the following line:

```
token.ThrowIfCancellationRequested();
```

will be there any change in the output?

E2.11 The following program creates a parent task and a nested task. It also allows you to cancel the nested task if you enter C quickly. Check whether you can predict the output.

```
using static System.Console;

WriteLine("Exercise 2.11");
var tokenSource = new CancellationTokenSource();
var token = tokenSource.Token;
var parent = Task.Factory.StartNew(
    () =>
    {
        var finalResult = string.Empty;
        try
        {
            if (token.IsCancellationRequested)
            {
                finalResult = "The cancellation request is
                 raised before the start of the parent task.";
                token.ThrowIfCancellationRequested();
            }
            WriteLine("The parent task has started.");

            // Creating a nested task
            var child = Task.Factory.StartNew(
                () =>
                {
                    WriteLine("The nested task has started.");
```

```
                    for (int i = 0; i < 10; i++)
                    {
                        token.ThrowIfCancellationRequested();
                        WriteLine($"\tThe nested task
                         prints:{i}");
                        Thread.Sleep(100);
                    }
                    return "The nested task has finished too.";
                }, token);

            finalResult = "Parent task: completed. Additional
             info: n/a.";

            // Updating the final result with the result of the
            // nested task
            finalResult = $"Parent task: completed.\t
             Additional info: {child.Result} ";

        }
        catch (AggregateException ae)
        {
            foreach (Exception e in ae.InnerExceptions)
            {
                WriteLine($"Caught error: {e.Message}");
            }
        }
        catch (OperationCanceledException oce)
        {
            WriteLine($"Error: {oce.Message}");
        }
        return finalResult;
    });
```

```
WriteLine("Enter c to cancel the nested task.");
char ch = ReadKey().KeyChar;
if (ch.Equals('c'))
{
    WriteLine("\nTask cancellation requested.");
    tokenSource.Cancel();
}

WriteLine($"Status: {parent.Result}");
WriteLine("End of the main thread.");
```

E2.12 If you execute the following code, can you predict the output?

```
using static System.Console;
TaskCompletionSource<int> tcs = new();
int value = 10;
var task1=Task.Run(() => value++);
Thread.Sleep(1000);
var task2=Task.Run(() =>
{
    Thread.Sleep(2000);
    tcs.SetResult(value*10);
}
);
Thread.Sleep(1000);
WriteLine($"The final result is:{tcs.Task.Result}");
```

E2.13 In Chapter 1 you solved exercise 1.6. Since you learned about implementing exception and cancellation scenarios, can you solve that exercise considering these scenarios?

Summary

This chapter continued the discussion of task programming, but this time the focus was on handling various special scenarios with different examples and case studies. In brief, it answered the following questions:

- How do you handle exceptions in a parallel programming environment?

- How can you support cancellations in a parallel programming environment?

- How can you monitor cancellations in your applications?

- How can you manage some I/O-bound tasks using the TaskCompletionSource class?

Solutions to Exercises

Here is a sample solution set for the exercises in this chapter.

E2.1

This program produces the following output:

```
Exercise 2.1
End
```

Additional Note: You do not observe the exception because the main thread did not encounter the exception; it was encountered by the task that was created by this main thread. I covered this topic using Demonstration 2 and Demonstration 3.

E2.2

This time you'll see the exception name. You may note that instead of seeing `System.DivideByZeroException`, you'll see `System.AggregateException` as follows:

```
Exercise 2.2
Encountered with System.AggregateException
End
```

E2.3

This program produces the following output:

```
Exercise 2.3
Caught error: invalid data
Caught error: insufficient memory
```

E2.4

The call to the statement `task1.Wait();` causes the `InvalidDataException`. As a result, control leaves the `try` block and produces the following output:

```
Exercise 2.4
Caught error: invalid data
```

E2.5

The program produces the following output:

```
Exercise 2.5 and Exercise 2.6
Caught inside DoSomething: invalid data
Caught inside main: insufficient memory
```

E2.6

The program produces the following output (see the explanation of E2.4 if required):

```
Exercise 2.5 and Exercise 2.6
Caught inside DoSomething: invalid data
```

E2.7

This program produces the following output:

```
Exercise 2.7
End
```

You may be wondering why are you not seeing the task's exception(s) in the output. This is because when you use the `WaitAny` method, the task's exception does not propagate to the `AggregateException`. I encourage you to read Stephen Clearly's blog post at `https://blog.stephencleary.com/2014/10/a-tour-of-task-part-5-wait.html` that summarizes the difference among `WaitAny`, `Wait`, and `WaitAll` as follows:

> *The semantics of WaitAny are a bit different than WaitAll and Wait: WaitAny merely waits for the first task to complete. It will not propagate that task's exception in an AggregateException. Rather, any task failures will need to be checked after WaitAny returns. WaitAny will return -1 on timeout, and will throw OperationCanceledException if the wait is cancelled.*

E2.8

This program may produce the following output:

```
Exercise 2.8
SomeTask's status: Faulted
The application ends here.
```

However, you may also notice that the program is stuck executing.
Why? Notice that when you evaluate the following condition, the
task may not be in the Running state (for example, it may be in the
WaitingForActivation state):

```
// Allowing some time so that the task can get up and running
while (someTask.Status != TaskStatus.Running)
{
  Thread.Sleep(10);
}
```

But inside the loop when you invoke the Sleep method, by that time,
the task may transition from the Running state to one of the terminating
states. As a result, the program will stuck here.

This is why to get a consistent output, you'd like to replace the
following segment:

```
// Allowing some time so that task can get up
// and running( Program can stuck here)
 while (someTask.Status != TaskStatus.Running)
 {
     Thread.Sleep(10);
 }

 // Waiting for the state change now
 while (someTask.Status == TaskStatus.Running)
 {
     Thread.Sleep(10);
 }
```

with the following one: `while (!someTask.IsCompleted) { }`

> **Note**   I already mentioned that you should avoid this kind of polling
> in the production code as it is inefficient.

E2.9

Here is some possible output:

```
Task cancellation initiated.
Cancelling the print activity.
The final status of printTask is: RanToCompletion
End of the main thread.
```

E2.10

This time the final task status should appear as Canceled. Here is some
sample output:

```
Task cancellation initiated.
The final status of printTask is: Canceled
End of the main thread.
```

E2.11

You already know that this program creates a parent task and a nested
task. It also allows you to cancel the nested task if you enter C quickly. As
a result, you may see different output. For example, if you do not intend to
cancel the nested task and press the Enter key at the end, you can see the
following output:

```
Exercise 2.11
Enter c to cancel the nested task.
The parent task has started.
```

```
The nested task has started.
        The nested task prints:0
        The nested task prints:1
        The nested task prints:2
        The nested task prints:3
        The nested task prints:4
        The nested task prints:5
        The nested task prints:6
        The nested task prints:7
        The nested task prints:8
        The nested task prints:9
```
Status: Parent task: completed. Additional info: The nested task has finished too.
```
End of the main thread.
```

On the other hand, depending on the time of cancellation, you can get different outputs. For example, if you press C almost at the beginning of the application, you will see the following:

```
Exercise 2.11
Enter c to cancel the nested task.
c
Task cancellation requested.
Error: The operation was canceled.
```
Status: The cancellation request is raised before the start of the parent task.
```
End of the main thread.
```

Otherwise, you may see something like the following:

```
Exercise 2.11
Enter c to cancel the nested task.
The parent task has started.
```

```
The nested task has started.
        The nested task prints:0
        The nested task prints:1
        The nested task prints:2
        The nested task prints:3
c
Task cancellation requested.
Caught error: A task was canceled.
Status: Parent task: completed. Additional info: n/a.
End of the main thread.
```

E2.12

You should see the following output:

```
The final result is: 110
```

[**Clue:** Notice that task1 updates the initial value to 11, but task2 further sets it as 11*10=110. The sleep statements are placed to preserve the order of evaluation.]

E2.13

I leave this exercise to you now. Good luck!

CHAPTER 3

Exploring Synchronization and Concurrent Collections

In a multithreaded environment, managing the shared data is a challenging activity. This is because multiple threads may try to perform the reading and writing operations simultaneously. If you do not coordinate them, you may see erroneous outcomes. Synchronization mechanisms help you control access to shared data to avoid inconsistent or erroneous outcomes.

This chapter discusses some useful synchronization techniques. It also covers the usage of concurrent collections in our applications. These concepts will help you make applications that can work seamlessly in a multithreaded environment. Since parallel programming is a subset of multithreading, understanding these concepts will help you a lot.

Synchronization

Synchronization is a vast topic, and there are many useful constructs. Depending on the situation, you may prefer one construct over another. One of my favorite authors is Joseph Albahari (the author of *C# in a*

© Vaskaran Sarcar 2024
V. Sarcar, *Parallel Programming with C# and .NET*,
https://doi.org/10.1007/979 8 8688-0400-5_3

Nutshell). He categorized the synchronization constructs as follows (see `https://www.albahari.com/threading/part2.aspx#_Synchronization`):

- **Simple blocking methods:** You already saw these methods. For example, `Thread.Sleep` and `Task.Wait` belong to this category.

- **Locking constructs:** Some examples in this category include the `lock` statements of `Mutex`, `Semaphore`, `SemaphoreSlim`, and so on. These are further categorized by exclusive locking and nonexclusive locking constructs. For example, `lock` and `Mutex` fall into exclusive locking constructs, whereas `Semaphore` and `SemaphoreSlim` fall into the other category.

- **Signaling constructs:** Event wait handles such as `AutoResetEvent`, `ManualResetEvent`, and `CountDownEvent` belong to this category.

- **Nonblocking synchronization constructs:** The `Interlocked` class and the `volatile` keyword are common examples in this category.

POINT TO NOTE

Discussing all of these constructs would make this chapter unnecessarily fat. In fact, to understand the content of the rest of the book and do the exercises, you may need to understand only a few of them. **So, I decided to cover at least one from each category.** However, if interested, you can refer to Appendix A where you'll find some additional material. Since you already saw me using `Thread.Sleep` and `Task.Wait`, let's focus on the remaining categories in this chapter.

Understanding Why We Need Synchronization

Before I discuss the synchronization primitives, I will present an erroneous program that shows why we need synchronization techniques.

An Erroneous Program

The following program tries to mimic a typical banking scenario where you see five different tasks perform some common operations: three of them perform the credit operations, and two of them perform the debit operations. Let's assume the credit amounts are $100, $200, and $300, whereas the debit amounts are $500 and $100. If you run these tasks one by one, the initial balance and the final balance will be the same. For example, if the initial balance is $0, after performing these operations, the final balance will also be $0. However, is this the case when these tasks run in a multithreaded environment?

Demonstration 1

Let's run the following program in a multithreaded environment and see the output:

```
using static System.Console;

Account account = new();
var credit100 = Task.Run(() => account.Credit(100));
var debit500 = Task.Run(() => account.Debit(500));
var credit200 = Task.Run(() => account.Credit(200));
var credit300 = Task.Run(() => account.Credit(300));
var debit100 = Task.Run(() => account.Debit(100));

Task.WaitAll(credit100, credit200, credit300, debit500,
 debit100);
WriteLine($"The current balance is ${account.Balance}");
```

```
#region Non-synchronized version
class Account
{
    public decimal Balance { get; set; }
    public void Credit(decimal amount)
    {
     Balance += amount;
     WriteLine($"The balance after the credit of ${amount} is
       ${Balance}");
    }
    public void Debit(decimal amount)
    {
     Balance -= amount;
     WriteLine($"The balance after the debit of ${amount} is
       ${Balance}");
    }
}
#endregion
```

Output

You may see different outputs on different executions. However, when I executed this program, most of the time, I got incorrect results. And on a few occasions, I saw that the final balance was $0; in those cases, also the intermediate results were wrong. Let me show you a sample:

```
The balance after the credit of $200 is $-500
The balance after the debit of $500 is $-500
The balance after the debit of $100 is $-300
The balance after the credit of $300 is $-200
The balance after the credit of $100 is $-500
The current balance is $-300
```

Analysis

Notice that multiple tasks were working on nonatomic operations that were not synchronized. This allowed multiple threads to enter the critical section of the code, and as a result, you see this incorrect result.

Q&A Session

Q3.1 How do the atomic operations work in a multithreaded environment?

Consider this line of code: `Balance += amount;`. What does it do? Surely, it increments the `Balance` by the `amount`. However, it may not be a single operation; instead, multiple steps can be involved as follows:

- **Step 1:** Load the current value of the `Balance` into a register.

- **Step 2**: Increment this current value by the amount (you may store the result in a temporary variable as well).

- **Step 3:** Store/set the updated value back to the `Balance`.

Now consider the case when a thread, say, thread A, starts executing these steps. Let's assume that it executes step 1 and step 2, but before executing step 3, it is preempted by another thread, say, thread B. Let's also assume that thread B completes all the steps without any interference from other threads. Now thread A resumes execution and overwrites the final value of `Balance`. This means the change made by thread B is lost.

Q3.2 What is a critical section?

In simple words, a critical section is a piece of code that you'd like to guard in a multithreaded environment. In this region/section, you coordinate access to the shared variables to produce the correct result. In a moment, I'll use the lock statement to make a critical section around my code. Let me show you a sample from the upcoming demonstration:

```
public void Credit(decimal amount)
{
    lock (_balanceLock)
    {
        Balance += amount;
        WriteLine($"The balance after credit ${amount} is
        {Balance} $");
    }
}
```

Here the lock keyword plays the role of a gatekeeper who allows only one thread to work in the critical section.

Using Lock Statements

Lock statements are usually used when we want exclusive access to a shared resource. The documentation states the following (see https://learn.microsoft.com/en-us/dotnet/csharp/language-reference/statements/lock).

> *The lock statement acquires the mutual-exclusion lock for a given object, executes a statement block, and then releases the lock. While a lock is held, the thread that holds the lock can again acquire and release the lock. Any other thread is blocked from acquiring the lock and waits until the lock is released. The lock statement ensures that at maximum only one thread executes its body at any time moment.*

Demonstration 2

The previous quote is self-explanatory. It ensures that while a thread is working in a critical section, no other thread can interfere with it. So, let's modify the Account class as follows:

```
#region Synchronized version using the lock statement
class Account
{
  public decimal Balance { get; set; }
  private readonly object _balanceLock = new();
  public void Credit(decimal amount)
  {
   lock (_balanceLock)
    {
    Balance += amount;
    WriteLine($"The balance after the credit of ${amount} is
     ${Balance}");
    }
   }
  public void Debit(decimal amount)
  {
   lock (_balanceLock)
   {
    Balance -= amount;
    WriteLine($"The balance after the debit of ${amount} is
     ${Balance}");
   }
  }
}
#endregion
```

Note   To avoid repetition, I did not show the complete program. However, you can download the project Demo2_UsingLock to run the complete program.

Output

Run this modified program again. Here is some sample output:

```
The balance after the credit of $100 is $100
The balance after the credit of $200 is $300
The balance after the debit of $500 is $-200
The balance after the credit of $300 is $100
The balance after the debit of $100 is $0
The current balance is $0
```

You may see different intermediate results, but each time you will see the final balance is $0 for sure.

Using Interlocked Classes

Using the lock statements, I solved the unwanted entries in the output. This is a common approach. However, you can adopt a different approach as well. To illustrate, this time I'll show you how to use the Interlocked class that provides atomic operations for variables that can be shared by multiple threads. By using this, you can enjoy **lock-free programming**.

Interlocked is a static class that has some useful methods such as Add, Increment, Decrement, Exchange, CompareExchange, and so on. You'll also see many overloaded versions. Figure 3-1 shows four overloads for the Add method.

```
- namespace System.Threading
  {
-   ...public static class Interlocked
    {
+     ...public static int Add(ref int location1, int value);
+     ...public static long Add(ref long location1, long value);
+     ...public static uint Add(ref uint location1, uint value);
+     ...public static ulong Add(ref ulong location1, ulong value);
```

Figure 3-1. *The overloaded Add methods in the Interlocked class*

Let me expand a method description:

```
//
// Summary:
//     Adds two 32-bit integers and replaces the first
// integer with the sum, as an atomic operation.
//
// Parameters:
//   location1:
//     A variable containing the first value to be added.
// The sum of the two values is stored in location1.
//
//   value:
//     The value to be added to the integer at location1.
//
// Returns:
//     The new value that was stored at location1 by this
// operation.
//
// Exceptions:
//   T:System.NullReferenceException:
//     The address of location1 is a null pointer.
public static int Add(ref int location1, int value);
```

You can see that this method can add two integers atomically. However, notice the presence of the ref parameter. Therefore, if you write something like this in the Account class:

```
public void Credit(int amount)
 {
      Interlocked.Add(ref Balance, amount);
 }
```

you'll see the compile-time error:

CS0206 A non ref-returning property or indexer may not be used as an out or ref value

Now you understand that if you want to use the Add method, you need to make some changes to the code.

Demonstration 3

Let's modify the Account class and introduce a backing field inside it as follows:

```
// The New Look of the Account Class
class Account
{
    // public decimal Balance { get; set; }
    private int _balance;
    public int Balance
    {
        get { return _balance; }
        set { _balance = value; }
    }

    public void Credit(int amount)
    {
        Interlocked.Add(ref _balance, amount);
    }
```

```
public void Debit(int amount)
{
    Interlocked.Add(ref _balance, -amount);
}
}
```

Note   To avoid repetition, I did not show the complete program. However, you can download the project Demo3_InterlockedOps to run the complete program.

Output

Run this modified program again. You will always see the following output:

```
The current balance is $0
```

You can see that this approach will produce the correct output consistently.

Q&A Session

Q3.3 You showed some task continuation examples in Chapter 1. By using that mechanism, can I avoid locking?

Yes, task continuations can indeed remove the necessity of using a lock or providing signals in certain scenarios. However, there are many situations where you'll reap benefits by using other synchronization constructs. The demonstrations that used the lock statements and the Interlocked class were good examples in this context. If required, you can combine different techniques in an application as well.

Signaling Using AutoResetEvent

Consider a multithreading environment where several threads try to access a shared resource. Now assume that any of those threads get access to this resource. Once the demand is fulfilled, this thread notifies others by saying that they can use this resource now. This kind of notification is known as **signaling**. This section discusses one signaling construct to demonstrate how different tasks (more accurately, threads) can coordinate their executions.

You are already familiar with locking mechanisms where, by releasing a lock, a thread notifies another thread that it can proceed. It is also one kind of signaling. However, this section describes a different construct (event wait handles) that uses a different kind of signaling. Let's see this.

POINT TO NOTE

I already told you that synchronization is a vast topic. To give you an idea of signaling using event wait handles, this chapter discusses the AutoResetEvent class only. See Appendix A for a discussion of the ManualResetEvent and the CountdownEvent classes.

In my city, if a passenger likes to use the metro railway service, he needs to purchase a ticket that comes in the form of a token. (Frequent travelers can purchase a card and top off the card as well.) Metro railway premises are highly secured. Passengers form a queue and enter the restricted area one by one by scanning their tokens. It is obvious that you need to form (or maintain) the queue if multiple passengers are waiting to enter the area at the same time; otherwise, you can disrupt the flow and cause chaos. **However, there is another characteristic in this scenario: the gate automatically closes once a passenger steps through. It is similar to a**

ticket turnstile in which by inserting a ticket only one passenger can pass through and then the gate closes automatically. AutoResetEvent perfectly mimics these scenarios. The documentation defines the AutoResetEvent class as follows (see https://learn.microsoft.com/en-us/dotnet/api/system.threading.autoresetevent?view=net-8.0):

> *Represents a thread synchronization event that, when signaled, releases one single waiting thread, and the event resets automatically. If no thread is waiting, the next thread that is set to the waiting state is immediately released, and the event resets automatically.*

Now the question arises: how to use AutoResetEvent? It is simple: you need to consider the following methods:

- **WaitOne**: A thread calls this method and enters the waiting (aka blocking) state.

- **Set**: An unblocked thread (that can access the AutoResetEvent instance) calls this method on it to release one blocked thread.

Do not worry! The upcoming example will make their usage clearer to you. Before I demonstrate the example, **let's see how to create an AutoResetEvent Instance.**

From the Visual Studio IDE, you can retrieve the following:

```
namespace System.Threading
{
    public sealed class AutoResetEvent : EventWaitHandle
    {
        public AutoResetEvent(bool initialState) :
         base(initialState,
         EventResetMode.AutoReset) { }
    }
}
```

This indicates you can create an AutoResetEvent instance as follows:

```
AutoResetEvent autoResetEvent = new(false);
```

Since the AutoResetEvent class derives from the EventWaitHandle class, you can write an equivalent code as follows:

```
EventWaitHandle autoResetEvent = new AutoResetEvent(false);
```

Interestingly, the EventWaitHandle class has several constructors, and each of them accepts EventResetMode as a parameter. Here is the simplest one:

```
public EventWaitHandle(bool initialState, EventResetMode mode);
```

This construct allows you to write another equivalent code as follows:

```
EventWaitHandle autoResetEvent = new (false,EventResetMode
    .AutoReset);
```

Finally, I assume I do not need to remind you that you can use the var keyword as well. For example, the following line of code is also valid:

```
var autoResetEvent = new AutoResetEvent(false);
```

Note   You may notice that while making an instance of the AutoResetEvent class, I passed false into the constructor. If you pass true into the constructor, the Set method on it is called immediately. In other words, you start with the signaled state, and a thread is released immediately. However, in my examples, I'll opt to pass false. This is because I have not seen any metro station where the officials allow the first customer to enter the restricted area without checking.

Demonstration 4

Let's consider a scenario where three potential customers want to enter a shopping mall (you can consider the metro railway station as well). *Let's assume that two customers have reached the entry gate almost at the same time. Shortly thereafter, the third customer also reaches the entry gate of this shopping mall.*

Either customer 1 or customer 2 will enter the mall first, and customer 3 should be the last one to enter. Let's see a program that mimics this scenario using AutoResetEvent.

```
using static System.Console;

var resetEvent = new AutoResetEvent(false);

WriteLine("Two customers are approaching  the mall.");
Task.Run(VisitMall);
Task.Run(VisitMall);

// Imposing some delay to mimic a real-world scenario
Thread.Sleep(2000);

WriteLine("Press any key to issue the signal from the main thread.");
ReadKey();
resetEvent.Set();
Thread.Sleep(1000);

// Reset is not required to close the gate

WriteLine("Press any key to issue another signal from the main
 thread.");
ReadKey();
resetEvent.Set();
Thread.Sleep(1000);
```

```
WriteLine("Another customer is approaching the mall.");
Task.Run(VisitMall);

WriteLine("Press any key to exit.");
ReadKey();

void VisitMall()
{
    // Imposing a small delay to mimic a real-world scenario
    Thread.Sleep(1000);
    WriteLine($"The customer {Task.CurrentId} is waiting for the
     entry pass.");
    resetEvent.WaitOne();
    WriteLine($"The customer {Task.CurrentId} enters the mall.");
}
```

Output

Here is some sample output (I pressed the Enter key to issue the signal):

```
Two customers are approaching the mall.
The customer 1 is waiting for the entry pass.
The customer 2 is waiting for the entry pass.
Press any key to issue the signal from the main thread.
The customer 1 enters the mall.
Press any key to issue another signal from the main thread.
The customer 2 enters the mall.
Another customer is approaching the mall.
Press any key to exit.
The customer 3 is waiting for the entry pass.
```

Analysis

This output reflects the following characteristics:

- This program essentially demonstrated one-way signaling where the worker threads were waiting for a signal from the main thread.

Note   You may note that the reverse flow is also possible. While solving the exercises, you will see a sample implementation (see the solution of E3.6) that demonstrates two-way signaling as well.

- Initially, both customer 1 and customer 2 were waiting for the entry pass, but once the main thread issued the signal, only customer 1 got the pass! **This depicts the fact that a signal could unblock only one waiting task (aka thread).**

- **Notice that the gate was closed automatically.** This is why no other customer could enter the mall automatically after customer 1 entered the mall. The second customer could enter the mall only when the main thread issued another signal.

- Now it makes sense why the third customer could not enter the mall yet! This customer can enter if and only if the main thread issues another signal.

Author's Note: I want you to note the last two points. While using ManualResetEvent, you'll notice a significant difference in this area. Let me show you some sample output. When I replaced the following line var resetEvent = new AutoResetEvent(false); with var resetEvent = new ManualResetEvent(false); , I got the following sample output (I pressed the Enter key to issue the signal):

```
Two customers are approaching the mall.
The customer 1 is waiting for the entry pass.
The customer 2 is waiting for the entry pass.
Press any key to issue the signal from the main thread.
The customer 1 enters the mall.
The customer 2 enters the mall.
Press any key to issue another signal from the main thread.
Another customer is approaching the mall.
Press any key to exit.
The customer 3 is waiting for the entry pass.
The customer 3 enters the mall.
```

Have you noticed the difference? Both customer 1 and customer 2 were able to enter the mall when the main thread issued the signal. In addition, customer 3 was also able to enter the mall because in between, the gate was not closed by calling the Reset method. However, do not worry! You'll see more discussion of them in Appendix A.

Q&A Session

Q3.4 It appears to me that every call to the Set method releases a thread. Is this correct?

Good question. Most of the time the answer is yes; however, there can be exceptional situations. In this context, Microsoft states the following (see the previously mentioned link):

> *There is no guarantee that every call to the Set method will release a thread. If two calls are too close together, so that the second call occurs before a thread has been released, only one thread is released. It's as if the second call did not happen.*

Q3.5 Will it be a problem when a thread calls the Set method when no other threads are waiting?

It should not cause any typical problems for you. In this case, the handle remains open until another thread calls `WaitOne`.

Q3.6 "In this case, the handle remains open until another thread calls `WaitOne`." Is there any specific thought behind this design choice?

Consider a scenario where two threads are participating in a multithreading environment. One thread calls the `Set` method, and another thread calls the `WaitOne` method simultaneously. However, assume that the `Set` method is executed just before the `Waitone` method. Let's assume that since there is no one waiting, you closed the gate now. However, in between, another thread invoked the `WaitOne` method; so it keeps waiting indefinitely. This is like a situation when you are waiting for a gate to be opened, but there is no queue. Now you understand that the proposed design prevents the race condition between threads.

Q3.7 I assume a situation where multiple threads will wait for the signals (and my code uses `AutoResetEvent`). Is it possible for me to call the Set method multiple times in advance to release them immediately?

When I showed you a sample output by using `ManualResetEvent`, you saw that this is possible. However, if your code uses `AutoResetEvent`, you need to remember the following.

If the `Set` method is called when there is no blocking thread, the handle stays open; however, it does not allow you to make multiple signals in advance. So, it does not matter how many times you release a signal in advance; when those threads appear, only one of them will be released immediately. As a result, the other threads will keep waiting for the signals.

Author's Note: Exercise 3.3 is made to demonstrate this scenario.

Concurrent Collections

Concurrent collections are an essential part of parallel programming. In a multithreaded environment, they fulfill the need for thread-safe collections. In fact, they are optimized for high-concurrency scenarios. Let's start discussing them.

System.Collections.Concurrent Namespace

I assume you are familiar with standard generic collections where you saw several types in the `System.Collections.Generic` namespace. However, concurrent collections are different from those ordinary collections. Here we'll focus on the `System.Collections.Concurrent` namespace that contains a limited number of types. In this section, I'll start the discussion of the `IProducerConsumerCollection<T>` interface. Later, I'll discuss the following types:

- `ConcurrentStack<T>`
- `ConcurrentQueue<T>`
- `ConcurrentDictionary<TKey,TValue>`
- `ConcurrentBag<T>`
- `BlockingCollection<T>`

You can safely assume that `ConcurrentStack<T>`, `ConcurrentQueue<T>`, and `ConcurrentDictionary<TKey,TValue>` are made for their nonconcurrent versions: `Stack<T>`, `Queue<T>`, and `Dictionary<TKey,TValue>`.

However, you can see that there are two additional concurrent classes called `ConcurrentBag<T>` and `BlockingCollection<T>`. You'll not find any nonconcurrent equivalent for them.

```
                      POINT TO NOTE
```

The `System.Collections.Concurrent` namespace contains a few
more types. I believe that a quick discussion on the mentioned types
will give you a fair idea about the usage of the concurrent collections.
If interested, you can learn about the remaining types from `https://`
`learn.microsoft.com/en-us/dotnet/api/system.collections.`
`concurrent?view=net-8.0`.

On the contrary, some classes do not have a counterpart in the
concurrent library. The `List<T>`, `SortedList<TKey,TValue>`, and `SortedD`
`ictionary<TKey,TValue>` are a few such examples.

IProducerConsumerCollection<T> Interface

This interface defines methods to work with thread-safe collections that are
intended for producer/consumer usage. In a producer/consumer collection,
a producer produces some items (for example, add items), and a consumer
consumes those items (for example, retrieves items while removing). If you
are familiar with stacks and queues, you already know this.

The following points that summarize some of the important
characteristics of the producer-consumer pattern:

- Developers use this pattern to decouple the process
  that produces items from the process that consumes
  those items.

- The production rate and consumption rate can be
  different.

- Normally, we use a queue to store the items. This
  is because the item that is produced first is usually
  consumed first as well.

The `ConcurrentQueue<T>`, `ConcurrentStack<T>`, and `ConcurrentBag<T>` classes implement the `IProducerConsumerCollection<T>` interface. If you investigate in Visual Studio, you'll see the screen in Figure 3-2.

```
namespace System.Collections.Concurrent
{
    public interface IProducerConsumerCollection<T> : IEnumerable<T>, IEnumerable, ICollection
    {
        void CopyTo(T[] array, int index);
        T[] ToArray();
        bool TryAdd(T item);
        bool TryTake([MaybeNullWhen(false)] out T item);
    }
}
```

Figure 3-2. *The IProducerConsumerCollection<T> interface inside the System.Collections.Concurrent namespace*

You can see that `IProducerConsumerCollection<T>` inherits from three more interfaces and contains four methods: `CopyTo`, `ToArray`, `TryAdd`, and `TryTake`. The last two will be useful for our upcoming discussions. Let's learn about them.

- The `TryAdd` method attempts to add an object to `IProducerConsumerCollection<T>`. If the object is added, the method returns `true`; otherwise, it returns `false`.

- The `TryTake` method attempts to remove and return an object from `IProducerConsumerCollection<T>`. The method returns `true` if the object is removed and returned successfully. Otherwise, it will return `false`. (You may note that the `item` parameter in the method signature is used to contain the removed object.)

You know that if a concrete class implements the `IProducerConsumerCollection<T>` interface, it must provide the implementations of the members in the interface. (Starting from C# 8.0, you can have default interface methods that can have some default implementation. However,

I am not talking about them here.) Since the ConcurrentQueue<T>, ConcurrentStack<T>, and ConcurrentBag<T> classes implement the IProducerConsumerCollection<T> interface, they must provide the implementation for the TryAdd and TryTake methods.

Let's see how the ConcurrentStack<T> class implements the TryAdd method. From Visual Studio, you can see the following explicit implementation:

```
bool IProducerConsumerCollection<T>.TryAdd(T item)
{
    Push(item);
    return true;
}
```

where the Push method is further defined as follows:

```
public void Push(T item)
{

    Node newNode = new Node(item);
    newNode._next = _head;
    if (Interlocked.CompareExchange(ref _head, newNode,
      newNode._next) != newNode._next)
    {

    PushCore(newNode, newNode);
}
```

You can see that in the case of a stack, the TryAdd method internally calls the Push method. The presence of the Interlocked operation in the Push method ensures that while using this method, you do not need to worry about the lock statements.

Similarly, if you investigate how the ConcurrentQueue<T> class implements the TryAdd method, you'll see the following:

```
bool IProducerConsumerCollection<T>.TryAdd(T item)
 {
     Enqueue(item);
     return true;
 }
```

You can see that in case of a queue, the TryAdd method internally calls the Enqueue method. On further study, you'll see that the Enqueue method is defined as follows:

```
    public void Enqueue(T item)
    {
        if (!_tail.TryEnqueue(item))
        {
            EnqueueSlow(item);
        }
    }
```

However, the EnqueueSlow method uses the lock statement as follows:

```
  private void EnqueueSlow(T item)
  {
     while (true)
     {
         ConcurrentQueueSegment<T> tail = _tail;

         // Try to append to the existing tail.
         if (tail.TryEnqueue(item))
         {
            break;
         }
```

```
lock (_crossSegmentLock)
{
// The remaining code is not shown
```

POINT TO NOTE

From these code segments, you can see that the `ConcurrentStack<T>` and `ConcurrentQueue<T>` classes implement the `TryAdd` method explicitly and expose the same functionality using specifically named public methods such as `Push` and `Enqueue`. You may also note that I have picked these code segments while executing my programs in .NET 8. However, if you investigate the same code in .NET 7, you'll see many supporting comments that can help you understand these functions better.

Have you seen any other important observations from these code segments? If not, do not worry! You'll see them in the next section when I'll summarize some other important points as well. For now, let's talk about the `TryTake` method.

In Figure 3-2, I showed you the `IProducerConsumerCollection<T>` interface details from the Visual Studio IDE. This figure showed that the `TryTake` method has the following signature:

```
bool TryTake([MaybeNullWhen(false)] out T item);
```

You understand that an implementer of `IProducerConsumerColle ction<T>` must provide the implementation for this method. I already investigated the `TryAdd` method in the `ConcurrentStack<T>` and `ConcurrentQueue<T>` classes. You can repeat a similar investigation and essentially learn the following:

- In the case of a stack, the `TryTake` method removes the most recently added element.

- In the case of a queue, the TryTake method removes the least recently added element.

- In the case of a bag, the TryTake method removes whatever element it can remove most efficiently.

Notable Characteristics

From our discussion on the concurrent collections so far, let me point out the notable characteristics. I suggest you read them carefully before you jump into the next section.

1. **When you see a concurrent collection for its noncurrent equivalent, you can find similarities.** It is obvious that there are some differences in the access mechanisms, but the general concept is the same. For example, both ConcurrentQueue<T> and Queue<T> support the first-in, first-out mechanism. So, if you are familiar with the Queue<T>, you can easily understand the ConcurrentQueue<T>.

2. **Consumers of these collections do not need to worry about the locks.** You may find that the necessary lock statements are provided internally in these structures. For example, when I showed you the TryAdd implementations in ConcurrentStack<T> and ConcurrentQueue<T>, you saw that the designers already used lock and interlocked internally in the respective places. This gives you the clue that Microsoft made concurrent collections by using the lock statements internally to make them thread-safe. In fact, while discussing concurrent dictionaries, Microsoft also ensures the

following (see https://learn.microsoft.com/en-us/dotnet/api/system.collections.concurrent.concurrentdictionary-2?view=net-8.0)

For modifications and write operations to the dictionary, Con currentDictionary<TKey,TValue> uses fine-grained locking to ensure thread safety.

POINT TO NOTE

In this context, I also encourage you to read the Microsoft blog at https://devblogs.microsoft.com/pfxteam/faq-are-all-of-the-new-concurrent-collections-lock-free/ to get more information. However, I suggest you read this blog once you are familiar with the common operations of these concurrent collections and acquire some basic ideas about memory barriers.

---

3. In the built-in implementations (that I showed you when I investigated the TryAdd method in ConcurrentStack<T> and ConcurrentQueue<T>), **you can also see how to use linked lists, which are conducive to lock-free or low-lock implementations**.

4. You saw that the ConcurrentStack<T> and ConcurrentQueue<T> classes implement the TryAdd method explicitly and expose the same functionality using specifically named public methods such as Push and Enqueue. **If you investigate the TryTake method, you'll have a similar observation. The only difference is that this time you'll see the methods TryPop (for the stack) and TryDequeue (for the queue).**

5. Shortly, you'll see the `ConcurrentDictionary<TKey,`
    `TValue>` class. It is the only concurrent collection
    that provides access to a specific item using a key.
    For example, if a dictionary contains 10 elements,
    you can get the fifth element (without removing it)
    using the key.

POINT TO NOTE

You may note that the `ConcurrentStack<T>`, `ConcurrentQueue<T>`, and
`ConcurrentBag<T>` classes also have a `TryPeek` method that you can use
to see the next item in the collection without removing it. However, you may
note that the `TryPeek` method in these classes lets us look only one item deep
into the collection, whereas the `ConcurrentDictionary<Tkey,TValue>`
class lets you see any item using the key.

---

6. About the `IProducerConsumerCollection<T>`
    interface, the official documentation states the
    following (see `https://learn.microsoft.com/en-`
    `us/dotnet/api/system.collections.concurrent.`
    `iproducerconsumercollection-1?view=net-8.0`):

*Defines methods to manipulate thread-safe collections
intended for producer/consumer usage. This interface provides a unified representation for producer/consumer collections so that higher level abstractions such as
BlockingCollection<T> can use the collection as the underlying storage mechanism.*

It is obvious that the `IProducerConsumerCollection<T>` types can be used based on your needs. In addition, this official documentation also states that **they can serve as backing storage(s) when you use them with the `BlockingCollection<T>` class.** (You will learn more about this when I discuss the `BlockingCollection<T>` class.)

Q&A Session

Q3.8 Why do we need concurrent collections when we can use common synchronization techniques such as lock statements to ensure thread safety?

Using a lock statement, you essentially turn a multithreaded code segment into a single-threaded code segment (at least within the lock statement). As a result, you essentially defeat the associated benefits of using a multithreaded application.

Q3.9 Does the use of a few lock statements matter for a simple application?

It is true that in the case of a tiny application, using a few lock statements does not matter much. However, what about an enterprise application? If you need to use the `lock` statements in several places, but you unfortunately miss one of them, you will receive an erroneous output. When multiple developers work on the same code base, this type of problem can occur easily. This is why though `lock` statements can make your code thread-safe, they may not always provide an ideal solution.

Q3.10 In that case, how can you make a better solution?

Notice that instead of working on a thread-unsafe data structure and guarding its usage by surrounding the `lock` statements by yourself, it would be better if you could directly work on the thread-safe data structures where the designers themselves ensure the thread-safety. The good news is that Microsoft provides you with this facility by providing you with concurrent collections, which is the topic of our discussion now.

ConcurrentStack<T>

This section demonstrates how to use the ConcurrentStack<T> class in a program. It is a thread-safe last in-first out (LIFO) collection. You already know that its nonconcurrent equivalent is Stack<T>. Let's exercise some programming now.

The following code creates an instance of this class:

```
var stack = new ConcurrentStack<int>();
```

The Push method inserts an element at the top of the stack. Here is a sample where I push three elements as follows:

```
stack.Push(1);
stack.Push(2);
stack.Push(3);
```

The stack contains three elements now. Let's examine two other useful methods.

- The TryPeek method attempts to return the top element from the stack without removing it.

- However, the TryPop method tries to remove the top element from the stack. Otherwise, it will return false.

Let's test these methods by appending the following code segment:

```
int top;
if (stack.TryPeek(out top))
    WriteLine($"{top} is on top now.");

if (stack.TryPop(out top))
    WriteLine($"{top} is popped now.");

if (stack.TryPeek(out top))
    WriteLine($"{top} is on top now.");
```

At this stage, if you run this program, you can see the following output:

```
3 is on top now.
3 is popped now.
2 is on top now.
```

The output confirms that the TryPeek did not remove the top element, whereas the TryPop method was able to pop the top element (which is 3 in our example).

There is a method for efficient popping, which is called TryPopRange. This method attempts to pop and return multiple elements from the top of ConcurrentStack<T> atomically. The simplest version of this method has the following signature:

```
public int TryPopRange(T[] items)
```

You can see that the return type of the TryPopRange is not a boolean, but it is an int. Keeping this in mind, you can write the following code that tries to pop five elements from the top of the stack and displays the result (in this code segment, items is a placeholder to hold the elements):

```
var items = new int[5];
if (stack.TryPopRange(items) > 0)
{
    foreach (int item in items)
    {
        Write($"{item}\t");
    }
}
```

You may be thinking that since our stack has two elements now, trying to pop more than two elements at this moment can cause an exception. **However, this assumption is not correct!** If you run this code segment, you won't receive any exception; instead, you'll see the following output:

```
2       1       0       0       0
```

You can see that 2 and 1 were popped successfully. What about the remaining zeros? You guessed it right! They are the default values of the array cells.

However, the TryPopRange method has another overload that has the following signature:

```
public int TryPopRange(T[] items, int startIndex, int count)
```

The parameters have their usual meaning (you can learn about them at https://learn.microsoft.com/en-us/dotnet/api/system.collections.concurrent.concurrentstack-1.trypoprange?view=net-8.0). Using this overloaded version, if you write the following code segment:

```
var items = new int[5];
if (stack.TryPopRange(items, 1, 3) > 0)
{
    foreach (int item in items)
    {
        Write($"{item}\t");
    }
}
```

You'll see the following output:

```
0       2       1       0       0
```

Notice that this time the top three elements from the stack are popped, and they are placed in the items array starting from index 1.

POINT TO NOTE

However, while using this overloaded version of TryPopRange, you need to be careful. If startIndex + count is greater than the length of items, you'll receive the System.ArgumentException exception.

If you need to add many elements to the stack, pushing one element at a time may not be a good idea. In this case, you can use an efficient method, called PushRange. About this method, Microsoft (states the following (see https://learn.microsoft.com/en-us/dotnet/api/system.collections.concurrent.concurrentstack-1.pushrange?view=net-8.0):

> ...*PushRange* guarantees that all of the elements will be added atomically, meaning that no other threads will be able to inject elements between the elements being pushed. Items at lower indices in the items array will be pushed before items at higher indices.

To illustrate, let me create an array of three integers and push them to our current stack as follows:

```
var newElements = new int[] { 10, 11, 12 };
stack.PushRange(newElements);
```

If you put a breakpoint and debug the code, you'll see the expected result (see Figure 3-3).

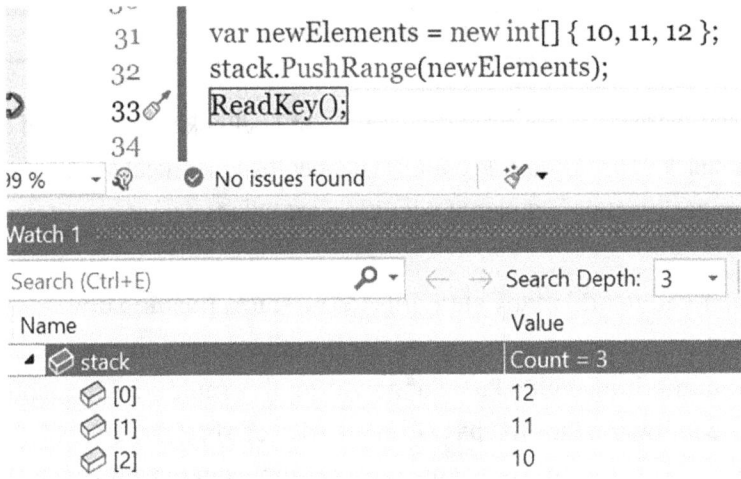

Figure 3-3. *The integers 10, 11, and 12 are pushed to the stack*

Note   You can download the project Understanding
ConcurrentStack to run the code segments that I discussed so far.

I assume you now have gotten an idea about the concurrent stack.
**Since you are learning about parallel programming, let's now exercise
a program where multiple tasks are involved in a multithreaded
environment.** In this example, you'll see the following namespace:

```
using System.Collections.Concurrent;
```

This is because we are working on the types that are available in this
namespace.

Note   In fact, in all programs in this section, you will see this
namespace.

176

Next, you will see me using the following code:

```
IProducerConsumerCollection<Car> cars = new
ConcurrentStack<Car>();
```

You can see that I used the polymorphic code while instantiating an instance of ConcurrentStack<Car>. Alternatively, I could instantiate this as follows: ConcurrentStack<Car> cars = new ConcurrentStack<Car>();. This approach could allow me to call class-specific methods such as Push, as well as TryPop on the cars instance. However, I did not opt for this approach because of the following reason:

- You can change the underlying data structure easily. For example, when I demonstrate to you the concurrent version of the Queue class, I will change only one line of code, which is as follows: IProducer ConsumerCollection<Car> cars= new Concurrent Queue<Car>();. There will be no other change in that demonstration.

Next, you'll see two different tasks (addBlackCarModelsTask and addNonBlackCarModelsTask) start running on separate threads. These tasks are used to push different Car instances where the Car class is defined as follows:

```
class Car(string model, string color)
{
    private string _model = model;
    private string _color = color;

    public override string ToString()
    {
        return $"[{_model},{_color}]";
    }
}
```

POINT TO NOTE

I have used a primary constructor in this class. This feature comes in C# 12. Here is the equivalent code that does not use the primary constructor in the Car class:

```
class Car
{
    private string _model;
    private string _color;
    public Car(string model, string color)
    {
        _model = model;
        _color = color;
    }
    public override string ToString()
    {
        return $"[{_model},{_color}]";
    }
}
```

You can learn more about primary constructors at https://learn. microsoft.com/en-us/dotnet/csharp/whats-new/tutorials/ primary-constructors.

To make the program short and simple, I used three simple methods. They are as follows:

- The AddBlackCarModels method is used to push the cars that have the black color.

- The AddNonBlackCarModels method is used to push the cars that do not have the black color.

- The RemoveCarModels method is used to remove the cars from the collection.

Once the cars are added to the stack, a third task, called removeCarsTask, is created to exercise the RemoveCarModels method. You should not have any trouble understanding the rest of the program now.

Demonstration 5

Here is the complete program:

POINTS TO NOTE

I want you to note the following points:

- To demonstrate the working mechanisms of different collections, I have used only a few cars in this demonstration and the upcoming demonstrations. So, you need not worry about the little bit of code duplication in these examples. In a real-life scenario, you can use common functionality to avoid code repetitions.

- For simplicity and to avoid more typing, I am using the terms *car models* and *cars* interchangeably. I hope that this will not trouble you much.

```
using static System.Console;
using System.Collections.Concurrent;

IProducerConsumerCollection<Car> cars = new
ConcurrentStack<Car>();

var addBlackCarModelsTask = Task.Run(AddBlackCarModels);
var addNonBlackCarModelsTask = Task.Run(AddNonBlackCarModels);
.Task.WaitAll(addBlackCarModelsTask, addNonBlackCarModelsTask);
```

```
WriteLine($"A total of {cars.Count} cars are added to the
    repository.");

WriteLine("Removing the items now...");
var removeCarsTask = Task.Run(RemoveCarModels);
removeCarsTask.Wait();
WriteLine($"A total of {cars.Count} cars are present in the
    repository now.");
void AddNonBlackCarModels()
{
    Car car;
    car = new("Hyundai Creta", "Pearl");
    WriteLine($"Adding: {car}");
    cars.TryAdd(car);
    Thread.Sleep(1000);

    car = new("Maruti Suzuki Alto 800", "Red");
    WriteLine($"Adding: {car}");
    cars.TryAdd(car);
    Thread.Sleep(1000);

    car = new("Toyota Fortuner Avant", "Bronze");
    WriteLine($"Adding: {car}");
    cars.TryAdd(car);
    Thread.Sleep(1000);
}

void AddBlackCarModels()
{
    Car car;
    car = new("Toyota Fortuner Attitude", "Black");
```

```
    WriteLine($"Adding: {car}");
    cars.TryAdd(car);
    Thread.Sleep(1000);

    car = new("Hyundai Creta Abyss", "Black");
    WriteLine($"Adding: {car}");
    cars.TryAdd(car);
    Thread.Sleep(1000);
}

void RemoveCarModels()
{
    foreach (Car car in cars)
    {
        cars.TryTake(out Car result);
        WriteLine($"Tried removing: {result}");
    }

}

// Using primary constructor
class Car(string model, string color)
{
    private string _model = model;
    private string _color = color;
    public override string ToString()
    {
        return $"[{_model}, {_color}]";
    }
}
```

Output

Here is some sample output:

```
Adding: [Toyota Fortuner Attitude, Black]
Adding: [Hyundai Creta, Pearl]
Adding: [Hyundai Creta Abyss, Black]
Adding: [Maruti Suzuki Alto 800, Red]
Adding: [Toyota Fortuner Avant, Bronze]
A total of 5 cars are added to the repository.
Removing the items now...
Tried removing: [Toyota Fortuner Avant, Bronze]
Tried removing: [Maruti Suzuki Alto 800, Red]
Tried removing: [Hyundai Creta Abyss, Black]
Tried removing: [Hyundai Creta, Pearl]
Tried removing: [Toyota Fortuner Attitude, Black]
A total of 0 cars are present in the repository now.
```

Analysis

You can see that all five car models were added to the stack, but they were removed in a last in first out (LIFO) fashion.

ConcurrentQueue<T>

The ConcurrentQueue<T> class is a thread-safe first in-first out (FIFO) collection. You already know that its nonconcurrent equivalent is Queue<T>. Earlier I told you if you are familiar with Queue<T>, you can easily understand ConcurrentQueue<T>. Let's verify some simple code segments that use some useful methods of this class.

The following code creates an instance of this class:

```
var queue = new ConcurrentQueue<int>();
```

While discussing the ConcurrentStack<T> class, you used the Push and TryPop methods. This time you will see the Enqueue and TryDequeue methods. The Enqueue method adds an element at the end of the queue (often called the *rear* end). Here is a sample of adding three elements:

```
queue.Enqueue(1);
queue.Enqueue(2);
queue.Enqueue(3);
```

The queue contains three elements now. Let's examine two other useful methods.

- The TryPeek method attempts to return the element from the beginning of the queue (often called the *front* end) without removing it.

- However, the TryDequeue method tries to remove the element from the front end. Otherwise, it will return false.

Let's test these methods by appending the following code segment:

```
int front;
if (queue.TryPeek(out front))
    WriteLine($"{front} is at the front now.");

if (queue.TryDequeue(out front))
    WriteLine($"{front} is removed now.");

if (queue.TryPeek(out front))
    WriteLine($"{front} is at the front now.");
```

At this stage, if you run this program, you can see the following output:

```
1 is at the front now.
1 is removed now.
2 is at the front now.
```

The output confirms that TryPeek did not remove the front element, whereas the TryDequeue method was able to remove the front element (which is 3 in our example).

Note   You can download the project UnderstandingConcurrent Queue to run these code segments that I discussed so far.

Let's now exercise a program where multiple tasks are involved in a multithreaded environment.

Demonstration 6

In the previous demonstration, you saw the following line:

```
IProducerConsumerCollection<Car> cars = new ConcurrentStack<Car>();
```

Replace this line with the following one (the key change is shown in bold):

```
IProducerConsumerCollection<Car> cars = new ConcurrentQueue<Car>();
```

There is no other change in this program. Since it is a small change, I do not show the entire program. You can download the project Demo6_ ConcurrentQueueDemo to see the complete program.

Output

Here is some sample output after running this program:

```
Adding: [Hyundai Creta, Pearl]
Adding: [Toyota Fortuner Attitude, Black]
Adding: [Maruti Suzuki Alto 800, Red]
Adding: [Hyundai Creta Abyss, Black]
Adding: [Toyota Fortuner Avant, Bronze]
```

```
A total of 5 cars are added to the repository.
Removing the items now...
Tried removing: [Hyundai Creta, Pearl]
Tried removing: [Toyota Fortuner Attitude, Black]
Tried removing: [Maruti Suzuki Alto 800, Red]
Tried removing: [Hyundai Creta Abyss, Black]
Tried removing: [Toyota Fortuner Avant, Bronze]
A total of 0 cars are present in the repository now.
```

Analysis

You can see all five different car models were added to the queue, and later, they were removed in first in first out (FIFO) fashion.

ConcurrentBag<T>

You have seen the concurrent versions of stacks and queues. However, if you are familiar with the concept of stack and queue data structure, you might have been a little bit bored. This time, let's learn about concurrent bags that do not guarantee the orderings. They are neither FIFO nor LIFO. Microsoft states the following about them (see https://learn. microsoft.com/en-us/dotnet/api/system.collections.concurrent.co ncurrentbag-1?view=net-8.0):

> *Bags are useful for storing objects when ordering doesn't matter, and unlike sets, bags support duplicates. ConcurrentBag<T> is a thread-safe bag implementation, optimized for scenarios where the same thread will be both producing and consuming data stored in the bag. ConcurrentBag<T> accepts null as a valid value for reference types.*

In the case of a concurrent stack, you saw the Push, TryPop, and TryPeek methods. In the case of a concurrent queue, you saw the Enqueue, TryDequeue, and TryPeek methods. In the case of a concurrent bag, you will see the Add, TryTake, and TryPeek methods in similar contexts.

However, before I show you the demonstration, let's understand the basic working mechanism. Let me tell you that it's a complex algorithm. (If you disagree with me, I suggest you see the implementation of the built-in method TrySteal.) However, I am trying to simplify this algorithm for you using some simple diagrams that you see shortly.

Before you see these diagrams, remember that internally each thread gets its own isolated storage (more specifically, its own private linked list). As a result, while adding the data, there is no conflict. In Figure 3-4, two threads add some items (using the Add method) in their own thread areas.

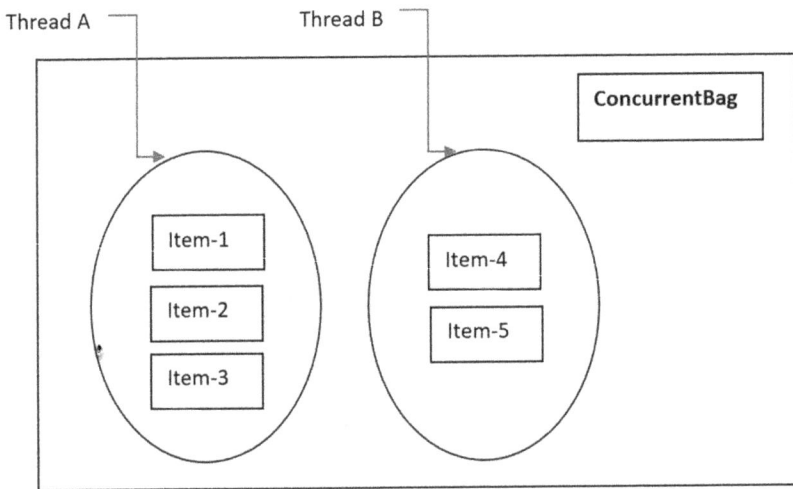

Figure 3-4. *The concurrent bag's status after the addition of five items by Thread A and Thread B*

By calling the TryTake method, a thread can remove an element from its storage area. Let's assume, Thread A calls TryTake once and removes Item-3. Let's also assume that Thread B calls the TryTake method twice. As a result, both Item 4 and Item 5 will be removed (one-by-one) from their storage areas. Figure 3-5 depicts this situation after these removals.

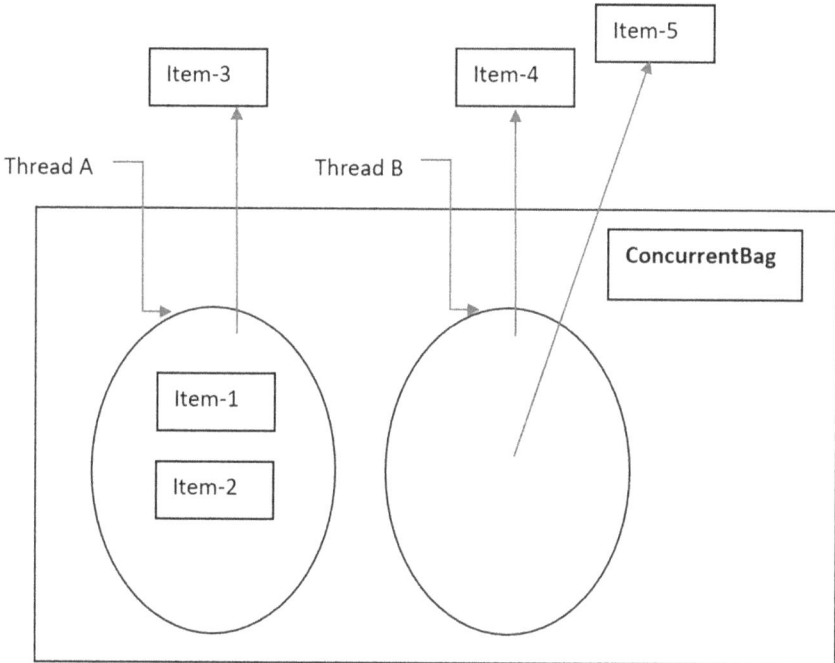

Figure 3-5.   *The concurrent bag's status after the removal of Item-3, Item-4, and Item-5*

Let's assume that Thread B calls the TryTake method once more. Since there is no item in its thread area, now it will try taking another item from its neighbor, i.e., Thread A's storage area (see Figure 3-6).

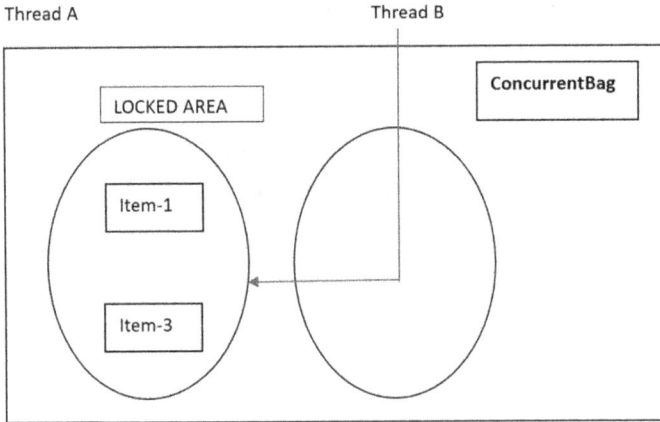

Figure 3-6. *Thread B is stealing an item from Thread A*

While taking this item, Thread A's storage area will be locked (if you see the implementation of TrySteal, you can see the Interlocked operation). As a result, this time the execution will be slower. In this algorithm, since one thread steals an item from another thread, this is often called a **work-stealing algorithm.**

In the upcoming demonstration, you'll see me using the TryTake method. This method attempts to remove and return an object from the concurrent bag. If you investigate the implementation in Visual Studio, you'll see the following:

```
public bool TryTake([MaybeNullWhen(false)] out T result)
{
    WorkStealingQueue? queue =
    GetCurrentThreadWorkStealingQueue(forceCreate: false);
    return (
      queue != null &&
      queue.TryLocalPop(out result)) ||
      TrySteal(out result, take: true);
}
```

On further investigation, you'll learn that TryLocalPop removes an item from the tail of the queue, and TrySteal is a local helper method to steal an item from any other nonempty thread. I hope that things are making sense to you!

However, most of the time, a thread adds items to its own storage area and removes items from its own storage area. Since there is no need to employ locks in these cases, the executions are very fast.

I assume that you have got the idea! Let's see the demonstration now. In the previous demonstration, you saw the following line:

```
IProducerConsumerCollection<Car> cars = new ConcurrentQueue<Car>();
```

This time you'll see the following (the key change is shown in bold):

```
IProducerConsumerCollection<Car> cars = new ConcurrentBag<Car>();
```

Note that ConcurrentBag<T> implements the TryAdd method of the IP roducerConsumerCollection<T> interface as follows:

```
bool IProducerConsumerCollection<T>.TryAdd(T item)
{
    Add(item);
    return true;
}
```

You can see that the TryAdd method internally calls the Add method. I used the TryAdd method in this demonstration to make it similar to the previous programs.

However, I slightly modified the methods. Earlier, you saw AddBlackCarModels and AddNonBlackCarModels. In that case, these AddXXX methods were performing the addition operations only; this time I renamed them to ProcessXXX (i.e., ProcessBlackCarModels and ProcessNonBlackCarModels). This is because to describe the working mechanism of a concurrent bag, I want the respective tasks to perform both the addition and removal operations. In addition, I also display the task IDs to verify which task performed the addition or the removal.

Demonstration 7

Here is the complete program. (There is no change in the Car class. It is not shown to avoid the repetition.)

```
using static System.Console;
using System.Collections.Concurrent;

IProducerConsumerCollection<Car> cars = new ConcurrentBag<Car>();

var addBlackCars = Task.Run(ProcessBlackCarModels);
var addNonBlackCars = Task.Run(ProcessNonBlackCarModels);
Task.WaitAll(addBlackCars, addNonBlackCars);
WriteLine($"At present, the repository contains {cars.Count}
 car(s).");

void ProcessNonBlackCarModels()
{
    Car car;
    car = new("Hyundai Creta", "Pearl");
    WriteLine($"Adding: {car} using task-{Task.CurrentId}");
    cars.TryAdd(car);
    Thread.Sleep(1000);

    car = new("Maruti Suzuki Alto 800", "Red");
    WriteLine($"Adding: {car} using task-{Task.CurrentId}");
    cars.TryAdd(car);
    Thread.Sleep(1000);
```

```
    car = new("Toyota Fortuner Avant", "Bronze");
    WriteLine($"Adding: {car} using task-{Task.CurrentId}");
    cars.TryAdd(car);
    Thread.Sleep(1000);

    WriteLine($"Task-{Task.CurrentId} will try removing one
     item now.");
    if (cars.Count > 0)
    {
        cars.TryTake(out Car removeCar);
        WriteLine($"Tried removing: {removeCar} using task-
         {Task.CurrentId}");
    }
}

void ProcessBlackCarModels()
{
    Car car;
    car = new("Toyota Fortuner Attitude", "Black");
    WriteLine($"Adding: {car} using task-{Task.CurrentId}");
    cars.TryAdd(car);
    Thread.Sleep(1000);

    car = new("Hyundai Creta Abyss", "Black");
    WriteLine($"Adding: {car} using task-{Task.CurrentId}");
    cars.TryAdd(car);

    // Putting a relatively long sleep so that the other
    // task can finish in between.
    Thread.Sleep(5000);

    WriteLine($"Task-{Task.CurrentId} will try removing three
     items now.");
```

```
for (int i = 0; i < 3; i++)
{
    if (cars.Count > 0)
     {
        cars.TryTake(out Car removeCar);
        WriteLine($"Tried removing: {removeCar} using task-
          {Task.CurrentId}");
    }
  }
}
```

```
// There is no change in the Car class. It is not shown to
// avoid the repetition.
```

Output

Here is some sample output after running this program:

```
Adding: [Toyota Fortuner Attitude, Black] using task-1
Adding: [Hyundai Creta, Pearl] using task-2
Adding: [Hyundai Creta Abyss, Black] using task-1
Adding: [Maruti Suzuki Alto 800, Red] using task-2
Adding: [Toyota Fortuner Avant, Bronze] using task-2
Task-2 will try removing one item now.
Tried removing: [Toyota Fortuner Avant, Bronze] using task-2
Task-1 will try removing three items now.
Tried removing: [Hyundai Creta Abyss, Black] using task-1
Tried removing: [Toyota Fortuner Attitude, Black] using task-1
Tried removing: [Hyundai Creta, Pearl] using task-1
At present, the repository contains 1 car(s).
```

Analysis

Notice that `task-1` added the black cars, and `task-2` added the nonblack cars. Later, `task-2` removed one car, and `task-1` removed three more cars. Here is the interesting part: while removing these cars, these tasks first attempt to remove the cars that were added by them. For example, `task-2` removed the car [Toyota Fortuner Avant, Bronze] because it was available in its private storage. However, `task-1` added only two black cars. This is why while removing, it first removed those black cars and then took another car from its neighbor and removed it as well.

Did you notice another interesting point? Each thread first tried to remove the items that were most recently added by them to their local list . However, while removing an item from a neighbor list, `task-1` removed the least recently added item from the neighbor's list.

Author's Note: Regarding the removal process, if interested, you can see the online discussion at `https://stackoverflow.com/questions/78382286/trytake-is-stealing-an-element-that-was-added-least-recently-on-another-thread/78387452#78387452`.

Q&A Session

Q3.11 How does `List<T>` differ from `ConcurrentBag<T>`?

`List<T>` is ordered, whereas `ConcurrentBag<T>` is unordered. However, the important thing to understand is that `ConcurrentBag<T>` is thread-safe, but the other one is not thread-safe. In a concurrent environment, instead of manually implementing the locking mechanism with `List<T>`, it is often advantageous to use a built-in thread-safe construct like `ConcurrentBag<T>`.

BlockingCollection<T>

Microsoft states the following about the `BlockingCollection<T>` class (see `https://learn.microsoft.com/en-us/dotnet/api/system.collections.concurrent.blockingcollection-1?view=net-8.0`):

> *Provides blocking and bounding capabilities for thread-safe collections that implement IProducerConsumerCollection<T>.*

Why do we need the blocking and bounding capabilities? Let me remind you that the core idea behind the producer-consumer pattern is that the producers produce some items and the consumers consume those items. However, the production and consumption rates can vary. As a result, you need to be prepared for the following situations:

- You cannot add an item if the underlying collection is full.

- You cannot remove an item if the underlying collection is empty.

This is why we need the blocking and bounding capabilities in a producer-consumer pattern.

Let's recollect how to use the built-in `TryAdd` and `TryTake` methods of the `IProducerConsumerCollection<T>` interface. When the `TryXXX` methods are unsuccessful, they return `false`. (For example, invoking the `TryTake` method on `ConcurrentQueue<T>` returns `false` if the queue is empty.)

However, sometimes you'd like the consumer to wait until an item is available or the producer to wait until a slot is available to place the produced item. How can you achieve this? You'll probably be tempted to make an overloaded version of these methods. However, the C# designers make your life easy! They have designed the `BlockingCollection<T>` type to support these scenarios.

Now the question is: how does BlockingCollection<T> help? It wraps any collection that implements IProducerConsumerCollection<T>. So, depending upon a user's choice, it can wrap any of the following types:

- ConcurrentQueue<T>

- ConcurrentStack<T>

- ConcurrentBag<T>

By default, it uses ConcurrentQueue<T>. As a result, now a consumer can take an item from the wrapped collection if an item is available. Otherwise, the consumer is blocked. Similarly, by limiting the size of the collection, you can block a producer when the collection is full. A collection limited in this manner is known as a **bounded blocking collection**.

POINT TO NOTE

The blocking collection is not itself a collection. It is just a wrapper around an underlying collection that implements the IProducerConsumerCollection<T> interface.

Let's see how to use the BlockingCollection<T> class. At the time of this writing, this class has the following constructors:

```
public BlockingCollection();
public BlockingCollection(IProducerConsumerCollection<T>
  collection);
public BlockingCollection(int boundedCapacity);
public BlockingCollection(IProducerConsumerCollection<T>
  collection, int boundedCapacity);
```

You can see that you can wrap a collection that implements `IProducer` `ConsumerCollection<T>`. At the same time, you can also limit the size (see the `boundedCapacity` parameters).

While using the `BlockingCollection<T>` class, you need to remember the following:

- First, you instantiate the class. You can also specify the underlying collection along with the size. In the upcoming demonstration, I used the following line: `BlockingCollection<Car> cars = new(3);`, so, in this case, the `ConcurrentQueue<Car>` with size 3 will be instantiated. If you want a concurrent bag, you can write something like the following: `BlockingCollection<Car> cars = new(new ConcurrentBag<Car>(), 3);`.

- To add (i.e., produce) an element to the underlying collection, you can use the `Add` or `TryAdd` method. I have used the `Add` method in the upcoming example. In addition, I invoked the `CompleteAdding` method to put an end marker after which no element can be added to the collection. The consumers can monitor the `IsCompleted` property to know when this collection is empty or if no more additions will be accepted.

- Similarly, to remove (i.e., consume) an element, you can use the `Take` or `TryTake` method. However, when I consume the items, I have used `GetConsumingEnumerable`, which helps me to consume the elements when they are available. In other words, you block the task if there is no element to consume, but you resume the task when an element is available.

BLOCKINGCOLLECTION<T>.ADD VS. BLOCKINGCOLLECTION<T>.TRYADD

The documentation at `https://learn.microsoft.com/en-us/dotnet/api/system.collections.concurrent.blockingcollection-1.add?view=net-8.0` states the following:

If a bounded capacity was specified when this instance of BlockingCollection<T> was initialized, a call to Add may block until space is available to store the provided item.

The documentation at `https://learn.microsoft.com/en-us/dotnet/api/system.collections.concurrent.blockingcollection-1.tryadd?view=net-8.0` states the following:

Tries to add the specified item to the BlockingCollection<T> within the specified time period, while observing a cancellation token.

You can see that the Add method and the TryAdd method are similar except for the second one, you can use a timeout parameter. A similar difference can be observed between the Take and TryTake methods.

Now you should not face any difficulty in understanding the following program that produces 10 similar cars and consumes them in parallel. You may note that in this program, the production rate is much higher than the consumption rate (a production takes a minimum of 200 milliseconds, whereas a consumption takes a minimum of 500 milliseconds).

POINT TO NOTE

There are a few more interesting properties and methods available inside the `BlockingCollection<T>` class. You can use them to manage different scenarios such as cancellations and timeouts as well. In the following program, I did not use them. However, you can learn about those remaining constructs at `https://learn.microsoft.com/en-us/dotnet/api/system.collections.concurrent.blockingcollection-1.-ctor?view=net-8.0`.

Demonstration 8

Here is the complete program (since there is no change in the Car class, it is not shown to avoid the repetition):

```
using static System.Console;
using System.Collections.Concurrent;

BlockingCollection<Car> cars = new(3);

var produceAndConsumeTask=Task.Run(ExerciseProducerConsumer);
produceAndConsumeTask.Wait();
WriteLine($"At present, the repository contains {cars.Count}
 car(s).");

void ExerciseProducerConsumer()
{
    var producerTask = Task.Run(ProduceCars);
    // Activating the producer a little bit early
    Thread.Sleep(300);
    var consumerTask = Task.Run(ConsumeCars);
    try
```

```
    {
        Task.WaitAll(producerTask, consumerTask);
    }
    catch (Exception ex)
    {
        WriteLine(ex.ToString());
    }
}

void ProduceCars()
{
    Car car;
    for(int i = 0;i<10;i++)
    {
        car = new($"{i}-Hyundai Creta", "Pearl");
        cars.Add(car);
        Thread.Sleep(200);
        WriteLine($"Produced: {car}");

    }
    // The following code prevents the consumer's foreach loop
    // from hanging
    cars.CompleteAdding();
    WriteLine($"+++ Production completed. +++");
}
void ConsumeCars()
{
    foreach (var car in cars.GetConsumingEnumerable())
    {
        WriteLine($"\tConsumed: {car}");
        Thread.Sleep(500);
    }
```

```
    WriteLine($"--- Consumption completed. ---");
}

// There is no change in the Car class. It is not shown to
// avoid the repetition.
```

Output

Here is some sample output after running this program:

```
Produced: [0-Hyundai Creta, Pearl]
        Consumed: [0-Hyundai Creta, Pearl]
Produced: [1-Hyundai Creta, Pearl]
Produced: [2-Hyundai Creta, Pearl]
        Consumed: [1-Hyundai Creta, Pearl]
Produced: [3-Hyundai Creta, Pearl]
Produced: [4-Hyundai Creta, Pearl]
        Consumed: [2-Hyundai Creta, Pearl]
Produced: [5-Hyundai Creta, Pearl]
        Consumed: [3-Hyundai Creta, Pearl]
Produced: [6-Hyundai Creta, Pearl]
        Consumed: [4-Hyundai Creta, Pearl]
Produced: [7-Hyundai Creta, Pearl]
        Consumed: [5-Hyundai Creta, Pearl]
Produced: [8-Hyundai Creta, Pearl]
        Consumed: [6-Hyundai Creta, Pearl]
Produced: [9-Hyundai Creta, Pearl]
+++ Production completed. +++
        Consumed: [7-Hyundai Creta, Pearl]
        Consumed: [8-Hyundai Creta, Pearl]
        Consumed: [9-Hyundai Creta, Pearl]
--- Consumption completed. ---
At present, the repository contains 0 car(s).
```

Analysis

Notice that though the production rate is much higher than the consumption rate, you never see more than three cars produced before the consumption starts. The **bounded blocking collection** blocked the producer task when three elements were already available to consume.

Author's Note: If the production rate is very fast, in some rare cases, it may appear to you that more than three cars are produced before the consumption starts. However, the consumption already started before you see that the "extra" car is produced. Ideally, you should never see a higher number of cars (such as five, six, or more) available before the consumption starts.

Note from Microsoft

Since `BlockingCollection<T>` implements the `IDisposable` interface, Microsoft suggests you dispose of the type once you finish the work. To dispose of this directly, you can call the `Dispose` method inside a `try/ catch` block. You can also dispose of the type indirectly via the language construct `using`. However, you should remember that the `Dispose` method is not thread-safe. To make the examples short and simple, I have ignored the concept of garbage collection in these programs.

ConcurrentDictionary<TKey,TValue>

This section demonstrates how to use the `ConcurrentDictionary<TKey,TV alue>` class in a program. It is a thread-safe collection of key/value pairs on which multiple threads can work concurrently. You already know that its nonconcurrent equivalent is `Dictionary<TKey,TValue> Stack<T>`.

Let's create a dictionary that contains countries with the most FIFA World Cup titles. The following code creates an instance of this class:

```
var fifaWCTitles = new ConcurrentDictionary<string, int>();
```

You will see methods for adding and removing elements. But before that, I'd like to mention that you can assign values for the key indexes as follows:

```
fifaWCTitles["Brazil"] = 5;
fifaWCTitles["Germany"] = 4;
fifaWCTitles["Argentina"] = 2; // Will be updated to 3 later
```

If you debug the code, you can see that the dictionary contains these three elements. Figure 3-7 shows an example.

Name	Value
▲ ⬡ fifaWCTitles	Count = 3
▷ ⬡ [0]	{[Argentina, 2]}
▷ ⬡ [1]	{[Germany, 4]}
▷ ⬡ [2]	{[Brazil, 5]}
▷ ⬡ Raw View	

Figure 3-7. *The dictionary contains three elements.*

To add an element to the dictionary, you can use the TryAdd method as well. This method attempts to add an element to the dictionary with the specified key and value. If the key already exists, this method returns false. At present, our dictionary does not have the key "Italy", so, the following code can add one more item to the dictionary:

```
fifaWCTitles.TryAdd("Italy", 4);
```

However, since the record of Argentina is already added, if you write something like the following:

```
fifaWCTitles.TryAdd("Argentina", 3); // will not update
```

it will not update the value for Argentina.

Then how do you update the value? You can try the AddOrUpdate method. The following code uses this method where you pass the existing key and its value for the first two parameters and a lambda expression as the third parameter:

```
fifaWCTitles.AddOrUpdate("Argentina", 2, (key, oldValue) => 3);
```

Using the code intelligence in Visual Studio, you can see that this lambda expression is used to generate a new value for an existing key based on the key's existing value.

To illustrate, if you replace the previous line of code with the following code segment:

```
fifaWCTitles.AddOrUpdate(
    "Argentina",
     2,
    (key, oldValue) =>
        {
            int newValue = 3;
            WriteLine($"{key}'s old value {oldValue} is
                updated to new value {newValue}.");
            return newValue;
        }
 );
```

executing this code segment, you can see the following output:

```
Argentina's old value 2 is updated to new value 3.
```

Let's check the current dictionary status in the debug mode (see Figure 3-8).

fifaWCTitles	Count = 4
▷ [0]	{[Argentina, 3]}
▷ [1]	{[Italy, 4]}
▷ [2]	{[Germany, 4]}
▷ [3]	{[Brazil, 5]}
▷ Raw View	

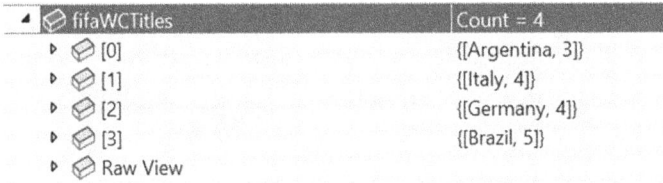

Figure 3-8. *The dictionary contains four elements with the updated record for Argentina*

You can see that the dictionary now contains four elements with the updated value for Argentina.

GetOrAdd is another useful method. If the key does not exist, using this method, you can add a new element to the dictionary as follows:

```
fifaWCTitles.GetOrAdd("France", 2); // Successful
```

If the key is present, this method returns the existing value for the key; otherwise, it will return the new value of the key. So, if I need to check the return value, I can write something like this:

```
int value=fifaWCTitles.GetOrAdd("France", 2); // Successful
WriteLine(value);
```

Anyway, you can easily understand that after adding the details of France, if you now write the following:

```
fifaWCTitles.GetOrAdd("France", 3); // Unsuccessful
```

it will not update the record.

OK, you have seen how to add elements to a concurrent dictionary or update an element in this dictionary. Let's try the removal operation as well. You guessed it right! Like the TryAdd method, there is a TryRemove method as well. The TryRemove method attempts to remove and return the value with the specified key from the dictionary. In the following code segment, I tried removing the records for France and Uruguay:

```
TryRemovingCountryDetails("France");
TryRemovingCountryDetails("Uruguay");

void TryRemovingCountryDetails(string country)
{
 var isRemoved = fifaWCTitles.TryRemove(country, out int
  removedValue);
 if (isRemoved)
 {
  WriteLine($"{country} with {removedValue} World Cup titles is
    deleted.");
 }
 else
 {
  WriteLine($"Could not remove the details of {country}");
 }
}
```

Since the key "France" is present in our dictionary, its record can be deleted. However, the dictionary did not contain any information about the key "Uruguay". So, you'll see the following output:

```
France with 2 World Cup titles is deleted.
Could not remove the details of Uruguay
```

Note   Download the UnderstandingConcurrentDictionary project to run these code segments that I discussed so far.

Are Atomicity and Thread-Safety Guaranteed?

For the update (and write) operations, the concurrent dictionary uses fine-grained locking to ensure thread safety. However, the documentation says the following about the built-in methods (see `https://learn.microsoft.com/en-us/dotnet/api/system.collections.concurrent.concurrentdictionary-2?view=net-8.0`):

> All these operations are atomic and are thread-safe with regards to all other operations on the ConcurrentDictionary< TKey,TValue> class. The only exceptions are the methods that accept a delegate, that is, AddOrUpdate and GetOrAdd. For modifications and write operations to the dictionary,

If you further scroll down the page, you will see the following warning message as well:

> All public and protected members of ConcurrentDictionary <TKey,TValue> are thread-safe and may be used concurrently from multiple threads. However, members accessed through one of the interfaces the ConcurrentDictionary<TKey,TValue> implements, including extension methods, are not guaranteed to be thread safe and may need to be synchronized by the caller.

Remember this information while using a concurrent dictionary in your program.

I assume you have some idea about the concurrent dictionary now. Since you are learning parallel programming, let's now exercise a program where multiple tasks are involved in a multithreaded environment.

Demonstration 9

The following is the complete program. (There is no change in the `Car` class. It is not shown here to avoid the repetition.)

```
using static System.Console;
using System.Collections.Concurrent;
```

```
ConcurrentDictionary<int, string> cars = new();

var addBlackCarModelsTask = Task.Run(AddBlackCarModels);
var addNonBlackCarModelsTask = Task.Run(AddNonBlackCarModels);
Task.WaitAll(addBlackCarModelsTask, addNonBlackCarModelsTask);
WriteLine($"A total of {cars.Count} cars are added to the
 repository.");

WriteLine("\nTrying to remove one item at random now.");
int random = new Random().Next(1, 6);
var removeCarsTask = Task.Run(()=>RemoveOneCar(random));
removeCarsTask.Wait();
WriteLine($"\nA total of {cars.Count} cars are present in the
 repository now.");
WriteLine("\nHere is the current content of the dictionary:");
foreach (var car in cars)
{
    WriteLine($"The key: {car.Key} has the value: {car.Value}");
}

void AddNonBlackCarModels()
{
    Car car;
    car = new("Hyundai Creta","Pearl");
    WriteLine($"Adding: {car}");
    cars.TryAdd(1,car.ToString());
    Thread.Sleep(1000);

    car = new("Maruti Suzuki Alto 800", "Red");
    WriteLine($"Adding: {car}");
    cars.TryAdd(2, car.ToString());
    Thread.Sleep(1000);
```

```
    car = new("Toyota Fortuner Avant", "Bronze");
    WriteLine($"Adding: {car}");
    cars.TryAdd(3, car.ToString());
    Thread.Sleep(1000);
}

void AddBlackCarModels()
{
    Car car;
    car = new("Toyota Fortuner Attitude", "Black");
    WriteLine($"Adding: {car}");
    cars.TryAdd(4, car.ToString());
    Thread.Sleep(1000);

    car = new("Hyundai Creta Abyss", "Black");
    WriteLine($"Adding: {car}");
    cars.TryAdd(5, car.ToString());
    Thread.Sleep(1000);
}

void RemoveOneCar(int key)
{
    var isRemoved = cars.TryRemove(key, out string removedValue);
    if (isRemoved)
    {
        WriteLine($"The key {key} with value: {removedValue} is
          deleted.");
    }
    else
    {
        WriteLine($"Could not remove the key: {key}");
    }
}
```

```
// There is no change in the Car class. It is not shown to
// avoid the repetition.
```

Output

Here is some sample output:

```
Adding: [Hyundai Creta, Pearl]
Adding: [Toyota Fortuner Attitude, Black]
Adding: [Hyundai Creta Abyss, Black]
Adding: [Maruti Suzuki Alto 800, Red]
Adding: [Toyota Fortuner Avant, Bronze]
A total of 5 cars are added to the repository.

Trying to remove one item at random now.
The key 4 with value: [Toyota Fortuner Attitude, Black] is
deleted.

A total of 4 cars are present in the repository now.

Here is the current content of the dictionary:
The key: 1 has the value: [Hyundai Creta, Pearl]
The key: 2 has the value: [Maruti Suzuki Alto 800, Red]
The key: 3 has the value: [Toyota Fortuner Avant, Bronze]
The key: 5 has the value: [Hyundai Creta Abyss, Black]
```

Analysis

You can see that at the beginning, two different tasks added five different cars simultaneously to the dictionary. Later, one car (that had key 4) was deleted at random.

Q&A Session

Q3.12 Should I always prefer concurrent collections over their counterpart?

It depends on the requirements of the application. As a general guideline, Microsoft suggests the following (see `https://learn.microsoft.com/en-us/dotnet/standard/collections/thread-safe/`):

> *When you write new code, use the concurrent collection classes to write multiple threads to the collection concurrently. If you're only reading from a shared collection, then you can use the classes in the* `System.Collections.Generic` *namespace.*

In the end, to make the code efficient, you want to use methods that can serve you best. You may remember that concurrent collections have some special methods (the `TryPop` method) that can help you perform atomic test-and-act operations that can provide you benefits in a multithreaded environment.

Exercises

E3.1 Can you predict the output of the following code?

```
using static System.Console;
using System.Collections.Concurrent;

var colorBag = new ConcurrentDictionary<int,string>();
colorBag.TryAdd(1, "Red");
colorBag.TryAdd(2, "Green");
string color=colorBag.GetOrAdd(2, "Blue");
WriteLine(color);
```

E3.2 Can you predict the output of the following code?

```
using static System.Console;
```

```
var resetEvent = new AutoResetEvent(true);

WriteLine("Two customers are approaching the mall.");
Task.Run(VisitMall);
Task.Run(VisitMall);

// Imposing some delay to mimic a real-world scenario
Thread.Sleep(2000);

WriteLine("Press any key to exit.");
ReadKey();

void VisitMall()
{
    // Imposing a small delay to mimic a real-world scenario
    Thread.Sleep(1000);
    WriteLine($"The customer {Task.CurrentId} is waiting for
     the entry pass.");
    resetEvent.WaitOne();
    WriteLine($"The customer {Task.CurrentId} enters the mall.");
}
```

E3.3 Let's make some changes to the previous program (E3.2) as follows (the changes are shown in comments):

```
using static System.Console;

// For Exercise 3.2
// var resetEvent = new AutoResetEvent(true);

// For Exercise 3.3
var resetEvent = new AutoResetEvent(false);
// Invoking the set method twice in advance
resetEvent.Set();
resetEvent.Set();

// There is no other change in the remaining code
```

You can see that the main thread invoked the Set method twice in advance. Will it help to release two upcoming worker threads immediately?

E3.4 Can you predict the output of the following code?

```
using static System.Console;
using System.Collections.Concurrent;

var stack = new ConcurrentStack<int>();
for(int i=1;i<=5;i++)
{
    stack.Push(i);
}
var items = new int[10];
if (stack.TryPopRange(items,1, 10) > 0)
{
    foreach (int item in items)
    {
        Write($"{item}\t");
    }
}
```

E3.5 Suppose an organization wants to fill its vacant posts. So, it announces an advertisement saying that interested people can apply for these posts by filling up an online form. However, each candidate needs to make an online payment of $5 to the organization's account number. You understand that many people can fill up the online form and pay the mentioned amount simultaneously. Assume that at a particular moment, 1,000 people tried to make the online payment. As a result, the organization should get $5000 in its account online. Can you write a program to mimic the scenario and verify the result?

E3.6 Demonstration 4 showed you an example of one-way signaling where the worker thread waited for a signal from the main thread. Now I want you to write a program that deals with two-way signaling using AutoResetEvent. You can consider a known scenario: during the billing process, any customer can raise a complaint. As a result, the billing process is paused until the issue is resolved. Can you write a program that mimics this scenario?

E3.7 Demonstration 8 in this chapter showed how to use a blocking collection. Can you update this program that allows you to pass a cancellation request as well?

Summary

This chapter started with a discussion on synchronization. It divided the synchronization constructs into four categories and showed you examples from each category including the lock statements, the Interlocked class, and signaling using AutoResetEvent. It also covered some blocking methods (this also belongs to the synchronization categories) such as Thread.Sleep and Task.Wait in various program segments.

Then the chapter focused on the concurrent collections and covered the important types such as ConcurrentStack<T>, ConcurrentQueue<T>, ConcurrentBag<T>, BlockingCollection<T>, and ConcurrentDictionary<TKey,TValue>. It also covered the IProducerConsumerCollection<T> interface and discussed the possible implementations of the producer-consumer pattern. You may find the chapter a little bit lengthy, but I sincerely believe that these discussions will help you a lot.

Solutions to Exercises

Here is a sample solution set for the exercises in this chapter.

E3.1

You will see the following output:

Green

Clue: Since key 2 was already added in the dictionary, you are seeing the existing value as Green, but not as Blue.

E3.2

This code will allow only one customer to enter the mall. Here is the sample output:

```
Two customers are approaching the mall.
The customer 2 is waiting for the entry pass.
The customer 1 is waiting for the entry pass.
The customer 2 enters the mall.
Press any key to exit.
```

(**Clue**: One customer was released immediately because AutoResetEvent was already in the signaled state.)

E3.3

No. Here is some sample output:

```
Two customers are approaching the mall.
The customer 2 is waiting for the entry pass.
The customer 1 is waiting for the entry pass.
The customer 2 enters the mall.
Press any key to exit.
```

(**Clue**: It does not matter how many times you release a signal in advance; when the threads appear, only one of them will be released immediately. This issue was discussed in the Q&A sessions; see the answer to Q3.7.)

E3.4

You'll see the following exception:

```
Unhandled exception. System.ArgumentException: The sum of the
startIndex and count arguments must be less than or equal to
the collection's Count.
```

```
// Other details such as line numbers etc. are not shown
```

E3.5

Here is a sample program:

```
using static System.Console;

Account account = new();
var tasks = new List<Task>();
for(int i=0;i<1000;i++)
{
    tasks.Add
     (
        Task.Run( () => account.Credit(5))
     );
}
Task.WaitAll([.. tasks]);
// Same as:
// Task.WaitAll(tasks.ToArray());
```

```
WriteLine($"The current balance is ${account.Balance}");

// The organization's account
class Account
{
    private int _balance;
    public int Balance
    {
        get { return _balance; }
        set { _balance = value; }
    }
    public void Credit(int amount)
    {
        Interlocked.Add(ref _balance, amount);
    }
    // The following method is not used in this program
    public void Debit(int amount)
    {
        Interlocked.Add(ref _balance, -amount);
    }
}
```

This program produces the following output:

```
The current balance is $5000
```

E3.6

Here is the sample program:

```
using static System.Console;

var billingEvent = new AutoResetEvent(false);
var complaintEventIfAny = new AutoResetEvent(false);
```

```
var billingTask = Task.Run(PrepareBill);

// Let the billing counter open first.
Thread.Sleep(2000);
WriteLine("The customer picks up the items and moves towards
  the billing counter.");

// Imposing some delay to mimic a real-world scenario
Thread.Sleep(1000);
billingEvent.Set();
WriteLine("The management waits if there is any complaint.");
complaintEventIfAny.WaitOne();
WriteLine("The management makes the customer happy.");

billingTask.Wait();
// Exception handling is not considered in this program

void PrepareBill()
{
    WriteLine("**The billing counter is waiting to serve the
     customer(s).**");
    billingEvent.WaitOne();
    WriteLine("**The billing counter starts functioning...**");
    int random = new Random().Next(1, 10);
    if (random > 3)
    {
        WriteLine($"The customer complains about a bill amount of
         ${random}");
    }
   complaintEventIfAny.Set();
    // Imposing a small delay to mimic a real-world scenario
    Thread.Sleep(2000);
    WriteLine("**The bill is generated.**");
}
```

Here is the sample output when the customer raises a complaint:

```
**The billing counter is waiting to serve the customer(s).**
The customer picks up the items and moves towards the billing
  counter.
**The billing counter starts functioning...**
The management waits if there is any complaint.
The customer complains about a bill amount of $9
The management makes the customer happy.
**The bill is generated.**
```

Here is more sample output when the customer does not raise a complaint:

```
**The billing counter is waiting to serve the customer(s).**
The customer picks up the items and moves towards the billing
  counter.
The management waits if there is any complaint.
**The billing counter starts functioning...**
The management makes the customer happy.
**The bill is generated.**
```

E3.7

I want you to do this exercise yourself.

CHAPTER 4

Working on Parallel Loops

C# developers are quite familiar with using foreach and for loops. By using these iteration statements, we can repeatedly execute a statement or a block of statements. This chapter primarily focuses on their parallel versions. It also helps you experiment with similar constructs that support parallel programming.

Revisiting Sequential Loops

Before we discuss parallel loops, let's analyze a common scenario where you would usually use a loop. For example, given the code List<int> numbers = Enumerable.Range(1, 10).ToList();, can you increase each number by 100 and display the result? Yes, you can do this in several ways. For example, you can use any of the following three approaches.

In the first approach, you use a foreach loop as follows:

```
// Approach: 1
foreach (int i in numbers)
{
  WriteLine($"Number:{i}, Incremented number: {i + 100}");
}
```

© Vaskaran Sarcar 2024
V. Sarcar, *Parallel Programming with C# and .NET*,
https://doi.org/10.1007/979-8-8688-0488-5_4

If you are a fan of the for loop, you can write something as follows (though this is less readable than the previous):

```
// Approach: 2
for (int i = 0; i < numbers.Count; i++)
{
    WriteLine($"Number:{numbers[i]}, Incremented number:
      {numbers[i] + 100}");
}
```

If you love the functional coding style, you can write the following equivalent code as well:

```
// Approach: 3
Numbers
 .ForEach
  (
    i => WriteLine($"Number:{i}, Incremented number: {i + 100}")
  );
```

I have shown how to use a foreach loop, a for loop, and a Foreach function in these approaches. However, notice that each approach follows the sequential execution.

Experimenting with Parallel Loops

Processing data sequentially does not matter much if the data set is small. However, if you need to loop through a large amount of data, sticking to the sequential approach is not a wise decision. The reason is obvious: it is time-consuming. So, to speed it up, you may want to achieve parallelism by segregating this data set into several parts and executing those parts in parallel. However, the good news is that you have built-in constructs that support the parallel versions of For and ForEach as well.

Introducing the Parallel Class

The Parallel class is made to provide these supports. Let's investigate this class. If you type Parallel and add a dot, you will see the screen in Figure 4-1.

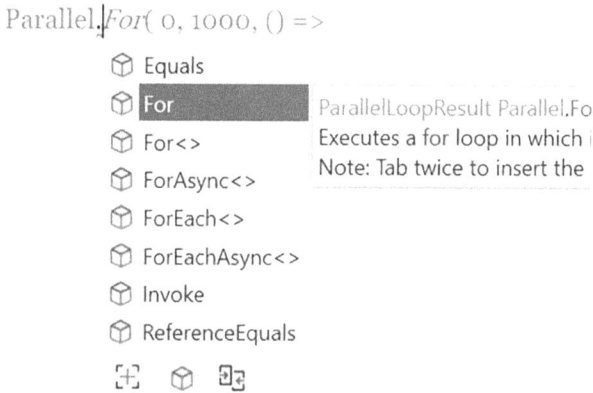

Parallel.|For(0, 1000, () =>

- Equals
- **For**   ParallelLoopResult Parallel.Fo
- For<>   Executes a for loop in which i
- ForAsync<>   Note: Tab twice to insert the
- ForEach<>
- ForEachAsync<>
- Invoke
- ReferenceEquals

Figure 4-1.   *The methods of the Parallel class*

Figure 4-1 shows you the presence of the following methods: For, ForEach, ForAsync, ForEachAsync, and Invoke in the Parallel class. These are the methods we'll focus on in this chapter. Since I have not discussed the async and await keywords yet, in this chapter, we'll cover the following:

- **Parallel.ForEach** (this is the parallel equivalent of the C# foreach loop)

- **Parallel.For** (this is the parallel equivalent of the C# for loop)

- **Parallel.Invoke** (this executes an array of delegates in parallel)

POINT TO REMEMBER

In the context of parallel programming, a few terms are often seen in different books, blogs, and/or articles. If you are unaware of those terms, understanding the topic or participating in a discussion forum can be challenging. It is obvious that once you finish this book, you'll have a fair idea about many of them. For now, let me remind (or introduce) you to a few common terms: you have seen task parallelism constructs in Chapter 1 and Chapter 2. Now you'll see data parallelism. The Task Parallel Library (TPL) supports data parallelism through the System.Threading.Tasks.Parallel class. The Parallel class with those task parallelism constructs is known as Task Parallel Library (TPL). In Chapter 3, you saw the concurrent collections, and in Chapter 5, you'll learn Parallel LINQ (PLINQ). In Appendix A, I'll talk about PFX, which can be written as TPL + PLINQ + concurrent collections.

Parallel.ForEach

Let's start with the parallel ForEach. There are many overloads of the Foreach method in the Parallel class (at the time of this writing, there are 20 overloads). Consider the following version that takes only two parameters:

```
public static ParallelLoopResult ForEach<TSource>(
 IEnumerable<TSource> source,
 Action<TSource> body)
{
    // Some code
}
```

As a result, given the code List<int> numbers = Enumerable. Range(1, 10).ToList();, you can now display the numbers using the parallel version of the foreach loop as follows:

```
// Approach: 4
Parallel.ForEach(
    numbers,
    i => WriteLine($"Number: {i}")
);
```

Parallel.For

At the time of this writing, there are 12 overloads for the parallel for loop. Take a look at the following form:

```
public static ParallelLoopResult For(int fromInclusive,
 int toExclusive, Action<int> body)
{
 // Some code
}
```

The first argument indicates the starting point (inclusive), and the next argument is used for the endpoint (exclusive). For example, to display the numbers between 1 to 10, you can write the following code:

```
// Approach: 5
Parallel
 .For
(
  1,
  11,
  i => WriteLine($"Number: {i}")
 );
```

Demonstration 1

Let's see a simple demonstration. While revisiting the sequential approaches, I incremented the numbers from 1 to 10 by 100. Now you have seen the parallel versions of the foreach and for loops. Let's verify whether these parallel loops work for us. In this program, I also print the task IDs to verify whether different tasks participate in this computation. Here is the complete program:

Note   In this demonstration, I have shown you the parallel loops only. However, by downloading the Demo1_ WorkingOnParallelLoops project, you can see their sequential versions as well. I have kept all of them in the same place for your ready reference.

```
using static System.Console;

List<int> numbers = Enumerable.Range(1, 10).ToList();

#region Parallel loops
WriteLine("\nUsing Parallel ForEach");
// Approach: 4
Parallel.ForEach(
    numbers,
    i => WriteLine($"Number:{i}, Incremented number:{i + 100},
        Id:{Task.CurrentId}")
);
WriteLine("Ending Parallel ForEach");

// Approach: 5
WriteLine("\nUsing Parallel For");
Parallel.For(
```

```
    1,
    numbers.Count + 1,
    i => WriteLine($"Number:{i}, Incremented number:{i + 100},
        Id:{Task.CurrentId}")
   );
WriteLine("Ending Parallel For");
#endregion
```

Output

Here is some sample output:

```
Using Parallel ForEach
Number:7, Incremented number:107, Id:4
Number:5, Incremented number:105, Id:3
Number:1, Incremented number:101, Id:1
Number:2, Incremented number:102, Id:1
Number:4, Incremented number:104, Id:1
Number:8, Incremented number:108, Id:4
Number:6, Incremented number:106, Id:3
Number:3, Incremented number:103, Id:2
Number:9, Incremented number:109, Id:5
Number:10, Incremented number:110, Id:1
Ending Parallel ForEach

Using Parallel For
Number:3, Incremented number:103, Id:8
Number:9, Incremented number:109, Id:11
Number:10, Incremented number:110, Id:11
Number:2, Incremented number:102, Id:11
Number:6, Incremented number:106, Id:11
Number:4, Incremented number:104, Id:8
Number:7, Incremented number:107, Id:10
```

```
Number:1, Incremented number:101, Id:7
Number:5, Incremented number:105, Id:9
Number:8, Incremented number:108, Id:11
Ending Parallel For
```

Analysis

The output confirmed the following characteristics:

- Different tasks participated in this program.

- Invoking the ForEach or ForAll method of the Parallel class caused these tasks to start automatically.

- If you keep executing this program, you'll always notice that the application finishes only after printing these numbers. This gives you a clue that these methods block until the work is complete.

Parallel.Invoke

The Parallel class has another useful method, called Invoke. The documentation states the following (see https://learn.microsoft.com/en-us/previous-versions/msp-n-p/ff963549(v=pandp.10)?redirected from=MSDN):

> **Parallel.Invoke** is the simplest expression of the parallel task pattern. It creates new parallel tasks for each delegate method that is in its **params** array argument list. The **Invoke** method returns when all the tasks are finished.

At the time of this writing, there are two overloads for the parallel Invoke method. Let me consider the following:

```
public static void Invoke(params Action[] actions)
```

Seeing this definition, you understand that we can pass a variable number of Action instances to the Invoke method. Let me create three such instances and pass them in the following program.

Demonstration 2

Here is the complete demonstration:

```
using static System.Console;

#region Parallel.Invoke
WriteLine("Using Parallel.Invoke method.");
Action greet = new(() => WriteLine($"Task {Task.CurrentId}
 says: Hello reader!"));
Action printMsg = new(() => WriteLine($"Task {Task.CurrentId}
 says: This is a beautiful day."));
Action suggest = new(() => WriteLine($"Task {Task.CurrentId}
 says: Relax now."));
Parallel.Invoke(greet,printMsg,suggest);
WriteLine("End Parallel.Invoke");
#endregion
```

Output

Here is some sample output:

```
Using Parallel.Invoke method.
Task 3 says: Hello reader!
Task 1 says: This is a beautiful day.
Task 2 says: Relax now.
End Parallel.Invoke
```

Q&A Session

Q4.1 I can see that task 1 finishes after task 3. Is this the expected behavior? I can also see that you did not wait for the tasks to be finished. Is this OK?

Yes. The documentation states the following (see `https://learn.microsoft.com/en-us/dotnet/api/system.threading.tasks.parallel.invoke?view=net-8.0`):

> *This method can be used to execute a set of operations, potentially in parallel. No guarantees are made about the order in which the operations execute or whether they execute in parallel. This method does not return until each of the provided operations has completed, regardless of whether completion occurs due to normal or exceptional termination.*

Q4.2 It appears to me that I could create separate tasks and wait for them to finish their executions instead of using `Parallel.Invoke`. Is this correct?

Nice observation. The documentation confirms the following (see `https://learn.microsoft.com/en-us/previous-versions/msp-n-p/ff963549(v=pandp.10)?redirectedfrom=MSDN`):

> *Internally, **Parallel.Invoke** creates new tasks and waits for them. It uses methods of the **Task** class to do this.*

If you study the mentioned link, you will understand that I could write an equivalent program as follows:

```
using static System.Console;

Task greet2 = Task.Factory.StartNew(
() => WriteLine($"Task {Task.CurrentId} says: Hello reader!"));

Task printMsg2 = Task.Factory.StartNew(
() => WriteLine($"Task {Task.CurrentId} says: This is a
beautiful day."));
```

```
Task suggest2 = Task.Factory.StartNew(
() => WriteLine($"Task {Task.CurrentId} says: Relax now."));

Task.WaitAll(greet2, printMsg2, suggest2);
```

However, notice that when you work with a large number of delegates, creating separate tasks for each delegate and managing them is not a good idea. Using Parallel.Invoke can help you! It will work efficiently in those cases as well.

Q4.3 When we use a sequential for loop, the step size need not be 1. For example, given the numbers 0 to 50, I can print the numbers 0, 5, 10, 15, ..., 45, and 50 using the following code:

```
int step = 5;
for (int i = 0; i <= 50; i += step)
{
    Write($"{i}\t");
}
```

How can I write an equivalent code using a parallel loop?
You can define a custom method. Here is a sample code fragment that uses a custom method, called InputDomain, that can be used to traverse the elements with a preferred step size (in this example, it is 5).

```
static IEnumerable<int> InputDomain(int start, int
endInclusive, int stepCounter)
{
    for (int i = start; i <= endInclusive; i += stepCounter)
    {
        yield return i;
    }
}
```

Having this function, I can now use `Parallel.Foreach` to print the numbers as follows:

```
Parallel.ForEach(
    InputDomain(0, 50, 5),
    i => Write($"{i}\t")
    );
```

You can download the project `Q&A_ParallelForWithCustomStep` to execute the complete program. Here is some sample output that was generated by executing this code:

```
15     5      0
35     40     45     50     10     20     25     30
```

Finally, you can also use the following code to get an equivalent output:

```
Parallel.ForEach(
  Enumerable
    .Range(0, 11)
    .Select(i => i * 5),
    i => Write($"{i}\t")
    );
```

Scenarios for Parallel Execution

Each scenario is not suitable for parallel execution. For example, if you execute a parallel for loop for a small number of iterations or use it to process a small data set, you may not see the benefit. In those cases, you may also notice that parallel execution is slower. To illustrate this, let's analyze the following case studies.

Case Study 1

Consider the numbers from 1 to 10. Now calculate the square of these numbers and display the result. Let's investigate the time taken when we use the following:

- A sequential foreach loop and
- A parallel foreach loop

Demonstration 3

Here is a sample program:

```
using System.Diagnostics;
using static System.Console;

WriteLine("Examining sequential versus parallel execution.");
List<int> input= Enumerable.Range(1, 10).ToList();

ExecuteSequentialFor(input);
ExecuteParallelFor(input);
void ExecuteSequentialFor(List<int> numbers)
{
    Stopwatch sw = Stopwatch.StartNew();

   foreach (int i in numbers)
    {
        Write($"{i * i}\t");
    }
    sw.Stop();
    WriteLine($"\nSequential execution(using foreach) time:
     {sw.ElapsedMilliseconds} ms\n");
}
```

```
WriteLine("_____");
void ExecuteParallelFor(List<int> numbers)
{
    Stopwatch sw = Stopwatch.StartNew();
    Parallel.ForEach(
        numbers,
        i => Write($"{i * i}\t")
    );
    sw.Stop();
    WriteLine($"\nParallel execution(using Parallel.ForEach)
     time: {sw.ElapsedMilliseconds} ms");
}
```

Output

I executed this program several times. In each case, my computer showed that sequential execution was faster. Here is some sample output:

```
Examining sequential versus parallel execution.
1    4    9    16    25    36    49    64    81    100
Sequential execution(using foreach) time: 0 ms

81   49   25   36    4    16    64    9     1    100
Parallel execution(using Parallel.ForEach) time:20 ms
```

Case Study 2

Now assume that in addition to printing the numbers, we are doing some other work as well. To mimic this activity, let me impose a small delay inside the loops and replace the previous loops (that are shown in Demonstration 3) with the following loops:

```
// New sequential loop

 foreach (int i in numbers)
  {
      // Imposing some delay to do some other work
      Thread.Sleep(500);
      Write($"{i * i}\t");
  }

// New Paralllel loop

Parallel.ForEach(
      numbers,
      i =>
      {
          // Imposing some delay to do some other work
          Thread.Sleep(500);
          Write($"{i * i}\t");
      }
    );

// There is no other change in the program
```

Run this modified program now. Here is some sample output:

```
Examining sequential versus parallel execution.
1     4     9     16    25    36    49    64    81    100
Sequential execution(using forech) time: 5093 ms

1     25    81    9     49    16    64    100   36    4
Parallel execution(using Parallel.ForEach) time:1081 ms
```

Since each iteration sleeps for 500 ms, there is no surprise that the sequential execution will take more than 5000 ms. **However, notice that this time parallel execution is almost five times faster than the sequential execution.**

Analysis

There is no doubt that the output can vary in your system. Still, from these case studies, the following points are evident:

- Not every scenario is suitable for parallel execution.

- A sequential execution can be faster than a parallel execution if the data set is small.

- On the other hand, when you work on a large data set or perform independent time-consuming (and blocking) operations, preferring parallel execution over sequential execution can provide you benefits.

POINT TO NOTE

Surely, parallelization, like any multithreaded code, will inherit complexities. It is because a multithreaded environment can be affected by many other factors such as thread creation, ensuring thread safety, workload distribution, context switching time, and so on. However, you'll learn that you can further fine-tune the parallel executions. I'll discuss this soon.

Useful Parameters

As mentioned, there are different overloads of `Parallel.For` and `Parallel.ForEach`. We have looked at some case studies with parallel foreach loops already. So, this time we'll do an upcoming analysis with parallel for loops.

Figure 4-2 shows the different parameters of `Parallel.For`.

```
public static class Parallel
{
    public static ParallelLoopResult For(int fromInclusive, int toExclusive, Action<int, ParallelLoopState> body);
    public static ParallelLoopResult For<TLocal>(int fromInclusive, int toExclusive, Func<TLocal> localInit, Func<int, ParallelLoopState, TLocal, TLocal>
    public static ParallelLoopResult For<TLocal>(int fromInclusive, int toExclusive, ParallelOptions parallelOptions, Func<TLocal> localInit, Func<int, Pa
    public static ParallelLoopResult For<TLocal>(long fromInclusive, long toExclusive, Func<TLocal> localInit, Func<long, ParallelLoopState, TLocal, TLo
    public static ParallelLoopResult For(long fromInclusive, long toExclusive, ParallelOptions parallelOptions, Action<long> body);
    public static ParallelLoopResult For(long fromInclusive, long toExclusive, ParallelOptions parallelOptions, Action<long, ParallelLoopState> body);
    public static ParallelLoopResult For<TLocal>(long fromInclusive, long toExclusive, ParallelOptions parallelOptions, Func<TLocal> localInit, Func<long
    public static ParallelLoopResult For(long fromInclusive, long toExclusive, Action<long, ParallelLoopState> body);
    public static ParallelLoopResult For(int fromInclusive, int toExclusive, ParallelOptions parallelOptions, Action<int> body);
    public static ParallelLoopResult For(int fromInclusive, int toExclusive, ParallelOptions parallelOptions, Action<int, ParallelLoopState> body);
    public static ParallelLoopResult For(int fromInclusive, int toExclusive, Action<int> body);
    public static ParallelLoopResult For(long fromInclusive, long toExclusive, Action<long> body);
```

Figure 4-2. *Different overloads of Parallel.For*

Figure 4-2 shows the presence of many different parameters. Most of them are very common, but there are a few new entries as well. Let's focus on the following two parameters:

- `ParallelLoopState`
- `ParallelOptions`

Understanding these parameters can help you use the parallel loops effectively.

Using ParallelLoopState

Using the `ParallelLoopState` parameter, you can monitor and/or manipulate the loop. I'll show you the usage of the following methods:

- `Stop`
- `Break`

Using Stop

Here is a sample demonstration where I tried to stop the loop at the seventh iteration using the `Stop` method. (You'll see that the `Break` method is commented inside this program. After we analyze the output, I'll comment out the `Stop` method and uncomment the `Break` method.)

235

Demonstration 4

Here is a sample demonstration:

```
using static System.Console;

var repeatedTask = Task.Run(() =>
{
    Parallel.For(
        1,
        16,
        (int i, ParallelLoopState state) =>
        {
            if (i == 7)
            {
                WriteLine($"Processing: {i} ID:{Task.
                    CurrentId}. About to interrupt the loop.");
                state.Stop();
                // state.Break();
            }
            Thread.Sleep(1000);
            WriteLine($"Processed: {i} ID:{Task.CurrentId}");
        });
});

repeatedTask.Wait();
WriteLine("End");
```

Output

The output can vary on different machines. However, let me show you some sample output:

```
Processing: 7 ID:2. About to interrupt the loop.
Processed: 1 ID:4
Processed: 4 ID:3
Processed: 10 ID:5
Processed: 7 ID:2
End
```

Using Break

Replace Stop() with Break() in the previous program now. Here is some sample output after this change (the output may vary on your computer):

```
Processing: 7 ID:4. About to interrupt the loop.
Processed: 1 ID:2
Processed: 4 ID:3
Processed: 10 ID:5
Processed: 7 ID:4
Processed: 2 ID:7
Processed: 5 ID:8
Processed: 3 ID:2
Processed: 6 ID:8
End
```

Q&A Session

Q4.4 How Break is different from Stop?

The documentation states the following (see https://learn. microsoft.com/en-us/dotnet/api/system.threading.tasks. parallelloopstate.break?view=net-8.0):

> *Break indicates that no iterations after the current iteration should be run. It effectively cancels any additional iterations of the loop. However, it does not stop any iterations that have already begun execution. For example, if Break is called from*

the 100th iteration of a parallel loop iterating from 0 to 1,000, all iterations less than 100 should still be run, but the iterations from 101 through to 1000 that have not yet started are not executed.

From the given output, you can verify this as well. You can see that when I called the Break method from iteration number 7, the numbers from 1 to 6 were processed successfully. But when I used the Stop method, this was not the case. In the output you can see the presence of 1 and 4, but {1,4} is only a subset of {1,2,3,4,5,6}. When you use the Stop method, this is an expected behavior.

Now you understand that when state.Break() is called, the loop ceases execution at the system's earliest convenience of all iterations beyond the current iteration. It does not stop the current or prior iterations. It's more like "Don't schedule any more iterations, but let the ones that have already started finish."

However, after invoking state.Stop(), the loop ceases execution of any more iterations at the system's earliest convenience, even if they are prior to the current iteration. It's more like "Stop all iterations as soon as possible."

In summary, Break is a polite request to wind down the loop after the current iteration, while Stop is a more immediate request to halt the loop.

Retrieving More Information

The parallel versions of for and foreach methods return a ParallelLoopResult object that exposes two useful properties called IsCompleted and LowestBreakIteration. They help you identify whether the loop ran to completion; if it did not, it can point to the cycle where it was broken. Here is a short description of them:

- IsCompleted: This property returns true if all iterations of the loop were executed, and false if the loop was exited early, by a call to either Break or Stop.

- LowestBreakIteration: This property returns the index of the first iteration of the loop for which Break was called. If Break was not called, this property returns null. This property is useful for understanding how much of the loop was completed before it was broken.

Let's see an example. While using the Break method, if you use the following version (changes are in bold) of the repeatedTask in Demonstration 4:

```
var repeatedTask = Task.Run(() =>
{
    ParallelLoopResult result =
    Parallel.For
    (
        1,
        16,
        (int i, ParallelLoopState state) =>
        {
            if (i == 7)
            {
                WriteLine($"Processing: {i} ID:{Task.
                 CurrentId}. About to interrupt the loop.");
                //state.Stop();
                state.Break();
            }
            Thread.Sleep(1000);
            WriteLine($"Processed: {i} ID:{Task.CurrentId}");
        }
    );
    WriteLine($"Loop completed? {result.IsCompleted}");
    // Retrieving more info if the loop is incomplete
    if (!result.IsCompleted)
```

```
    {
        if (result.LowestBreakIteration != null)
        {
            WriteLine($"The lowest break iteration:
              {result.LowestBreakIteration}");
        }
        else
        {
            WriteLine("The Stop() method was called.");
        }
    }
});
```

You can see an output like the following (notice the important changes in bold):

```
Processing: 7  ID:3. About to interrupt the loop.
Processed: 1   ID:2
Processed: 4   ID:4
Processed: 10  ID:5
Processed: 7   ID:3
Processed: 2   ID:7
Processed: 3   ID:2
Processed: 5   ID:8
Processed: 6   ID:8
Loop completed? False
The lowest break iteration: 7
End
```

But if you use the Stop method (instead of the Break method), you can see an output like the following (notice the important changes in bold):

```
Processing: 7 ID:4. About to interrupt the loop.
Processed: 4 ID:3
```

Processed: 1 ID:2

Processed: 10 ID:5

Processed: 7 ID:4

Loop completed? False

The Stop() method was called.

End

Note   Download the Demo4_ParallelLoopState_Modified
project to see the complete program from the Apress website.

Using ParallelOptions

Let's discuss the ParallelOptions class. This class has three useful properties:

- TaskScheduler: This property gets or sets the
  TaskScheduler that is used to schedule the tasks.
  The TaskScheduler is responsible for managing
  how and when tasks are executed. You may also
  note that by default methods on the Parallel class
  are non-cancelable, use the default task scheduler
  (TaskScheduler.Default), and attempt to use all the
  available processors. By using ParallelOptions, you
  can override these defaults.

- MaxDegreeOfParallelism: This property gets or sets
  the maximum number of concurrent tasks enabled by
  the ParallelOptions instance. It allows you to limit
  the number of concurrent operations run by Parallel
  methods, which can be useful to prevent overloading
  the system with too many tasks.

- CancellationToken: This property gets or sets the CancellationToken associated with this ParallelOptions instance. A CancellationToken allows the cooperative cancellation of the parallel operation. It can be used to request that the operation be canceled, although it's up to the operation to check the cancellation token and respond appropriately.

Since .NET provides a default TaskScheduler instance, normally you do not need to worry about it. Let's focus on the other two parameters. I'll start the discussion with MaxDegreeOfParallelism.

By executing the following code on my computer:

```
using static System.Console;

var repeatedTask2 = Task.Run(() =>
{
    Parallel.For(
        1,
        10,
        i =>
        {
            WriteLine($"Processed:{i} with the task
                ID:[{Task.CurrentId}]");
        });
});

repeatedTask2.Wait();
```

I see the following sample output:

```
Processed:5 with the task ID:[4]
Processed:6 with the task ID:[4]
Processed:8 with the task ID:[4]
Processed:9 with the task ID:[4]
```

```
Processed:2 with the task ID:[4]
Processed:4 with the task ID:[4]
Processed:7 with the task ID:[5]
Processed:1 with the task ID:[2]
Processed:3 with the task ID:[3]
```

It is not a surprise to see different task IDs. The four task IDs represent four different tasks in this output. Interestingly, you can control the number of tasks. How? Let's see the following demonstration.

Demonstration 5

In the following program, I create an instance of ParallelOptions where I limit the maximum number of concurrent tasks to 2 and pass it to the parallel for loop as follows:

```
using static System.Console;

ParallelOptions parallelOptions = new()
{
    MaxDegreeOfParallelism = 2
};

var repeatedTask2 = Task.Run(() =>
{
  Parallel.For(
    1,
    10,
    parallelOptions,
    i =>
    {
```

```
      WriteLine($"Processed:{i} with the task ID: [{Task.
        CurrentId}]");
    });
});

repeatedTask2.Wait();
```

Output

Here is some sample output that I got by executing this program:

```
Processed:5 with the task ID:[2]
Processed:1 with the task ID:[3]
Processed:6 with the task ID:[2]
Processed:7 with the task ID:[2]
Processed:8 with the task ID:[2]
Processed:2 with the task ID:[3]
Processed:3 with the task ID:[3]
Processed:4 with the task ID:[3]
Processed:9 with the task ID:[2]
```

Analysis

This time there are only two different task IDs present in this output. The official documentation says the following (see https://learn.microsoft. com/en-us/dotnet/api/system.threading.tasks.paralleloptions. maxdegreeofparallelism?view=net-8.0#system-threading-tasks- paralleloptions-maxdegreeofparallelism):

> *A positive property value limits the number of concurrent operations to the set value. If it is -1, there is no limit on the number of concurrently running operations (with the exception of the ForEachAsync method, where -1 means ProcessorCount).*

Now you understand that you can set the value as -1, but not -2, -3, and so forth. It's a design decision.

You have seen the usefulness of the Paralleloptions class where I used MaxDegreeOfParallelism. The MaxDegreeOfParallelism property in .NET can be set to -1, indicating no limit on concurrent tasks, with the system optimizing based on available resources. Any other negative value is invalid and will cause a System.ArgumentOutOfRangeException to occur. You can use the CancellationToken property to manage cancellations. It is coming next.

Managing Cancellations

In a concurrent environment, managing tasks is an important activity. Since any task can exercise a parallel loop, you may want to know how to cancel a parallel loop.

Following the Previous Approach

Using the knowledge you learned in Chapter 2, you may attempt to cancel the task that executes a parallel loop as follows:

```
using static System.Console;

CancellationTokenSource cts = new();
CancellationToken token = cts.Token;

#region The previous approach that you learned in Chapter 2
var repeatedTask = Task.Run(() =>
{
    Parallel.For(
        1,
        50,
        (i) =>
```

```
    {
        token.ThrowIfCancellationRequested();
        WriteLine($"Processed: {i}");
        Thread.Sleep(1000);
    });

}, token);
#endregion
// Some other code (for example, you can initiate a
// cancellation or wait for the task to finish its execution)
```

Recommended Approach

Though the previous code works, it is interesting to note that there are alternative approaches as well. To cancel a parallel loop, the official documentation recommends the following (see https://learn. microsoft.com/en-us/dotnet/standard/parallel-programming/how-to-cancel-a-parallel-for-or-foreach-loop?redirectedfrom=MSDN):

> *In a parallel loop, you supply the CancellationToken to the method in the ParallelOptions parameter and then enclose the parallel call in a try-catch block.*

Following Microsoft's suggestion, I create a ParallelOptions instance and pass this instance inside repeatedTask in the next demonstration. I also display the corresponding task IDs in this program.

Demonstration 6

Here is the complete program with the important changes in bold:

```
using static System.Console;
```

```
CancellationTokenSource cts = new();
CancellationToken token = cts.Token;

#region The recommended approach
ParallelOptions parallelOptions = new()
{
    CancellationToken = token
};

var repeatedTask = Task.Run(() =>
{
    Parallel.For
    (
        1,
        50,
        parallelOptions,
        i =>
        {
            WriteLine($"Processed ={i}  ID:{Task.CurrentId}");
            Thread.Sleep(1000);
        }
    );

});
#endregion

try
{

    WriteLine("Press c to cancel");
    var input = ReadKey().KeyChar;
    if (input.Equals('c'))
        cts.Cancel();
```

```
    repeatedTask.Wait(token);
}

catch (OperationCanceledException oce)
{
    WriteLine($"\nCaught error due to cancellation: {oce.
     Message} ");
}

catch (AggregateException ae)
{
    ae.Handle(e =>
    {
        WriteLine($"\nCaught error:  {e.Message}");
        return true;
    });
}

finally
{
    cts.Dispose();
}

WriteLine("The application ends now.");
```

Output

Here is some sample output that triggered a cancellation while the application was running:

```
Press c to cancel
Processed: 25   ID:5
Processed: 1    ID:3
Processed: 37   ID:4
```

```
Processed: 13   ID:2
Processed: 49   ID:6
Processed: 14   ID:2
Processed: 2   ID:9
Processed: 38   ID:8
Processed: 26   ID:10
c
Caught error due to cancellation: The operation was canceled.
The application ends now.
```

Q&A Session

Q4.5 In this demonstration, you have used Wait(token) instead of Wait(). Is there any specific thought behind this design?

In this demonstration, the use of the Wait(token) method makes more sense to me. It also shows a similar pattern of outputs if you do not follow the recommended approach (for canceling the parallel loop).

However, if you replace this method with the Wait method and **do not follow the recommended approach**, you may see output like the following:

```
Press c to cancel
Processed: 1
Processed: 13
Processed: 37
Processed: 25
Processed: 49c
Caught error:  One or more errors occurred. (The operation was
canceled.) (The operation was canceled.) (The operation was
canceled.) (The operation was canceled.) (The operation was
canceled.)

The application ends now.
```

You can see lots of cancellations in this output. Does this look good? For me, the answer is no because only one message was sufficient to understand that something was canceled in between the executions.

Note   I placed a sample project, named Demo_RepeatingSameError, in the Chapter4 folder to give you an idea about this kind of output. You can download this project from the Apress website. You may also note that the output may vary based on your computer.

Handling Exceptions

The documentation states the following (see https://learn.microsoft. com/en-us/dotnet/standard/parallel-programming/how-to-handle-exceptions-in-parallel-loops):

> *The Parallel.For and Parallel.ForEach overloads do not have any special mechanism to handle exceptions that might be thrown. In this respect, they resemble regular for and foreach loops (For and For Each in Visual Basic); an unhandled exception causes the loop to terminate as soon as all currently running iterations finish.*

This is why while executing a parallel loop, you must handle the possible exceptions.

In Chapter 2, you learned about handling exceptions. You learned that you can wrap the possible exceptions in a System.AggregateException. The same idea applies here as well. I will now add a few lines of code to the previous demonstration to show you a modified program.

Demonstration 7

Here I will apply some dummy logic to generate an exception. The logic is as follows:

- If the processing number is greater than 45, I generate a random number. If this random number is an even number, I generate an exception.

POINT TO NOTE

In this example scenario, I am throwing the exception based on a random value. This makes the discussion easy. I often use a similar logic in different programs to demonstrate various concepts. However, since the Random class is not thread-safe, in a typical application, you may need to use a lock statement surrounding the random value. However, this approach will limit the concurrency. So, a better idea is to generate separate Random instances for each thread using the ThreadLocal<T> class. You'll see a sample program that uses Threadlocal<T> shortly.

Here is the complete program:

```
using static System.Console;

CancellationTokenSource cts = new();
CancellationToken token = cts.Token;

ParallelOptions parallelOptions = new()
{
    CancellationToken = token
};
```

```
var repeatedTask = Task.Run(() =>
{
    Parallel.For(
        1,
        50,
        parallelOptions,
        i =>
        {
            WriteLine($"Processed: {i}  ID:{Task.CurrentId}");
            Thread.Sleep(1000);
            // A dummy logic to generate an exception randomly
            if (i > 45)
            {
                int random = new Random().Next(1, 11);
                if (random % 2 == 0)
                {
                    throw new Exception($" While processing the
                        number {i}, the random value was: {random}");
                }
            }
        });
});

try
{
    // Let us allow the loop to be executed for some time
    Thread.Sleep(1000);
    WriteLine("Press c to cancel");
    var input = ReadKey().KeyChar;
    if (input.Equals('c'))
        cts.Cancel();
```

```
    repeatedTask.Wait(token);
}

catch (AggregateException ae)
{
    ae.Handle(e =>
    {
        WriteLine($"\nCaught error:  {e.Message}");
        return true;
    });
}

catch (OperationCanceledException oce)
{
    WriteLine($"\nCaught error due to cancellation: {oce.
     Message} ");
}
finally
{
    cts.Dispose();
}

WriteLine("\nThe application ends now.");
```

Output

Once again, you may see different output on your computer. However, I am including some sample output for your reference.

```
The application ends now.
Processed: 1   ID:14
Processed: 37  ID:16
Processed: 25  ID:15
Processed: 13  ID:13
```

```
Processed: 49   ID:17
Press c to cancel
Processed: 38   ID:20
Processed: 26   ID:19
Processed: 14   ID:13
Processed: 2   ID:21
Processed: 4   ID:18
Caught error: One or more errors occurred. ( While processing
the  number 49, the random value was: 8)

The application ends now.
```

You may note that I *did not* trigger a cancellation request while running the application. I pressed the Enter key only after the program stopped printing the messages in the console window.

Fine-Tuning

You can fine-tune a parallel loop using some built-in constructs. Let's use the concept of a parallel for loop to calculate the factorial of 10. Once we analyze the output, you'll see its fine-tuned version.

POINT TO NOTE

You may wonder why we need to use a parallel loop to calculate this small computation. It is because opting for a parallel loop can be beneficial for certain scenarios such as when you are handling a large amount of data (say one million) or you are dealing with some time-consuming operations. However, consider the fact that since I am showing you the output of each demonstration, printing those large numbers of data is not only boring, it is time-consuming as well. So, I considered this simple example to show you a possible implementation, and later I'll fine-tune it.

To understand the code, read the following points:

- In this program, the variable factorial is shared among multiple threads/tasks.

- Since I exercise a parallel loop, I need to provide a synchronization mechanism to access this variable. To ensure this, I used a lock statement before updating this variable.

You should not have any trouble understanding the following code now:

```
using System.Diagnostics;
using static System.Console;

int n = 10;
object lockObject = new();
var stopWatch1 = Stopwatch.StartNew();
int factorial = 1;
Parallel.For(
    1,
    n + 1,
    (x) =>
    {
        lock (lockObject)
        {
            factorial *= x;
        }
    }
);
stopWatch1.Stop();
WriteLine($"The factorial of {n} is {factorial}");
```

```
WriteLine($"The elapsed time (Ticks): {stopWatch1.
ElapsedTicks}");
WriteLine("_____");
```

Once I execute this program, my computer shows the following output:

```
The factorial of 10 is 3628800
The elapsed time (Ticks): 334679
```

Using Thread-Local Variables

Let's fine-tune this program. Notice that in the previous demonstration, I needed to use a lock statement to provide the synchronization mechanism where only one thread can update the factorial variable at a particular time. However, this approach suffers a typical problem when each thread tries to access the shared variable many times.

How can you limit the access to this variable? You can calculate a partial product on each thread, and then you can work on those partial products inside the lock statement. This approach helps you avoid the overhead of synchronizing a large number of accesses to the shared variable. As a result, you will improve the overall performance of the application.

To implement this idea, I used the thread-local data in the following program. Let's see what Microsoft says about it. The documentation states the following (see https://learn.microsoft.com/en-us/dotnet/standard/parallel-programming/how-to-write-a-parallel-for-loop-with-thread-local-variables):

> By using thread-local data, you can avoid the overhead of synchronizing a large number of accesses to shared state. Instead of writing to a shared resource on each iteration, you compute and store the value until all iterations for the task are complete. You can then write the final result once to the shared resource, or pass it to another method.

Now I use a different overload of the `Parallel.For` loop that can use the thread-local variable. It has the following signature:

```
public static ParallelLoopResult For<TLocal>(
    int fromInclusive,
    int toExclusive,
    Func<TLocal> localInit,
    Func<int, ParallelLoopState, TLocal, TLocal> body,
    Action<TLocal> localFinally
)
```

Let's understand the parameters:

As usual, the **first two parameters** specify the starting and ending points for the iteration values.

The **third parameter** represents the function delegate that returns the initial state of the local data for each task. Notice that `localInit` is a `Func<TResult>` type where `TResult` is the type of the variable that will store the thread-local state. Its type is defined by the generic type argument supplied when you call the generic version of this `For` loop. You understand that in our example, it is `Int32`. The type argument tells the compiler the type of the temporary variable that will be used to store the thread-local state. In this example, the expression `() => 1` initializes the thread-local variable to one.

The **fourth parameter** defines the logic of this loop. Since its signature is (`Func<int, ParallelLoopState, TLocal, TLocal>`), I can use a lambda expression as follows:

```
(int num, ParallelLoopState state, int subFact) =>
{
    return num * subFact;
}
```

Here the first parameter (num) is the value of the loop counter for that iteration of the loop. The second parameter is a ParallelLoopState object (state) that can be used to break out of the loop. To make the example simple, I did not use the state variable in this example. The third parameter is the thread-local variable. Notice that the return type is also an int here.

The return value of this lambda iteration is used to initialize subFact on each subsequent iteration of the loop. You can consider this last parameter as a value that is passed to each iteration and then passed to the localFinally delegate when the last iteration is complete.

The **fifth parameter** defines the method that is called once after all the iterations on a particular thread have been completed. You'll see me using the lock statement here. As a result, I could avoid writing to the factorial variable multiple times on each iteration of the loop.

Demonstration 8

Let's take a look at the complete program and measure the elapsed time for this fine-tuned program:

```
using System.Diagnostics;
using static System.Console;

int n = 10;
object lockObject = new();
WriteLine($"Calculating the factorial of a number.");

var stopWatch2 = Stopwatch.StartNew();
int factorial2 = 1;

Parallel.For(
    1,
    n + 1,
    () => 1,
```

```
   (int num, ParallelLoopState state, int subFact) =>
   {
       return num * subFact;
   },
   subFact =>
   {
       lock (lockObject)
       {
           factorial2 *= subFact;
       }
   }
 );
stopWatch2.Stop();
WriteLine($"Using thread-local data, the factorial of {n} is
 {factorial2}");
WriteLine($"After fine-tuning, the elapsed time is {stopWatch2.
 ElapsedTicks} timer ticks.");
```

Output

Here is some sample output:

```
Using thread-local data, the factorial of 10 is 3628800
After fine-tuning, the elapsed time is 41516 timer ticks.
```

You can see that **this fine-tuned version is almost seven times faster than the previous program**. Though the output may vary, using thread-local data inside a parallel for loop can help you improve the performance of an application.

Using Partition-Local Variables

When I was discussing `Parallel.For`, you saw the term **thread-local variable**. If you work with `Parallel.ForEach`, you may see the term **partition-local variable**. The documentation states the following (see https://learn.microsoft.com/en-us/dotnet/standard/parallel-programming/how-to-write-a-parallel-foreach-loop-with-partition-local-variables):

> *When a ForEach loop executes, it divides its source collection into multiple partitions. Each partition has its own copy of the partition-local variable. A partition-local variable is similar to a thread-local variable, except that multiple partitions can run on a single thread.*

Using the concept that you learned in Demonstration 8, you should not find trouble while using partition-local variables inside the `Parallel.ForEach` method. I leave this exercise to you.

Note that I used this concept while solving exercise E4.6. If needed, you can refer to that program or follow the previously mentioned link to get more clarity on the topic.

Additional Note

The scenario in Demonstration 8 can be handled by Parallel LINQ (PLINQ) as well. Once you learn about it in Chapter 5, you can write the following equivalent code:

```
int n = 10;
#region Using PLINQ

var stopWatch3 = Stopwatch.StartNew();
int factorial3 = ParallelEnumerable
    .Range(1, 10)
    .AsParallel()
```

```
    .Aggregate(1, (subFact, nxtNumber) => subFact * nxtNumber);
stopWatch3.Stop();
WriteLine($"Using PLINQ, the factorial of {n} is {factorial3}");
WriteLine($"Now the elapsed time is {stopWatch3.ElapsedTicks}
  timer ticks.");
#endregion
```

Here is some sample output that I got by running this code:

```
Using PLINQ, the factorial of 10 is 3628800
Now the elapsed time is 26709 timer ticks.
```

Notice that the code is both simple and efficient. In fact, it produced the best performance so far. However, it is obvious that the performance may vary on your computer.

PLINQ has a rich set of functionalities that can help you perform all the necessary steps that you'd like to do to parallelize your work. For example, PLINQ can partition the work into tasks, execute those tasks on different threads, and gather the results into a single output sequence. So, using PLINQ, you can avoid the burden of partitioning the work and output collating from different threads.

Note   When you download the project Demo8_UsingThreadLocalData, you'll see that I have kept all the code segments: the first one does not use the thread-local data, the second one uses the thread-local data, and the final one uses PLINQ. As a result, you can compare the results instantly on your computer.

Q&A Session

Q4.6 It can help me if you explain thread-local storage with a simple example.

If you think about Demonstration 7 and Demonstration 8, you'll understand that to limit the access to the shared variable, I needed to fine-tune the application. How did I do this? While making the computation on each thread, I wanted to keep the data isolated. In simple words, while one thread was doing the computation, I needed to prevent other threads from interfering with it. This is why I needed to consider thread-local storages/variables.

It is useful to note that you can implement thread-local storage in different ways. Some of the common approaches in this context include marking a static field with the `ThreadStaticAttribute` using `ThreadLocal<T>` class and using `AsyncLocal<T>` (useful for asynchronous programming).

I recommend you refer to `https://learn.microsoft.com/en-us/dotnet/standard/threading/thread-local-storage-thread-relative-static-fields-and-data-slots` to learn more. The documentation also suggests the following:

> *You can use the System.Threading.ThreadLocal<T> class to create thread-local objects that are initialized lazily when the object is first consumed.*

To illustrate a simple example, let me show you an example using the `ThreadLocal<T>` class. See the following program where I create two different tasks and each task receives the same initial value before they make some changes to it (notice that I also wait for these tasks to complete their executions before closing the application):

POINT TO NOTE

If you are reading about the ThreadLocal<T> class for the first time, I
recommend you visit https://learn.microsoft.com/en-us/dotnet/
api/system.threading.threadlocal-1?view=net-8.0 to see the
different constructors and parameters available in this class. In this program,
I have used the constructor that accepts a Func<T> parameter. In addition,
I used the Value property to get and set the value of the instance of the
current thread.

```
using static System.Console;
WriteLine("Understanding the ThreadLocal<T> class.");

var flag = new ThreadLocal<int>(() => 50);

var task1 = Task.Run(
    () =>
        {
            WriteLine($" Task1 received the value:{flag.Value}");
            flag.Value += 25;
            WriteLine($" Task1 changed the value to {flag.Value}");
        }
    );

var task2 = Task.Run(
    () =>
        {
            WriteLine($"\tTask2 received the value:{flag.Value}");
            flag.Value += 50;
            WriteLine($"\tTask2 changed the value to {flag.Value}");
        }
    );
```

```
Task.WaitAll(task1, task2);

WriteLine($"Before closing the application, the main thread
 contains the value: {flag.Value}");
```

Run the program now. Here is some sample output:

```
Understanding the ThreadLocal<T> class.
 Task1 received the value: 50
 Task1 changed the value to 75
         Task2 received the value: 50
         Task2 changed the value to 100
Before closing the application, the main thread contains the
 value: 50
```

You can see that each task received 50 as the initial value, and later, they changed this value inside them. However, those changes did not impact this value inside the main thread.

Note   The Q&A_UnderstandingThreadLocal project contains this program. You can download it from the Apress website.

Q4.7 In Demonstration 8, you initialized the thread-local variable to 1 by using the expression () => 1. Since you worked with an int, it was OK. I am curious to know how to initialize when you work with a reference type or user-defined value type.

It is similar. You can write something like ()=> UserDefinedClass.

Reviewing Different Coding Styles

Congratulations! You are about to finish another useful chapter. Before you move into the next chapter, I'd like to draw your attention to a few coding styles. I have included this section to avoid any confusion if you see similar code in the future.

Throughout this book, to generate numbers, I used the Enumerable class. For example, to generate the numbers from 1 to 10, I used the following syntax:

```
List<int> numbers = Enumerable.Range(1, 10).ToList();
```

Or this:

```
var numbers = Enumerable.Range(1, 10).ToList();
```

In the first case, I explicitly mentioned the type(List<int>). In the second case, I let the compiler infer the type. Both are fine. But as you progress more on the topic and learn PLINQ (or use LINQ), you'll understand that LINQ or PLINQ follows functional programming, which is nothing but declarative programming. So, if you are biased toward functional/declarative programming, you may prefer to use var instead of explicitly mentioning the type. I leave this preference to you.

In this context, note that C# 12 (available with .NET 8) was released in November 2023 with some exciting features, and one of them is collection expressions. Using this new feature, I showed you some alternative code in Chapter 1 (you can refer to Demonstration 4 and Exercise 1.6 in that chapter) as well.

Let's take a quick look at the different approaches that show equivalent code.

Approach 1:

```
List<int> numbers = Enumerable.Range(1, 10).ToList();
```

Approach 2:

```
var numbers = Enumerable.Range(1, 10).ToList();
```

Approach 3:

```
List<int> numbers = [.. Enumerable.Range(1, 10)];
```

But the following line will cause a compile-time error:

```
var numbers4 = [.. Enumerable.Range(1, 10).ToList()];
```

I often follow Approach 1 and Approach 2 to support backward compatibility. But to make you familiar with the new syntax, in some cases, I have used Approach 3 as well.

Introducing the ParallelEnumerable Class

There is a class called ParallelEnumerable that is the parallel equivalent of the Enumerable class. So, you can write something like the following as well:

Approach 4:

```
List<int> numbers = ParallelEnumerable.Range(1, 10).ToList();
```

Interestingly, if you use the previous line of code, Visual Studio will suggest you prefer Approach 3 and write something like the following:

Approach 5:

```
List<int> numbers = [.. ParallelEnumerable.Range(1, 10)];
```

You will see many useful methods inside this class for querying objects that implement ParallelQuery{TSource}. You'll see me using this class when I discuss parallel LINQ (PLINQ) queries in Chapter 5.

POINT TO NOTE

The `Enumerable` class provides methods for querying objects that implement `IEnumerable<T>`. The `ParallelEnumerable` class provides methods for querying objects that implement `ParallelQuery{TSource}`.

If you're interested, you can learn more about the class by referring to the documentation: `https://learn.microsoft.com/en-us/dotnet/api/system.linq.parallelenumerable?view=net-8.0`.

Exercises

Check your understanding by attempting the following exercises:

REMINDER

As mentioned, for all the code examples, the Implicit Global Usings setting was enabled in Visual Studio. This is why you will not see me mentioning some other namespaces that were available by default. You can safely assume that all other necessary namespaces are available for these code segments in this exercise. The same comment applies to all exercises in this book.

E4.1 True or False?

a) A parallel loop is always faster than the corresponding sequential loop.

b) The methods of the `Parallel` class improve CPU-bound tasks but not the I/O-bound tasks.

    c) Thread-local variables can be used to fine-tune a parallel loop.

    d) While instantiating the `ParallelOptions` class, you can set `MaxDegreeOfParallelism` to -1.

E4.2 The following program prints the position of the characters of the string "abcde":

```
using static System.Console;

string input = "abcde";
int position = 0;
foreach (char c in input)
{
    WriteLine($"{c} is in position:{position++}");
}
```

    Can you write an equivalent program using `Parallel.ForEach`?

    (**Hint:** You can use the following overload of the `ForEach` method:
```
public static ParallelLoopResult ForEach<TSource>(IEnumerable
<TSource> source, Action<TSource, ParallelLoopState, long>
body);)
```

E4.3 Can you give an example where you'd like to use the `Stop` or `Break` method? These methods are very similar. Can you give an example where you'd prefer one over the other?

E4.4 Can you predict the output of the following program?

```
using static System.Console;

try
{
    Action greet = new(() =>
    {
        WriteLine($"Hello reader! Started: {Task.CurrentId}");
```

```
        Thread.Sleep(500);
        WriteLine($"Have a nice day! Finished: {Task.
         CurrentId}");
    }
    );

    Action printMsg = new(() =>
    {
        WriteLine($"Trying to print a message. Started: {Task.
         CurrentId}");
        throw new InvalidOperationException("invalid
         operation");
    });

    Action sayBusy= new(() =>
    {
        WriteLine($"I'm performing a lengthy operation.
         Started: {Task.CurrentId}");
        Thread.Sleep(1500);
        WriteLine($"I am free now! Finished: {Task.CurrentId}");
    });

    Parallel.Invoke(greet, printMsg,sayBusy);
}
catch(AggregateException ae)
{
    foreach(Exception e in ae.InnerExceptions)
    {
        WriteLine($"Error: {e.Message}");
    }
}
```

E4.5 Can you predict the output of the following program?

```
using static System.Console;

try
{
    ParallelOptions parallelOptions = new()
    {
      MaxDegreeOfParallelism = 0
    };
    List<int> numbers = [.. ParallelEnumerable.Range(1, 10)];
    var repeatedTask = Task.Run(() =>
    {
        Parallel.ForEach(
            numbers,
            parallelOptions,
             i =>
             {
                 WriteLine($"Processed the number: {i}");
             });
    });
    repeatedTask.Wait();
}
catch (AggregateException ae)
{
    foreach (Exception e in ae.InnerExceptions)
    {
        WriteLine($"Error: {e.Message}");
    }
}
```

```
catch (ArgumentOutOfRangeException e)
{
    WriteLine($"Caught error: {e.Message}");
}
```

E4.6 In this chapter, you saw me calculating the factorial of 10 using a parallel `for` loop. This time I want you to calculate the sum of the numbers from 1 to 1000. However, I want you to do this exercise using a parallel `foreach` loop. If possible, once you complete this exercise, fine-tune your application and compare the output as well.

Summary

This chapter started with a quick recap of sequential loops and then focused on their parallel equivalents. It also analyzed some case studies to evaluate whether a parallel loop is beneficial compared to its counterpart (i.e., a sequential loop). In brief, it answered the following questions:

- How can you execute parallel loops in C#?

- How do you use `Parallel.ForEach`, `Parallel.For`, and `Parallel.Invoke` in an application?

- How can you manage a parallel loop using the `ParallelLoopState` and `ParallelOptions` parameters?

- How can you handle exceptions and manage cancellations while executing a parallel loop?

- How can you fine-tune a parallel loop using thread-local data?

Solutions to Exercises

Here are the solutions for the exercises in this chapter.

E4.1

The answers are as follows:

a) A parallel loop is always faster than the corresponding sequential loop. (**False**)

b) The methods of the `Parallel` class improve CPU-bound tasks but not I/O-bound tasks. (**True**)

c) Thread-local variables can be used to fine-tune a parallel loop. (**True**)

d) While instantiating the `ParallelOptions` class, you can set `MaxDegreeOfParallelism` to -1. (**True**)

E4.2

The following program shows the sequential as well as the parallel version:

```
using static System.Console;

#region The sequential version
string input = "abcde";
int position = 0;
foreach (char c in input)
{
    WriteLine($"{c} is in position:{position++}");
}
#endregion
```

```
WriteLine("========");

#region The parallel version

Parallel.ForEach
  (
   input,
   (char c, ParallelLoopState state, long position) =>
    {
      WriteLine($"{c} is in position:{position++}");
     }
  );
#endregion
```

Here is some sample output for your reference:

```
a is in position:0
b is in position:1
c is in position:2
d is in position:3
e is in position:4
========
b is in position:1
c is in position:2
d is in position:3
a is in position:0
e is in position:4
```

E4.3

You often see their presence in search-based algorithms.

Yes, they are indeed very similar. Let's see what the official documentation says about them. In the case of the Stop method, Microsoft states the following (see `https://learn.microsoft.com/en-us/dotnet/api/system.threading.tasks.parallelloopstate.stop?view=net-8.0`):

> *Communicates that the Parallel loop should cease execution at the system's earliest convenience.*

However, in the case of the Break method, Microsoft states the following (see `https://learn.microsoft.com/en-us/dotnet/api/system.threading.tasks.parallelloopstate.break?view=net-8.0#system-threading-tasks-parallelloopstate-break`):

> *Communicates that the Parallel loop should cease execution **of iterations beyond the current iteration** at the system's earliest convenience.*

Now consider the case where you search for a particular element in a data structure using a parallel for loop. Typically, you can use either the Stop method or the Break method. However, in a search-based algorithm, if you find the required element, you can immediately stop the search operation.

Consider another case where you discovered a typical fault and, as a result, continuing the application does not make sense. So, in such cases, I'd like to use the Stop method.

E4.4

Here is some sample output:

```
Trying to print a message. Started: 1
I'm performing a lengthy operation. Started: 2
Hello reader! Started: 3
Have a nice day! Finished: 3
I am free now! Finished: 2
Error: invalid operation
```

Explanation: Notice that you are seeing the exception at the end of the output. The documentation confirms the following (see `https://learn.microsoft.com/en-us/previous-versions/msp-n-p/ff963549(v=pand p.10)?redirectedfrom=MSDN`):

> *Any exceptions that occur during the execution of Parallel. Invoke are **deferred and rethrown when all tasks finish**. All exceptions are rethrown as inner exceptions of an AggregateException instance.*

E4.5

You should see the following output:

```
Caught error: MaxDegreeOfParallelism ('0') must be a non-zero
value. (Parameter 'MaxDegreeOfParallelism')
Actual value was 0.
```

Additional Note: You are not allowed to set the value of the `MaxDegreeOfParallelism` property to zero or to a value that is less than -1; you'll see the `ArgumentOutOfRangeException`. However, you can set the value to -1. The documentation states the following (see `https://learn.microsoft.com/en-us/dotnet/api/system.threading.tasks.paralleloptions.maxdegreeofparallelism?view=net-8.0#system-threading-tasks-paralleloptions-maxdegreeofparallelism`):

> *A positive property value limits the number of concurrent operations to the set value. If it is -1, there is no limit on the number of concurrently running operations (with the exception of the ForEachAsync method, where -1 means ProcessorCount).*

E4.6

Here is a sample implementation and its fine-tuned version:

```
using System.Diagnostics;
using static System.Console;

List<int> numbers = [.. ParallelEnumerable.Range(1, 1000)];

WriteLine($"Calculating the sum of 1 to 1000.");
#region Without using thread local variable
var stopWatch = Stopwatch.StartNew();
int total = 0;
Parallel.ForEach(
    numbers,
    (x) =>
    {
        Interlocked.Add(ref total, x);
    }
);
stopWatch.Stop();
WriteLine($"The sum is: {total}");
WriteLine($"The elapsed time is {stopWatch.ElapsedTicks} timer
  ticks.");
WriteLine("_____");
#endregion

WriteLine($"Fine-tuning the application now.");

#region Using thread local variable
stopWatch = Stopwatch.StartNew();
total = 0;
Parallel.ForEach(
    numbers,
```

```
    () =>0,
    (int num, ParallelLoopState state, int subTotal) =>
    {
        return num + subTotal;
    },
  subTotal =>
  {
      Interlocked.Add(ref total, subTotal);
  }
);
stopWatch.Stop();
WriteLine($"The sum is: {total}");
WriteLine($"Now the elapsed time is {stopWatch.ElapsedTicks}
 timer ticks.");

#endregion
```

Here is some sample output:

```
Calculating the sum of 1 to 1000.
The sum is:  500500
The elapsed time is 258695 timer ticks.
_____

Fine-tuning the application now.
The sum is:  500500
Now the elapsed time is 31290 timer ticks.
```

CHAPTER 5

Parallel LINQ

Language-Integrated Query (LINQ) was an important addition to .NET. Parallel LINQ (PLINQ) is its parallel implementation, which is an integral part of parallel programming. This chapter attempts to simplify the topic for you.

Prerequisite Knowledge

In this section, I'll demystify some important characteristics of PLINQ. Careful study of this section will help you understand the topic better.

Imperative vs. Declarative Programming

It is useful for PLINQ users to understand the difference between the imperative and declarative styles of coding. If you already know about them, you can skip this section. Otherwise, keep reading.

The imperative style of programming (also known as algorithmic programming) describes *how* to solve the problem by defining a sequence of commands or operations. This style of programming is characterized by explicit control flow and mutable state. For example, one may suggest: "Do this step, then do that step, and then get the result." Imperative programming is a step-by-step approach. Object-oriented programming languages such as C#, C++, Visual Basic, and Java are designed primarily to support imperative programming. This is why I assume you are familiar with this coding style.

© Vaskaran Sarcar 2024
V. Sarcar, *Parallel Programming with C# and .NET*,
https://doi.org/10.1007/979-8-8688-0488-5_5

By contrast, declarative programming focuses on the result without trying to control the flow of the program. Instead of describing how to get the result, developers focus on *what* needs to be done. More specifically, in declarative programming, developers focus on defining the desired outcome instead of specifying step-by-step instructions and let the language or framework handle the implementation details. This is why declarative programming is often associated with higher-level abstractions, such as functions or expressions, and it encourages immutability and data-driven approaches. Languages like SQL, HTML/ CSS, and functional programming languages like Haskell and F# exemplify declarative programming

The good news is that though C# is primarily object-oriented, it supports functional programming as well. It has many functional features, and some of them are common as well. To follow declarative programming, functional programmers use expressions, not statements. If you are familiar with LINQ, you have seen this before. Since functional programming is merely a form of declarative programming. you can say that C# supports declarative programming as well.

PLINQ Supports Declarative Programming

Now if you need to exercise parallel programming, probably you would like to partition the work into multiple tasks, execute those tasks on different threads, and then merge the results. The good news is that all this is done by the underlying framework that PLINQ uses. This is why it is declarative, not imperative.

Understanding LINQ Is Beneficial

The Microsoft documentation states the following (see `https://learn.microsoft.com/en-us/dotnet/standard/parallel-programming/introduction-to-plinq`):

> *PLINQ implements the full set of LINQ standard query operators as extension methods for the System.Linq namespace and has additional operators for parallel operations. PLINQ combines the simplicity and readability of LINQ syntax with the power of parallel programming.*

So, LINQ can help you learn and use PLINQ easily. Let me elaborate:

- LINQ follows the functional style of coding. It is declarative in nature, operates on an in-memory `IEnumerable` or `IEnumerable<T>` data source, and supports deferred execution. **PLINQ continues this legacy: it does the same.**

- Then how does the LINQ and PLINQ differ? PLINQ does the necessary things on your behalf to achieve parallelism: it partitions the data source into segments and executes queries on each segment on separate threads in parallel using multiple processors. This is why particular parallel queries can be significantly faster than the corresponding sequential queries.

The Path Toward Parallelism

If you are familiar with LINQ queries, then you can impose parallelism on them easily. How? You simply use the extension method `AsParallel` as the entry point for PLINQ.

To illustrate, let's consider the following code. Given a list of numbers, this code picks numbers that are divisible by 5:

```
using static System.Console;
const int count = 30;
var numbers = Enumerable.Range(0, count);

// Using LINQ
var divisibleByFive=
    numbers
    .Where(x => x % 5 == 0);

WriteLine("\nNumbers divisible by 5 are:");
foreach(var x in divisibleByFive)
{
    Write($"{x}\t");
}
```

It is not a surprise that this code can produce the following output:

```
Numbers divisible by 5 are:
0       5       10      15      20      25
```

Converting LINQ into PLINQ Using AsParallel

If you want to use a PLINQ query, you can use the AsParallel extension method in the previous LINQ query as follows:

```
var divisibleByFive=
    numbers
    .AsParallel()
    .Where(x => x % 5 == 0);
// There is no other change in the previous program
```

Upon executing, this modified code can produce different output. Here is a sample:

```
Numbers divisible by 5 are:
0        10       20       25       5        15
```

Note   You can safely assume that the output will vary on your computer.

Using the ParallelEnumerable Class

Since I used the Enumerable class in the previous program, I used AsParallel() to make it parallel. Since the ParallelEnumerable class is the parallel equivalent of Enumerable, I could start with the ParallelEnumerable class as well. For example, I could write something like the following:

```
numbers = ParallelEnumerable
          .Range(0, 30)
          .Where(x => x % 5 == 0);

// There is no other change in the previous program
```

Upon executing this query, my computer produces the following output:

```
Numbers divisible by 5 are:
0       5        10       20        25        15
```

Upon executing similar code, you may expect to see unordered output in a parallel environment. This is OK. However, you must note that **sequential output does not specify that the corresponding code did not execute in parallel. In addition, it is also possible that a PLINQ query**

followed sequential execution. Why? Microsoft states the following (see
`https://learn.microsoft.com/en-us/dotnet/standard/parallel-`
`programming/introduction-to-plinq#parallel-vs-sequential-`
`queries`):

> *If PLINQ has a choice between a potentially expensive parallel*
> *algorithm or an inexpensive sequential algorithm, it chooses*
> *the sequential algorithm by default.*

So, a computer can produce ordered output as well as unordered
output for a query. However, if you are sure that running a query in parallel
mode is beneficial, you can instruct PLINQ to force parallelism by using
WithExecutionMethod. PLINQ can also help you control the degree of
parallelism. This is helpful when you work with I/O-intensive operations.
I'll discuss this in a moment.

Note   You can download the project Demo_LinqToPlinq to
compare the different approaches and their corresponding results.

Introducing ForAll

Notice that when you use Enumerable.Range(0, count);, the
Range method returns an IEnumerable<int>. But when you use
ParallelEnumerable.Range(0, count);, the Range method returns
ParallelQuery<int>. You should keep this point in mind. In fact, if you
investigate the following query:

```
divisibleByFive =
    numbers
    .AsParallel()
    .Where(x => x % 5 == 0);
```

you'll see that the AsParallel method also returns a
ParallelQuery<int>, which is an important class. Refer to

https://learn.microsoft.com/en-us/dotnet/api/system.linq.para
llelquery-1?view=net-8.0, which states that ParallelQuery<Tsource>
represents a parallel sequence, and this class inherits from ParallelQuey
and IEnumerable<TSource>. There you'll also find many useful methods
and extension methods.

Among these methods, I often like to use the ForAll extension method
in my code. Let me write a simple query in the following program:

```
using static System.Console;
const int count = 30;
WriteLine("\nNumbers divisible by 5 are:");
ParallelEnumerable
    .Range(0, count)
    .Where(x => x % 5 == 0)
    .ForAll(num=>Write($"{num}\t"));
```

Here is some sample output of this program:

```
Numbers divisible by 5 are:
0       10      25      5       20      15
```

Author's Note: When you download Demo_LinqToPlinq, you can see this
code segment as well.

As a C# developer, you are familiar with foreach and for loops. You
also learned about their parallel versions in Chapter 3. This time you saw
the ForAll method and learned that this method also helps you invoke a
specified action for each element of a source in parallel.

Now, you may wonder whether to use ForAll or Foreach or For.
Let's refer to https://learn.microsoft.com/en-us/dotnet/standard/
parallel-programming/potential-pitfalls-with-plinq#prefer-
forall-to-foreach-when-it-is-possible to find Microsoft's thoughts on
this. The documentation suggests the following:

*Use the ForAll method to enable each thread to output its own
results.*

Q&A Session

Q5.1 Why does Microsoft suggest using ForAll to ForEach?

When you consume a parallel query result inside a foreach loop, the query result needs to be merged back into a thread and accessed serially by an enumerator. Though this step is essential for certain situations, it is not mandatory for every situation. So, you understand that by avoiding the merging step, the performance can be improved. ForAll does the same thing, but it does not require the merge step at the end.

This is why Microsoft says the following (see https://learn. microsoft.com/en-us/dotnet/standard/parallel-programming/ potential-pitfalls-with-plinq):

> *The same issue applies to Parallel.ForEach. In other words, source.AsParallel().Where().**ForAll**(...) should be strongly preferred to Parallel.**ForEach**(source.AsParallel().Where(), ...).*

Getting Familiar with PLINQ

Let's now explore PLINQ in more detail. You understand that though LINQ supports declarative programming, the execution is sequential. But when you deal with a lot of data, you may be interested in parallel execution. PLINQ is made for this. So, it's time for some more coding. Let's start.

The First Program

In the following program, I generate some numbers using Enumerable's Range method. After this, you will see a PLINQ query that checks whether a number is divisible by 5. If so, it increments the number by 100. This query will also show you the different task IDs that will be involved in the process. Finally, I display the numbers using a traditional foreach loop.

Note   Later you will see me using the ForAll function instead of using a foreach loop or a ForEach function. Since this is just the beginning, let's learn slowly.

Demonstration 1

Here is the complete program:

```
using static System.Console;

WriteLine("Introduction to PLINQ.");

var numbers = Enumerable.Range(1, 27);
// The query to get the new numbers.
var newNumbers =
    numbers
     .AsParallel()
     .Where(x => x % 5 == 0)
     .Select(num =>
     {
         WriteLine($" Processing: {num} ID:{Task.CurrentId}");
         return num + 100;
     });

WriteLine("The changed numbers are as follows:");
foreach (var number in newNumbers)
{
    Write($"{number}\t");
}
```

Output

Here is some sample output:

```
Introduction to PLINQ.
The changed numbers are as follows:
 Processing: 15 ID:4
 Processing: 10 ID:3
 Processing: 25 ID:5
 Processing: 5 ID:2
 Processing: 20 ID:4
110      115      125      105      120
```

Analysis

You can see that the PLINQ query processed the numbers in parallel. Notice that five numbers are updated and four different tasks (IDS 2,3,4 and 5) were involved in this process.

If you execute the program again, you may notice that these numbers appear in a different order. This is fine. It is because you cannot predict the processing order in advance.

Q&A Session

Q5.2 The last line in the previous output showed elements in an unordered fashion. I understand that in a parallel environment, this is an expected output. However, I am curious to know while using PLINQ, is it possible to control the order of the elements in the output?

Yes. If you update the query using AsOrdered() as follows:

```
var newNumbers =
    numbers
     .AsParallel()
     .AsOrdered()
```

```
.Where(x => x % 5 == 0)
.Select(num =>
{
    WriteLine($" Processing: {num} ID:{Task.CurrentId}");
    return num + 100;
});
```

you can see that the output is as follows (notice that the elements are ordered in the final line):

```
// Previous lines of output are not shown to focus on this
// discussion
105     110     115     120     125
```

Q5.3 What is the reason behind printing "The changed numbers as follows" text before "processing...." even though in code it is written on top?

This is because you observed a deferred execution where we do not evaluate an expression until a realized value is required. Microsoft says the following (see `https://learn.microsoft.com/en-us/dotnet/standard/linq/deferred-execution-lazy-evaluation`):

Deferred execution can greatly improve performance when you have to manipulate large data collections, especially in programs that contain a series of chained queries or manipulations.

However, certain query operators (and their corresponding functions for method syntax) promote immediate execution. In this context, Microsoft states the following:

Immediate execution means that the data source is read and the operation is performed once. All the standard query operators that return a scalar result execute immediately. You can force a query to execute immediately using the Enumerable.

ToList or Enumerable.ToArray methods. Immediate execution provides reuse of query results, not query declaration. The results are retrieved once, then stored for future use.

So, if you want to perform an immediate execution, you can update the query where you append ToList() as follows:

```
var newNumbers =
    numbers
     .AsParallel()
     .Where(x => x % 5 == 0)
     .Select(num =>
     {
         WriteLine($" Processing: {num} ID:{Task.CurrentId}");
         return num + 100;
     })
     .ToList();
```

After this change, you can execute the program again to get output that looks like this:

```
Introduction to PLINQ.
Processing: 10 ID:3
 Processing: 25 ID:5
 Processing: 5 ID:2
 Processing: 15 ID:4
 Processing: 20 ID:4
The changed numbers are as follows:
105     110     115     120     125
```

Notice that to get the ordered output, I did not need to use the AsOrdered extension method as well.

Do Parallel Queries Run Faster Than Sequential Queries?

The interesting point is that an attempt to make a parallel query does not guarantee that it will be faster than the corresponding sequential query. In fact, if you use an expensive partitioning strategy, it can significantly slow down the execution. So, it is important to understand the complexities of a query before you try to make it parallel.

To illustrate more on this, let me show you some sample programs. Go through the next three programs (Demonstration 2 to Demonstration 4).

Demonstration 2

Here I measure the execution time for three equivalent code segments. Given some numbers, each part displays those numbers that are divisible by 5. The first code segment uses the traditional foreach loop, the next code segment uses one LINQ query, and the final one uses a PLINQ query as follows:

```
using System.Diagnostics;
using static System.Console;

var numbers = Enumerable.Range(0, 31);

Stopwatch sw;
sw = Stopwatch.StartNew();
WriteLine("Numbers divisible by 5 are (using foreach loop):");
foreach (int num in numbers)
{
    if (num % 5 == 0)
    {
        Write($"{num}\t");
    }
}
```

291

```
sw.Stop();
WriteLine($"Time taken:{sw.ElapsedMilliseconds} ms");

sw = Stopwatch.StartNew();

WriteLine("\nNumbers divisible by 5 are (using LINQ and the
 ForEach function):");
numbers
    .Where(num => num % 5 == 0)
    .ToList()
    .ForEach(num => Write($"{num}\t"));

sw.Stop();
WriteLine($"Time taken:{sw.ElapsedMilliseconds} ms");

sw = Stopwatch.StartNew();

WriteLine("\nNumbers divisible by 5 are (using PLINQ and the
 ForAll function):");
numbers
    .AsParallel()
    .Where(num => num % 5 == 0)
    .ForAll(num => Write($"{num}\t"));

sw.Stop();
WriteLine($"Time taken:{sw.ElapsedMilliseconds} ms");
```

Output

Most of the time, on my computer, the code block that used the PLINQ query took more time to execute compared to other code segments. Let me include one of those samples for your reference:

```
Numbers divisible by 5 are (using foreach loop):
0       5       10      15      20      25      30      Time
taken:12 ms

Numbers divisible by 5 are (using LINQ and the ForEach function):
0       5       10      15      20      25      30      Time
taken:3 ms

Numbers divisible by 5 are (using PLINQ and the ForAll function):
5       20      25      30      10      0       15      Time
taken:23 ms
```

Analysis

You can easily assume that it was due to the overhead associated with parallel processing. However, since my data set was very small, I could not get much benefit when I opted for parallel processing.

POINT TO NOTE

I have measured the performance using ElapsedMilliseconds. The documentation at https://learn.microsoft.com/en-us/dotnet/standard/parallel-programming/how-to-measure-plinq-query-performance suggests that for more fine-grained measurement, you should use ElapsedTicks instead of ElapsedMilliseconds. It also states the following:

To get a deeper and richer view of the interaction of the query threads with one another and with other running processes, use the Concurrency Visualizer.

Our primary goal in this chapter is to understand the fundamentals of PLINQ. The discussion of the Concurrency Visualizer is beyond the scope of this book.

Q&A Session

Q5.4 In Demonstration 2, the PLINQ query used the ForAll function instead of ForEach. Is there any specific thought behind this?

Since I did not need to merge the results at the end (see Q&A Session 5.1), following Microsoft's suggestion, I preferred ForAll over ForEach.

Demonstration 3

Now consider the following program that uses a time-consuming method GetResult in LINQ:

```
using System.Diagnostics;
using static System.Console;

Stopwatch sw = Stopwatch.StartNew();
var numbers = Enumerable.Range(0, 4);

var results =
    numbers
    .Select(x => GetResult(x + 1));

results
    .ToList()
    .ForEach(x => WriteLine(x + "\t"));

sw.Stop();
WriteLine($"Time taken: {sw.ElapsedMilliseconds} ms");

static int GetResult(int number)
{
    int waitTimeMs = number * 1000;
    // Simulating the delay
    Thread.Sleep(waitTimeMs);
    return waitTimeMs;
}
```

Output

You can easily predict that the execution time will not be less than (1000+2000+3000+4000) ms. I have included some sample output for you:

1000

2000

3000

4000

Time taken: 10098 ms

Enabling Parallelization

If you are using a multicore machine, an equivalent PLINQ query can improve the performance. So, let's enable parallelization by updating the previous query as follows:

```
// There is no change in the previous code
var results =
    numbers
    .AsParallel()
    .Select(x => GetResult(x + 1));
// There is no change in the remaining code
```

Output

Execute the program one more time. Here is some sample output:

1000

2000

3000

4000

Time taken: 4075 ms

Analysis

You can see that the program is almost 2.5 times faster now. The time difference between the approaches will increase if you keep increasing the numbers.

Demonstrations 2 and 3 also show that certain PLINQ queries can improve the performance of a program, but the same is not true for all PLINQ queries.

Note   In this context, I encourage you to read Igor Ostrovsky's thoughts at `https://devblogs.microsoft.com/pfxteam/plinq-queries-that-run-sequentially/`.

Q&A Session

Q5.5 In Demonstration 3, you have used the following code segment:

```
var results =
    numbers
    .Select(x => GetResult(x+1));

results
    .ToList()
    .ForEach(x => WriteLine(x + "\t"));
```

But it appears to me that you could use a single query as follows:

```
numbers
.Select(x => GetResult(x + 1))
.ToList()
.ForEach(x => WriteLine(x + "\t"));
```

Is there any specific reason behind this?

Nice observation. The ToList method forces an immediate execution, but I opted for a deferred execution.

Q5.6 In Demonstration 3, you have the ForEach function instead of a foreach loop. Do you think ForEach is better than foreach?

No. In fact, foreach is probably more readable than ForEach. But I have found ForEach helpful in certain scenarios because of the following reasons:

- You can reduce the code length.

- Once you start composing functions using method chaining, you'll find it is more readable at the end of a long chain. In fact, in the case of parallel programming, you may notice a similar coding style.

In Demonstration 3, since you're already converting the results to a list with ToList(), using ForEach is a reasonable choice. However, if you didn't need to convert to a list and wanted more control over the loop, foreach might be a better choice.

Note   In Demonstration 3, I have not changed the Foreach function only for an easy comparison between a LINQ query and its equivalent PLINQ query. However, following Microsoft's suggestion, I'd recommend using the ForAll function instead of the ForEach function whenever possible, particularly to enable each thread to output its own results.

Q5.7 The ForEach function is defined in the List<T> class only. Similar support is not available for other data structures. So, it appears to me that its usage is limited. Is this correct?

You can define an extension method to provide similar support for other data structures as well. If interested, you can download the project Demo_TraversingDictionaryUsingForEach where you see a sample implementation.

Author's Note: I showed this program in my other book *Introducing Functional Programming Using C#*, also published by Apress.

Forcing Parallelism and Controlling the Degree

As mentioned, in some situations, PLINQ can run the query sequentially. However, if you are sure that running a query in parallel mode is beneficial, you can instruct PLINQ to force parallelism. PLINQ can also help you control the degree of parallelism. This is helpful when you work with I/O-intensive operations. Let's examine them.

Demonstration 4

In Demonstration 2, we analyzed the performance of three equivalent code segments. Let's append one more code segment in that demonstration. You may note that using this code, I try to force parallelism as well as control the degree of parallelism using two useful methods, called WithExecutionMode and WithDegreeOfParallelism. Here I'll append the following code segment in Demonstration 2 and measure the execution time one more time:

```
// The previous code is shown in demonstration 2
sw = Stopwatch.StartNew();
WriteLine("\nNumbers divisible by 5 are(using PLINQ(dop-4):");
numbers
    .AsParallel()
    .WithExecutionMode(ParallelExecutionMode.ForceParallelism)
    .WithDegreeOfParallelism(4)
    .Where(num => num % 5 == 0)
```

```
    .ForAll(num => Write($"{num}\t"));
sw.Stop();
WriteLine($"Time taken:{sw.ElapsedMilliseconds} ms");
```

Output

My computer shows a significant performance gain for the added code segment. Here is some sample output (see the bold portion):

```
Numbers divisible by 5 are (using foreach loop):
0       5       10      15      20      25      30  Time taken:14 ms

Numbers divisible by 5 are (using LINQ and the ForEach function):
0       5       10      15      20      25      30  Time taken:1 ms

Numbers divisible by 5 are (using PLINQ and the ForAll function):
10      15      25      30      0       5       20  Time taken:22 ms
```

Numbers divisible by 5 are(using PLINQ(dop-4):
25   20   30   10   15   0   5   Time taken:1 ms

POINT TO NOTE

The documentation suggests the following (see `https://learn.`
`microsoft.com/en-us/dotnet/standard/parallel-programming/`
`introduction-to-plinq#parallel-vs-sequential-queries`):

In cases where a query is performing a significant amount of non-compute-bound work such as File I/O, it might be beneficial to specify a degree of parallelism greater than the number of cores on the machine.

I assume that careful study of this section gives you fundamental ideas about PLINQ. It's time to explore more about this topic. Continue reading.

Merging Data

In a concurrent environment, you will deal with multiple threads. Exercising parallel queries, you can divide complex work into multiple parts and execute those parts in different threads. Upon completion, you may want to merge the results. Briefly, these are the steps:

- Partition the data into multiple parts.

- Multiple threads work on these parts and produce the corresponding results.

- Finally, collect these results and combine (aka merge) them. In other words, consumers consume the results that are produced by these threads.

The last step is common but not mandatory for every situation. Typically, it depends on the operations that you perform on the application.

For example, you may want to consume these results on a particular thread using a foreach loop. This case requires you to merge these results before you exercise the loop. But, if displaying the output is the only concern, then ForAll can be a better choice.

Merge Options

Now the question is **if needed, how do you merge the data?** The answer to this question can lead us to various approaches such as the following:

- Buffer all the data before you merge. Then pass the whole set of data to the consuming thread.

- Buffer the data chunk by chunk and yield those chunks periodically to the consuming thread.

- Yield the elements as soon as they are available. Notice that in this approach you do not need to maintain any buffer before you send the data to the consuming thread. This is analogous to "streaming" the data.

To exercise these options, you can use the `WithMergeOptions` method. This is an extension method that accepts `ParallelMergeOptions` as a parameter. On further investigation, you can see that `ParallelMergeOption` is an enumeration type and has four members: `Default`, `NotBuffered`, `AutoBuffered`, and `FullyBuffered`. If you expand the `Default` member, you can see that the default merge type is auto-buffered. Figure 5-1 shows a sample screenshot for reference.

```
namespace System.Linq
{
    public enum ParallelMergeOptions
    {
        //
        // Summary:
        //     Use the default merge type, which is AutoBuffered.
        Default = 0,
        NotBuffered = 1,
        AutoBuffered = 2,
        FullyBuffered = 3
    }
}
```

Figure 5-1. *The members of ParallelMergeOptions*

Demonstration 5

Let's see a demonstration. The goal of the demonstration is to exercise different merge options and investigate the results.

Using a PLINQ query, the following program produces some data. While producing the data, it uses the `FullyBuffered` option. Here you will see the following query:

```
var incrementedvalues =
    numbers
    .AsParallel()
```

```
.WithMergeOptions(ParallelMergeOptions.FullyBuffered)
.Select(x =>
{
    var temp = Math.Pow(x,2);
    Write($"[{temp}]");
    return temp;
});
```

You can see that I have used a square bracket ([ ]) to mark the data being produced by the program.

Later, you'll see a foreach loop to consume this data. It is as follows:

```
foreach (var number in incrementedvalues)
{
    Write($"{number} \t");
}
```

You understand that this is a simple demonstration that follows a parallel producer-consumer pattern. Let's see the complete program:

```
using static System.Console;

List<int> numbers = Enumerable.Range(1, 25).ToList();

WriteLine("Making square.");
var incrementedvalues =
    numbers
    .AsParallel()
    .WithMergeOptions(ParallelMergeOptions.FullyBuffered)
    .Select(x =>
    {
        var temp = Math.Pow(x,2);
        Write($"[{temp}]");
```

```
        return temp;
    });

foreach (var number in incrementedvalues)
{
    Write($"{number} \t");
}
```

Output

Here is some sample output:

```
Making square.
[196][1][400][64][81][100][121][144][225][441][4][256][289]
[324][361][169][484][9][529][16][25][576][625][36][49]1      4
9       16      25      36      49      64      81
100     121     144     169     196     225     256     289
324     361     400     441     484     529     576     625
```

The output shows that after producing all the data, the program started consuming that data. Now change the option to NotBuffered. So, here is the updated query:

```
var incrementedvalues =
    numbers
    .AsParallel()
    .WithMergeOptions(ParallelMergeOptions.NotBuffered)
    .Select(x =>
    {
        var temp = Math.Pow(x,2);
        Write($"[{temp}]");
        return temp;
    });
```

Here is some sample output for this change:

```
Making square.
[400][1][196][64][441][484][225][81][4][529][576][100][9]
[16]1   [121][256][289][324][361][144][625][25]64        [169]
[36]196    400     [49]4    81      225      441     9
100     256     484     16      121     289     529     25
144     324     576     36      169     361     625     49
```

The output shows that the program started consuming the data (for example, see 1 came before [121], 64 came before [169], and so on) before all the data was produced.

Suggestions

Before I finish this section, I'd like you to notice the operators that you use in a query. These are good indicators of what kind of buffer is required. For example, Reverse or OrderBy cannot yield any element until the complete data is generated. On the contrary, ForAll can yield the elements immediately. It does not require any buffer.

Q&A Session

Q5.8 I understand that in some special queries, I may need to generate the complete data before yielding them. In those cases, I need to use the FullyBuffered option. But what happens if I choose a different option? For example, I'd like to know instead of choosing the FullyBuffered option what happens if I choose a different option such as NotBuffered. Will it cause a compile-time error?

No. In those cases, the request will be ignored. Here is an example. Replace the PLINQ query in the previous program with the following one (see the change in bold):

```
var orderedList =
    numbers
    .AsParallel()
    .WithMergeOptions(ParallelMergeOptions.NotBuffered)
    .Select(x =>
    {
        var temp = Math.Pow(x, 2);
        Write($"[{temp}]");
        return temp;
    })
    .OrderDescending();
```

Here is some sample output after this change:

```
[1][196][225][256][289][400][441][484][529][576][625]
[324][361][4][9][16][25][64][36][49][81][100][121][144]
[169]625    576        529      484      441      400      361
324      289      256      225      196      169      144      121
100     81       64       49       36       25       16       9
4       1
```

You can see that the data consumption started only after all the data was produced.

Note that since PLINQ is intelligent enough, you do not need to specify the merge options in most of these cases. But through testing and experience, you may decide that in certain cases, opting for a nondefault option is beneficial. For example, to make the user interface more responsive, you may opt for those nondefault options.

Managing Special Scenarios

In Chapter 2, you learned about handling exceptions and managing cancellations in task programming. Those concepts are applicable when you use PLINQ as well. Let's look at some case studies.

Handling Exceptions

Read the following points to understand the upcoming program:

- At first, the program generates some numbers.

- Once that is done, it uses a PLINQ query that performs multiple things.

- First, it filters the numbers that are divisible by 10.

- Then, it calculates a square of those numbers. For example, once it finds the number 10, it will make it 10*10=100.

- The final part of the query displays the calculated value in the console.

- To display the calculated values, I use the `ForAll` method because I do not need to order the output.

- I create an exceptional situation whenever the transformed number is greater than 6400. In this case, the program throws a custom exception. I named this exception `ExceedsCustomLimitException` for easy readability.

Now understand that since the PLINQ query raises an exception, I need to handle the situation. The following program handles the situation using the concept you learned about in Chapter 2. This is the reason you will see a `catch` block to handle `AggregateException` in this program too.

Demonstration 6

Here is the complete program:

```
using static System.Console;
using CustomExceptions;

var numbers = Enumerable.Range(0, 100);
try
{

    numbers
    .AsParallel()
    .Where(x => x % 10 == 0)
    .Select(
      x =>
       {
          int temp = x * x;
          if (temp > 6400)
             throw new ExceedsCustomLimitException($"The
               calculated value {temp} exceeds 6400");
          WriteLine($"{x} is processed by task:[{Task.CurrentId}]");
         return temp;
       }
    )
    .ForAll(num => WriteLine($"The calculated number is: {num}"));
}

catch (AggregateException ae)
{
    // Approach-1
    foreach (Exception e in ae.InnerExceptions)
```

```
    {
        WriteLine($"Error Type: {e.GetType().Name}, Message:
        {e.Message}");
    }

    //// Approach-2
    // ae.Handle(e =>
    // {
    //     WriteLine($"Error Type:{e.GetType().Name},
    //     Message:{e.Message}");
    //     return true;
    // });
}

namespace CustomExceptions
{
    public class ExceedsCustomLimitException : Exception
    {
        public ExceedsCustomLimitException()
        {
            // Some other code, if any
        }

        public ExceedsCustomLimitException(string message)
            : base(message)
        {
            // Some other code, if any
        }

        public ExceedsCustomLimitException(string message,
         Exception inner): base(message, inner)
        {
```

```
        // Some other code, if any
    }
  }
}
```

Output

Here is some sample output:

```
30 is processed by task:[3]
80 is processed by task:[5]
The calculated number is: 6400
50 is processed by task:[4]
The calculated number is: 2500
60 is processed by task:[4]
The calculated number is: 3600
0 is processed by task:[2]
The calculated number is: 900
70 is processed by task:[4]
40 is processed by task:[3]
The calculated number is: 1600
The calculated number is: 4900
The calculated number is: 0
10 is processed by task:[2]
The calculated number is: 100
20 is processed by task:[2]
The calculated number is: 400
Error Type: ExceedsCustomLimitException, Message: The
 calculated value 8100 exceeds 6400
```

Handling Cancellations

You can manage cancellation operations as well. The approach is almost the same as you saw in Chapter 2. To show you a sample case study on cancellations while a PLINQ query is executing, I will modify the previous program (Demonstration 6) now.

Since this program intends to handle both exceptions and cancellations, I updated the logic a little bit as well. Let's review the important changes.

In Demonstration 6, whenever the calculated number was greater than 6400, I threw a custom exception. This time I do not check only the calculated number. Instead, I generate (and check) a random number as well. If this random number is an even number and the calculated value is greater than 6400, I throw the custom exception. However, if the random number is an odd number and the calculated value is greater than 6400, I trigger a cancellation. This is why you'll see the following code in the upcoming program:

```
if (temp > 6400)
{
 if (random % 2 == 0)
 {
  throw new ExceedsCustomLimitException($"The calculated value
   {temp} exceeds 6400");
 }
 else
 {
  cancellationTokenSource.Cancel();
 }
}
```

To handle a cancellation scenario, the program creates a CancellationToken instance. So, you see the following lines:

```
CancellationTokenSource cancellationTokenSource = new();
CancellationToken token = cancellationTokenSource.Token;
```

But the most important part is to understand how you associate the CancellationToken instance to the query. You will see the use of the extension method WithCancellation as follows:

```
numbers
 .AsParallel()
 .Where(x => x % 10 == 0)
 .WithCancellation(token)
 .Select(
   x =>
   {
   // Some code here
   }
 );
```

This time you may need a catch block to handle the OperationCanceledException. So, you'll also see the following block:

```
catch (OperationCanceledException oce)
{
    WriteLine($"Error:{oce.Message}");
}
```

You should not have a problem understanding the remaining part of the program. Let's look at it now.

Demonstration 7

Here is the complete program. Notice the important changes in bold.

```
using static System.Console;
using CustomExceptions;

var numbers = Enumerable.Range(0, 100);
CancellationTokenSource cancellationTokenSource = new();
CancellationToken token = cancellationTokenSource.Token;
try
{
    numbers
     .AsParallel()
     .Where(x => x % 10 == 0)
     .WithCancellation(token)
     .Select(
        x =>
          {
                int temp = x * x;
                int random = new Random().Next(0, 2);
                if (temp > 6400)
                {
                    if (random % 2 == 0)
                    {
                        throw new ExceedsCustomLimit
                          Exception($"The calculated value {temp}
                          exceeds 6400");
                    }
                    else
                    {
                        cancellationTokenSource.Cancel();
                    }
                }
```

```
                WriteLine($"{x} is processed by task:[{Task.
                  CurrentId}]");
                return temp;
            }
      )
    .ForAll(num => WriteLine($"The calculated number is: {num}"));
}

catch (AggregateException ae)
{
    // Approach-1
    foreach (Exception e in ae.InnerExceptions)
    {
        WriteLine($"Error Type: {e.GetType().Name}, Message:
         {e.Message}");
    }

    //// Approach-2
    // ae.Handle(e =>
    // {
    //      WriteLine($"Error Type:{e.GetType().Name},
            Message:{e.Message}");
    //      return true;
    // });
}
catch (OperationCanceledException oce)
{
    WriteLine($"Error: {oce.Message}");
}

// The CustomExceptions namespace is the same. It is not shown
// again to avoid repetition.
```

Note   You can download the project Demo7_ManagingCancellations from the Apress website to see the complete implementation. It is in the Chapter 5 folder.

Output

Here is some sample output I got when a cancellation was triggered:

```
30 is processed by task:[3]
80 is processed by task:[5]
The calculated number is: 6400
50 is processed by task:[4]
The calculated number is: 2500
The calculated number is: 900
60 is processed by task:[4]
0 is processed by task:[2]
The calculated number is: 0
The calculated number is: 3600
70 is processed by task:[4]
The calculated number is: 4900
10 is processed by task:[2]
The calculated number is: 100
90 is processed by task:[5]
40 is processed by task:[3]
The calculated number is: 1600
The calculated number is: 8100
20 is processed by task:[2]
The calculated number is: 400
Error: The query has been canceled via the token supplied to
  WithCancellation.
```

Author's Note: Whenever the program raises the other exception (`ExceedsCustomLimitException`), you should expect to see similar output as shown in Demonstration 6. So, I did not present the output again.

Q&A Session

Q5.9 If I handle a cancellation in the user code, do I need to use `WithCancellation` in the query definition?

No. However, Microsoft does not want you to avoid using this. The documentation states the following (see `https://learn.microsoft.com/en-us/dotnet/standard/parallel-programming/how-to-cancel-a-plinq-query`):

> *When you handle the cancellation in user code, you do not have to use WithCancellation in the query definition. However, we recommend that you do use WithCancellation, because WithCancellation has no effect on query performance and it enables the cancellation to be handled by query operators and your user code.*

MICROSOFT'S RECOMMENDATION

I recommend that you visit `https://learn.microsoft.com/en-us/dotnet/standard/parallel-programming/how-to-cancel-a-plinq-query`. There you can find some additional information as well as some useful guidelines on this topic.

Exercising Aggregation

Aggregation operations are common in programming. Using an aggregation function, you can compute a single value from a collection of values. LINQ queries are very efficient in such cases. Let me show you a few code segments that will support my claim.

Example 1:

Given the numbers 1 to 10, the following code creates the squares of each number and calculates the sum of those squares:

```
using static System.Console;
int sum = Enumerable
    .Range(1, 10)
    .Sum(x => x * x);
WriteLine($"The sum of squares:{sum}");
```

Example 2:

Given these numbers, you can also find the maximum number using the following code:

```
int max = Enumerable
    .Range(1, 10)
    .Max();
WriteLine($"Maximum:{max}");
```

In this example, if you replace the Max function with Average, you can calculate the average of these numbers as well.

You may note that the methods Sum, Max, and Average are nothing but ready-made extension methods to help you perform aggregation operations.

Sequential Custom Aggregation

Instead of using specialized aggregation methods, you can use a general method called Aggregate. This method allows you to perform custom aggregation. Here is a sample that can also display the sum of the squares for the numbers 1 to 10 (I have chosen the initial accumulator value, or the seed value 0):

```
int total = Enumerable
    .Range(1, 10)
    .Select(x => x * x)
    .Aggregate(0, (subTotal, nxtNumber) => subTotal + nxtNumber);
WriteLine($"The sum of squares: {total}");
```

If you want to see the intermediate values, I can further modify the query as follows:

```
int total = Enumerable
    .Range(1, 10)
    .Select(x => x * x)
    .Aggregate(0,(subTotal,nxtNumber) =>
    {
        int temp = subTotal+ nxtNumber;
        WriteLine($"{subTotal}+{nxtNumber}={temp}");
        return temp;
    });
WriteLine($"The sum of squares: {total}");
```

This time you can see the following output, which is very clear:

```
0+1=1
1+4=5
5+9=14
14+16=30
30+25=55
55+36=91
91+49=140
140+64=204
204+81=285
285+100=385
The sum of squares: 385
```

Till now, you have seen some aggregation operations that perform sequential executions. **Now the question is: how can we perform custom aggregation in a parallel environment?** The following section answers this question.

Parallel Custom Aggregation

Inside the `ParallelEnumerable` class, you'll see several overloads of the `Aggregate` method; see Figure 5-2.

```
1   *Assembly System.Linq.Parallel, Version=8.8.0.8, Culture=neutral, PublicKeyToken=b03f5f7f11d50a3a
4
5     #nullable enable
6
7   *using
11
12  namespace System.Linq
13  {
14      public static class ParallelEnumerable
19      {
20          public static TSource Aggregate<TSource>(this ParallelQuery<TSource> source, Func<TSource, TSource, TSource> func);
52          public static TAccumulate Aggregate<TSource, TAccumulate>(this ParallelQuery<TSource> source, TAccumulate seed, Func<TAccumulate, TS
91          public static TResult Aggregate<TSource, TAccumulate, TResult>(this ParallelQuery<TSource> source, Func<TAccumulate> seedFactory, Fu
141         public static TResult Aggregate<TSource, TAccumulate, TResult>(this ParallelQuery<TSource> source, TAccumulate seed, Func<TAccumulat
191         public static TResult Aggregate<TSource, TAccumulate, TResult>(this ParallelQuery<TSource> source, TAccumulate seed, Func<TAccumulat
```

Figure 5-2. *Overloads of aggregation methods*

The interesting point is that if you look into these methods, you'll find overloads that are not available in the sequential implementation. Let me pick a complex version that is particularly designed to work in a parallel environment. Here it is:

```
public static TResult Aggregate<TSource, TAccumulate, TResult>(
  this ParallelQuery<TSource> source,
  TAccumulate seed,
  Func<TAccumulate, TSource, TAccumulate> updateAccumulatorFunc,
    Func<TAccumulate, TAccumulate, TAccumulate> combineAccumulatorsFunc,
    Func<TAccumulate, TResult> resultSelector)
{
// Implementation is not shown here
```

Before I show you an application of this method, I suggest you read the method definition, which can be easily seen in Visual Studio. This description will help you understand the method. In brief, it works like this:

- You choose a seed value.

- You partition the data (source) into several subpartitions and apply an accumulator function on each element of these partitions.

- Each subpartition will yield elements. Another accumulator function will work on these yielded elements.

- The final accumulator value will be transformed into a result value.

In the upcoming program, I keep the supporting comments to help you match these steps.

Demonstration 8

It is a time for another demonstration where you exercise custom aggregation in a parallel environment. The last time you calculated $1^2+2^2+ ...+10.^2$ This time you compute the same in a parallel environment. Here is the complete program:

```
using static System.Console;
int parallelSum = ParallelEnumerable
    .Range(1, 10)
    .Select(x => x * x)
    .Aggregate(
        // initialize subtotal/ seed value.
        0,
        // Executes this on each thread
```

```
        (subTotal, nxtNumber) =>
        {
            int temp = subTotal + nxtNumber;
            WriteLine($"subTotal={subTotal}, next number=
             {nxtNumber}, temp={temp} id:[{Task.CurrentId}]");
            return temp;
        },
        // Aggregating the subtotals from all threads
        (total, subTotal) =>
        {
            int temp2 = total + subTotal;
            WriteLine($"total={total},subTotal={subTotal},temp2
             ={temp2}");
            return temp2;
        },
        // Processing the final result(if required) before
        // you return
        total => total
    );
WriteLine($"The sum of squares: {parallelSum}");
```

Output

As always, the output will vary on your computer. Here is some sample output that was produced on my computer:

```
subTotal=0, next number=16,temp=16 id:[3]
subTotal=0, next number=81,temp=81 id:[5]
subTotal=0, next number=49,temp=49 id:[4]
subTotal=0, next number=1,temp=1 id:[2]
subTotal=16, next number=25,temp=41 id:[3]
```

```
subTotal=81, next number=100,temp=181 id:[5]
subTotal=49, next number=64,temp=113 id:[4]
subTotal=1, next number=4,temp=5 id:[2]
subTotal=41, next number=36,temp=77 id:[3]
subTotal=5, next number=9,temp=14 id:[2]
total=14,subTotal=77,temp2=91
total=91,subTotal=113,temp2=204
total=204,subTotal=181,temp2=385
The sum of squares: 385
```

Analysis

Notice that four tasks (IDs 2, 3, 4, and 5) performed the computation as follows:

- Task ID 2 computes its final subtotal as 14 (see the last appearance of id:[2]).

- Task ID 3 computes its final subtotal as 77.

- Task ID 4 computes its final subtotal as 113.

- Task ID 5 computes its final subtotal as 181.

Later these subtotals are added to compute the final total.

Q&A Session

Q5.10 In the previous demonstration, you did not use the AsParallel method inside the query. Was that intentional?

You already learned that the ParallelEnumerable class is the parallel equivalent of Enumerable. In addition, notice that Enumerable. Range(1, 10) returns IEnumerable<int>, but Enumerable.Range(1, 10). AsParallel() returns ParallelQuery<int>. Using ParallelEnumerable. Range(1,10), you already got a ParallelQuery<int> as well. Since I used ParallelEnumerable.Range already, it was not needed for me to write something like `ParallelEnumerable.Range (1,10).AsParallel()` inside the query. However, you may note that the program can still work despite this redundant call.

Exercises

E5.1 Pick the correct statements from the following set of statements:

a) A parallel query is always faster than a sequential query.

b) PLINQ follows declarative programming.

c) `WithDegreeOfParallelism` is an extension method that can be used to set the degree of parallelism in a parallel query.

d) The `ForAll` extension method does not require a merge step at the end.

e) If we use the `ForAll` method, the order of execution is deterministic.

f) If you specify a merge option such as `AutoBuffered` in a PLINQ query, the system may ignore the request, if necessary.

E5.2 Can you write a program that uses a PLINQ query to find prime numbers between 1 and 100?

E5.3 Can you predict the output of the following sequential query (notice that a few lines are commented here)?

```
using static System.Console;

int numberAbove20ComesFirst =
    Enumerable
    .Range(1, 50)
```

```
// .AsParallel()
// .WithExecutionMode(ParallelExecutionMode.ForceParallelism)
// .WithDegreeOfParallelism(4)
.Where(x => x % 2 == 0)
.Aggregate
 (
    20,
    (tempHighest, next) =>
    {
        if (tempHighest > 20)
        {
            return tempHighest;
        }
        else
        {
            int temp = tempHighest >= next ?
              tempHighest : next;
            WriteLine($"seed={tempHighest},
              next={next},temp={temp}");
            return temp;
        }
    }
 );

WriteLine($"The number above 20 that appears first is:
 {numberAbove20ComesFirst}");
```

E5.4 Uncomment the following portion in the previous program:

```
// .AsParallel()
// .WithExecutionMode(ParallelExecutionMode.ForceParallelism)
// .WithDegreeOfParallelism(4)
```

Can you predict the output now?

E5.5 Can you predict the output of the following program?

```
using static System.Console;

var numbers = Enumerable.Range(0, 100);
CancellationTokenSource cts = new();
CancellationToken token = cts.Token;

var cancellationTask = Task.Run(() =>
{
    // We'll trigger a cancellation request shortly
    Thread.Sleep(300);
    cts.Cancel();
});

var anotherTask = Task.Run(SomeMethod, token);
anotherTask.Wait();
WriteLine("End of the main thread.");

void SomeMethod()
{
    try
    {
        numbers
        .AsParallel()
        .Where(x => x % 10 == 0)
        .WithCancellation(token)
        .Select(
            x =>
            {
                token.ThrowIfCancellationRequested();
                Thread.Sleep(100);
                return x;
```

```
        }
      )
        .ForAll(num=>WriteLine($"The processed number is:
        {num}"));
  }
  catch (AggregateException ae)
  {
      foreach (Exception e in ae.InnerExceptions)
      {
          WriteLine($"Error Type:{e.GetType().Name},
          Message:{e.Message}");
      }
  }
  catch (OperationCanceledException oce)
  {
      WriteLine($"Error:{oce.Message}");
  }
}
```

E5.6 You have learned about parallel custom aggregation in this chapter. Can you calculate the factorial of 10 using the same concept?

Summary

This chapter started with some prerequisite discussions that can help you understand PLINQ better. Then it showed you how to convert a sequential query into a parallel query. After this, it discussed different aspects of PLINQ. In brief, it answered the following questions:

- Why is PLINQ declarative?

- Why are some PLINQ queries faster than sequential queries (and vice versa)?

- How can you force parallelism in a query?

- How can you exercise different merge options before outputting the result?

- How can you handle exceptions, and how can you handle exceptions while exercising a PLINQ query?

- How can use apply aggregation in a parallel environment?

Solutions to Exercises

Here are the solutions for the exercises in this chapter.

E5.1

The answers are shown in bold as follows:

a) A parallel query is always faster than a sequential query. (**False**)

b) PLINQ follows declarative programming. (**True**)

c) `WithDegreeOfParallelism` is an extension method that can be used to set the degree of parallelism in a parallel query. (**True**)

d) The `ForAll` extension method does not require a merge step at the end. (**True**)

e) If we use the `ForAll` method, the order of execution is deterministic. (**False**)

f) If you specify a merge option such as `AutoBuffered` in a PLINQ query, the system may ignore the request, if necessary. (**True**)

E5.2

Here is a sample program:

```
using static System.Console;

const int count = 100;
var numbers = Enumerable.Range(1, count);

var primes = numbers
    .AsParallel()
    .Where(x =>
    {
        if (x == 1) return false;
        if (x == 2) return true;
        var boundary = (int)Math.Floor(Math.Sqrt(x));
        for (int i = 2; i <= boundary; i++)
        {
            if (x % i == 0) return false;
        }
        return true;
    });
WriteLine("Prime numbers are:");
primes
    .ToList()
    .ForEach(primes => Write(primes + "\t"));
```

This program produces the following output:

```
Prime numbers are:
2    3    5    7    11   13    17   19  23    29    31    37    41
43    47    53    59    61    67    71    73    79    83    89    97
```

Code explanation: A number is prime if it is divisible by 1 and the number itself. For example, 41 is divisible by 1 and 41 only. This is why to check whether a number, say 41, is a prime number, you can loop through 1 to 41 and find that you have not received more than two factors. But instead of looping up to a given number (say n), mathematically, we can prove that testing up to the square root of n should be enough for us. This is why I started looping from 2 and testing up to the square root of the given count (i.e., 100).

E5.3

The output of this program is predictable. The final value will always be 22. The following output clearly shows that the control followed the sequential execution:

```
seed=20, next=2,temp=20
seed=20, next=4,temp=20
seed=20, next=6,temp=20
seed=20, next=8,temp=20
seed=20, next=10,temp=20
seed=20, next=12,temp=20
seed=20, next=14,temp=20
seed=20, next=16,temp=20
seed=20, next=18,temp=20
seed=20, next=20,temp=20
seed=20, next=22,temp=22
The number above 20 that appears first is: 22
```

E5.4

After this modification, the output of the program is unpredictable. Here is some sample output that appears on my computer:

```
seed=20, next=14,temp=20
seed=20, next=28,temp=28
```

The number that is greater than 20 that appears first is 28.

However, remember that since we are exercising a parallel query without preserving the order, the numbers can be processed in random order. For example, when I executed the same program online at SharpLab (https://sharplab.io), I saw the following output:

```
seed=20, next=2,temp=20
seed=20, next=4,temp=20
seed=20, next=6,temp=20
seed=20, next=8,temp=20
seed=20, next=10,temp=20
seed=20, next=12,temp=20
seed=20, next=40,temp=40
The number above 20 that appears first is: 40
```

E5.5

Once again, there is no doubt that the output can vary. But I want you to notice how a cancellation request is handled in this code. You may note that I imposed some forced delay so that the cancellation fires while the query is executing. Here is some sample output on my computer:

```
The processed number is: 0
The processed number is: 80
The processed number is: 30
The processed number is: 90
```

The processed number is: 40
The processed number is: 10
The processed number is: 20
Error: The query has been canceled via the token supplied to
 WithCancellation.
End of the main thread.

POINTS TO NOTE

Note the following points:

1. To see similar output, you may need to adjust the sleep time
   to ensure the cancellation triggers while the query starts
   executing.

2. Notice that the main thread did not call SomeMethod. It was
   invoked by a separate task (another task). This is why the main
   thread did not suffer from any unhandled exception. You can
   also see that the OperationCanceledException is already
   handled inside SomeMethod. This is why you could catch this
   exception instantly.

Additional Note: The absence of this catch block (that handles
OperationCanceledException) inside the SomeMethod could cause the
following: Unhandled exception. System.AggregateException: One
or more errors occurred. (A task was canceled.) It is because this
case requires you to guard the Wait() call inside the main thread. Here is
a sample:

```
// There is no change in the previous code
var anotherTask = Task.Run(SomeMethod, token);
//anotherTask.Wait();
try
{
```

```
    anotherTask.Wait();
}
catch (AggregateException ae)
{
 foreach (Exception e in ae.InnerExceptions)
 {
  WriteLine($"Error Type: {e.GetType().Name}, Message:
   {e.Message}");
 }
}
// There is no change in the remaining code
```

E5.6

Here is a sample program. I kept printing intermediate outputs and task IDs for your better understanding:

```
using static System.Console;
int n = 10;
int factorial = ParallelEnumerable
    .Range(1, n)
    .Aggregate(
        // initialize subtotal/ seed value.
        1,
        // Executes this on each thread
        (partialResult, nxtNumber) =>
        {
            int temp = partialResult * nxtNumber;
            WriteLine($"The partial value: {partialResult},
             next number: {nxtNumber},  temp: {temp} id:
             [{Task.CurrentId}]");
```

```
            return temp;
        },
        // Aggregating the subtotals from all threads
        (finalResult, individualResult) =>
        {
            int temp2 = finalResult * individualResult;
            WriteLine($"The final result: {finalResult},
              individual result: {individualResult}, temp2:
              {temp2}");
            return temp2;
        },
        // Processing the final result
        total => total
    );
WriteLine($"The factorial of {n} is {factorial}");
```

Here is some sample output:

```
The partial value: 1, next number: 4, temp: 4 id: [3]
The partial value: 1, next number: 9, temp: 9 id: [5]
The partial value: 1, next number: 1, temp: 1 id: [2]
The partial value: 1, next number: 7, temp: 7 id: [4]
The partial value: 7, next number: 8, temp: 56 id: [4]
The partial value: 9, next number: 10, temp: 90 id: [5]
The partial value: 1, next number: 2, temp: 2 id: [2]
The partial value: 2, next number: 3, temp: 6 id: [2]
The partial value: 4, next number: 5, temp: 20 id: [3]
The partial value: 20, next number: 6, temp: 120 id: [3]
The final result: 6, individual result: 120, temp2: 720
The final result: 720, individual result: 56, temp2: 40320
The final result: 40320, individual result: 90, temp2: 3628800
The factorial of 10 is 3628800
```

CHAPTER 6

Simplifying Asynchronous Programming

Just like while preparing your breakfast you perform many activities in parallel, in the coding world while developing an application, you will want to develop applications that execute things in parallel. This is why nowadays you can listen to your favorite song while downloading another song on your mobile phone. No one wants to be blocked from doing a task while waiting until another task is complete. We all want to do multiple activities simultaneously rather than executing them one after the other. Fast-paced modern applications use asynchronous code to match real-world situations like this.

So, what is asynchronous programming? In programming terminology, we can say the following: **if a calling thread invokes a long-running task, it does not wait for its completion. Instead, it comes back to the caller to invoke another task (or continue the remaining work). Meanwhile, the invoked task will keep running. If needed, the initial caller can again go back to the previous task to continue. The process can continue until the tasks are finished.**

© Vaskaran Sarcar 2024
V. Sarcar, *Parallel Programming with C# and .NET*,
https://doi.org/10.1007/979-8-8688-0488-5_6

In the past, asynchronous programming was considered a challenging activity, but now things are easy! C# 5.0 introduced two useful keywords to do this: `async` and `await`. This chapter discusses the programs that benefit from using them.

Introduction to async and await

Asynchronous programming was possible in earlier versions of C#; however, you needed to perform a lot of work to make it happen. Though the Task Parallel Library (TPL) simplified things for us, there were always possibilities for improvement. The `async` and `await` keywords were introduced to fill those gaps.

To illustrate, let's consider a synchronous method that returns a number, say 100:

```
// Synchronous version
static int GetHundred()
{
    WriteLine("The method is arranging the number.");
    Task.Delay(1500);
    WriteLine("The method resumes.");
    return 100;
}
```

It is simple and easy to understand. Now let me show an asynchronous version of it using `async` and `await`. It is as follows (notice the changes in bold):

```
// Asynchronous version
static async Task<int> GetHundredAsync()
{
    WriteLine("The method is arranging the number.");
    await Task.Delay(1500);
```

```
    WriteLine("The method resumes.");
    return 100;
}
```

You can see the following changes:

- The word Async is added to the method name.

- The return type is now Task<int>.

- The method signature now includes the async keyword.

- There is an await keyword inside this method.

You may wonder about these changes. Let's discuss them one by one. I'll discuss the await keyword shortly. First, let's examine the async keyword.

Author's Note: I often see the terms await keyword, await expression, await operator, and await statement used interchangeably across different articles/blogs and resources. For example, if you like to see the details of the await keyword at https://learn.microsoft.com/en-us/dotnet/csharp/language-reference/keywords/, you will be redirected to https://learn.microsoft.com/en-us/dotnet/csharp/language-reference/operators/await, which uses the term await operator.

Understanding async

You can use the async modifier to make an asynchronous method. Before we dive into the details, let's start with the naming convention.

Naming Convention

The documentation states the following (see `https://learn.microsoft.com/en-us/dotnet/csharp/asynchronous-programming/task-asynchronous-programming-model`):

> *The name of an async method, by convention, ends with an "Async" suffix.*

You understand that I have followed this naming convention for the async method.

Return Types and Parameters

You may be wondering about the return type! You may think that since the return type of the asynchronous method (GetHundred**Async**) is Task<int>, you must create a task and return it from the method body. But instead of returning a Task<int>, it returned 100, which is an ordinary int. How was this possible? It was possible because I used the async keyword in the method signature.

Typically, when you mark a method with the async keyword, the method can have any of the following return types:

- Task<Result>
- Task
- void

Normally, inside an async method, you'll see the await operator as well.

```
┌──────────────────────────────────────────────────────────┐
│                     POINT TO NOTE                         │
└──────────────────────────────────────────────────────────┘
```

Before you read further, I want you to remember the following points:

- If you use the void return type, the method cannot be awaited. As a result, the caller of this void returning method will not be able to catch any exception that the invoked method can throw.

- In addition, any type that has an accessible GetAwaiter method can be used as a return type as well. ValueType<TResult> is such an example. I'll talk about it later.

- The documentation at https://learn.microsoft.com/ en-us/dotnet/csharp/asynchronous-programming/ async-return-types talks about a few more return types. For example, the IAsyncEnumerable<T> type is used for an async method that returns an async stream. This online link also talks about other types such as IAsyncAction and IAsyncAction<TResult> that are specific to Windows workloads. For now, let's make things as simple as possible and keep learning about the essentials.

I want you to remember one final point before you leave this section. If your async method's return type is either void or Task, the return statement is just return and is optional. For example, the following method can compile successfully without the return statement.

```
static async Task SomeTaskAsync()
{
    WriteLine("SomeTaskAsync is called.");
    await Task.Delay(1000);
    WriteLine("SomeTaskAsync is completed now.");
```

```
// The following return statement is optional
// return;
}
```

Async Restrictions

While using the async methods, you need to remember a few more restrictions that are as follows:

- An async method cannot declare in, ref, or out parameters. However, that method can call methods that have such parameters.

- Though an async method can call methods with ref return values, it can't return a value by reference.

Q&A Session

Q6.1 Why does an async method support a limited number of types?

Typically, you use an async method that awaits a long-running operation. It allows a caller to invoke the method and get the control back quickly. However, normally, when the control returns, the async methods are not finished and you do not know about the final result. You understand that, in this case, the incomplete method needs to resume to produce the final value. So, it makes sense that an async method considers Task or Task<TResult> as a return type. In addition, if you do not care about the return value, it makes sense to have a void return type as well.

Understanding await

Let's discuss the await keyword now. Using it you can start a task in a nonblocking way and **then continue the execution when that task is completed**. Microsoft states the following (see https://learn.microsoft.com/en-us/dotnet/csharp/language-reference/operators/await):

> *The await operator suspends evaluation of the enclosing async method until the asynchronous operation represented by its operand completes. When the asynchronous operation completes, the await operator returns the result of the operation, if any.*

Earlier, you saw the asynchronous method called GetHundredAsync. Now the question is how do you consume this method? The answer is as follows: int result = await GetHundredAsync();.

Notice that the GetHundredAsync method returns a Task<int>, but the result is an int. How does the compiler allow this? The await keyword has done this magic by unwrapping from Task<int> to int.

The next question is if GetHundredAsync is a time-consuming method, how can you write better code? See the following sample, which comes from the upcoming demonstration:

```
Task<int> getValue = GetHundredAsync();
WriteLine("The main thread continues.");
// Consuming the return value which is an int
int result = await getValue;
WriteLine($"The invoked task returns: {result}");
```

Let's understand the flow now. First, the calling thread invokes GetHundredAsync. So, the control goes there and starts executing. After going there, when it sees the line await Task.Delay(1500);, the enclosing async method (i.e., GetHundredAsync) is suspended (control resumes here when the delay is over). Meanwhile, the control comes back to the calling thread. So, the calling thread becomes free.

As a result, the calling thread starts executing again until it needs the return value of GetHundredAsync. This is why it can now process the line WriteLine("The main thread continues.");.

Next, the calling thread sees the following line:

```
int result = await getValue;
```

Since this line contains the await operator, this time the calling thread needs to wait for the completion of the getValue task. Once the task is completed, the calling thread can resume. This means you do not need to call the Start method on the task explicitly (yes, it is still hot!).

POINT TO REMEMBER

If you mark a method as async, you can apply the await keyword. Then the compiler will do all the heavy work for you to ensure that the method gets split into smaller pieces. In other words, the await keyword helps you mark a point in the method where that method can be suspended or split up.

Demonstration 1

It's time for a demonstration to cross-verify our understanding. Here is the complete program:

```
using static System.Console;

WriteLine("The main thread starts.");
```

```
Task<int> getValue = GetHundredAsync();
WriteLine("The main thread continues.");
// Consuming the return value which is an int
int result = await getValue;
WriteLine($"The invoked task returns: {result}");
WriteLine("The main thread ends.");

// Asynchronous version
static async Task<int> GetHundredAsync()
{
    WriteLine("The method is arranging the number.");
    await Task.Delay(1500);
    WriteLine("The method resumes.");
    return 100;
}
```

Output

Here is some sample output:

```
The main thread starts.
The method is arranging the number.
The main thread continues.
The method resumes.
The invoked task returns: 100
The main thread ends.
```

Analysis

Let me remind you that in the case of asynchronous programming, we do not want the calling thread to be blocked. If the calling thread is not blocked, how can the invoked method (which is called by the calling thread) continue? You understand that we need another thread for the invoked method to continue.

To investigate this, let's put some breakpoints in this program and analyze them. First, while debugging, launch the thread window by selecting the **Debug** menu, selecting **Windows**, and then selecting **Threads**, as shown in Figure 6-1.

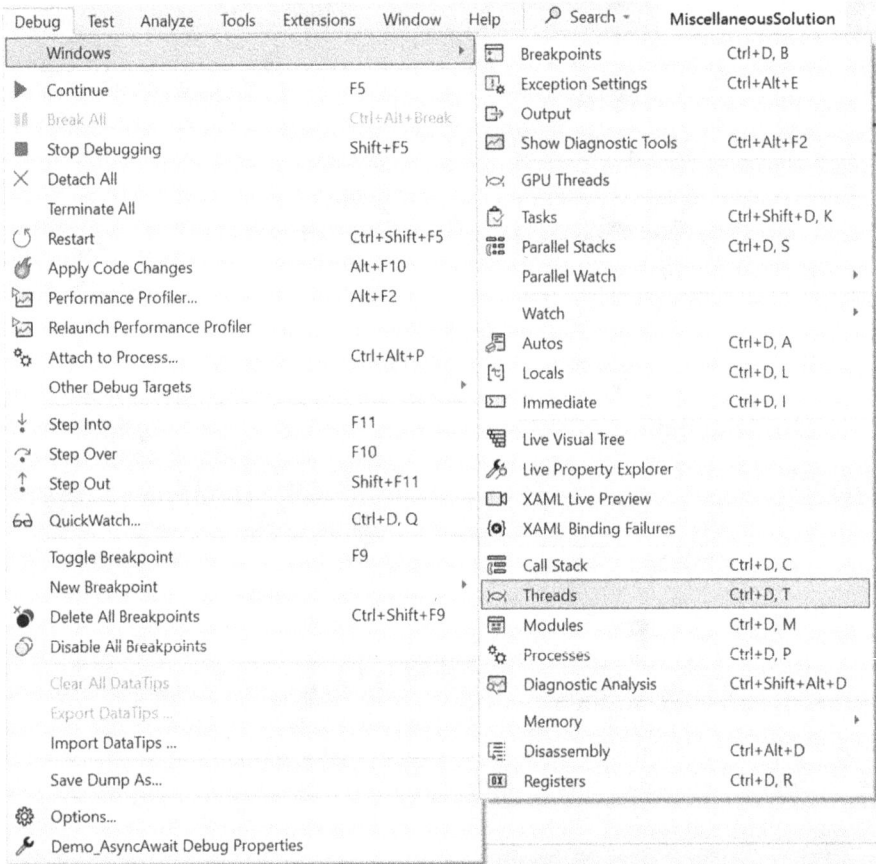

Figure 6-1. *Launching the Threads window while debugging*

Notice that while the control (aka instruction pointer) hits the line `WriteLine("The invoked task returns:{result}")`; the following snapshot shows that both the main thread and the worker thread are running (see Figure 6-2).

```
19        Task<int> getValue = GetHundredAsync();
20        WriteLine("The main thread continues.");
21        // Consuming the return value which is an int
22        int result = await getValue;
23        WriteLine($"The invoked task returns: {result}");
24        #endregion
25
26        WriteLine("The main thread ends.");
27
28        // Asynchronous version
```

99 %   ·   No issues found

Threads

Search   Group by: Process ID   · Columns ·

ID▲	Managed ID	Category	Name	Location
Process ID: 5740 (8 threads)				
228	8	Worker Thread	.NET TP Worker	System.Private.CoreLib.dll!Interop.Kernel32.GetQueuedCo...
5580	4	Worker Thread	.NET TP Worker	Demo1_AsyncAwaitBasics.dll!Program.<Main>$
8196	6	Worker Thread	.NET TP Worker	System.Private.CoreLib.dll!Interop.Kernel32.GetQueuedCo...
8480	10	Worker Thread	.NET Timer	System.Private.CoreLib.dll!System.Threading.WaitHandle.V...
13768	9	Worker Thread	.NET TP Worker	System.Private.CoreLib.dll!Interop.Kernel32.GetQueuedCo...
15372	7	Worker Thread	.NET ThreadPool IO	System.Private.CoreLib.dll!System.Threading.PortableThrea...
15428	5	Worker Thread	.NET TP Gate	System.Private.CoreLib.dll!System.Threading.WaitHandle.V...
15856	1	Main Thread	Main Thread	System.Private.CoreLib.dll!System.Threading.Monitor.Wait...

Figure 6-2. *The main thread is running along with the worker thread*

Figure 6-2 shows that multiple threads start running while the program executes.

Q&A Session

Q6.2 What do you mean by a "hot" task?

A task is *hot* if you do not need to call the Start method on the Task object. In technical terms, these are initiated and their task status is an enumeration value other than TaskStatus.Created. So, these are active tasks.

When you create Task instances using the public Task constructors, those are cold tasks because they are scheduled only when you call the Start method on those instances.

Q6.3 I can see that multiple threads are involved in the previous program. Does this mean that asynchronous programming inherently uses multithreading?

Yes.

Q6.4 When should I prefer the void return type over the Task return type (and vice versa)?

Note that a returned task represents ongoing work. A task encapsulates the required information about the state of the process. It is often useful to know the final outcome because any process can raise an exception. To illustrate, consider the following program:

```
using static System.Console;

WriteLine("The main thread starts executing.");
Task getTask=SomeTaskAsync();
WriteLine("The main thread resumes.");
await getTask;

static async Task SomeTaskAsync()
{
    WriteLine("SomeTaskAsync is called.");
    await Task.Delay(1000);
    WriteLine("SomeTaskAsync is completed now.");
    // The following return statement is optional
    // return;
}
```

Here is some sample output from this program:

```
The main thread starts executing.
SomeTaskAsync is called.
The main thread resumes.
SomeTaskAsync is completed now.
```

You can see that the program lets you know when the invoked task (SomeTaskAsync) was completed. This is because you awaited the returned task (see the line await getTask;) to know the final result.

Note   You can download the Discussing_AsyncReturnTypes project to exercise this program.

However, if you opt for the void return type (instead of Task), the caller may not know about the final result of the invoked task. So, the void return type is useful when you do not care about a result or you do not show any interest in knowing whether the method executes successfully. This is why its usage is rare. However, the void return type can be useful for the event handlers that can be used as a "fire-and-forget" operation such as initiating an async program.

POINT TO NOTE

Stephen Cleary's blog is a nice resource for learning (see https://blog.stephencleary.com/2013/01/async-oop-0-introduction.html). Though it was written a long time ago, I still believe that reading those materials can help you a lot. You may note that he likes to use the term "fire-and-forget" sensibly. In reply to a question on stack overflow (see https://stackoverflow.com/questions/17659603/async-void-asp-net-and-count-of-outstanding-operations/17660475#17660475), he said the following: "I personally never use this phrase for async void methods. For one thing, the error handling semantics most certainly do not fit in with the phrase 'fire and forget'; I half-jokingly refer to async void methods as 'fire and crash'. A true async 'fire and forget' method would be an async Task method where you ignore the returned Task rather than waiting for it."

Await Restrictions

While using the await keyword in your code, you need to remember the following restrictions:

Restriction 1: You cannot use await without async inside a method, lambda expression, or anonymous method. For example, if you write something like the following:

```
class Sample
{
    public void SomeMethod()
    {
        // Some code, if any
        await Task.Delay(1000); //Error CS4033
        // Some other code, if any
    }
}
```

you'll see the following error:

```
Error CS4033 The 'await' operator can only be used within an
async method. Consider marking this method with the 'async'
modifier and changing its return type to 'Task'.
```

Restriction 2: You cannot use await in an unsafe context. For example, if you write something like the following:

```
unsafe
{
    // Some code, if any
    await Task.Delay(1000); // Error CS4004

    // Some code
    // Task.Delay(1000); // OK
}
```

346

you'll see the following error:

```
Error CS4004 Cannot await in an unsafe context
```

Restriction 3: You cannot use await inside a lock. For example, if you write something like the following:

```
class Foo
{
    private readonly object _padLock = new();
    public async void SomeMethod()
    {
        lock (_padLock)
        {
            // Do the synchronous operations, if any
            // Trying to do an asynchronous operation now
            await Task.Delay(1000); // Error CS1996
        }
    }
}
```

you'll see the following error:

```
Error CS1996 Cannot await in the body of a lock statement
```

Finally, I want you to note the following code block:

```
try
{
    // do something
    throw new Exception("Forceful exception.");
}
catch (Exception e)
{
    await Task.Delay(1000);
```

```
    // Do something else
}
finally
{
    await Task.Delay(1000);
    // Do something else
}
```

From C# 6.0 onward this code will compile. However, C# 5.0 will complain about it.

Note   You can download the Await_Restrictions project to exercise these code segments.

Q&A Session

Q6.5 I understand that I cannot use the await operator inside a lock. However, I'll like to know whether there is any workaround.

The very first thing you should understand is how the asynchronous programming model works with the async and await keywords. You may try to design your application in a way that can avoid this need. Otherwise, you can try the following verbose code where I used the lock statement multiple times and processed the asynchronous code separately (I kept the comments for your reference):

```
public async void SomeMethod()
{
    lock (_padLock)
    {
        // Do the synchronous operations
        // and prepare for the asynchronous operation
```

```
    }

    // Doing the asynchronous operation now
    await Task.Delay(1000);
    // Lock again, if required
    lock (_padLock)
    {
        // Do the remaining synchronous operations
    }
}
```

State Machines Are Behind the Scenes

Consider the following program where you see the use of three await keywords. One of them is at the beginning of the file, and the other two are placed inside the ExecuteLongTaskAsync() method.

```
using System;
using System.Threading.Tasks;
using static System.Console;

WriteLine("Main thread starts.");

var getValue = ExecuteLongTaskAsync();
WriteLine("Main thread continues.");
int result = await getValue;
WriteLine($"The long task returns: {result}");
WriteLine("Main thread ends.");

static async Task<int> ExecuteLongTaskAsync()
{
    WriteLine("Long running method starts.");
    Random random = new();
```

```
await Task.Delay(500);
WriteLine("Long running method resumes.");
await Task.Delay(700);
WriteLine("Long running method resumes again.");
return random.Next(1, 100);
}
```

Let's investigate the IL code. To show you the IL code, I used **SharpLab** (https://sharplab.io/) here. First, I want you to notice the bold portions in the following segment (do not worry; I'll show you better readable code shortly):

```
// Previous lines not shown
.class nested private auto ansi sealed beforefieldinit
'<<Main>$>d__0'
        extends [System.Runtime]System.Object
        implements [System.Runtime]System.Runtime.CompilerServices.
        IAsyncStateMachine
    {
        .custom instance void [System.Runtime]System.Runtime.
        CompilerServices.CompilerGeneratedAttribute::.ctor() = (
            01 00 00 00
        )
        // Fields
        .field public int32 '<>1__state'
        .field public valuetype [System.Runtime]System.Runtime.
        CompilerServices.AsyncTaskMethodBuilder '<>t__builder'
        .field public string[] args
        .field private class [System.Runtime]System.Threading.
        Tasks.Task`1<int32> '<getValue>5__1'
        .field private int32 '<result>5__2'
```

```
.field private int32 '<>s__3'
.field private valuetype [System.Runtime]System.
Runtime.CompilerServices.TaskAwaiter`1<int32> '<>u__1'

// Methods
.method public hidebysig specialname rtspecialname
    instance void .ctor () cil managed
{
    // Method begins at RVA 0x20e9
    // Code size 8 (0x8)
    .maxstack 8

    IL_0000: ldarg.0
    IL_0001: call instance void [System.Runtime]
     System.Object::.ctor()
    IL_0006: nop
    IL_0007: ret
} // end of method '<<Main>$>d__0'::.ctor

// Remaining code skipped
```

In this code, you notice a sealed class, named <<Main>$>d__0 (but not the Main method). You can also see that this class extends Object and implements IAsyncStateMachine. What does this mean? It shows that behind the scenes, there is a state machine. **So, the first thing to understand is that the compiler has generated a temporary object for you**. On further investigation, you'll understand the following things:

- These fields exist for the variables inside the function.

- These states will be preserved on the state machine.

Let's learn about the IAsyncStateMachine interface. Visual Studio shows the following details:

```
namespace System.Runtime.CompilerServices
```

```
{
    //
    // Summary:
    // Represents state machines that are generated for
    // asynchronous methods. This type is intended for compiler
    // use only.
    public interface IAsyncStateMachine
    {
        //
        // Summary:
        // Moves the state machine to its next state.
            void MoveNext();
        //
        // Summary:
        // Configures the state machine with a heap-allocated
            replica.
        //
        // Parameters:
        // stateMachine:
        // The heap-allocated replica.
            void SetStateMachine(IAsyncStateMachine stateMachine);
    }
}
```

The associated comments are self-explanatory. For now, our focus will be on the MoveNext method in the decompiled code.

Let's investigate the other details now. Since the IL code is not readable enough, for our further investigation, let's choose C# (instead of IL) under Decompile in SharpLab as shown in Figure 6-3.

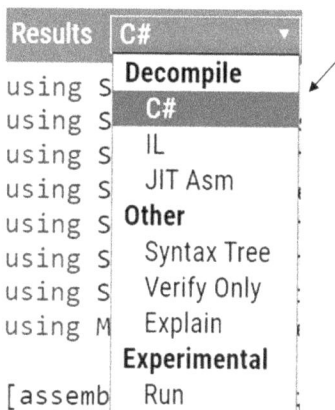

Figure 6-3. *Opting for the C# option instead of IL under the Decompile tab in SharpLab*

This time you can see a better readable code. Let's first investigate the entry points of the code where you saw one await expression. Figure 6-4 shows a partial snapshot of this. You can see that it contains a TaskAwaiter<int> instance called awaiter in the MoveNext method as shown in Figure 6-4.

```
[StructLayout(LayoutKind.Auto)]
[CompilerGenerated]
private struct <<Main>$>d__0 : IAsyncStateMachine
{
    public int <>1__state;

    public AsyncTaskMethodBuilder <>t__builder;

    private TaskAwaiter<int> <>u__1;

    private void MoveNext()
    {
        int num = <>1__state;
        try
        {
            TaskAwaiter<int> awaiter;
            if (num != 0)
            {
                Console.WriteLine("Main thread starts.");
                Task<int> task = <<Main>$>g__ExecuteLongTaskAsy
                Console.WriteLine("Main thread continues.");
                awaiter = task.GetAwaiter();
                if (!awaiter.IsCompleted)
                {
                    num = (<>1__state = 0);
                    <>u__1 = awaiter;
```

Figure 6-4. *One TaskAwaiter<int> instance is present inside the MoveNext method*

Now focus on the ExecuteLongTaskAsync() method and notice the arrow tips shown in Figure 6-5.

```
Results  C#              ▼                                                        D

[CompilerGenerated]
private sealed class <<<Main>$>g__ExecuteLongTaskAsync|0_0>d : IAsyncStateMachine
{
    public int <>1__state;

    public AsyncTaskMethodBuilder<int> <>t__builder;

    private Random <random>5__1;

    private TaskAwaiter <>u__1;

    private void MoveNext()
    {
        int num = <>1__state;
        int result;
        try
        {
            TaskAwaiter awaiter;
            TaskAwaiter awaiter2;
            if (num != 0)
            {
                if (num == 1)
                {
                    awaiter = <>u__1;
                    <>u__1 = default(TaskAwaiter);
                    num = (<>1__state = -1);
                    goto IL_00fb;
                }
                Console.WriteLine("Long running method starts.");
                <random>5__1 = new Random();
                awaiter2 = Task.Delay(500).GetAwaiter();
                if (!awaiter2.IsCompleted)
```

Figure 6-5. *Two TaskAwaiter<int> instances are present inside the MoveNext method*

You can see that this time there are two TaskAwaiter instances (awaiter and awaiter2) inside the MoveNext() method. These two instances reflect that there are two await keywords inside the ExecuteLongTaskAsync method.

POINT TO NOTE

Now you understand that if a method contains one await keyword, the method is divided into two parts. If there are multiple await keywords inside the method, the method is divided into multiple parts accordingly.

Next, refer to the arrows in Figure 6-6.

```
{
    if (num == 1)
    {
        awaiter = <>u__1;
        <>u__1 = default(TaskAwaiter);
        num = (<>1__state = -1);
        goto IL_00fb;
    }
    Console.WriteLine("Long running method starts.");
    <random>5__1 = new Random();
    awaiter2 = Task.Delay(500).GetAwaiter();
    if (!awaiter2.IsCompleted)
    {
        num = (<>1__state = 0);
        <>u__1 = awaiter2;
        <<<Main>$>g__ExecuteLongTaskAsync|0_0>d stateMachine = this;
        <>t__builder.AwaitUnsafeOnCompleted(ref awaiter2, ref stateMachine);
        return;
    }
}
else
{
    awaiter2 = <>u__1;
    <>u__1 = default(TaskAwaiter);
    num = (<>1__state = -1);
}
awaiter2.GetResult();
Console.WriteLine("Long running method resumes.");
awaiter = Task.Delay(700).GetAwaiter();
if (!awaiter.IsCompleted)
{
    num = (<>1__state = 1);
    <>u__1 = awaiter;
    <<<Main>$>g__ExecuteLongTaskAsync|0_0>d stateMachine = this;
    <>t__builder.AwaitUnsafeOnCompleted(ref awaiter, ref stateMachine);
    return;
}
goto IL_00fb;
IL_00fb:
awaiter.GetResult();
Console.WriteLine("Long running method resumes again.");
result = <random>5__1.Next(1, 100);
}
catch (Exception exception)
```

Figure 6-6. *The* ExecuteLongTaskAsync() *method is sliced through*
awaiter2 and awaiter

Figure 6-6 reveals the following observations:

- Notice the code segment where you see the if block: if (!awaiter2.IsCompleted){..}. It shows that if awaiter2 is not completed, there is a certain logic to ensure that once the thread is back, it can resume the execution from the intended point. If you scroll down, you can also notice that a similar logic is implemented for awaiter as well. Anyway, you understand that these are things by which states are preserved, and they help a thread to resume execution from an intended point.

- You can see that the line Long running method resumes. appears after the line awaiter2.GetResult(). You can also see that the line Long running method resumes again. comes after the line awaiter. GetResult(). This code format indicates that once a particular awaiter is completed, you can get the result and process the next part.

POINT TO NOTE

The previous bullet point indicates that the await keyword slices the method into parts.

Q&A Session

Q6.6 How can I distinguish between asynchronous and parallel programming?

Let's first consider some real-world examples. Suppose you set up an office that delivers different products to customers. In your office, there is a customer care executive. When a client dials the customer support number, this executive officer picks up the call, listens to the issue, and tries to solve the issue. Now think of a situation when multiple customers try to get help almost at the same time. Obviously, one of them can connect to the executive, but others need to wait. How do you interpret this situation? Surely, it's not a pleasant experience for your customers. So, you decide to hire another customer care executive to serve your customers fast. For example, if there are two executives, those two officers can serve two customers at the same time, aka in parallel. This is equivalent to parallel programming with a dual-core machine.

Now imagine a slightly different situation where the customer care executive listens to the problem, takes a note, and provides a ticket number to the customer. He also ensures the customer that the problem will be solved (or the ticket will be resolved) as soon as possible and that the company will inform the customer about the resolution via an email or a phone call. You can see that, in this case, though the problem is not solved immediately, the customer care executive can serve more customers in a specified time frame. This is equivalent to asynchronous programming. The benefit is obvious: the customers do not need to stay on the call until the problem is solved. As a result, the customer can do other work while the company executive tries to find a solution to the problem.

Another real-life situation in this category is when you order something from a grocery store and then start checking your email. You know the delivery person will deliver the order on time and you do not need to stop working while waiting for it.

So, if you combine these two models, the response time can be very fast. For example, if multiple support executives listen to multiple customers, provide some tickets, and assure them about the resolutions, the customers will have a better experience. We try to do this in programming. In fact, the terms *asynchronous programming* and *parallel programming* are related to each other. The Visual Studio Magazine summarized this as follows (see `https://visualstudiomagazine.com/articles/2011/03/24/wccsp_asynchronous-programming.aspx`):

*Asynchronous programming is a means of parallel program-
ming in which a unit of work runs separately from the main
application thread and notifies the calling thread of its completion, failure or progress.*

**Q6.7 Seeing your explanation, I get the feeling that in the previous
chapters we also exercised asynchronous programming. Is this
correct?**

True. In fact, when you create a new thread from a calling thread and
run both threads, surely you are doing things asynchronously. But the
focus of this chapter is on the `async` and `await` keywords, particularly how
to simplify asynchronous programming using these keywords.

Author's Note: This `async-await` programming model in C# can be
called other things in other programming languages. For example, C++
developers often use the term *coroutines* in a similar context. The wiki page
at `https://en.wikipedia.org/wiki/Coroutine` states the following:

*C# 2.0 added semi-coroutine (generator) functionality through
the iterator pattern and yield keyword. C# 5.0 includes await
syntax support.*

Task.Run vs. Task.Factory.StartNew

This section compares the `Task.Run` and `Task.Factory.StartNew`
methods using some small and valid code segments. In these code
segments, my focus will be on the return types. To make things fast, instead
of using the `var` type and then using the `GetType` method to determine the
type, I'll explicitly show you the type in these code segments. Let's begin.

Task.Factory.StartNew Treats Ordinary Lambdas and Asynchronous Lambdas Differently

Notice that in Code Segment 1, task1 is of type Task<int>. You can see that the return type int is wrapped with an additional layer.

Code Segment 1:

```
// Notice that task1 is a Task<int>
Task<int> task1 = Task.Factory.StartNew(
    () =>
    {
        return 100;
    }
);
```

Code Segment 2:

Now I make the lambda async. As a result, the return type becomes Task<Task<int>>. You can see that the return type int is now wrapped with one more additional layer.

```
// Notice that task2 is a Task<Task<int>> [ for applying async]
Task<Task<int>> task2 = Task.Factory.StartNew(
    async() =>
    {
        return 100;
    }
);
```

These code segments show that Task.Factory.StartNew treats ordinary lambdas and asynchronous lambdas differently.

Task.Run Treats Ordinary Lambdas and Asynchronous Lambdas Uniformly

Now start analyzing similar code with the Task.Run method. For example, see the following code segments (Code Segments 3 and 4) with supportive comments. In both cases, you see the return type as Task<int>.

Code Segment 3:

```
// Notice that task3 is a Task<int>.

Task<int> task3 = Task.Run(
    () =>
    {
        return 100;
    }
);
```

Code Segment 4:

```
// Notice that task4 is also a Task<int>.

Task<int> task4 = Task.Run(
    async () =>
    {
        return 100;
    }
);
```

You can see that when you pass an async lambda inside the Run method, there is no change in the return type.

POINT TO NOTE

Code Segments 3 and 4 show that `Task.Run` treats ordinary lambdas and asynchronous lambdas uniformly.

Unwrapping Using the Unwrap Method

While using the `StartNew` method, you can apply the `Unwrap` method as follows:

Code Segment 5:

```
Task<int> task5 = Task.Factory.StartNew(
    async () =>
    {
        return 100;
    }
).Unwrap();
```

See that you have unwrapped from `Task<Task<int>>` to `Task<int>`.

Unwrapping Using await

You can use `await` as an unwrapper. For example, see the following code:

Code Segment 6:

```
// await is unwrapping the layer
int task6 = await Task.Run(
    () =>
    {
        return 100;
    }
);
```

You can see that task6 is now an int, but not a Task<int>.

Code Segment 7:

As you have already seen, the Run method treats ordinary lambdas and asynchronous lambdas uniformly. Applying await in the following code helps you get the return type int again.

```
// await is unwrapping the layer
int task7 = await Task.Run(
    async() =>
    {
        await Task.Delay(100);
        return 100;
    }
);
```

Note   You can test these code segments by downloading the project UnderstandingTaskDotRun from the Apress website.

Asynchronous Construction

While using the async and await keywords, you need to follow certain restrictions. Acknowledging them will help you understand this section easily. Let's start.

For our upcoming discussions, I'll use a class called Repository that is defined as follows:

```
class Repository
{
    public static async Task<int> GetDataAsync()
    {
```

```
        await Task.Delay(1000);
        return new Random().Next(1, 10);
    }
}
```

Given this code, **the C# compiler does not complain if you invoke a task inside a constructor as follows:**

```
class Sample
{
    private int _flag;
    public Sample()
    {
        Task.Run(
            async () =>
            {
                _flag = await Repository.GetDataAsync();
                WriteLine($"The flag is set to {_flag} now");
            }
        );
    }
}
```

Interestingly, the C# compiler also allows you to call an asynchronous method from the constructor. This is why the following code will compile as well (Later, you'll see that this is not recommended):

```
class Sample
{
    public int Flag { get; set; }

    private async void InitializeAsync()
    {
```

```
        Flag = await Repository.GetDataAsync();
        WriteLine($"The flag is set to {Flag} now");
    }
    public Sample()
    {
        InitializeAsync();
    }
}
```

However, C# does not allow you to mark a constructor with the
async keyword. This means you cannot use the await keyword in the
constructor too. For your reference, consider the following code that
will not compile (you'll see multiple compile-time errors for this code
segment):

```
class Sample
{
    public int Flag { get; set; }

    // Error
    public async Sample()
    {
        Flag = await Repository.GetDataAsync();
        WriteLine($"The flag is set to {Flag} now");
    }

}
```

Then how can you perform an asynchronous initialization? Let's
investigate some possible approaches and the associated pros and cons.

POINT TO REMEMBER

Using the await operator, you can wait until the async operation is completed. When an async method returns a Task or Task<T>, you can handle the exceptions easily. Since you cannot use the async and await operators inside the constructor, asynchronous initialization is a challenging activity. This section discusses the possible approaches that can handle the situation.

Approach 1

Since you cannot construct everything asynchronously, you can attempt to segregate the asynchronous initialization part from its counterpart. For example, you call a constructor to perform the usual initialization (for the synchronous part), and then you invoke a method that can perform the asynchronous initialization (for the asynchronous part).

Demonstration 2

Here is a sample demonstration:

POINT TO NOTE

I made the InitializeAsync method's return type Task<Sample>. It is because you cannot await on this method if its return type is void.

```
using static System.Console;

WriteLine("Examining an async initialization.");
```

```
Sample sample = new();
// Performing async initialization and unwrapping Task<Sample>
// to Sample
sample = await sample.InitializeAsync();
sample.GetFlagValue();

class Sample
{
    private int _flag;

    public Sample()
    {
        // Performing sequential construction here
    }

    public async Task<Sample> InitializeAsync()
    {
        _flag = await Repository.GetDataAsync();
        WriteLine($"The flag is set to {_flag} now.");
        // Some other code, if any
        return this;
    }

    public void GetFlagValue()
    {
        WriteLine($"The current flag value is {_flag}.");
    }
}

// The Repository class is not shown again to avoid repetition.
```

Output

Here is some sample output from my computer:

```
Examining an async initialization.
The flag is set to 1 now.
The current flag value is 1.
```

Analysis

You can see that the usage of the Sample class is troublesome. This is because you need to use a traditional constructor along with the intended method for the complete initialization of a class. If you forget to call any of them, you will see an unintended result. This is misleading in the sense that a constructor did not perform the complete initialization. In addition, you cannot invoke the async initialization part before getting a Sample instance that performs the sequential initialization. So, **this is not a recommended approach.**

Approach 2

You already learned that the C# compiler allows you to call an asynchronous method from the constructor. Let's use this concept in the following program and analyze it.

Demonstration 3

Here is a sample program:

```
using static System.Console;

WriteLine("Examining an async initialization.");

Sample sample = new();
sample.GetFlagValue();
```

```
ReadKey();

class Sample
{
    private int _flag;
    public Sample()
    {
        InitializeAsync();
    }
    private async void InitializeAsync()
    {
        _flag = await Repository.GetDataAsync();
        WriteLine($"The flag is set to {_flag} now.");
    }

    public void GetFlagValue()
    {
        WriteLine($"The current flag value is {_flag}.");
    }
}
// The Repository class is not shown again to avoid repetition.
```

Output

Here is some sample output from my computer (I did not press any key
until I saw the last line of output):

```
Examining an async initialization.
The current flag value is 0.
The flag is set to 8 now.
```

Analysis

You can see that when the GetFlagValue method was called, the updated flag value (_flag) was not set. This is because when the constructor completed, the instance was still being asynchronously initialized, and you did not know when the asynchronous initialization would complete.

By introducing a delay before calling the GetFlagValue method, you can increase the possibility of getting the intended output. To illustrate, when I introduce a two-second delay before I invoke the GetFlagValue method as follows:

```
using static System.Console;

WriteLine("Examining async initialization");

Sample sample = new();
Thread.Sleep(2000);
sample.GetFlagValue();

//There is no other change in the remaining code
```

I see the intended output on my computer. Here is a sample for your reference:

```
Examining an async initialization.
The flag is set to 7 now.
The current flag value is 7.
```

However, you know the purpose of a constructor. When a call returns from the constructor, you expect to see the fully initialized object. It should not be the case that you get the fully initialized object at some undefined point of time in the future. At the same time, you also expect that the initialization process will not encounter an exception. Otherwise, you must handle it properly.

To illustrate, suppose you surround the object construction code inside a try-catch block and exercise the code as follows:

```
WriteLine("Examining async initialization");

try
{
    Sample sample = new();
    Thread.Sleep(2000);
    sample.GetFlagValue();
}
catch (Exception e)
{
    WriteLine(e.Message);
}
ReadKey();

class Sample
{
    private int _flag;
    public Sample()
    {
        InitializeAsync();
    }
    private async void InitializeAsync()
    {
        _flag = await Repository.GetDataAsync();
        WriteLine($"The flag is set to {_flag} now.");
        // The calling thread cannot catch the following
        // exception which can be raised due to some logic
        // throw new InvalidOperationException("Invalid ops!");
    }

// There is no change in the remaining code
```

This try-catch block is not sufficient to handle the exception that can be raised by the InitializeAsync method (notice that the asynchronous method has the void return type). You can see that handling exceptions inside the InitializeAsync method is another concern. So, **this is not a recommended approach either.**

Let's see another approach now.

Approach 3 (Using a Static Method aka Factory)

To address the limitations of the previous approaches, you can employ the factory pattern. Let's analyze it further.

Demonstration 4

This program uses a static method to perform the complete initialization. Here is a sample program:

```
using static System.Console;

WriteLine("Examining an async initialization.");

// Sample sample = new(); // Error now

// Performing async initialization and unwrapping Task<Sample>
// to Sample
Sample sample = await Sample.InitializeAsync();
sample.GetFlagValue();

class Sample
{
    private int _flag;
    private Sample()
```

```
    {
        // Do something here, if required
    }

    // Doing the initialization work here
    public static async Task<Sample> InitializeAsync()
    {
        Sample sample = new()
        {
            _flag = await Repository.GetDataAsync()
        };

        WriteLine($"The flag is set to {sample._flag} now.");
        return sample;
    }

    public void GetFlagValue()
    {
        WriteLine($"The current flag value is {_flag}.");
    }
}

// The Repository class is not shown again to avoid repetition.
```

Output

Here is some sample output:

```
Examining an async initialization.
The flag is set to 2 now.
The current flag value is 2.
```

Analysis

You can see that this solves the problems of the previous approaches. Notice that in this program, the GetFlagValue method always displays the updated value of the flag variable (_flag). In addition, if you surround the following code using a try-catch block inside the main thread as follows:

```
try
{
    // Performing async initialization and unwrapping
    // Task<Sample> to Sample
    Sample sample = await Sample.InitializeAsync();
    sample.GetFlagValue();
}
catch (Exception e)
{
    WriteLine(e.Message);
}
```

then you can catch any exception that can be raised by the InitializeAsync method. This is a common approach for an asynchronous construction.

Q&A Session

Q6.8 I can see that you have made the constructor private. Was this intentional?

Yes. In this case, I'd also like to prohibit the direct usage of the constructor so that readers know there is only one way to initialize. Interestingly, if you are familiar with the singleton design pattern, you are already familiar with this approach.

Approach 4 (Lazy Initialization)

If an object creation is a time-consuming or costly operation, you may delay the instantiation process. The idea is that unless you need the object, you should avoid the construction process. This tactic is helpful when you deal with shared resources that are typically large.

Understanding Lazy<T>

Surely, you can employ a custom logic to implement the concept. However, the good news is that the Lazy<T> class can help in this context. Let's get a quick overview of it.

This time the Sample class has the following look:

```
class Sample
{
    public int Flag { get; init; }
    public Sample(int  flag)
    {
        Flag = flag;
    }
    // It also can have some big data such as:
    // public int[] Data = new int[5000];

}
```

You can always make an object of Foo using this approach: var sample2 = new Foo(10);.

When you'd like to construct an object of Foo lazily, you will see several constructors. At the time of this writing, I can see what's shown in Figure 6-7.

```
public Lazy();
public Lazy(bool isThreadSafe);
public Lazy(Func<T> valueFactory);
public Lazy(LazyThreadSafetyMode mode);
public Lazy(T value);
public Lazy(Func<T> valueFactory, bool isThreadSafe);
public Lazy(Func<T> valueFactory, LazyThreadSafetyMode mode);
```

Figure 6-7. *Available constructors for lazy initializations*

To instantiate a Sample object lazily, let's use the third constructor as follows:

```
var sample1 = new Lazy<Sample>(
    () => { return new Sample(5); }
    );
```

In this case, the large object (i.e., sample1) is not constructed until you access the Flag property. By using Value (gets the lazily initialized value of the current Lazy<T> instance) inside a lazily initialized object, you can access the class properties (in this example, it is Flag).

Demonstration 5

Let's debug the following program to verify this:

```
using static System.Console;

var sample1 = new Lazy<Sample>(
    () => { return new Sample(5); }
    );

var sample2 = new Sample(10);
ReadKey();
WriteLine(sample1.Value.Flag);
ReadKey();

class Sample
{
```

```
public int Flag { get; init; }
public Sample(int  flag)
{
    Flag = flag;
}
// It also can have some big data such as:
// public int[] Data = new int[5000];
}
```

Analysis

Figure 6-8 shows when the control hits the breakpoint at line 8.

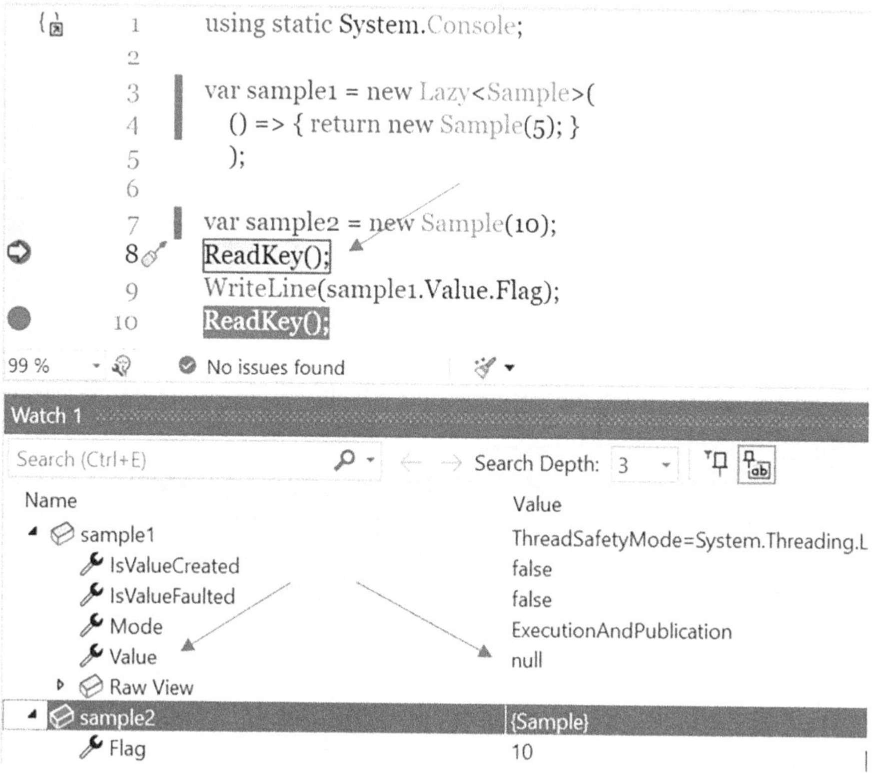

Figure 6-8. *The sample2 instance is ready, but the sample1 instance is not ready yet*

You can see that the sample2 instance was created, but the sample1 instance is not ready yet. In addition, notice that the Value property of the sample1 instance is null at this stage.

Let's continue the execution. (Since I used ReadKey to pause the execution, you need to press F5 and any key to proceed further.) Now control hits the breakpoint at line 10. This time notice the Watch window as show in Figure 6-9.

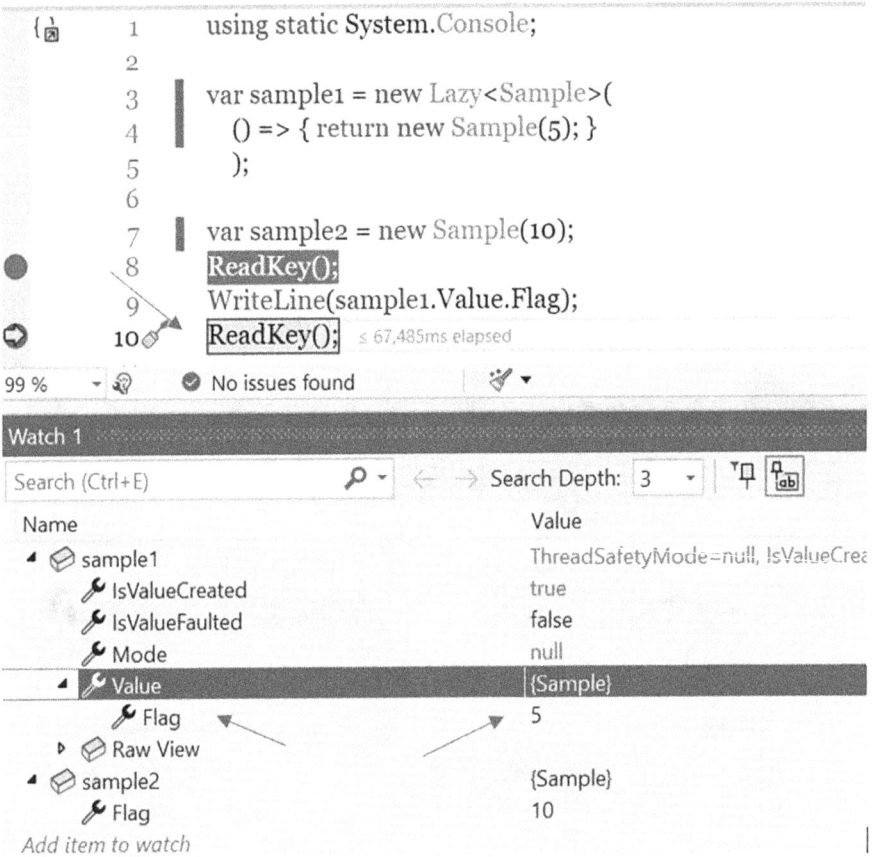

Figure 6-9. *The construction process of the sample1 instance is completed now*

You can see that once you access the Value property, the sample1 instance is constructed. This is why the Value property of the sample1 instance is not null anymore.

Using Lazy<Task<T>> for Async Construction

You saw Lazy<Sample> in the previous demonstration. However, note that Lazy<T> **does not support asynchronous initialization**. This causes obvious problems when the initialization involves long-running tasks or I/O operations. For example, while downloading a large file from a remote server, blocking the main thread will cause a poor user experience for sure.

Why doesn't Lazy<T> support asynchronous initialization? At https://devblogs.microsoft.com/pfxteam/asynclazyt/, Stephen Toub, a partner software engineer from Microsoft, answers this question as follows:

> *Lazy<T> is all about caching a value and synchronizing multiple threads attempting to get at that cached value, whereas we have another type in the .NET Framework focused on representing an asynchronous operation and making its result available in the future: Task<T>. Rather than building asynchronous semantics into Lazy<T>, you can instead combine the power of Lazy<T> and Task<T> to get the best of both types!*

Let's exercise an asynchronous initialization using Lazy<Task<Sample>> now. In the upcoming program, you'll see the following code block inside the Sample class:

```
private static Lazy<Task<Sample>> InitializeAsync =
   new(
         async () =>
         {
             int data = await Repository.GetDataAsync();
             return new Sample(data);
         }
     );
```

```
┌─────────────────────────────────────────────────┐
│                 POINT TO NOTE                   │
└─────────────────────────────────────────────────┘
```

Notice that I return a `Sample` object that is wrapped as `Task<Sample>`.
Why? This is because there is an `async` lambda, and it does this wrapping,
which you already learned about. In other words, if the lambda is not `async`,
then the program will intend to work with `Lazy<Sample>`, but not with
`Lazy<Task<Sample>>`.

Using this code block is easy. You'll see the following `public` method
(inside the `Sample` class) that can be invoked from the client code:

```
public static async void GetFlagValue()
{
    var sample = await InitializeAsync.Value;
    WriteLine($"The current flag value is {sample._flag}.");
}
```

Demonstration 6

Here is a sample demonstration:

```
using static System.Console;

WriteLine("Examining async lazy Initialization");
Sample.GetFlagValue();
ReadKey();

class Sample
{
    private int _flag;
    private Sample(int flag)
    {
        _flag = flag;
    }
```

```
    private static Lazy<Task<Sample>> InitializeAsync = new(
      async () =>
      {
          int data = await Repository.GetDataAsync();
          return new Sample(data);
      }
    );
    public static async void GetFlagValue()
    {
        var sample = await InitializeAsync.Value;
        WriteLine($"The current flag value is {sample._flag}.");
    }
}

// The Repository class is not shown again to avoid repetition.
```

Output

Here is some sample output:

```
Examining async lazy Initialization
The current flag value is 3.
```

Using Nito.AsyncEx Library

If you read Stephen Cleary's blog at https://blog.stephencleary.
com/2013/01/async-oop-2-constructors.html or Stephen Toub's article
at https://devblogs.microsoft.com/pfxteam/asynclazyt/, you'll see
the type AsyncLazy<T> that essentially simplifies the "appearance" of
the code. By adding the Nito.AsyncEx namespace (I used version 5.1.2)

in my codebase, I can get such a type and write the equivalent code for InitializeAsync as follows (I prefixed the word *Nito* in this case so that you can compare InitializeAsync and NitoInitializeAsync easily):

```
private static AsyncLazy<Sample> NitoInitializeAsync = new(
  async () =>
  {
    int data = await Repository.GetDataAsync();
    return new Sample(data);
  }
);
```

In this case, I need to update the following method as follows(the old code is shown in comment for the comparison purposes):

```
public static async void GetFlagValue()
{
 //var sample = await InitializeAsync.Value;
 var sample = await NitoInitializeAsync;
 WriteLine($"The current flag value is {sample._flag}.");
}
```

With these changes, if you run the program, you'll see similar output once again.

Note   Download the Demo6A_LazyInitializationAsync UsingNito project from the Apress website to see the complete program.

Introducing ValueTasks

You've been learning about tasks since the beginning of the book; they are fundamental to asynchronous programming. The Task and Task<TResult> classes help us a lot when we exercise asynchronous programming. From C# 5.0 onward we have the async and await keywords as well. While describing the C# 5.0 key features, the documentation at https://learn. microsoft.com/en-us/dotnet/csharp/whats-new/csharp-version-history#c-version-40 states the following:

> *... async and await are the real stars of this release.*

This chapter showed how these keywords made asynchronous programming easier.

One major improvement came in C# 7.0 where we saw the usage of ValueTask and ValueTask<TResult>. The AsTask method helps you retrieve a Task object from a ValueTask object. Obviously, an instance of ValueTask<Result> can be awaited as well.

The Task class is very flexible and provides lots of benefits. So, you may be wondering why we need the ValueTask instance.

In most cases, by invoking an asynchronous operation, you'll be awaiting for a resulting task. Just like you pay less for a product that has a limited number of features, you'd use ValueTask when you do not need all the features of the Task class.

Don't forget that Task is a class. So, it is heap-allocated. If you create lots of Task instances, you put extra pressure on the garbage collector (GC) for allocations and deallocations. It surely affects the performance of the application. In this context, you may note that ValueTask is of type struct, but not class.

Keeping the previous points in mind, you may try to implement a caching mechanism. However, let me tell you that it is not feasible to cache everything in every situation.

┌───┐
│   **POINT TO NOTE**   │
└───┘

In this context, I suggest you read Microsoft's suggested article called "Understanding the Whys, Whats, and Whens of ValueTask" at https://devblogs.microsoft.com/dotnet/understanding-the-whys-whats-and-whens-of-valuetask/ to learn more about this.

Consuming ValueTasks

Here is a synchronous method that returns a ValueTask<int>:

```
// Synchronous method
ValueTask<int> SomeMethod()
{
    // Some other code, if any
    return new ValueTask<int>(50);
}
```

You can consume this method as follows:

```
var task1 = SomeMethod();
WriteLine($"Received: {task1.Result}");
```

There is no surprise that you'll see the following output: Received: 50.

You can convert a ValueTask<Result> instance into a Task<Result> instance using AsTask. For example, the following code:

```
var task2 =
    SomeMethod()
    .AsTask()
    .ContinueWith
    (
```

```
    t => WriteLine($"The latest value is: {t.Result + 10}")
  );
task2.Wait();
```

can produce the following output: The latest value is: 60.

Let's consider an asynchronous method now. The following method returns a ValueTask<int> as well:

```
// Asynchronous method
async ValueTask<int> SomeMethodAsync()
{
    await Task.Delay(100);
    //return new ValueTask<int>(100); // Error now
    return 100; // OK
}
```

You can consume this method as follows:

```
int result = await SomeMethodAsync();
WriteLine($"Got: {result}");
```

which can produce the following output: Got: 100.

Note   You can download the project UnderstandingValueTask to run these code segments and verify the output.

Q&A Session

Q6.9 Should I replace Task and Task<TResult> with ValueTask and ValueTask<TResult> in my asynchronous APIs?

No. By default, you should always prefer Task or Task<TResult>. Unless you are really concerned about performance, Task or Task<TResult> is still preferred.

Also note that there are certain restrictions when you use `ValueTask` or `ValueTask<TResult>` in your programs; otherwise, the result will be undefined.

Q6.10 What are the restrictions of using a `ValueTask` or `ValueTask<TResult>` in my programs?

According to the documentation at `https://learn.microsoft.com/en-us/dotnet/api/system.threading.tasks.valuetask-1?view=net-8.0`, if you perform any of the following operations, the result will be undefined:

- Awaiting the instance multiple times

- Calling `AsTask` multiple times

- Using `.Result` or `.GetAwaiter().GetResult()` when the operation hasn't yet completed, or using them multiple times

- Using more than one of these techniques to consume the instance

Q6.11 When should I use `ValueTask` or `ValueTask<TResult>`?

I suggest you follow Stephen Toub's suggestion. After a long discussion, he gave us the short rule as follows (see `https://devblogs.microsoft.com/dotnet/understanding-the-whys-whats-and-whens-of-valuetask/`):

With a ValueTask or a ValueTask<TResult>, you should either await it directly (optionally with .ConfigureAwait (false)) or call AsTask() on it directly, and then never use it again.

Reviewing Exceptions

Before you finish this chapter, I want to draw your attention to a special characteristic of an `await` expression. I first made the following class with two almost identical methods to demonstrate this. However, the first one is a normal method, and the second one is an `async` method. Let's look into the class:

```
class InvalidClass
{
    public static string UnknownUserDenied(string user)
    {
        throw new UnauthorizedAccessException($"{user} is
          unauthorized");
    }

    public static async Task<string> UnknownUserDeniedAsync
    (string user)
    {
        await Task.Delay(1000);
        throw new UnauthorizedAccessException($"{user} is
          unauthorized");
    }
}
```

Now let's execute the following code from the main thread:

```
using static System.Console;

WriteLine("Reviewing Exceptions.");

try
{
    var validateTask = Task.Run(() =>
```

```
    InvalidClass.UnknownUserDenied("abc"));
   WriteLine(validateTask.Result);
}
catch (Exception e)
{
   WriteLine($"Exception type: {e.GetType()}, Message:
   {e.Message}");
}
```

Upon running this program, you'll see the following output:

```
Reviewing Exceptions.
Exception type: System.AggregateException, Message: One or more
 errors occurred. (abc is unauthorized)
```

I assume you are not surprised. You have seen a lot of discussion on AggregateException , and you know how to deal with it. For example, if you replace the existing catch block with the following one:

```
catch (AggregateException ae)
{
   foreach (Exception e in ae.InnerExceptions)
   {
       WriteLine($"Exception type: {e.GetType()}, Message:
       {e.Message}");
   }
}
```

you will see the specific exception(s) as follows:

```
Reviewing Exceptions.
Exception type: System.UnauthorizedAccessException, Message:
 abc is unauthorized
```

Now replace the previous `try-catch` block with the following one:

```
try
{
    var validateAsyncTask = await
        InvalidClass.UnknownUserDeniedAsync("abc");
}
catch (Exception e)
{
    WriteLine($"Exception type: {e.GetType()}, Message:
    {e.Message}");
}
```

Upon running this program, you'll see the following output:

```
Reviewing Exceptions.
Exception type: System.UnauthorizedAccessException, Message:
 abc is unauthorized
```

Notice that this time you are seeing the `UnauthorizedAccessException` directly. How is this possible? Let's see what Microsoft states about it. The documentation at `https://learn.microsoft.com/en-us/dotnet/csharp/asynchronous-programming/` states the following:

> *When code awaits a faulted task, the first exception in the AggregateException.InnerExceptions collection is rethrown.*

Now you understand that the `await` keyword has done this magic! It helps you pick the first exception inside the `AggregateException`.

Note   Download the `Demo_ReviewingExceptions` project to see the complete program that contains the discussed code segments.

Congratulations! You have finished the final chapter of the book. It's time to check your understanding by attempting the following exercises.

Author's Note: Once I finished writing this book, I found that Stephen Toub and Scott Hanselman recently discussed some useful stuff at `https://www.youtube.com/watch?v=R-z2Hv-7nxk`. This is another good resource for learning about `async/await`.

Exercises

Check your understanding by attempting the following exercises:

Note   You can assume that in addition to the default settings, the statement: `using static System.Console;` has also been added at the beginning of all the following exercises.

E6.1 Can you predict the output of the following code?

```
var task1 = Task.Run(
    async () =>
    {
        await Task.Delay(1000);
        return "Hello";
    });
WriteLine(task1.Result);
```

E6.2 If you replace `Task.Run` with `Task.Factory.StartNew` in the previous code, will you see the same output?

E6.3 Can you predict the output of the following code?

```
var task3A = new ValueTask<int>(10);

var task3B = task3A.ContinueWith(
    (t) =>
```

```
    {
        int temp = task3A.Result;
        return ++temp;
    }
);
WriteLine($"The final result is: {task3B.Result}");
```

E6.4 Can you predict the output of the following code?

```
string result = await GetWeatherReportAsync();
WriteLine(result);

async ValueTask<string> GetWeatherReportAsync()
{
    await Task.Delay(100);
    return "This is a beautiful day!";
}
```

E6.5 Can you predict the output of the following code?

```
var number= await GetNumberAsync().AsTask();
WriteLine($"Got the number: {number}");

async ValueTask<int> GetNumberAsync()
{
    await Task.Delay(100);
    return new ValueTask<int>(50);
}
```

E6.6 Can you compile the following code?

```
var task6 = Task.Run(
    async () =>
    {
        await Task.Delay(1000);
```

```
        return new ValueTask<int>(10);

    });
WriteLine($"Task 6 returns: {task6.GetAwaiter().GetResult()}");
```

E6.7 Can you compile the following code?

```
var task7 = Task.Run(
    async () =>
    {
        await Task.Delay(1000);
        return new ValueTask<int>(20).AsTask();
    });
WriteLine($"Task 7 returns: {await task7.GetAwaiter().
 GetResult()}");
```

E6.8 Can you predict the output of the following code?

```
var task8 =
    Task.Factory.StartNew(
    async () =>
    {
        await Task.Delay(1000);
        return Task.Run(()=>"Hello");
    });
WriteLine($"Task 8 returns:{await await task8.Result}");
```

E6.9 Demonstration 1 showed you an asynchronous program using the async and await keywords. Can you write an equivalent program using a task-based continuation?

E6.10: Write a program that requests the content of a web page. Ensure that your program demonstrates the power of the async and await keywords.

Hint: Write an async function that accepts a URL that can be passed to the GetStringAsync method. Before you print the content, ensure that the calling thread is not blocked while the function is working. You may note that starting in .NET 6, the WebClient class is deprecated. So, try using the HttpClient class in this program.

E6.11 Add the cancellation capability to the previous program (E6.10).

E6.12 Can you summarize the benefits of using the async and await keywords?

Summary

The Task class and the derived Task<TResult> were introduced to make asynchronous programming easy. Still, there were challenges. To overcome those challenges and make things simpler, C# 5 introduced the async and await keywords, and C# 7.0 came up with ValueTask and ValueTask<TResult>. These are integral parts of asynchronous programming nowadays. This chapter discussed them using various code segments and complete programs. Upon completion of this chapter, you should not find difficulties in answering the following questions:

- How do the async and await keywords make asynchronous programming easy?

- What are the restrictions associated with the async and await keywords?

- How does the Task.Factory.StartNew and Task.Run methods treat ordinary lambdas and asynchronous lambdas?

- How should you perform asynchronous initializations?

- Why ValueTasks were introduced? How do they help?

- How can you consume the ValueTasks?

- What are the restrictions associated with the ValueTasks?

Solutions to Exercises

Here is a sample solution set for the exercises in this chapter.

E6.1

You should see the following output: Hello.

E6.2

No. This time you'll see the following:

System.Runtime.CompilerServices.AsyncTaskMethodBuilder`1+AsyncS
tateMachineBox`1[System.String,Program+<>c+<<<Main>$>b__0_1>d]

Clue: You have seen that Task.Factory.StartNew treats async lambdas differently. To see the output Hello, you can either use the Unwrap method as follows:

```
var task2 = Task.Factory.StartNew(
    async () =>
    {
        await Task.Delay(1000);
        return "Hello";
    }).Unwrap();
WriteLine(task2.Result);
```

or, use one more await keyword as follows:

```
var task2 = await Task.Factory.StartNew(
    async () =>
    {
        await Task.Delay(1000);
        return "Hello";
    });
WriteLine(task2.Result);
```

E6.3

This program will not compile. You will see the following error:

```
CS1061 'ValueTask<int>' does not contain a definition
for 'ContinueWith' and no accessible extension method
'ContinueWith' accepting a first argument of type
'ValueTask<int>' could be found (are you missing a using
directive or an assembly reference?)
```

Additional Note: You can replace the line:

```
var task3B = task3A.ContinueWith(  // Error CS1061
```

with the following line that uses the AsTask method:

```
var task3B = task3A.AsTask().ContinueWith(  //OK
```

and get output as follows:

```
The final result is: 11
```

E6.4

You should see the following output: This is a beautiful day!

E6.5

This code will not compile because the method implementation is incorrect. Here is some sample output for your reference:

CS4016 Since this is an async method, the return expression must be of type 'int' rather than 'ValueTask<int>'

So, if you replace the existing method with the following method:

```
async ValueTask<int> GetNumberAsync()
{
    await Task.Delay(100);
    //return new ValueTask<int>(50); // Error CS4016
    return 50; // OK
}
```

you can see the following output:

    Got the number: 50

E6.6

Yes. Notice that this time you are passing the async lambda inside the Task.Run method and task6 is of type Task<ValueTask<int>>. This code will produce the following output:

    Task 6 returns: 10

You may also note that if you write something like the following:

```
var task6 = Task.Run(
    async () =>
    {
        await Task.Delay(1000);
        return 10; // OK too
        //return new ValueTask<int>(10); // OK
    });
```

you'll see the same output, but this time task6 is a Task<int>.

E6.7

Yes. This code will produce the following output:

```
Task 7 returns: 20
```

E6.8

This time task8 is of type Task<Task<Task<string>>>. So, do not be surprised about the two await keywords in the following expression: await await task8.Result. By using them, you can unwrap the type Task<Task<Task<string>>> twice to get the output:

```
    Task 8 returns: Hello
```

E6.9

The following program shows you a task-based continuation example. It is similar to Demonstration 1. You may note that, in this case, you observe a slightly different output where the line "The method resumes. " appears before the line "The main thread continues.". Why? In this program, I'm synchronously waiting for the continuation task to complete.

However, in Demonstration 1, the control returned to the calling thread as soon as it hit the first await expression (and it did not wait for the method to be completed). For an easy comparison, I have kept both code segments and the associated output.

```
using static System.Console;

WriteLine("The main thread starts.");

WriteLine("-----------------------------------");
```

```csharp
#region Calling the asynchronous code (Used in  demo 1)
Task<int> getValue = GetHundredAsync();
WriteLine("The main thread continues.");
// Consuming the return value which is an int
int result1 = await getValue;
WriteLine($"The invoked task returns: {result1}");
#endregion
WriteLine("-------------------------------------");

#region Task-based asynchronous equivalent
Task<int> result = GetHundred();
WriteLine("The main thread continues.");
var remainingTask = result.ContinueWith(
    t => WriteLine($"The invoked task returns: {t.Result}")
);
remainingTask.Wait();
#endregion

WriteLine("-------------------------------------");

WriteLine("The main thread ends.");

// Asynchronous version
static async Task<int> GetHundredAsync()
{
    WriteLine("The method is arranging the number.");
    await Task.Delay(1500);
    WriteLine("The method resumes.");
    return 100;
}

// Synchronous version
static Task<int> GetHundred()
```

```
{
    WriteLine("The method is arranging the number.");
    Task.Delay(1500);
    WriteLine("The method resumes.");
    return Task.Run(() => 100);
}
```

This program produces the following output:

```
The main thread starts.
-------------------------------------
The method is arranging the number.
The main thread continues.
The method resumes.
The invoked task returns: 100
-------------------------------------
The method is arranging the number.
The method resumes.
The main thread continues.
The invoked task returns: 100
-------------------------------------
The main thread ends.
```

E6.10

Here is a sample program where I arbitrarily chose the URL https://www.
aboutamazon.in/what-we-do/amazon-pay:

```
using static System.Console;

WriteLine("Exercise 6.10");
string url = "https://www.aboutamazon.in/what-we-do/
 amazon-pay";
```

```
var webContent = PrintContents(url);
WriteLine("Shortly, you'll see the content...");
WriteLine(webContent.Result);
ReadKey();

static async Task<string> PrintContents(string url)
{
    var client = new HttpClient();
    var contents = await client.GetStringAsync(url);
    return contents;
}
```

Since the output is long, I've condensed it (I highlighted a portion in bold so that you can verify the content):

```
Exercise 6.10
Shortly, you'll see the content...
<!DOCTYPE html>
<html class="PageDefault" lang="en">

// Intermediate output skipped

    <div class="HubPage1-content">

    <div class="HubPage1-description">
                Amazon Pay simplifies daily life and fulfills
                the aspirations of every Indian by solving their
                payment and financial needs. It offers a trusted,
                convenient, and rewarding way for millions of cash
                customers to make digital payments, both on Amazon
                and at offline stores. It is also used by millions
                of merchants every day to provide their customers
                with a simple, safe, and reliable method to pay.
    </div>
```

```
    </div> <!-- END HubPage1-content -->
</div> <!-- END HubPage1-container -->

// Remaining output is skipped too
```

E6.11

I leave this exercise to you.

Hint: This time consider using an overloaded version of GetStringAsync that accepts both the URL and the CancellationToken as parameters.

E6.12

The following list includes some of the key benefits of this:

- You write less code.

- You do not need continuations that are based on anonymous callbacks.

- The asynchronous code that uses async and await keywords looks very similar to its counterpart, i.e., the synchronous version.

- The exception handling becomes easier.

APPENDIX A

Supplementary Notes

A *multicore* machine can execute multiple threads simultaneously. With the advancement of technology, most computers have multicore processors nowadays. To make fast-paced applications, you can take advantage of the hardware and parallelize your code by distributing the work among these cores. Throughout this book, you explored the possibilities using various C# constructs. This appendix includes some additional information, useful suggestions, and supplementary materials for you.

PFX Overview

When you jump into parallel programming in C#, you will often hear the acronym PFX. This stands for the Parallel Framework (often called Parallel Framework Extensions) in C#.

You may be wondering why didn't I mention PFX earlier. This is because PFX includes lots of constructs, and I didn't want to overwhelm you. Since you have completed Chapters 1–6, you can realize that you've learned most of these components.

Data Structures

At `https://learn.microsoft.com/en-us/dotnet/standard/parallel-programming/data-structures-for-parallel-programming`, Microsoft talks briefly about the following data structures that are useful for parallel programming.

© Vaskaran Sarcar 2024
V. Sarcar, *Parallel Programming with C# and .NET*,
https://doi.org/10.1007/979-8-8688-0488-5

- Concurrent collection classes

- Lightweight synchronization primitives such as `SemaphoreSlim`, `CountdownEvent`, `ManualResetEventSlim`, `Barrier`, `SpinLock`, and `SpinWait`

- Types for lazy initialization such as `System.Lazy<T>`, `System.Threading.ThreadLocal<T>`, and `System.Threading.LazyInitializer`

- Aggregate exceptions (`System.AggregateException` type)

You learned about concurrent collections in Chapter 3, `Lazy<T>` in Chapter 6, and `AggregateException` in Chapter 2. This means we have already covered many of these components. Though the book does not try to cover all of them, this appendix will cover a few more synchronization primitives such as `SemaphoreSlim`, `CountdownEvent`, and `ManualResetEventSlim`.

PFX Components

When .NET Framework 4.0 was released, Microsoft stated the following (`https://learn.microsoft.com/en-us/archive/msdn-magazine/2009/september/what%E2%80%99s-new-in-the-base-class-libraries-in-net-framework-4`):

> *Another major new addition to the BCL in .NET 4 is the Parallel Extensions (PFX) feature that is being delivered by the Parallel Computing Platform team. PFX include the Task Parallel Library (TPL), Coordination Data Structures, Concurrent Collections and Parallel LINQ (PLINQ)—all of which will make it easier to write code that can take advantage of multicore machines.*

Since the task parallelism constructs and the `Parallel` class are known together as the Task Parallel Library (TPL), you can say that PFX essentially encompasses the following:

- The task parallelism constructs (you learned about many of these in Chapter 1 and Chapter 2)

- The `Parallel` class (you learned about this class in Chapter 3)

- The coordination data structures including concurrent collections (you learned these structures in Chapter 2 and Chapter 3)

- Parallel LINQ (PLINQ) (you learned about this in Chapter 5)

How Does PFX Help?

At a high level, parallel programming involves the following steps:

1. Partitioning the "big" work into "smaller works"

2. Exercising those "small works" in parallel

3. Collecting and organizing the results properly

This can be done using classic multithreading constructs, but things are not straightforward. The PFX libraries were designed to make things easier for you.

Partitioning Strategies

While exercising parallelism, there are two partitioning strategies:

- Partitioning the data (data parallelism)

- Partitioning the tasks (task parallelism)

As the name implies, in the case of data parallelism, the source collection is partitioned so that different threads can work on those segments concurrently. TPL supports this concept through the `Parallel` class. More specifically, PFX provides a basic form of structured parallelism via `Parallel.For`, `Parallel.ForEach`, and `Parallel.Invoke`.

However, in case of task parallelism, the independent tasks run concurrently.

POINT TO NOTE

Data parallelism tends to be *structured* because the parallel work units start and finish in the same place in the program. On the contrary, task parallelism tends to be *unstructured*, because the parallel work units may start and finish in different places.

Q&A Session

QApp1.1 My understanding is that the `Parallel` class helps me to segregate the work but I need to gather the result. However, in the case of task parallelism, I need to partition the work too. Is that correct?

I appreciate your observation. You are correct.

More on Synchronization Constructs

In Chapter 3 we divided the synchronization constructs into four categories and discussed one from each category. Here you'll see a few more useful constructs. You can use them as needed.

Signaling Using ManualResetEvent

You already learned signaling using AutoResetEvent. Demonstration 4 in Chapter 3 showed you a sample implementation as well. This time you'll learn about ManualResetEvent. I also showed you in Chapter 3 that when I replaced the line var resetEvent = new AutoResetEvent(false); with var resetEvent = new ManualResetEvent(false); I got the following output:

```
Two customers are approaching the mall.
The customer 1 is waiting for the entry pass.
The customer 2 is waiting for the entry pass.
Press any key to issue the signal from the main thread.
The customer 1 enters the mall.
The customer 2 enters the mall.
Press any key to issue another signal from the main thread.
Another customer is approaching the mall.
Press any key to exit.
The customer 3 is waiting for the entry pass.
The customer 3 enters the mall.
```

Then I pointed out the difference between the outputs. In this output, both customer 1 and customer 2 were able to enter the mall when the main thread issued the signal. In addition, customer 3 was also able to enter the mall because, in between, the gate was not closed.

Now the question is: how to close the gate? You need to call the Reset method. Let's look at the following program.

Demonstration 1

Here is a sample implementation for you:

```
using static System.Console;

var resetEvent = new ManualResetEvent(false);
```

```
WriteLine("Two customers are approaching the mall.");
Task.Run(VisitMall);
Task.Run(VisitMall);

// Imposing some delay to mimic a real-world scenario
Thread.Sleep(2000);

WriteLine("Press any key to issue the signal from the main
 thread.");
ReadKey();
resetEvent.Set();
Thread.Sleep(1000);

// Reset will restrict the new task to continue
WriteLine("Resetting the signal now.");
resetEvent.Reset();

WriteLine("Another customer is approaching the mall.");
Task.Run(VisitMall);

WriteLine("Press any key to exit.");
ReadKey();

void VisitMall()
{
    // Imposing a small delay to mimic a real-world scenario
    Thread.Sleep(1000);
    WriteLine($"The customer {Task.CurrentId} is waiting for
     the entry pass.");
    resetEvent.WaitOne();
    WriteLine($"The customer {Task.CurrentId} enters the mall.");
}
```

Output

Here is a sample output (I pressed the Enter key to issue the signals):

```
Two customers are approaching the mall.
The customer 1 is waiting for the entry pass.
The customer 2 is waiting for the entry pass.
Press any key to issue the signal from the main thread.
The customer 1 enters the mall.
The customer 2 enters the mall.
Resetting the signal now.
Another customer is approaching the mall.
Press any key to exit.
The customer 3 is waiting for the entry pass.
```

Analysis

You can see that when the gate opened, customer 1 and customer 2 both entered the mall. However, the gate was closed shortly after that. This is why customer 3 could not enter the mall.

Q&A Session

QApp1.2 While discussing AutoResetEvent, you talked about a real-world scenario. How can I relate a real-world scenario to ManualResetEvent?

In my city, when I go to the cinema, I usually see an entire family or group of people enter the movie hall with a single ticket. It means that a group of people can pass the entry gate together. Look at the previous demonstration now. You can see that when the main thread issued the signal, the waiting customers entered the mall together as well.

Signaling Using ManualResetEventSlim

ManualResetEventSlim is a lightweight alternative to ManualResetEvent. Let's make the following changes in the previous demonstration:

- Replace the line var resetEvent = new ManualResetEvent(false); with var resetEvent = new ManualResetEventSlim(false);.

- This time replace the WaitOne method with the Wait method inside the VisitMall method. This Wait method blocks the current thread until the current ManualResetEventSlim is set. This change is required because this slim version does not subclass WaitHandle.

Demonstration 2

Since there are only two minor changes, I am not showing you the complete program here. You can download the Demo2_ManualResetEventSlim project from the Apress website to see the complete program and execute it.

Output

Once you make these changes, you'll see similar output to what was shown in the previous demonstration.

Q&A Session

QApp1.3 When should I prefer ManualResetEventSlim over ManualResetEvent (and vice versa)?

You should prefer ManualResetEventSlim when you expect a short waiting time. However, you may note that though the lightweight synchronization types normally provide better performance, they cannot be used for interprocess synchronization. In other words, you can use them in single applications.

You can find additional information at https://learn.microsoft. com/en-us/dotnet/api/system.threading.manualreseteventslim?view =net-8.0.

> *ManualResetEventSlim uses busy spinning for a short time while it waits for the event to become signaled. When wait times are short, spinning can be much less expensive than waiting by using wait handles. However, if the event does not become signaled within a certain period of time, ManualResetEventSlim resorts to a regular event handle wait.*

Signaling Using CountdownEvent

Using ManualResetEvent, you make one thread superior. Here one thread can release several blocked threads. CountdownEvent can be used for a reverse scenario where multiple threads collectively release one blocked thread. In other words, a thread is unblocked when it receives signals from multiple threads.

To show you an example, let me talk about our metro railway stations one more time. I have told you that only one passenger can pass through a gate at a time, but I did not mention that there are multiple gates through which passengers can enter or exit. During the festive seasons or office hours, the metro officials open those gates to control the crowd. However, an ordinary shop may not have this option. To control the crowd, they may need to restrict the entries.

Suppose that a well-known company has announced that its next-generation product is about to be launched on a particular day. Let's assume that on the day of the release, customers are approaching a local shop, which is not very big! Let's further assume that initially, the gatekeeper allows the customers. However, to control the crowd, the gatekeeper needs to close the gate shortly. He decides to open the gate for a new customer if at least three current customers exit from the shop. The upcoming program demonstrates this situation. Here are the key characteristics of this program:

- The main thread (gatekeeper) waits to receive signals from three worker threads (customers). It blocks itself by calling the Wait method.

- Each of these worker threads issues a signal by invoking the Signal method.

Demonstration 3

Here is the demonstration:

```
using static System.Console;

var countdownEvent = new CountdownEvent(3);

WriteLine("Five customers are trying to enter the mall.");
for (int i = 0; i < 5; i++)
{
    Task.Run(VisitMall);
}
WriteLine($"The gatekeeper waits for {countdownEvent.
 CurrentCount} customers to exit.");
countdownEvent.Wait();
WriteLine($"The gatekeeper got {countdownEvent.InitialCount}
 signals.");
WriteLine("A new customer can enter the mall now.");
WriteLine("Press any key to exit.");
ReadKey();
```

```
void VisitMall()
{
    int random = new Random().Next(1, 5);
    Thread.Sleep(1000);
    WriteLine($"The customer {Task.CurrentId} starts
     purchasing.");
    Thread.Sleep(random* 500);
    WriteLine($"-----The customer {Task.CurrentId} is
     exiting now.");
    countdownEvent.Signal();
}
```

Output

Here is some sample output:

```
Five customers are trying to enter the mall.
The gatekeeper waits for 3 customers to exit.
The customer 3 starts purchasing.
The customer 2 starts purchasing.
The customer 1 starts purchasing.
The customer 4 starts purchasing.
-----The customer 3 is exiting now.
The customer 5 starts purchasing.
-----The customer 1 is exiting now.
-----The customer 4 is exiting now.
The gatekeeper got 3 signals.
A new customer can enter the mall now.
Press any key to exit.
-----The customer 2 is exiting now.
-----The customer 5 is exiting now.
```

413

Additional Note

The CountdownEvent class has many other useful methods with their usual meaning. For example, you can use the AddCount method to increment the CountdownEvents current count by one. You can also use the overloaded version AddCount(int signalCount) to increment the current count by a specified number. However, while using the AddCount method, you need to be careful; if you use this method when the CountdownEvents current count is zero, you will observe the following error message:

```
System.InvalidOperationException: 'The event is already
signaled and cannot be incremented.'
```

Therefore, you can consider using the TryAddCount method in such a context. I suggest you experiment with the other methods as well.

POINT TO NOTE

Ideally, you should try to release the resources whenever possible. The same rule applies when you use the ManualResetEventSlim class or the CountdownEvent class. However, I do not discuss garbage collection in this book. To focus on the key areas of the discussion and make the code short and simple, I ignored this suggestion.

Using Mutex

A mutex is another useful synchronization primitive; it is similar to the lock statements. The documentation at https://learn.microsoft.com/en-us/dotnet/api/system.threading.mutex?view=net-8.0 states the following:

Mutex is a synchronization primitive that grants exclusive access to the shared resource to only one thread. If a thread acquires a mutex, the second thread that wants to acquire that mutex is suspended until the first thread releases the mutex.

Demonstration 1 in Chapter 3 showed you an erroneous program. We corrected the program by modifying the Account class in Demonstration 2 of that chapter. To ensure synchronized access, we used lock statements in the modified version of the Account class. This time I'll show you another program that uses a different version of the Account class using the Mutex class.

Demonstration 4

Let's understand the changes in this new version of the Account class step-by-step.

- The Account class has a Mutex object. It also contains a Boolean variable, called _lockBalance.

- Inside the Credit method, the _lockBalance variable is used as follows: _lockBalance = _mutex.WaitOne(); Using this line, you try to block the current thread until the current WaitHandle receives a signal. If the method returns true, you can perform the intended operation. In simple words, you block the current thread until you get ownership of the mutex. Otherwise, you cannot operate.

POINT TO NOTE

A calling thread can be unblocked in any of the following cases:

Case 1: When the WaitOne method returns true. This means that no one owns the mutex at that moment.

Case 2: When a specified time limit is elapsed. You can specify this time-out interval to an overloaded version of the WaitOne method.

- If you get the ownership, after performing the intended job, you must release the mutex by calling the ReleaseMutex method. Similar to a lock statement, a mutex is released only from the thread that acquired the lock. Now you understand that the WaitOne method is used to lock and ReleaseMutex is used to unlock.

- The Debit method is similar. However, as per the name, it debits from the balance.

Since there is no change in the client code and the namespace, I am not showing them again to avoid repetition. You can download the project Demo4_Mutex to execute the complete program. In that program, I also kept all the different variations of the Account class in the commented code. You already saw these variations in other examples, but I'm showing them again for reference.

I assume you will not have any difficulty understanding the following code that shows the modified version of the Account class:

```
#region Using mutex
class Account
{
    public decimal Balance { get; set; }
    private readonly Mutex _mutex = new();
    private bool _lockBalance;
    public void Credit(decimal amount)
    {
        _lockBalance = _mutex.WaitOne();
        if (_lockBalance)
        {
            try
            {
```

```
            Balance += amount;
            WriteLine($"The balance after the credit of
             ${amount} is ${Balance}");
        }
        finally
        {
            if (_lockBalance) _mutex.ReleaseMutex();
        }
    }
    else
    {
        WriteLine($"Could not credit: {amount}");
    }
}
public void Debit(decimal amount)
{
    _lockBalance = _mutex.WaitOne();
    if (_lockBalance)
    {
        try
        {

            Balance -= amount;
            WriteLine($"The balance after the debit of
             ${amount} is ${Balance}");
        }
        finally
        {
            if (_lockBalance) _mutex.ReleaseMutex();
        }
    }
```

```
        else
        {
            WriteLine($"Could not debit: {amount}");
        }
    }
}
#endregion
```

Output

Here is some sample output:

```
The balance after the credit of $200 is $200
The balance after the debit of $500 is $-300
The balance after the credit of $100 is $-200
The balance after the credit of $300 is $100
The balance after the debit of $100 is $0
The current balance is $0
```

Additional Note

The Mutex class is a powerful synchronization primitive. You can use it for interprocess communications as well. I recommend that you read the documentation at https://learn.microsoft.com/en-us/dotnet/api/system.threading.mutex?view=net-8.0 to learn more about the Mutex class.

Q&A Session

QApp1.4 Can you show me an example where a mutex is used for interprocess communication?

As suggested, if you read the documentation at the previous link, you'll see that mutexes can be any of the following types:

- Unnamed local mutexes

- Named system mutexes

For the interprocess communication, you'll use a named system mutex that can be created by providing a name to the constructor. (You can learn more about the "naming" from the previously mentioned link.)

Let's look at a sample program where you'd like to ensure only one instance of a program can run at a time. Before executing the program, here is the flow:

- First, the `OpenExisting` method tries to open the specified named mutex. If the mutex does not exist, it'll throw an exception, named `WaitHandleCannotBeOpenedException`.

- If you encounter the exception, you understand that mutex does not exist; so, you create a mutex inside the `catch` block.

- Once the mutex is available, you try to get it before launching the application.

The remaining code should be easy for you because you're already familiar with the `WaitOne` and the `ReleaseMutex` methods. However, this time I passed 5 sec as a parameter to the `WaitOne` method to avoid an indefinite waiting time. Here is the complete program:

```
using static System.Console;

const string appName = "MyApp";
Mutex mutex;
try
{
    mutex = Mutex.OpenExisting(appName);
    // If the previous line succeeds, we can run the following line.
```

```
    WriteLine($"An instance of the application {appName} is
     already running!");
    return;
}
catch (WaitHandleCannotBeOpenedException)
{
  // Since the mutex is unavailable, we can create it
    mutex = new(false, appName);
}

// The mutex is already created. Trying to get it before
// launching the app.

bool getMutex = mutex.WaitOne(5000);
if (getMutex)
{
    try
    {
        // Launching the application now
        LaunchApplication();
    }
    finally
    {
        WriteLine($"Press the 'Enter' key to close the app.");
        ReadKey();
        mutex.ReleaseMutex();
    }
}
```

```
void LaunchApplication()
{
    WriteLine($"Starting the {appName} application");
    // Do something, if needed
}
```

Once you run this program, you'll see the following output:

```
Starting the MyApp application
Press the 'Enter' key to close the app.
```

Do not press the Enter key now. Instead, try to launch the same program from the command line. This time, you'll see the screen in Figure App-1.

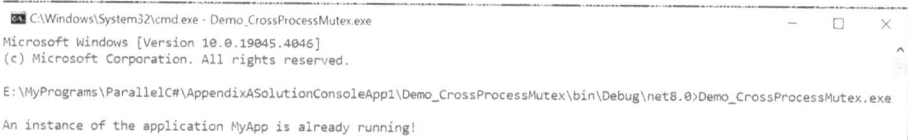

```
C:\Windows\System32\cmd.exe - Demo_CrossProcessMutex.exe                                    —    □    ×
Microsoft Windows [Version 10.0.19045.4046]
(c) Microsoft Corporation. All rights reserved.

E:\MyPrograms\ParallelC#\AppendixASolutionConsoleApp1\Demo_CrossProcessMutex\bin\Debug\net8.0>Demo_CrossProcessMutex.exe

An instance of the application MyApp is already running!
```

Figure App-1. *Trying to launch the same application from the command line*

You can also use multiple command prompts to verify the scenario. I believe that you have got the idea!

Author's Note: If you first launch the application from the command prompt, you should not try to run the application from Visual Studio again. Instead, you can launch another command prompt to verify the scenario. Figure App-2 shows an example.

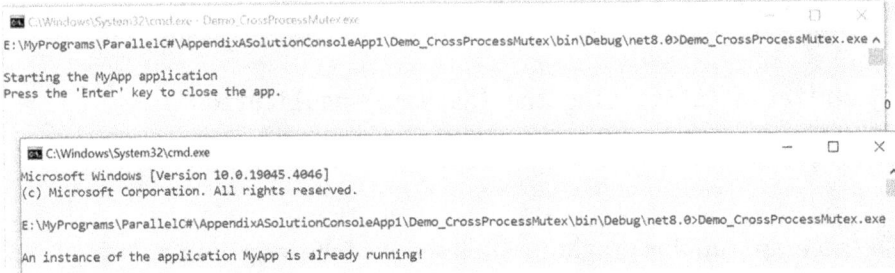

Figure App-2. *Trying to launch the same application from two different command prompts*

You can download the `Demo_CrossProcessMutex` project from the Apress website to execute this program.

Using SemaphoreSlim

Consider a typical appointment booking scenario in a doctor's office or a hospital. At any time, different numbers of patients can try to connect to the office over the phone to book an appointment. However, you know that there are a limited number of help-desk members who can pick up the calls to schedule an appointment. To demonstrate an example, let's assume that there are only two such members who can answer the incoming calls. As a result, at any time a maximum of two patients' appointment booking procedures can happen, and other callers need to wait to get their turn. The use of semaphores perfectly suits this scenario.

In this context, you can use either the `Semaphore` or `SemaphoreSlim` class. As per the name, the latter one is a slim and optimized version of the first. However, this slim version cannot be used if you want to handle interprocess communications. In the upcoming example, I'm going to use the optimized version, i.e., `SemaphoreSlim`.

How does the semaphore work? See the following points:

- A semaphore's count denotes the number of spaces (in our example, the available help-desk members). This count is increased when a thread releases the semaphore and is decreased when a thread enters the semaphore.

- Microsoft ensures (see https://learn.microsoft. com/en-us/dotnet/standard/threading/semaphore- and-semaphoreslim) that there is no guaranteed order, such as last-in, first-out (LIFO) or first-in, first-out (FIFO) in which blocked threads enter the semaphore.

- The Release method is used to release the semaphore. Both the Semaphore and SemaphoreSlim classes have the Release method.

- While using the Semaphore class, by calling the WaitOne method (this is inherited from the WaitHandle class), you can block the current thread until the current WaitHandle receives a signal. However, I am using the SemaphoreSlim class in the upcoming program; so, you'll see me using the Wait method (it also blocks the current thread until it enters the semaphore).

Let us understand the code now. The SemaphoreSlim class has the following constructors:

```
public SemaphoreSlim(int initialCount);
public SemaphoreSlim(int initialCount, int maxCount);
```

The initialCount parameter is used to indicate the initial number of requests for the semaphore that can be granted concurrently. The other version is used when you set the initial count along with the maximum count that can be granted.

Let's assume the patients start calling for the appointments before the help-desk members have arrived. They eagerly wait for someone to answer their call or get an appointment. To represent this situation, I create the following semaphore with a maximum count of two and an initial count of zero. (Since in our case two help-desk members can book the appointment, I set the maximum count to two.)

```
SemaphoreSlim semSlim = new(0, 2);
```

Once the help-desk members are available, the booking procedure starts. Now two people can schedule the appointment. So, you'll see the following code segment with supporting messages for your reference:

```
// Restore the Slimaphore count to its maximum value.
WriteLine("The helpdesk members have arrived and the booking
   procedure has started. ");
semSlim.Release(2);
helpdeskMemberCount = semSlim.CurrentCount;
```

The remaining part is easy. Let's see a sample demonstration that uses the SemaphoreSlim class.

Demonstration 5

Here is the complete program:

```
using static System.Console;

SemaphoreSlim semSlim = new(0, 2);

for (int i = 1; i <= 5; i++)
{
    _ = Task.Run(() => Appointment.BookAppointment(semSlim));
}
```

```
// Let the patients wait
Thread.Sleep(2000);
int helpdeskMemberCount = semSlim.CurrentCount;
WriteLine($"Currently, {helpdeskMemberCount} helpdesk member(s)
 are available.");
WriteLine("Please wait...");
// Restore the Slimaphore count to its maximum value.
WriteLine("The helpdesk members have arrived and the booking
 procedure has started. ");
semSlim.Release(2);
helpdeskMemberCount = semSlim.CurrentCount;

ReadKey();

class Appointment
{
  public static void BookAppointment(SemaphoreSlim sem)
   {
    try
    {
     int patientId = Task.CurrentId.HasValue ? (int)Task.
      CurrentId : 0;
     WriteLine($"Patient: {patientId} calls for an appointment
      booking.");
     sem.Wait();
     WriteLine($"**Patient: {patientId} is getting the
      appointment. **");
     // The booking time for different patients can be different
     Thread.Sleep(patientId * 500);
     WriteLine($"\tPatient: {patientId} disconnects the call.");
     sem.Release();
    }
```

```
    catch (Exception e)
    {
     WriteLine($"Something went wrong: {e.Message}");
    }
   }
}
```

Output

Here is some sample output:

```
Patient: 2 calls for an appointment booking.
Patient: 4 calls for an appointment booking.
Patient: 1 calls for an appointment booking.
Patient: 3 calls for an appointment booking.
Patient: 5 calls for an appointment booking.
Currently, 0 helpdesk member(s) are available.
Please wait...
The helpdesk members have arrived and the booking procedure has
started.
**Patient: 2 is getting the appointment. **
**Patient: 4 is getting the appointment. **
        Patient: 2 disconnects the call.
**Patient: 1 is getting the appointment. **
        Patient: 1 disconnects the call.
**Patient: 3 is getting the appointment. **
        Patient: 4 disconnects the call.
**Patient: 5 is getting the appointment. **
        Patient: 3 disconnects the call.
        Patient: 5 disconnects the call.
```

Q&A Session

QApp1.5 It appears to me that a semaphore with an initial count of 1 is similar to a lock (or mutex). Is this correct?

Yes, these look similar. However, you should remember that the thread that obtained the lock is the only one that can release the lock. However, a semaphore does not have an owner; any thread can call `Release` on it.

Avoiding Deadlocks

Up until now, you have seen many synchronization primitives. I assume that you understand the async programming model as well. I recommend that you read the online documentation at `https://learn.microsoft.com/en-us/dotnet/csharp/asynchronous-programming/async-scenarios` to get some additional advice from Microsoft. Its suggestion is that you write code that awaits tasks in a nonblocking manner. A blocking call eventually may lead to a deadlock situation. This is why Microsoft suggests that you do the following:

- Use `await` instead of `Task.Wait` or `Task.Result` when you want to retrieve the result of a background task.

- Use `await Task.WhenAny` instead of `Task.WaitAny` when you want to wait for a task to complete.

- Use `await Task.WhenAll` instead of `Task.WaitAll` when you want to wait for all tasks to complete.

- Use `Task.Delay` instead of `Thread.Sleep`.

In this book, you started experimenting with parallel programming using tasks. So, I needed to use the constructs like `Task.Wait`, `Task.WaitAny`, `Task.WaitAll`, or `Task.Result` in my demonstrations. In a simple application, finding a deadlock is relatively easy. So, you do not need to worry much. However, for an enterprise edition, it's better to keep these suggestions in mind.

More on Async/Await

In earlier days, you'd see the use of asynchronous programming models (also known as APMs or `IAsyncResult` patterns) and event-based asynchronous patterns (EAPs). I also discussed them in my book *Design Patterns in C# 2nd Edition* (Apress, 2020). However, these are considered obsolete patterns nowadays. This is why this book does not discuss them.

What are the alternatives? Microsoft says the following (see `https://learn.microsoft.com/en-us/dotnet/standard/asynchronous-programming-patterns/task-based-asynchronous-pattern-tap`):

> *In .NET, the task-based asynchronous pattern is the recommended asynchronous design pattern for new development.*

This is why you are about to see the discussions on TAP.

Task-Based Asynchronous Patterns

To qualify for a task-based asynchronous pattern (TAP) pattern, Microsoft has detailed guidelines (see `https://learn.microsoft.com/en-us/dotnet/standard/asynchronous-programming-patterns/task-based-asynchronous-pattern-tap`). However, for a simple application, you do not have to worry about all those details. For your quick reference, I have summarized the important ones here:

- TAP is based on `Task` and `Task<Result>`. So, the asynchronous methods inside TAP return awaitable types such as `Task`, `Task<TResult>`, `ValueTask`, and `ValueTask<TResult>`.

- If you have an asynchronous method that does not return awaitable types, you can use names like `StartXXX`, `BeginXXX`, or any other verb.

- You already know that the asynchronous methods normally have the `Async` suffix. You should maintain the same convention when you implement the TAP pattern.

- However, there are a few exceptions to the previous rule, such as when you use combinators such as `WhenAll` or `WhenAny`.

- Consumers of a TAP method always work with hot running tasks. It means that they never call the `Start` method on them.

- The return type of a TAP method depends on the corresponding synchronous method. For example, if a synchronous method returns `void`, the corresponding asynchronous method returns `Task`. But if the synchronous method returns `TResult`, the corresponding asynchronous method will return `Task<TResult>`.

- You should also note that Microsoft suggests you consider the `async void` only for the event handlers (see `https://learn.microsoft.com/en-us/dotnet/csharp/asynchronous-programming/async-scenarios`). Any other users do not follow the TAP model. In addition, the `async void` methods are difficult to test and any exception raised by them cannot be caught outside of that method.

- The TAP-based asynchronous method can perform a small number of synchronous operations, but it should return to the caller as quickly as possible. This is not a problem for you. It is because you are familiar with the `await` keyword now. However, keep in mind that this point is very important when you work with I/O-bound tasks.

- The parameters of an asynchronous method and its corresponding synchronous method should match. These parameters also follow the same order.

- There are some exceptional cases when the previous rule is not applicable. For example, this rule does not hold for `ref` and `out` parameters. In fact, Microsoft suggests (see the detailed guideline link that is mentioned at the beginning of this section) to avoid them in your implementation by stating the following:

*Any data that would have been returned through an out or ref parameter should instead be returned as part of the **TResult** returned by **Task< TResult>**, and should use a tuple or a custom data structure to accommodate multiple values.*

- Providing progress notifications and/or cancellation tokens is optional for you. But Microsoft suggests you consider adding a `CancellationToken` parameter for the TAP method even if the corresponding synchronous method does not have such a parameter.

Case Study

To bring more clarity to the topic, let's do some hands-on exercises. Suppose, someone has written a program where the program prints some numbers sequentially by calling a simple method, named `PrintNumbers`. You understand that a real-world scenario may deal with complex methods, which are time-consuming as well. To mimic the situation, I simulated some delay inside this method.

Here is the program:

```
using static System.Console;

var printTask = Task.Run(() => PrintNumbers(10));
try
{
    WriteLine($"Printed up to the number: {printTask.Result}");
}
catch (AggregateException ae)
{
    foreach (Exception e in ae.InnerExceptions)
    {
        WriteLine($"Encountered error: {ae.Message}");
    }
}

WriteLine("End of the main thread.");

// The following method is synchronous.

static int PrintNumbers(int limit)
{
    int currentNumber = 0;
    WriteLine("The printing task starts now.");

    for (int i = 0; i < limit; i++)
    {
        Write($"PrintNumbers prints {i}\n");
        currentNumber = i;
        // Simulating some delay for some other activities, if any
        Thread.Sleep(500);
    }
    return currentNumber;
}
```

Note   You can download the project Demo_WithoutTAP to execute
this program.

You should not be surprised that you are expected to see the
following output:

```
The printing task starts now.
PrintNumbers prints 0
PrintNumbers prints 1
PrintNumbers prints 2
PrintNumbers prints 3
PrintNumbers prints 4
PrintNumbers prints 5
PrintNumbers prints 6
PrintNumbers prints 7
PrintNumbers prints 8
PrintNumbers prints 9
Printed up to the number: 9
End of the main thread.
```

Though the program is simple, the problem is obvious. Now we are
considering only 10 elements, but if we need to deal with thousands of
elements, the execution time is longer. Also, you may need to cancel
the program due to some typical reasons. So, your job is to make an
asynchronous version of the method that supports cancellations as well.
Can you do this?

I am sure that you can make an application using the concepts of
tasks that you learned at the beginning of the book. **However, this time, I
want you to make an asynchronous version of the PrintNumber method
and follow the TAP pattern.** Can you make it? Let's search for a sample
solution.

Demonstration 6

In the upcoming program, you'll see the use of the following method:

```
static async Task<int> PrintNumbersAsync(int limit,
 CancellationToken token)
{
    int currentNumber = 0;
    WriteLine("The printing task starts now.");
    for (int i = 0; i < limit; i++)
    {
        token.ThrowIfCancellationRequested();
        Write($"PrintNumbersAsync prints {i}\n");
        currentNumber = i;
        // Simulating some delay
        await Task.Delay(500, token);
    }
    return currentNumber;
}
```

Let us verify whether this method follows the TAP pattern. You already see the use of the async and await keywords. In addition, we can confirm the following points:

- The method returns a Task<TResult> type. Here it is Task<int>.

- The method name has the Async suffix.

- This method accepts the same parameter (i.e., limit) as its synchronous version does.

- In addition, it supports the cancellation activity.

Note   You can handle the possible exceptions inside this task. However, I preferred to handle them inside the main thread.

You can see the criteria for following the TAP pattern is satisfied. Let's see the sample program that demonstrates the usage of PrintNumbersAsync. It is as follows:

```
using static System.Console;

WriteLine("Task-based asynchronous pattern (TAP)
  demonstration.");

var tokenSource = new CancellationTokenSource();
var token = tokenSource.Token;

var printTask = Task.Run(() => PrintNumbersAsync(10, token));

WriteLine("Enter c to cancel the task.");
var input = ReadKey();
if (input.KeyChar.Equals('c'))
{
    WriteLine("\nTask cancellation requested.");
    tokenSource.Cancel();
}

try
{
    WriteLine($"Printed up to the number: {printTask.Result}");
}
catch (AggregateException ae)
{
    foreach (Exception e in ae.InnerExceptions)
    {
```

```
        WriteLine($"Encountered error: {e.Message}");
    }
}

WriteLine("End of the main thread.");

// The PrintNumbersAsync is placed here. It is not shown again
// to avoid the repetition.
```

Note   You can download the Demo_TAP project to see and execute the complete program.

Output

Here is the output I got when I initiated a cancellation request while the program was running:

```
Task-based asynchronous pattern (TAP) demonstration.
Enter c to cancel the task.
The printing task starts now.
PrintNumbersAsync prints 0
PrintNumbersAsync prints 1
PrintNumbersAsync prints 2
PrintNumbersAsync prints 3
c
Task cancellation requested.
Encountered error: A task was canceled.
End of the main thread.
```

Q&A Session

QApp1.6 Why should a TAP-based asynchronous method return to the caller as quickly as possible?

Here are some specific reasons behind this:

- If the method spends too much time on a time-consuming synchronous operation, the responsiveness of the application is affected, and the ultimate benefit of using asynchronous programming is lost.

- Consider another typical scenario when you concurrently launch multiple asynchronous methods. In this case, if one of these tasks performs a time-consuming synchronous operation, other asynchronous operations are delayed. As a result, the overall benefit of concurrency is lost as well.

In fact, you can easily understand the importance of quick returns when you consider the out-of-process calls. I assume that you'll also agree that if a UI thread calls a web page or a database, it should not block itself for the invoked operation to be completed.

QApp1.7 What happens if a consumer calls the Start method on a hot task?

A hot task is an active task. So, calling the Start method on such a task causes an InvalidOperationException to occur. For example, if you write something like the following:

```
// The previous code is the same
var printTask = Task.Run(() => PrintNumbersAsync(10, token));
printTask.Start();
// The remaining code is the same
```

and execute the program again, you'll see the error in the output. Here is a sample:

```
// The previous lines in the output are not shown
System.InvalidOperationException: Start may not be called on a
 promise-style task.
//The remaining lines in the output are not shown
```

QApp1.8 I can see that you have not shown the progress status of this application. Was it intentional? If not, how can I support progress reporting in a similar application?

Support for cancellation and progress reporting are both optional for TAP. You can use none of them, any of them, or both. So, four possible overloads for a particular asynchronous method are possible. Since Microsoft suggests we consider the support for cancellation, I have shown an application that fulfils the minimum criterion (and recommendation).

QApp1.9 When an async method does not have the await keyword, I see the following warning message: "CS1998 This async method lacks 'await' operators and will run synchronously. Consider using the 'await' operator to await non-blocking API calls, or 'await Task.Run(...)' to do CPU-bound work on a background thread." I'd like to know the reason behind this.

Microsoft does not want you to do this. This is very inefficient because, in this case, for the async method, the C# compiler unnecessarily generates a state machine that is of no use.

QApp1.10 I am interested in displaying the progress reporting. How can I support the concept in the previous demonstration?

Normally, to support progress reporting, developers use the IProgress<T> interface. Usually, you pass it as a parameter to the asynchronous method and name the parameter progress. However, you can exercise a simple logic to incorporate the progress reporting in this program. For example, see the updated method with the key changes in bold:

```csharp
static async Task<int> PrintNumbersAsync(int limit,
 CancellationToken token)
{
    int total = 0;
    WriteLine("The printing task starts now.");
    for (int i = 0; i < limit; i++)
    {
        token.ThrowIfCancellationRequested();
        #region Old code
        // Write($"PrintNumbersAsync prints {i}\n");
        #endregion

        #region New code to display progress
        Write($"PrintNumbersAsync prints {i}");
        Write($"\tCompleted {(i + 1) * 100 / limit}%\n");
        #endregion

        total = i;
        // Simulating some delay
        await Task.Delay(500, token);
    }
    return total;
}
```

Now execute the program again. Here is some sample output for you:

```
Task-based asynchronous pattern (TAP) demonstration.
Enter c to cancel the task.
The printing task starts now.
PrintNumbersAsync prints 0        Completed 10%
PrintNumbersAsync prints 1        Completed 20%
PrintNumbersAsync prints 2        Completed 30%
PrintNumbersAsync prints 3        Completed 40%
c
```

```
Task cancellation requested.
Encountered error: A task was canceled.
End of the main thread.
```

Note   You can download the Demo_TAP_WithProgressReporting project to see and execute the complete program.

What's Next?

Parallel programming is a vast topic, and it is almost impossible to cover everything in a book. Also, this book is already fat! So, before I finish this book, I'll provide a few more words about the next steps:

- Throughout the book, I used many different built-in functions. There are many overloads available for these methods. You should explore them as well.

- This book covers many synchronization constructs. Still, there are many more. Based on the needs of your application, you may want to know about others as well. There are plenty of online and offline materials to serve you in this context.

- You saw me using the built-in task-based combinator Task.Run throughout this book. I want you to explore other constructs such as Task.FromResult, Task. WhenAll, and Task.WhenAny as well. Particularly, you have seen the last two when I talked about deadlock avoidance. You can get help from https:// learn.microsoft.com/en-us/dotnet/standard/

```
asynchronous-programming-patterns/consuming-
the-task-based-asynchronous-pattern#using-the-
built-in-task-based-combinators.
```

- The new features can make the coding easy. So, I suggest you keep track of the latest features. C# 12 included several interesting features, and you have already seen the usage of the collection expressions, optional parameters in lambda expressions, and private constructors in this book.

POINT TO NOTE

However, the key point is to understand that new features will keep evolving; whatever is new today will be outdated tomorrow. On the contrary, the activity that involves understanding the fundamentals or core constructs is long-lasting and evergreen. This is why this book puts more emphasis on helping you understand the essentials of parallel programming and how the important constructs are evolving.

A Personal Appeal

Over the years, I have seen a general trend in my books. When you like the book, you send me messages, write nice emails, and motivate me with your kind words and suggestions. Unfortunately, many of them do not reach review platforms like Amazon and others. However, when the opposite happens, I see all the criticisms on those pages.

Undoubtedly, these criticisms help me to write better. But it is also helpful for me to know what you liked in the book. These constructive suggestions help me to keep that information in an updated edition of the book.

So, I have a request for you: you can always point out the improvement areas of this work, but at the same time, please let me know about the areas you liked. I am sure that you also know that it is always easy to criticize, but an artistic view and open mind are required to discover the true efforts that are associated with any kind of work.

Thank you and happy coding!

APPENDIX B

Recommended Reading

This appendix lists some useful resources including paid courses. I have gotten many new insights from them. I believe that they will be equally effective for you.

Books

The following list includes two books. In this list, the first one is my favorite. The second one is quite old but still helpful.

- *C# 12 in a Nutshell* by Joseph Albahari (O'Reilly Media, 2023)

- *Pro .NET 4 Parallel Programming in C#* by Adam Freeman (Apress, 2010)

I have learned many things from Stephen Cleary's blogs/articles. However, I have not read his book on this topic yet. If interested, you may look at the following one as well:

- *Concurrency in C# Cookbook: Asynchronous, Parallel, and Multithreaded Programming Second Edition* (O'Reilly Media, 2019)

© Vaskaran Sarcar 2024
V. Sarcar, *Parallel Programming with C# and .NET*,
https://doi.org/10.1007/979-8-8688-0488-5

Courses

The following list includes helpful online courses. The first one covers a wide number of topics whereas the other courses cover a limited number of topics. At the time of this writing, none of them is free. However, you may get a promotional discount occasionally on these courses.

- `www.udemy.com/course/parallel-dotnet/learn/lecture/5645430#overview`

- `www.linkedin.com/learning/advanced-threading-in-c-sharp`

- `www.linkedin.com/learning/advanced-c-sharp-thread-safe-data-with-concurrent-collections`

Other Resources

In each chapter, you have seen various online resources in the discussions and the "Q&A Sessions." If interested, you can have a detailed look at those resources to learn more about them. However, I recommend that you start with the following one: `https://learn.microsoft.com/en-us/dotnet/standard/parallel-programming/`.

APPENDIX C

Other Books by the Author

The following list includes my other Apress books:

- *Introducing Functional Programming Using C#* (Apress, 2023)

- *Simple and Efficient Programming in C# Second Edition* (Apress, 2022)

- *Test Your Skills in C# Programming* (Apress, 2022)

- *Java Design Patterns Third Edition* (Apress, 2022)

- *Simple and Efficient Programming in C#* (Apress, 2021)

- *Design Patterns in C# Second Edition* (Apress, 2020)

- *Getting Started with Advanced C#* (Apress, 2020)

- *Interactive Object-Oriented Programming in Java Second Edition* (Apress, 2019)

- *Java Design Patterns Second Edition* (Apress, 2019)

- *Design Patterns in C#* (Apress, 2018)

© Vaskaran Sarcar 2024
V. Sarcar, *Parallel Programming with C# and .NET*,
https://doi.org/10.1007/979-8-8688-0488-5

- *Interactive C#* (Apress, 2017)

- *Interactive Object-Oriented Programming in Java* (Apress, 2016)

- *Java Design Patterns* (Apress, 2016)

The following list includes my non-Apress books:

- *Python Bookcamp* (Amazon, 2021)

- *Operating System: Computer Science Interview Series* (Createspace, 2014)

To learn more about these books, you can refer to `https://amazon.com/author/vaskaran_sarcar` or to `https://link.springer.com/search?new-search=true&query=vaskaran+sarcar&content-type=book&dateFrom=&dateTo=&sortBy=newestFirst`.

Index

A

AddBlackCarModels method, 180, 191

Add methods, 150–152, 191, 198, 199

AddNonBlackCarModels method, 180, 191

AddOrUpdate method, 204

AggregateException, 79–80, 84, 388, 389

Aggregation methods, 316, 318

Aggregation operations, 315, 316, 318

AsParallel method, 284, 321

AsTask, 383, 384, 395

Async and await keywords, 349, 392, 428

async method, 336–340, 346, 387

Async-await programming model, 359

Asynchronous construction
async and await keywords, 363, 365
await operator, 366

Asynchronous initialization, 365, 366, 370, 379

Asynchronous programming, 333, 358, 359, 383
analyze, 342
await keyword, 334, 335, 339, 346
await operator, 340
challenging activity, 334
demonstration, 340
documentation, 337
fire-and-forget operation, 345
long-running operation, 338
naming convention, 336
output, 341
restrictions, 338
return statement, 337
return types, 336
type, 336
void return type, 345
worker thread are running, 342

Asynchronous programming models (APMs), 428

AutoResetEvent class, 144, 154–156, 161

await expression, 335, 353, 387, 397

Await_Restrictions project, 348

© Vaskaran Sarcar 2024
V. Sarcar, *Parallel Programming with C# and .NET*,
https://doi.org/10.1007/979-8-8688-0488-5